THE SOCIAL SELF

The Sydney Symposium of Social Psychology series

This book is Volume 4 in the Sydney Symposium of Social Psychology series. The aim of the *Sydney Symposia of Social Psychology* is to provide new, integrative insights into key areas of contemporary research. Held every year at the University of New South Wales, Sydney, each Symposium deals with an important integrative theme in social psychology, and the invited participants are leading researchers in the field from around the world. Each contribution is extensively discussed during the Symposium, and is subsequently thoroughly revised into book chapters that are published in the volumes in this series. The themes of forthcoming Sydney Symposia are announced, and contributions from interested participants are invited around June every year. For further details see website at www.sydneysymposium.unsw.edu.au

Previous Sydney Symposium of Social Psychology volumes:

SSSP 1. FEELING AND THINKING: THE ROLE OF AFFECT IN SOCIAL COGNITION* (Edited by J. P. FORGAS). Contributors: Robert Zajonc *(Stanford)*, Jim Blascovich & Wendy Mendes *(UCSanta Barbara)*, Craig Smith & Leslie Kirby *(Vanderbilt)*, Eric Eich & Dawn Macauley *(British Columbia)*, Len Berkowitz et al. *(Wisconsin)*, Leonard Martin *(Georgia)*, Daniel Gilbert *(Harvard)*, Herbert Bless *(Mannheim)*, Klaus Fiedler *(Heidelberg)*, Joseph Forgas *(UNSW)*, Carolin Showers *(Wisconsin)*, Tony Greenwald, Marzu Banaji et al. *(U.Washington/Yale)*, Mark Leary *(Wake Forest)*, Paula Niedenthal & Jamin Halberstadt *(Indiana)*.

Comments on 'Feeling and Thinking':

"At last a project that brings together the central findings and theories concerning the interface of social cognition and affect. This important new volume is sure to become the sourcebook . . . must reading for anyone interested in the vital role of affect in social life." Prof. Tory Higgins, Columbia University

"I am filled with admiration for the contribution I believe this book makes to our understanding of affect and cognition . . . " Prof. Ellen Berscheid, University of Minnesota

"I can't imagine a more interesting collection of affect researchers under one roof! Joseph Forgas has brought together the best minds in psychology, young and old, to reflect on the interface between emotion and thought . . . this volume will make you wish you had traveled to Sydney to attend the original symposium. Excellent investigators showcase their best work." Prof. Peter Salovey, Yale University.

SSSP 2. THE SOCIAL MIND: COGNITIVE AND MOTIVATIONAL ASPECTS OF IN-TERPERSONAL BEHAVIOR* (Edited by J. P. FORGAS, K. R. WILLIAMS, & LADD WHEELER). Contributors: William & Claire McGuire *(Yale)*, Susan Andersen *(NYU)*, Roy Baumeister *(Case Western)*, Joel Cooper *(Princeton)*, Bill Crano *(Claremont)*, Garth Fletcher *(Canterbury)*, Joseph Forgas *(UNSW)*, Pascal Huguet *(Clermont)*, Mike Hogg *(Queensland)*, Martin Kaplan *(N. Illinois)*, Norb Kerr *(Michigan State)*, John Nezlek *(William & Mary)*, Fred Rhodewalt *(Utah)*, Astrid Schuetz *(Chemnitz)*, Constantine Sedikides *(Southampton)*, Jeffrey Simpson *(Texas A&M)*, Richard Sorrentino *(Western Ontario)*, Dianne Tice *(Case Western)*, Kip Williams & Ladd Wheeler *(UNSW)*.

Comments on 'The Social Mind':

"At last . . . a compelling answer to the question of what is 'social' about social cognition. The editors have assembled a stellar cast of researchers . . . and the result is eye-opening and mind-expanding . . . the contributors to this project make a convincing case that, for human beings, mental life IS social life." Prof. Marilynn B. Brewer, Ohio State University

"The Sydney Symposium has once again collected some of social psychology's best researchers, and allowed them to . . . explore how the world within the mind represents, creates, interacts with, and is influenced by the world without. The bridge between social relations and social cognition has never been sturdier, and scientists on both sides of the divide won't want to miss this. . . ." Prof. Daniel Gilbert, Harvard University

* Volumes from the first two Symposia were published by Cambridge University Press.

SSSP 3. SOCIAL INFLUENCE: DIRECT AND INDIRECT PROCESSES** (Edited by J. P. FORGAS & K. E. WILLIAMS). Contributors: Robert Cialdini *(Arizona State)*, Eric Knowles, Shanon Butler & Jay Linn *(Arkansas)*, Bibb Latane *(Florida Atlantic)*, Martin Bourgeois *(Wyoming)*, Mark Schaller *(British Columbia)*, Ap Dijksterhuis *(Nijmegen)*, James Tedeschi *(SUNY-Albany)*, Richard Petty *(Ohio State)*, Joseph Forgas *(UNSW)*, Herbert Bless *(Mannheim)*, Fritz Strack *(Wurzburg)*, Eva Walther *(Heidelberg)*, Sik Hung Ng *(Hong Kong)*, Thomas Mussweiler *(Wurzburg)*, Kipling Williams *(Macquarie)*, Lara Dolnik *(UNSW)*, Charles Stangor & Gretchen Sechrist *(Maryland)*, John Jost *(Stanford)*, Deborah Terry & Michael Hogg *(Queensland)*, Stephen Harkins *(Northeastern)*, Barbara David & John Turner *(Australian National University)*, Robin Martin *(Queensland)*, Miles Hewstone *(Cardiff)*, Russell Spears & Tom Postmes *(Amsterdam)*, Martin Lea *(Manchester)*, Susan Watt *(Amsterdam)*.

Comments on 'Social Influence':

"What a great new book. . . . In this cutting edge volume, . . . social cognition meets social influence, and the result is a big step forward for social psychology." Prof. David Myers, Hope College

"This Sydney Symposium volume, the third in a series, showcases the best research done by a collection of stellar scholars in social influence . . . from subliminal and cognitive effects to interpersonal and socio-cultural effects. [This book] will be of great interest to anyone concerned with social influence phenomena—students, researchers, practitioners and laypersons alike." Prof. Elizabeth Loftus, University of Washington

** Volume three of the Symposia was published by Psychology Press.

THE SOCIAL SELF
Cognitive, Interpersonal, and Intergroup Perspectives

Edited by

Joseph P. Forgas
University of New South Wales

and Kipling D. Williams
Macquarie University

Psychology Press
New York • London • Hove

Published in 2002 by
Psychology Press
29 West 35th Street
New York, NY 10001

Published in Great Britain by
Psychology Press
27 Church Road
Hove, East Sussex
BN3 2FA

10 9 8 7 6 5 4 3 2 1

Library of Congress Cataloging-in-Publication Data
The social self : introduction and overview / [edited by] Joseph P. Forgas and Kipling D.
   Williams.
      p. cm. — (Sydney Symposium of Social Psychology series)
   Includes bibliographical references and index.
      ISBN 1-84169-062-7 — 1-84169-082-1 (pbk.)
      1. Self—Congresses. 2. Self—Social aspects—Congresses. I. Forgas, Joseph P.
II. Williams, Kipling D. III. Series.

BF697.5.S65 S63 2002
I55.2—dc21   2002017834

To Stephanie Moylan

Contents

III. INTERGROUP, COLLECTIVE, AND CULTURAL
ASPECTS OF THE SELF

About the Editors

Joseph P. Forgas received his DPhil and subsequently a DSc from the University of Oxford. He is currently Scientia Professor of Psychology at the University of New South Wales, Sydney, Australia. He has also spent various periods of time working at the Universities of Giessen, Heidelberg, Stanford, Mannheim, and Oxford. His enduring interest is in studying the role of cognitive and affective processes in interpersonal behavior. His current project investigates how mood states can influence everyday social judgments and social interaction strategies. He has published some 14 books and over 130 articles and chapters in this area. He has been elected Fellow of the Academy of Social Science in Australia, the American Psychological Society, and of the Society of Personality and Social Psychology, and he is recipient of the Alexander von Humboldt Research Prize (Germany) and a Special Investigator Award from the Australian Research Council.

Kipling D. Williams received his BS at the University of Washington, where he began his research career testing whether rats preferred to work or free-ride for their food. He then received his MA and PhD in Social Psychology at The Ohio State University. There, he began his collaboration with Bibb Latané and Stephen Harkins, working on the causes and consequences of social loafing. Before coming to Macquarie University, Professor Williams taught at Drake University, University of Washington, Purdue University, University of Toledo, and the University of New South Wales. His recent research focus is on ostracism—being excluded and ignored, on which his book, "Ostracism—The Power of Silence" will be published in 2001. He also has interests in psychology and law, including research on the tactic of stealing thunder, eyewitness accuracy, and the impact of crime heinousness on jury verdicts.

Contributors

Art Aron, Department of Psychology, State University of New York, Stony Brook, USA.

Roy F. Baumeister, Department of Psychology, Case Western Reserve University, USA.

Monica Biernat, Department of Psychology, University of Kansas, USA.

Marilynn B. Brewer, Department of Psychology, Ohio State University, USA.

Natalie Ciarocco, Department of Psychology, Case Western Reserve University, USA.

Anna Clark, Department of Psychology, University of Melbourne, Australia.

Joel Cooper, Department of Psychology, Princeton University, USA.

Christian S. Crandall, Department of Psychology, University of Kansas, USA.

Scott Eidelman, Department of Psychology, University of Kansas, USA.

Amy Eshleman, Department of Psychology, Wagner College, USA.

Joseph P. Forgas, School of Psychology, University of New South Wales, Australia.

Kathleen Fuegen, Department of Psychology, University of Kansas, USA.

Thomas Gilovich, Department of Psychology, Cornell University, USA.

Edward R. Hirt, Department of Psychology, Indiana University– Bloomington, USA.

Michael A. Hogg, Department of Psychology, University of Queensland, Australia.

William Ickes, Department of Psychology, University of Texas at Arlington, USA.

Emiko Kashima, Discipline of Psychology, Swinburne University of Technology, Australia.

Yoshihisa Kashima, Department of Psychology, University of Melbourne, Australia.

Marianne LaFrance, Department of Psychology, Yale University, USA.

Mark R. Leary, Department of Psychology, Wake Forest University, USA.

Diane M. Mackie, Department of Psychology, University of California, Santa Barbara, USA.

Bertram F. Malle, Department of Psychology, University of Oregon, USA.

Sean M. McCrea, Department of Psychology, Indiana University– Bloomington, USA.

Stephanie J. Moylan, School of Psychology, University of New South Wales, Australia.

Laurie T. O' Brien, Department of Psychology, University of Kansas, USA.

Sabine Otten, Department of Social Psychology, Friedrich-Schiller-University Jena, Germany.

Cynthia L. Pickett, Department of Psychology, University of Illinois, USA.

Frederick Rhodewalt, Department of Psychology, University of Utah, USA.

Brandon J. Schmeichel, Department of Psychology, Case Western Reserve University, USA.

Constantine Sedikides, Department of Psychology, University of Southampton, England.

Eliot R. Smith, Department of Psychology, Purdue University, USA.

Dianne M. Tice, Department of Psychology, Case Western Reserve University, USA.

Michael Tragakis, Department of Psychology, University of Utah, USA.

Linda R. Tropp, Department of Psychology, Boston College, USA.

Jean M. Twenge, Department of Psychology, Case Western Reserve University, USA.

Kipling D. Williams, Department of Psychology, Macquarie University, Australia.

Stephen C. Wright, Department of Psychology, University of California, Santa Cruz, USA.

Preface

The self remains one of the most important, yet least understood concepts in psychology. Philosophers and writers have long been intrigued by the nature and origins of that elusive entity, the core of our sense of unique individual existence, selfhood. In our age of rampant individualism and unprecedented emphasis on personal identity and achievement, interest in the psychology of the self is at an all-time high. The issue of how an adequate and adaptive sense of selfhood is formed, maintained, and presented to others is of considerable interest not only to psychologists, but also to clinicians, educators, criminologists, policy analysts, and a variety of applied professionals. Problems and defects in selfhood have at various times been used to explain mental illness, educational under-achievement, criminality, relationship breakdowns, and a variety of other personal and social ills and problems. Indeed, the ability to develop and maintain a consistent and functional sense of the self in the increasingly superficial and anonymous interpersonal context of modern mass societies is widely believed to be one of the cornerstones of personal and social success.

The main objective of this book is to provide an informative, scholarly yet readable overview of recent advances in research on the self, and to integrate current developments that focus on the personal, interpersonal, and intergroup aspects of selfhood. Indeed, we want to advocate a greatly expanded and more integrated conceptualization of the self than is common in the existing literature. The chapters selected for inclusion in this volume argue that a proper understanding of the self requires an integrated analysis of the intra-psychic, interpersonal, and collective influences that jointly shape our sense of personal identity and selfhood. The mechanisms that produce unique social selves include both direct and indirect processes that can operate at the psychological, interpersonal, and socio-cultural levels. In other words, this book advocates a new, expanded conceptualization of the social self that makes use not only of the latest developments in research on social cognition and social motivation, but also links these processes to higher-level interpersonal and intergroup variables.

The chapters also offer important new insights into the role that a sense of self plays in a variety of everyday social judgments and behaviors. The contributions to this book will address a number of intriguing questions with profound practical implications, such as: What are the cognitive mechanisms that shape our mental representations about the self? How do interpersonal experiences impact on self-representations? Why do people often overestimate the amount of scrutiny they receive from others? How do we decide which standards to use when evaluating ourselves? How and why do affective states influence self-conceptions, and how does affect impact on people's self-disclosure strategies? When and why is self-handicapping a useful strategy to protect the self-concept? How does social rejection and ostracism impact on the self, and how do people cope with such experiences? What is the role of folk-theories and cultural conventions in the way people think about themselves? Why do people sometimes assimilate the self into reference groups, and sometimes contrast themselves against such groups? How do group memberships influence the sense of self, and how does selfhood in turn impact on intergroup relations?

Naturally, no single book could possibly include everything that is interesting and exciting in contemporary research on the self. In assembling this collection and selecting and inviting our contributors, we aimed to achieve a comprehensive and representative coverage, but of course we cannot claim to have fully sampled all of the relevant areas. The chapters are arranged into three sections, dealing with (1) the indvidual and intrapsychic aspects of the self, (2) interpersonal and relational aspects of the self, and (3) intergroup, collective and cultural aspects of the self. The first, introductory chapter presents a historical overview of self research, and outlines the case for a more comprehensive and integrative conceptualization of the field (Forgas & Williams).

The chapters in Part I discuss some of the fundamental cognitive processes involved in self-construction (Smith), the judgmental strategies people rely on in self-judgments (Gilovich), and the different comparison standards used in self-evaluations (Biernat, Eidelman, & Fuegen). The role of affect in self-judgments and self-disclosure is considered (Forgas & Moylan), and the role of self-handicapping in maintaining the self is discussed (Hirt & McCrea; and Rhodewalt & Tragakis). Part II looks at fundamental interpersonal processes in self-construction (Leary), and the way rejection and social exclusion impact on the self (Baumeister, Twenge, & Ciarocco; Tice, Twenge, & Schmeichel). Individualistic and interpersonal approaches to the self are contrasted (Ickes; Kashima), and the role of cultural and folk-theories (Malle) and communicative acts (LaFrance) in self-construction are analyzed. Finally, Part III considers the role of group and collective influences on the self, including group identification processes (Brewer & Pickett) and the role of the self as a determinant of responses to ingroups and outgroups (Otten; Crandall, O'Brien, & Eshleman; and Mackie & Smith). Identification with ingroup members as a source of vicarious dissonance processes is discussed (Cooper & Hogg), and the consequences of including ingroups in the self are considered (Wright, Aron, & Tropp).

The final chapter by Sedikides offers an overall conceptual integration of the themes covered in the above contributions.

THE SYDNEY SYMPOSIUM
OF SOCIAL PSYCHOLOGY SERIES

This book is the fourth volume in the Sydney Symposium of Social Psychology series, held every year at the University of New South Wales, Sydney. Perhaps a few words are in order about the origins of this volume, and the Sydney Symposium of Social Psychology series in general. First, we should emphasize that this is not simply an edited book in the usual sense. The objective of the Sydney Symposia is to provide new, integrative understanding in important areas of social psychology by inviting leading researchers in a particular field to a three-day residential Symposium in Sydney. This Symposium has received generous financial support from the University of New South Wales as well as Macquarie University, allowing the careful selection and funding of a small group of leading researchers as contributors. Draft papers by all contributors are prepared and circulated well in advance of the symposium and are placed on a dedicated website. Thus, participants had an opportunity to review and revise their papers in the light of everybody else's draft contribution even before they arrived in Sydney.

The critical part of the preparation of this book has been the intensive three-day face-to-face meeting between all invited contributors. Sydney Symposia are characterized by open, free-ranging, intensive and critical discussion between all participants, with the objective to explore points of integration and contrast between the proposed papers. A further revision of each chapter was prepared soon after the Symposium, incorporating many of the shared points that emerged in our discussions. Thanks to these collaborative procedures, the book does not simply consist of a set of chapters prepared in isolation. Rather, this Sydney Symposium volume represents a collaborative effort by a leading group of international researchers intent on producing a comprehensive and up-to-date review of research on the social self. We hope that the published papers will succeed in conveying some of the sense of fun and excitement we all shared during the Symposium. For more information on the Sydney Symposium series and details of our past and future projects please see our website www.sydneysymposium.unsw.edu.au.

Three previous volumes of the Sydney Symposium series have been published. The first, *Feeling and Thinking: The Role of Affect in Social Cognition* was edited by Joseph Forgas, and was published by Cambridge University Press, New York, 2000 (ISBN 0-52164-223-X). This book explored the role that affective states play in social cognition and social behavior, with contributions by Robert Zajonc, Jim Blascovich, Craig Smith, Eric Eich, Len Berkowitz, Leonard

Martin, Daniel Gilbert, Herbert Bless, Klaus Fiedler, Joseph Forgas, Carolin Showers, Tony Greenwald, Mahzarin Banaji, Mark Leary, Paula Niedenthal. and Jamin Halberstadt, among others. The second volume, *The Social Mind: Cognitive and Motivational Aspects of Interpersonal Behavior* was also published by Cambridge University Press (2001; ISBN 0-52177-092-0), and featured chapters by William and Claire McGuire, Susan Andersen, Roy Baumeister, Joel Cooper, Bill Crano, Garth Fletcher, Joseph Forgas, Pascal Huguet, Mike Hogg, Martin Kaplan, Norb Kerr, John Nezlek, Fred Rhodewalt, Astrid Schuetz, Constantine Sedikides, Jeffrey Simpson, Richard Sorrentino, Dianne Tice, Kip Williams, Ladd Wheeler, and others. The third Sydney Symposium volume edited by Joseph Forgas and Kip Williams was entitled *Social Influence: Direct and Indirect Processes* and was published by Psychology Press (2001; ISBN 1-84169-039-2), with contributions by Bob Cialdini, Bibb Latane, Martin Bourgeois, Mark Schaller, Ap Disjksterhuis, Jim Tedeschi, Richard Petty, Joseph Forgas, Herbert Bless, Fritz Strack, Sik Hung Ng, Kip Williams, Charles Stangor, Debbie Terry, Michael Hogg, Stephen Harkins, John Turner, Barbara David, Russell Spears, and others.

Given its comprehensive coverage, this book should be useful both as a basic reference book, and as an informative textbook to be used in advanced courses dealing with the self. The main target audience for this book comprises researchers, students. and professionals in all areas of the social and behavioral sciences, such as social, cognitive, clinical, counselling, personality, organizational and applied psychology, as well as sociology, communication studies, and cognitive science. The book is written in a readable yet scholarly style, and students both at the undergraduate and at the graduate level should find it an engaging overview of the field and thus useful as a textbook in courses dealing with the self. The book should also be of particular interest to people working in applied areas where using and understanding the self is important, such as clinical, counselling, educational, forensic, marketing, advertising and organisational psychology, and health psychology.

We want to express our thanks to people and organizations who helped to make the Sydney Symposium of Social Psychology, and this fourth volume in particular, a reality. Producing a complex multi-authored book such as this is a lengthy and sometimes challenging task. We have been very fortunate to work with such an excellent and cooperative group of contributors. Our first thanks must go to them. Because of their help and professionalism, we were able to finish this project on schedule. Past friendships have not frayed, and we are all still on speaking terms; indeed, we hope that working together on this book has been as positive an experience for them as it has been for us.

The idea of organizing the Sydney Symposia owes much to discussions with, and encouragement by Kevin McConkey, and subsequent support by Chris Fell, Sally Andrews, Peter Lovibond, and numerous others at the University of New South Wales. We want to express our gratitude to Paul Dukes, Ken Silver, and Jill Standing at Psychology Press who have been consistently helpful, efficient, and supportive through all the stages of producing this book. Our colleagues at the School of Psychology at UNSW, and at Macquarie University, Simon Laham, Rebekah East, Norman Chan, Cassandra Govan, Carla Walton, Carol Yap, Vera Thomson, and others have helped with advice, support, and sheer hard work to share the burden of preparing and organizing the symposium and the ensuing book. We also wish to acknowledge financial support from the Australian Research Council, the University of New South Wales, and Macquarie University, support that was of course essential to get this project off the ground. Most of all, we are grateful for the love and support of our families who have put up with us during the many months of work that went into producing this book.

We are obliged to finish this preface on a rather sad note. We dedicate this book to Dr. Stephanie Moylan, who has been a long-term friend and colleague to us at the University of New South Wales. Stephanie has been involved in the Sydney Symposium series since its inception, and has made an invaluable contribution to its success for the past four years. After a brief battle with cancer, Stephanie died a tragic and premature death a few months ago. Stephanie has been that rare individual, a kind, generous and deeply spiritual person whose eternal good cheer, humor, and countless examples of selfless kindness touched deeply the lives of everyone who knew her. We shall miss her more than words can say.

Joseph P. Forgas and Kipling D. Williams
Sydney, April 2002

1

The Social Self
Introduction and Overview

JOSEPH P. FORGAS
KIPLING D. WILLIAMS

INTRODUCTION

What is this mysterious entity we call "the self"? How does it arise, how do everyday experiences shape it, and how do people go about maintaining and enhancing a positive sense of selfhood? And how in

---

This work was supported by a Special Investigator award from the Australian Research Council, the Research Prize by the Alexander von Humboldt Foundation to Joseph P. Forgas, and an Australian Research Council grant to Kipling D. Williams. The contribution of Stephanie Moylan, Lisa Zadro, Cassie Govan, Simon Laham, and Norman Chan to this project is gratefully acknowledged.

Address for correspondence: Joseph P. Forgas, at the School of Psychology, University of New South Wales, Sydney 2052, Australia. E-mail: jp.forgas@unsw.edu.au

turn does a sense of self shape our thinking, judgments and behaviors? Questions such as these constitute some of the most enduring puzzles in all of psychology. Despite the massive advances in experimental psychology in recent years, the self remains one of those imponderables that we still cannot fully understand. As Pinker (1997) wrote recently, "What or where is the unified centre of sentience that comes into and goes out of existence, that changes over time but remains the same entity, and that has a supreme moral worth?" (p. 558). Psychological theorizing about the self often emphasizes distinctions between various self-components, such as the material, social, and spiritual aspects of the self (James, 1890/1950); the conflict between id, ego, and superego as in Freud's theorizing; and the links between actual and various ideal selves (Higgins, 1987). In contrast, much contemporary research, including many of the papers presented here, focuses on more specific objectives, such as the understanding of particular self-processes that link the psychological, interpersonal, and collective aspects of the self-system (Sedikides & Brewer, 2001).

A better understanding of the notion of selfhood is not merely of passing theoretical interest. Ever since the first emergence of the philosophy of the enlightenment in the eighteenth century, and the rapid adoption of the values and ideology of individualism in most developed industrialized countries since then, a better understanding of the way people think about themselves has also become an important practical problem. Cultivating and regulating the self-concept and developing appropriate levels of self-esteem are now also seen as critical issues for public policy, educational planning, and social engineering. Policy analysts, social workers, and psychologists now share an abiding interest in understanding how selfhood is created and maintained in our daily interactions. There is much evidence that in modern individualist societies many symptoms of social maladjustment, mental illness, violence, and criminality may be linked to inadequately developed or threatened selfhood (Baumeister, 1999; Williams, 2001).

The aim of this book is to survey some of the most recent advances in research on the self and to identify emerging, integrative principles that can help us develop a more comprehensive understanding of this elusive concept. Consistent with most contemporary theorizing (Sedikides & Brewer, 2001), the contributions to this book will also address three complementary aspects of the self: the self as an intrapsychic phenomenon (Part I), the influence of interpersonal and relational variables on the self (Part II), and the links between collective, intergroup phenomena on the self (Part III). Within each of these sections, leading international researchers present their most recent integrative theories and empirical research on the self. However excellent each of the individual chapters are, as editors, our hope is that the total contribution of this book will indeed amount to more than the sum of its parts. We believe that a proper understanding of the self can only be achieved by considering the interaction of the individual, relational, and collective aspects of the self as a dynamic self-system. This theme was also represented in an earlier volume of the Sydney Symposium of Social Psychology series, *The Social Mind* (Forgas, Williams, & Wheeler, 2001). In this introductory chapter, we want to offer some general theoretical and historical comments about the psychology of the self before outlining the structure and introducing the content of the book.

THE EVOLUTIONARY ORIGINS OF THE SELF

One view that is gaining popularity in recent psychological theorizing emphasizes the evolutionary origins of psychological phenomena (Buss, 1999). In evolutionary terms, we may think about the human mind as a complex, modular information processing device that was shaped by evolution to facilitate the solution of specific problems (Pinker, 1997). Accordingly, we may consider the emergence of a distinct sense of selfhood as either one of the many "mind modules" that developed because they confer distinct survival advantages over evolutionary time, or possibly, a mere by-product of such evolutionary pressures (Buss, 1999). What were the evolutionary pressures most likely to have produced the universal human capacity to conceive of and maintain a distinct sense of self?

One plausible suggestion is that having a clear and stable representational and motivational system focused on the self confers distinct evolutionary advantages because it makes sophisticated interaction with other members of our species more predictable and manageable. Humans are an intrinsically social and gregarious species, and there can be little doubt that much of our evolutionary success is due to our highly sophisticated ability to interact with each other. The human capacity for cooperation and complex, coordinated interaction largely depends on our cognitive, computational ability to represent, plan, and predict the behaviors of others and ourselves and to internalize the norms of the groups to which we belong (see also Crandall, O'Brien, & Eshleman; Malle; this volume). Indeed, there are some suggestions that the evolution of an immensely powerful computational device, the human brain, was itself a consequence of the need to manage ever-more complex interaction processes within successful emerging human groups (Pinker, 1997).

As phenomenological social psychologists such as Heider (1958) also observed, perhaps the most fundamental problem faced by human beings is to understand and predict the behaviors of others (see also Malle, this volume). This is largely accomplished by moving from observations of external behaviors to inferences about the internal causes of those behaviors, a task that is made possible by assuming that the subjective world of other people is similar to our own. A well-defined sense of self may thus be a powerful aid in solving the problem of inter-subjectivity: what are other people like? What do they think? Why do they act as they do? In other words, it is through having a clear concept of ourselves as agents and social actors that we are able to mentally model and represent the subjective worlds of others. The phenomenological sense of agency and selfhood thus appears to provide a powerful and universal model for understanding others (Heider, 1958). Convergent evidence from developmental psychology also suggests that children tend to develop a distinct "theory of mind" as well as a distinct sense of selfhood by about age three (Wellman, 1990). It is these developments that make it possible for people to rely on their subjective experiences to draw inferences about the internal states, desires, and intentions of others (Bless & Forgas, 2000).

Having a sense of self may also be adaptive for another reason. As a "mind module" and a distinct computational and representational device, the self allows us to systematize and accumulate the various kinds of social information and feedback we receive from others, and thus helps to modify our behaviors so as to optimize the way people respond to us. Leary (this volume) suggested that in a profoundly social species such as humans the need to constantly monitor signs of acceptance and rejection from others—what he called the operation of a "sociometer"—is indeed one of the most fundamental functions of the self. Others, such as Baumeister, Twenge, and Ciarocco, and Tice, Twenge, and Schmeichel (this volume) have shown how rejection and exclusion often produce maladaptive and self-defeating behavior patterns, attesting to the critical importance of interpersonal feedback to selfhood (see also Williams, 2001).

Thus, it appears that having a clear sense of self may have evolved to solve at least two kinds of adaptational problems. The self is the repository of the social feedback we receive from others, and is thus a major influence guiding successful and adaptive interpersonal strategies. The notion of self is also useful because it allows us to model and understand the internal, subjective worlds of others, making it easier to infer intentions and causes that lay behind observed behaviors, thus improving our interaction efficacy (Heider, 1958). There are plausible arguments, then, why the human self may be considered as an evolved psychological mechanism that gave humans improved behavioral flexibility and a superior ability to engage in complex, coordinated interactions with others (Buss, 1999; Pinker, 1997). Of course, the processes whereby integrated selves are constructed and the way symbolic processes enable human beings to create enduring representations of themselves can be inordinately complex. Symbolic interactionist theorists, such as George Herbert Mead and Charles Cooley and psychologists such as William James have done much of the early work to elucidate these mechanisms.

THE SELF AS A SYMBOLIC SOCIAL CONSTRUCTION: THE SYMBOLIC INTERACTIONIST TRADITION

Our sense of selfhood is one of the most private, unique, and special characteristics we all possess; yet at the same time, the self is also a fundamentally social creation, a product of our interactions with others (see also Ickes; Kashima, Kashima, & Clark; LaFrance; this volume). Symbolic interactionist theorists such as George Herbert Mead provided a unique insight into this paradox. According to Mead, the self is a product of the symbolic representations about ourselves that we construct on the basis of interactions with others. One of the paradoxical characteristics of the self is that it is an object to itself; it is both the observer and the observed (Mead, 1934/1970). William James (1890/1950) proposed a somewhat similar idea by distinguishing between the "I" self as the active agent of experience, the "thinker," and the "me" self as the object of experience, the target of observation and thought. But how can an individual get outside himself (experientially) in such a way as to become an object to himself?

It is the uniquely human ability to construct enduring symbolic representations of ourselves and others based on direct interpersonal experiences that is the essential prerequisite for a distinct sense of selfhood to develop, according to Mead. Thus, "the individual experiences himself . . . not directly, but only indirectly from the particular standpoints of other individual members of the same social group, or from the generalized standpoints of the social group as whole to which he belongs" (1934/1970, p. 138). Along the same lines, James (1890/1950) also believed that the "social me" is in essence the repository of others' reactions to us; people may thus process a multiplicity of selves incorporating the reactions they receive from a multiplicity of interaction partners. Remarkably, these insights about the social construction of the self have received strong confirmation in contemporary self research, as the chapters here by Biernat and Eidelman; Brewer and Pickett; Cooper and Hogg; Otten; and Wright, Aron, and Tropp illustrate.

For Mead, a person

> enters his own experience as a self . . . not by becoming a subject to himself, but only insofar as he first becomes an object to himself just as other individuals are objects to him . . . and he becomes an object to himself only by taking the attitudes of other individuals toward himself within a social environment . . . the importance of what we term "communication" lies in the fact that it provides a form of behavior in which the organism or the indvidual may become an object to himself. (1934/1970, p. 138)

In other words, the genesis of the self can be found in social interaction and communication, and it arises as a function of the accumulated reactions we receive from others (see also chapter by LaFrance, this volume). Thus, it is impossible to conceive of a self arising outside of social experience (Mead, 1934/ 1970). At the same time, the self is also an intrapsychic individual construct, the sum total of our accumulated symbolic representations and memories about ourselves. This symbolic interactionist analysis of the self as a symbolic social construction has received strong support from experimental social psychology.

Seminal experiments by Jones and his colleagues (e.g., Jones, Davis & Gergen, 1961) have shown that self-presentations that are successful and validated by the responses of others are incorporated into the self, but unsuccessful self-presentations are excluded.

However, as does James' (1890/1950), Mead's conception of the self recognizes that the self incorporates both a socially determined component, the "me," and a uniquely individual, subjective component, the "I." "The 'I' is the response of the organism to the attitudes of the others; the 'me' is the organized set of attitudes of others which one himself assumes" (p. 175). "Me" is the sum total of a person's perception and knowledge of how others see and respond to him/her. However, the "I" remains a fundamentally subjective and indeterminate entity, one that infuses a sense of freedom, flexibility, and uniqueness into how the self is conceived. It is the "I's" sometimes unexpected responses to social situations that provide a source of creativity, change and innovation to social life. The dynamic relationship between the "I" and the socialized "me" continues to be the focus of recent influential self-regulatory theories, such as Higgins' (1987) self-discepancy model.

In other words, although the self is to some extent a social construction, in turn, the social world is also an individual's construction. Within Mead's system, neither the social nor the individual realms have primacy. Rather, both social worlds and individual selves emerge in the course of symbolic interaction between individuals. Every encounter we have with others is the crucible within which individual selves and social systems are created, maintained, or changed.

As a number of contributors to this volume will show, the exploration of the precise nature of the interaction between the individual and the interpersonal, social aspects of the self has remained one of the key research questions to this day (see also Forgas et al., 2001; Sedikides & Brewer, 2001). How do social and cultural experiences actually produce the cognitive representational patterns of the self (Kashima et al.; Smith; this volume)? How do people shift the social standards they judge themselves by as a function of subtle contextual changes (Biernat & Eidelman, this volume)? How does the self respond to rejection and exclusion by others (Baumeister et al.; Leary; Tice et al.; this volume)? What are the processes people use to make judgments (and misjudgments) about the way they appear to others (Forgas; Gilovich; this volume)? How do we use our membership in important groups to construct a stable and positive sense of self (Brewer & Pickett; Cooper & Hogg; Otten; Wright et al.; this volume)?

Clearly, the subjective, phenomenological experience of the individual, and the external, interpersonal, social, and cultural information we continuously receive relevant to the self are in an organic, interactive relationship. Sometimes, the collective self is a source of individual self-definitions, and sometimes, it is the individual self that serves as a source of definining the collective self. This can occur, for example, when ingroups are novel, ambiguous, or loosely defined and we use self-knowledge to assign meaning to the group (Otten, this volume). As Mead (1934/1970), and more recently Sedikides and Brewer (2001), argued, emphasizing the social to the exclusion of the individual would be just as misleading as focusing on the subjective self to the exclusion of the social self. People's subjective representations about how others see them may be wildly inaccurate, as Gilovich's work on the spotlight effect (this volume) shows, yet concern with feedback from others remains a crucial determinant of self-conceptions (Crandall et al.; Leary; Tice et al.; Baumeister et al.; Rhodewalt & Tragakis; Hirt & McCrea; this volume).

INTEGRATIVE THEMES: LINKING THE INDIVIDUAL, RELATIONAL, AND COLLECTIVE ASPECTS OF THE SELF

Although it has been clearly recognized at least since Mead's (1934/1970) work that the self is a product of the interaction of individual cognitive and symbolic mechanisms with interpersonal and group influences, empirical research on this interaction is a much more recent phenomenon (Bless & Forgas, 2000; Forgas et al., 2001). Several chapters here focus on the precise mechanisms that are responsible for the way individual and collective aspects of the self interact. For example, Smith (this volume) outlines a connectionist distributed parallel processing theory that can account for the emergent quality of subjective self-representations produced by the ever-changing social inputs we receive from others. Kashima et al. cover somewhat similar ground by analyzing the interface between sociocultural variables and self-construction. Although social inputs about the self may change quite rapidly, the cumulatively established connection weights that ultimately determine subjective self-perceptions are more stable and change only gradually. This may account for the fact that individual and social self-conceptions (the way we see ourselves, and the way others see us) may sometimes be temporarily disjointed (see also Gilovich, this volume). Different contextual inputs should activate different patterns of weighting individual and social self-attributes, producing different self-responses.

The processes whereby social feedback becomes gradually incorporated into the phenomenological self are especially fascinating and are addressed in several chapters here. As Biernat and Eidelman and also Brewer and Pickett (this volume), argue, quite subtle contextual cues can play a critical role in determining whether people will assimilate into or contrast themselves with important reference groups. Some judgments—for example, those calling for objective rankings—produce assimilation to the reference group, while subjective judgments may produce judgments that contrast the self against the group norm. Thus, women may see themselves as "good leaders" when the judgment is subjective and calls for an implicit comparison with other women, but see themselves as "poor leaders" when objective rankings are required implying comparison with males. Interpersonal communicative acts such as smiling can also be the vehicle that people use to enhance the relational self and present a positive, socially valued image of themselves to the outside world (LaFrance, this volume). Other variables, such as the temporary salience and relevance of group identifications also impact on the extent to which relational and group identities are incorporated into the self (e.g., Cooper & Hogg; Otten; Wright et al.; this volume).

However, simple identification with the group is not necessarily a universal self-construction strategy, as Brewer and Pickett argue. Rather, people seem to be motivated to achieve the right balance between belonging to and identifying with significant groups, at the same time maintaining an optimal level of individuality within the group. The correct level of this "optimal distinctiveness" is dynamically determined as a function of a variety of contextual and personal characteristics, as research by Brewer and her colleagues has shown. Of course, self-representations are not simply the product of cold, rational cognitive processes. Of all the numerous knowledge domains we possess, knowledge about the self is perhaps the one most heavily influenced by powerful motivational forces. The way we think about ourselves is profoundly important to all of us, and the almost universal need to protect and enhance the self is one of the most enduring influences on self-construction and self-regulation (Higgins, 1987).

A number of chapters address the affective and motivational characteristics of the self in this volume (e.g., Forgas; Hirt & McCraea; Mackie & Smith; Rhodewalt & Tragakis; Wright et al.). A particularly intriguing question is how individuals respond when the self is threatened by negative feedback received from others. To the extent that the self is at least partly a social construction (Mead, 1934/1970), negative feedback from others can be especially threatening and difficult to deal with. Leary's (this volume) "sociometer theory" suggests that the continuous monitoring of feedback from others is one of the primary functions of the self-system. Nevertheless, experiences of negative feedback, rejection, and exclusion are frequently unavoidable in social life. How do people cope with such experiences? The chapters by Baumeister et al. and by Tice et al. (this volume) suggest that social exclusion often produces negative, maladaptive behaviors. Thus, excluded and rejected people seem to engage in more antisocial, aggressive acts both toward the sources of exclusion and toward neutral, innocent others than do others. Further, the likelihood of positive, altruistic, prosocial behaviors seems to decrease as a consequence of social exclusion and rejection. In a way, the work of Tice et al. and Baumeister et al. suggests that aggressive or antisocial behavior following rejection can be seen as a "clumsy attempt to reaffirm autonomy" (Sedikides, this volume). Both Tice et al. and Baumeister et al. (this volume) also report that these responses were not accompanied by reports of negative affectivity. This is rather a surprising result, and may well be due to the fact that excluded and rejected persons may be particularly unwilling or unable to admit to feeling upset about being ostracised (Williams, 2001).

One of the more fascinating motivated strategies designed to protect the self is self-handicapping. Self-handicapping is a fundamentally paradoxical mechanism, as self-protection can only be achieved at the cost of increasing the real likelihood of failure at important achievement tasks. So why do people engage in such a self-defeating strategy? Although self-handicapping may at first appear counterproductive, in fact, as both Rhodewalt and Tragakis, and Hirt and McCrea (this volume) suggest, it may seem reasonable from the subjective perspective of the individual employing it. When people have ambiguous or unclear causal understanding of what produces success in achievement tasks, believe that competence is a stable and unalterable characteristic, and expect the likelihood of failure to be high, self-handicapping may serve to protect the self from the damaging consequences of what appears as inevitable failure.

The role of group memberships in the creation and maintenance of meaningful selves has been analyzed by Tajfel (e.g., Tajfel & Forgas, 1981), who showed that identification with groups can become a source of a positive sense of self and may produce a universal motivation designed to ensure that the groups we belong to are positively distinguished from outgroups. Ingroup favoritism and discrimination against outgroups can thus serve the purpose of self-enhancement. This idea has undergone numerous theoretical revisions in recent years, as researchers attempted to disentangle the complex cognitive and motivational processes involved. We now know that the degree of identification with an ingroup appears to be dependent on a number of contextual factors. Too little identification can be just as problematic as too much identification according to the work of Brewer and Pickett (this volume). Identifying with a group can also be an effective mechanism for producing self-change according to Cooper and Hogg (this volume), and groups are also an important source of many of our attitudes (Crandall et al., this volume). When individuals become members of new and unfamiliar groups, there is a tendency for the individual self to expand and infuse the collective self. The resulting favoritism and altruism toward the new ingroup represents an interesting byproduct of self-enhancement, according to the analysis by Otten (this volume).

OVERVIEW OF THE VOLUME

Contributions to this volume have been organized into three distinct parts, dealing with the role of (1) intra-individual, (2) interpersonal, relational and (3) collective and group variables in the construction and maintenance of the self.

PART I. INDIVIDUAL AND INTRAPSYCHIC ASPECTS OF THE SELF

After this introductory chapter, the first contribution looking at intra-individual processes by Eliot Smith offers a cognitive conceptualization of how one's social self can be constantly revised and constructed. Smith notes that although most accepted theories about social self in psychology advocate a fluid, ever-changing view of the self as existing in interaction with the groups to which one belongs, the precise cognitive mechanism for how self and social identity change and affect our behaviors is still lacking. Smith presents the "distributed connectionist" model that assumes that conceptions of the social self are continuously reconstructed within a distributed parallel processing system of representations that is highly sensitive to contextual influences. In support of this model, Smith and his colleagues use a reaction time paradigm to show that shared traits and attitudes with an ingroup produce faster responses. Furthermore (see also chapter by Wright et al., this volume), a distributed network of self/other conceptualizations also influences close relationships. This line of work, then, provides a model of the cognitive mechanisms by which social identity and self-categorization may be constructed, suggesting that social selves are partly defined by the groups to which we belong, and they are fluid and sensitive to the situational context.

The next chapter by Gilovich asks the question: How do we decide how much attention others pay to the way we look, sound, and behave? As reactions by others are so central to the self, there are many situations when estimating the extent to which we attract attention is crucial. Gilovich suggests that people often overestimate how much attention others pay to them. The existence of this "spotlight effect" may well be an adaptive strategy to monitor social evaluations by members of a highly gregarious species such as humans. Gilovich suggests that social actors estimate the level of attention they receive using an anchoring and adjustment strategy. Subtle changes in the salience and accessibility of the self serve as an anchor, and the actor's ability and willingness to undertake the cognitively costly adjustment of his/her subjective experience determines the size of the spotlight effect. In several ingenuous experiments, Gilovich shows that our awareness of ourselves as we appear to others is essentially the product of sociocognitive judgmental processes that obey the same rules as do many other inferential social judgments.

In the third chapter in this section, Biernat and Eidelman suggest that mental representations about the self partly depend on the implicit comparisons people make with relevant "standard" groups. Thus, some judgments may invoke comparing the individual with the standards of his/her group, while other judgments call for absolute evaluations. Ratings on subjective scales are more likely to be based on implicit ingroup comparisons (i.e., a person's perceived position within the reference group), whereas objective judgments are independent of stereotyped ingroup norms. For example, Biernat and Eidelman report that female Army trainees evaluate themselves on traits such as leadership with reference to their gender group when subjective measures are used but shift to more stereotyped gender-based assessments when objective measures are used. Thus, men and women may rate themselves as similarly on leadership qualities on subjective scales, but on objective measures men rate themselves higher than do women. Such shifting standards do have wide-ranging implications for our self-concept, as people more identified with their ingroup are more likely to rely on within-group comparisons.

The next chapter by Joseph Forgas also suggests that self-concept and self-esteem are the product of shifting social judgments and inferences, and affect is an important influence on self-judgments. The chapter reviews cognitive theories of affective influences on judgments, including Forgas' (in press) Affect Infusion model that predicts that mood effects on self-judgments largely depend on the kind of processing strategies people adopt in a particular task. Surprisingly, self-judgments are more influenced by mood when the task requires more elaborate processing and allows greater scope for mood-primed thoughts to infuse the outcome. Thus, mood effects are greater when judgments concern more peripheral rather than central aspects of the self (see Sedikides, this volume). Mood also has a greater influence on self-judgments by low self-esteem individuals who may have a more unstable, uncertain concept of themselves. However, mood effects can be eliminated or reversed when a targeted, motivated processing strategy is used. Forgas also shows that moods also influence how people disclose intimate information about themselves, confirming that moods play an important role both in self-related cognition and communication.

Hirt and McCrea review interesting evidence suggesting that human beings possess a variety of mental self-protection mechanisms designed to maintain and bolster a positive sense of the self. How can we locate self-handicapping as a protective mechanism in this armory of self-affirmational resources? ask Hirt and McCrea. Self-handicapping is an intrinsically costly strategy because it necessarily involves task failure; so why should people choose this form of self-defense? Perhaps a unique feature of self-handicapping, suggest Hirt and McCrea, is that it also allows us to maintain our belief of ability and competence in a domain that is important to us. Other forms of self-protection, although capable of boosting global self-esteem, do not offer specific protection against negative information about ability following task failure. Several interesting studies reported by Hirt and McCrea found that high self-handicapping men rated themselves higher on specific ability than others despite their objective failure. Hirt and McCrea also suggest that affect seems to play a key role in triggering self-protective strategies (see also chapter by Forgas).

Rhodewalt and Tragakis argue that self-handicapping is a key intra-psychic strategy people employ to construct and maintain a positive self-concept. Rhodewalt and Tragakis describe an integrated model of the self-handicapping process, identifying both the antecedents (proximal and distal motives) and the consequences of this strategy. Self-handicapping appears to be based on an implicit belief that competency and abilities are fixed rather that incremental. Because self-handicappers see past successes as not causally linked to effort, they do not believe that increased effort will improve outcomes. In these circumstances, preparing for expected failure by self-handicapping may indeed appear a reasonable strategy. Rhodewalt and Tragakis report a series of empirical studies showing that high self-esteem self-handicappers were more likely to engage in self-aggrandizing attributions when successful and external attributions when failing. It appears then that self-handicapping is most likely when people have insecure self-conceptions, believe that abilities are fixed and immutable, and expect their abilities to be publicly challenged.

PART II. INTERPERSONAL AND RELATIONAL ASPECTS OF THE SELF

The second part of the book looks at the relationship between interpersonal processes and the self. Mark Leary reviews various interpersonal approaches to the self, such as terror management theory, sociometer theory, and dominance theory. Leary's sociometer theory assumes that people continuously monitor the degree to which they are accepted or rejected by others, and self-esteem is the measure they use to gauge their success in this enterprise. Considerable evidence indeed suggests that acceptance or rejection by others has a major and direct effect on self-esteem, an idea also included in the works of Charles Cooley, George Herbert Mead, and William James many decades ago. Ultimately, Leary's sociometer theory represents perhaps the most realistic and powerful conceptualization of how such an interpersonal evaluation system might operate. Alternative models, such as dominance theory and terror management theory, seem to account for some, but not all, of the phenomena predicted by sociometer theory. The interpersonal role of self is also the focus of Baumeister, Twenge, and Ciarocco's chapter, which suggests that the social self is essentially a tool for facilitating our ability to form and maintain rewarding social interactions. Indeed, the need to belong and to interact with others is one of the most fundamental evolutionary characteristics of our species. However, modern mass societies are not ideally constituted to provide us with rewarding interactions. Rejection, exclusion, and social isolation are all too common and can have catastrophic consequences. Baumeister et al. present a series of experiments exploring how inner, psychological processes mediate behavioral responses to rejection and exclusion. Social exclusion produced a strong increase in antisocial behaviors such as aggressiveness and cheating, and a corresponding reduction in prosocial behaviors such as helping. Rejection temporarily impaired reasoning ability, caused temporal disorientation, and interfered with retrieval (but not with encoding) processes. Surprisingly, negative affect was not implicated in these responses to exclusion. However, as Baumeister et al. note, because exclusion and rejection are embarrassing and shameful events, it is possible and perhaps likely that excluded people were unwilling or unable to admit to emotional distress in their verbal reports.

The link between social exclusion and antisocial behavior is also the theme of Tice, Twenge, and Schmeichel's chapter. Does rejection produce aggression, or is it antisocial behavior that produces rejection? After all, it would be far more adaptive to respond to rejection with positive, prosocial behaviors rather than risk further rejection by behaving in an antisocial manner. Research by Tice and her colleagues suggests that social exclusion can increase aggressive, antisocial tendencies especially in response to provocation; surprisingly, however, excluded persons also respond more aggressively to neutral, innocent persons. Excluded people were also more likely to break rules, engage in risky, unorthodox behaviors, produce antagonistic responses in a prisoner's dilemma game, and were less willing to engage in adaptive, prosocial behaviors. Again, negative affect was not reported; however, excluded individuals may have been unwilling to admit that they were upset.

In the next chapter, Bertram Malle suggests that simple folk theories about mind and interpersonal behavior offer a rich source of information about the self. Malle finds that there are notable differences in how actors and observers attend to social interactions, which behaviors they attempt to explain, and how they explain them. A series of ingenuous studies explored folk theories of mind and behavior as manifested in participants' daily records of their thoughts about their everyday encounters, the explanations people give to others in everyday conversations, and reflections about social events as described in twentieth-century novels. Malle argues that a full understanding of the real social cognitive processes individuals engage in as they construct a representation of themselves requires close attention to such naturalistic folk explanations. It is such private mental conversations with ourselves that form the basis of people's attempts to distinguish themselves from others, and to coordinate action and communication with others.

Self-processes can be analyzed either in terms of intrapsychic variables as discussed in Part I of this book or in terms of interpersonal processes as suggested by contributions to Part II. In his chapter, William Ickes presents a provocative metatheoretical analysis contrasting the individualistic social cognitive approach to the self with more interpersonal approaches. Because the social cognition paradigm looks at individuals alone, it often oversimplifies and over-emphasizes cognition, and produces research that is sometimes artificial and unimportant when compared to *social* cognition that occurs when people interact face-to-face. Ickes advocates an intersubjective research paradigm that studies perceptions, cognitions, and behavioral interactions within a dyadic (or larger group) setting. Ickes argues that this paradigm is not only richer and more complex, but is also more appropriate for understanding the social self in its natural surroundings.

Interpersonal communication is a key process in maintaining the self-concept, a process first described by Mead (1934/1970). Marianne LaFrance argues in her chapter that communicative acts such as smiling play an important role in the public display and definition of the self. According to LaFrance, smiling by women is not always a reflection of felt emotions as much as it is a self-display guided by gender norms, situational constraints, and emotion repair. As such, the emotional aspect of the social self is not revealed through one's smiles, but rather smiles reveal the obligations and roles that are thrust upon the social self. LaFrance uses both laboratory experiments and meta-analyses to show that women smile more often, smile more with strangers than friends, and smile more when others are dealing with negative emotions than do men. However, women also often report that not smiling makes them feel uncomfortable and that others would perceive them badly for not smiling. LaFrance outlines her Expressivity Demand Theory that maintains that the obligation to present a pleasant and nurturing self is felt more strongly by women, and is managed and controlled largely by smiling.

Kashima, Kashima, and Clark in their chapter return to Mead's conception of the thoroughly socialized self and suggest that the use of symbolic interpersonal processes in self-definition have received insufficient attention in psychological research. The capacity to represent ourselves as objects—a representation of the representer, or metarepresentation—underlies both self-recognition and symbol use, and has probably emerged as a result of evolutionary processes. Kashima et al. suggest that as early hominids developed, the need for ever-more elaborate shared symbolic representations was necessary to make group life possible. It is the symbolic products of a shared culture that make the construction of self-representations possible. Kashima et al. show that this interaction of individual representations and culturally shared symbols in the construction of the self can be simulated using a parallel distributed processing architecture. In essence, this models the processes first described by Mead (1934/1970) representing how meaningful cultural symbols are simultaneously represented within individual minds and also across individuals as collective representations. Thus, representations of the individual self can differentiate members of individualistic (e.g., United States, Australia) from collectivist (Japan) cultures, and women were found to score higher than men on measures of the relational self (see also LaFrance, this volume). In other words, interpersonal conditions shape the way individual, relational, and collective aspects of the self are symbolically constructed.

PART III. INTERGROUP, CULTURAL, AND COLLECTIVE ASPECTS OF THE SELF

In the third section, the links between the self, and groups and collective phenomena are explored. Following Tajfel, Brewer and Pickett see social identity as that part of the self-concept that is derived from an individual's membership in valued social groups. Reducing uncertainty, and the need for security and safety may be alternative motivations that drive ingroup identification (see also Leary, this volume). Brewer and Pickett suggest that the need to identify with a group is counterbalanced by an opposing need to be independent of, and distinctive from, ingroups. We need to "belong," but we also need to be "different." According to this dynamic "optimal distinctiveness" theory, social identities are activated to help us achieve an optimal balance between inclusion in, yet adequate individual differentiation from, reference groups. Research by the authors supports the optimal distinctiveness model by showing that when either distinctiveness or inclusiveness motives are invoked, people will shift their social identifications so as to restore optimal distinctiveness. In other words, social identities are managed so as to achieve a contextually optimal balance between assimilation to, and differentiation from, reference groups. Thus, the self-systems operate as a dynamic source of countervailing motivations, designed to achieve and maintain an optimal balance between inclusion in, yet differentiation from, the groups to which we belong.

Sabine Otten explores the role of the self in social cognitive explanations for ingroup favoritism such as in the minimal group paradigm. Motives such as self-esteem enhancement or uncertainty reduction have received mixed support, and Otten believes that it may not be necessary to invoke such motivational explanations for the ingroup favoritism effect. Ingroup favoritism, Otten argues, may simply be the default strategy when individuals find themselves in a minimal group, rather than the outcome of motivated social processes. Specifically, positive feelings about the self may be automatically projected to otherwise meaningless groups to which we belong. Otten's studies using subliminal priming and spontaneous trait inference tasks found that novel ingroups were immediately associated with positive affect, whereas novel outgroups were linked to neutral rather than negative affect. Novel ingroups thus acquire meaning because characteristics of the self are generalized to the group as a whole. Outgroups that cannot profit from an association with the self are typically seen as less positive. Otten and her colleagues also found that on ill-defined dimensions the ingroup is evaluated according to the self-stereotype. These results indicate the high relevance of self-anchoring in the process of defining an ingroup, without the need to assume motivated processes as some intergroup theories do (e.g., Tajfel & Forgas, 1981).

Crandall, O'Brien, and Eshleman resurrect Sherif's Group Norm Theory to argue that an individual's social self consists in large part of attitudes that fit the norms of the groups to which the individual belongs. The process of acquiring these attitudes occurs in stages as the individual first joins the group, feels pressure to adopt normative attitudes, and finally internalizes these attitudes. Crandall and his colleagues focus on prejudice and explore attitudes toward different groups, including those who do and do not attract justifiable negative evaluations. There was a strong relationship between expressions of prejudice and normative perceptions of Kansas University students' attitudes. In other words, expressions of prejudice fit the norms of prejudice. Crandall and his colleagues find that individuals who try hardest to suppress their personal prejudices in order to fit into the larger group are also most likely to voice the strongest held prejudices against groups that they believe it is okay to dislike. Crandall et al. argue that high prejudice suppressors are simply individuals caught in that difficult stage of group membership, a stage in which they are trying their hardest to mirror the norms of their group, fighting their own previously held attitudes. This chapter presents a particularly convincing case for the inclusion of the study of attitudes in understanding the content and nature of the social self.

Mackie and Smith explore the nature of prejudice from the perspective of emotions felt at the group level. Classic approaches to prejudice assumed that negative affect and dislike are the underlying causes of discrimination. These explanations do little to clarify why one outgroup attracts fear or contempt while another becomes the target of anger and that there is an impulse to move against some groups and away from others. Mackie and Smith suggest that based on the context in which the emotions are experienced, various negative emotions can result in distinctly different types of prejudice and action tendencies. Thus, fear produces one type of prejudice that leads to avoidance, but anger produces prejudice that leads to confrontation. Because group memberships form part of the self (see also Brewer & Pickett; Wright et al.; Smith; and Otten, this volume), events may trigger group-based emotions and action tendencies experienced on behalf of the group, regardless of whether the individual self is implicated or not. Finally, the authors propose that just as individual emotions are self-regulatory, intergroup emotions have a social regulatory function. Thus, people may respond with different emotions and actions to the same outgroup depending on contextual factors and appraisals.

Cooper and Hogg present a new look at cognitive dissonance theory; asking if individuals closely aligned with a group may not also experience dissonance and then attitude change when confronted with another group member's attitude-inconsistent behavior. Such "vicarious dissonance" is based on an expansion of the concept of the social self, suggesting that the same mechanisms that serve to maintain the consistency of the self also operate with respect to the groups to which we belong. In several clever studies, the authors show that individuals who highly identify with their group change their attitudes away from their own (and the group's) attitude when they hear (or simply know) that a group member is giving a speech advocating this counter-attitudinal position. Whereas individuals can be misled into misattributing their dissonance arousal to another source of discomfort, those who experience vicarious dissonance do not respond in this way. These intriguing findings suggest that an extended conceptualization of the social self (see also Wright et al.) offers promising avenues for integrating theories of individual cognitive dissonance processes and theories of group behavior such as social identity theory.

Wright, Aron, and Tropp in the final chapter in this section present a thoughtful analysis of how the concept of self may be used to integrate research on groups and on close relationships, thus providing a link between Part II and Part III. Wright et al. (as do Smith and Cooper & Hogg) note that the social self is shaped both by the groups to which one belongs (see also chapters by Brewer & Pickett; Cooper & Hogg; Otten) and identification with loved ones in close relationships. Wright et al. (this volume) also note that the idea of self-expansion has several interesting implications for intergroup relations. For example (see also Smith, this volume), individuals seem to assimilate ingroup members into their extended concept selfhood, and self-expansion might even apply to acquiring an outgroup's ways of perceiving and behaving. Wright et al. show, for example, that cross-group friendships lead to marked improvements in intergroup attitudes. In several studies, the authors show that even the knowledge that an ingroup member holds a close friendship with an outgroup member leads to improvements in attitudes toward that outgroup. Wright et al.'s self/other inclusion hypothesis suggests a crucial link between relationship research and group research, with self-expansion as the key variable.

SUMMARY

In his summary review chapter, Sedikides integrates the contributions to this volume in terms of the traditional tripartite model of the self—distinguishing between the individual, the interpersonal, and the collective aspects of the self. Sedikides shows how the various chapters not only illustrate these three complementary aspects of the self, but also enrich and challenge it. For example, the juxtaposition of the subjective and intersubjective, the individual and the social aspects of the self is a recurring theme in several metatheoretical chapters (e.g., Ickes; Kashima et al.; Malle; Smith). Comparing and contrasting these two approaches helps us better understand both paradigms, according to Sedikides. For example, Brewer and Pickett point out that achieving an "optimal distinctiveness" from the group is the outcome of a delicate, dynamic process where identification with, and distinctiveness from, valued groups is carefully calibrated. Others show that people may often be mistaken about how others see them (Gilovich), and the process of incorporating social information into the phenomenological self involves slow, gradual changes to our system of self-representations (Smith). Sedikides also suggests that concern with the motivated character of self-construction is another overarching theme within this book. People seem to employ a variety of strategies to monitor social feedback (Leary), to actively create conditions allowing them to preserve a positive self-concept (Hirt & McCrea; Rhodewalt & Tragakis), and to respond in motivated ways to negative feedback and rejection (Tice et al.; Baumeister et al.). Sometimes, it is positive self-assessment that drives the tendency to enhance otherwise "empty" groups we belong to (Otten).

As we have noted earlier, there continues to be a lively debate in contemporary self-research between those who believe that the self is best understood either at the individual/intrapsychic, relational, or intergroup levels. We hope that this volume will make a constructive contribution by focusing on integrative themes across the three approaches and emphasizing the psychological processes that link these different levels of explanation.

REFERENCES

Baumeister, R. F. (1999). *Evil: Inside human violence and cruelty.* New York: Freeman.

Bless, H., & Forgas, J. P. (Eds.). (2000). *The message within: The role of subjective experience in social cognition and behavior.* Philadelphia: Psychology Press.

Buss, D. M. (1999). *Evolutionary psychology.* Boston: Allyn & Bacon.

Forgas, J. P. (in press). Feeling and doing: Mood effects on interpersonal behavior. *Psychological Inquiry.*

Forgas, J. P., Williams, K. D., & Wheeler, L. (Eds.). (2001). *The social mind: Cognitive and motivational aspects of interpersonal behavior* (Vol. 2 in the Sydney Symposium of Social Psychology Series). New York: Cambridge University Press.

Heider, F. (1958). *The psychology of interpersonal relations.* New York: Wiley.

Higgins, E. T. (1987). Self-discrepancy: A theory relating self and affect. *Psychological Review, 94,* 319–340.

James, W. (1890/1950). *The principles of psychology (Vol. 1).* New York: Dover.

Jones, E. E. Davis, K.E. & Gergen, K. (1961). Role playing variations and their informational value for person perception. *Journal of Abnormal and Social Psychology, 63,* 302–310.

Mead, G. H. (1934/1970). *Mind, self and society.* Chicago: The University of Chicago Press.

Pinker, S. (1997). *How the mind works.* London: Penguin.

Sedikides, C., & Brewer, M. (Eds.). (2001). *Individual self, relational self, collective self.* Philadelphia: Psychology Press.

Tajfel, H., & Forgas, J. P. (1981). Social categorization: Cognitions, values and groups. In J. P. Forgas (Ed.), *Social cognition: Perspectives on everyday understanding* (pp. 113–140). London & New York: Academic Press.

Wellman, H. (1990). *The child's theory of mind.* Cambridge, MA: MIT Press.

Williams, K. D. (2001). *Ostracism: The power of silence.* New York: Guilford.

PART I

INDIVIDUAL AND INTRAPSYCHIC ASPECTS OF THE SELF

2

Overlapping Mental Representations of Self and Group
Evidence and Implications

ELIOT R. SMITH

Introduction
Connectionism
Autoassociative Connectionist Memory
Reconstruction of the Social Self
The Reconstructed Self and Intergroup Relations
Conclusion

INTRODUCTION

*T*his chapter will span several apparently quite disparate levels of analysis, including (a) detailed models of mental process and representation (specifically, connectionist models); (b) psychological phenomena regarding the social self (specifically, patterns of response times for self-descriptiveness judgments); (c) social and intergroup phenomena (specifically, identification with a social group and its consequences); with (d) some speculative links to evolution, self-regulation, close relationships, and so on (see Ickes, this volume, for another metatheoretical perspective on conceptualizing the social self).

The author is grateful to Diane Mackie for comments on earlier drafts of this chapter and for ongoing collaboration, as well as to the other participants in the Fourth Sydney Symposium of Social Psychology for valuable ideas and suggestions.

Address for correspondence: Eliot R. Smith, Department of Psychological Sciences, Purdue University, West Lafayette, IN 47907-1364, USA. E-mail: esmith@psych.purdue.edu

I hope to elucidate some connections among these levels, making the case that they are highly relevant to each other. In a nutshell, the basic argument of the chapter is this. Social identity theory and self-categorization theory, currently the most well-developed approaches to intergroup phenomena, rest on the assumption that intergroup behavior depends crucially on the psychological self. They postulate that the psychological self is flexible, and depending on the context may extend beyond the isolated individual to incorporate relationships with other people and identification with social groups. However, the underlying mechanisms of this "incorporation" or "overlap" have not been theoretically explicated in detail. The connectionist approach to mental representation can fill this gap. I will present a connectionist framework that can account for the flexibility and context sensitivity of the self (and other mental representations) and, in turn, the ways that a salient group membership and identification can alter the psychological representation of the self.

CONNECTIONISM

In cognitive and developmental psychology (McClelland & Rumelhart, 1986; Elman et al., 1996) and now increasingly in social psychology (Read & Miller, 1998), connectionist models are being explored and developed as a fundamental alternative to more traditional types of models of mental representation. This represents a true shift in the guiding metaphor for understanding cognition, from *computation* to *biology*. The computational metaphor dominated since mid-century, aided by the development of modern computers and the ascendancy of the cognitive perspective within psychology. But with an increasing recognition that cognition evolved for the control of adaptive behavior, a more biologically based approach to thinking about cognition has taken hold (Brooks, 1991; Smith & Semin, 2000). Connectionist models are a part of this newer thinking, insofar as they are biologically inspired (although in most cases far from faithful to the detailed workings of biological neurons).

Connectionist models or, more specifically, distributed connectionist models are most easily described in terms of their contrasts with more familiar types of models that draw on the computational metaphor (see Smith, 1998 for a more detailed presentation). *Symbolic* models include all those most familiar in social psychological theory (schemas, associative networks, Storage Bins, and the like). *Localist connectionist* (parallel constraint satisfaction) models constituted the first generation of connectionist models applied in social psychology (e.g., Shultz & Lepper, 1996; Kunda & Thagard, 1996). In both of these types of models, complete representations are constructed from individually semantically meaningful nodes by outside processes. For example, one might be assumed to form a representation by taking nodes representing, say, a person and several behaviors that the person had performed, and connecting these nodes with linkages that bind them together into a complete symbolic structure. This process resembles the combination of individually meaningful words to form a sentence. Like words on a page of text, the nodes themselves are passive bearers of information rather than active processing units.

In contrast, in *distributed connectionist* models any meaningful representation is a *pattern* of activation across a number of nodes (Smith, 1996, 1998). No single node has any fixed meaning (unlike the "person" node in the above example). Conversely, the same units participate in many different patterns that represent different objects or concepts (a property termed *superposition*). A familiar analogy is the individual pixels on a TV screen. No one pixel has any fixed meaning, but by taking on different patterns of color and illumination, the set of pixels can collectively represent a very large number of different meaningful images. Nodes are active processing units rather than passive information bearers that have to be assembled by external procedures. The nodes are richly interconnected and send signals to each other over these connections. The connections are relatively permanent (although their strengths may change with time as described below) rather than being dynamically created like a symbolic structure.

Connectionist networks not only are vehicles for representation but also actively process information. Specifically, each unit has a property termed *activation* that is assumed to change from moment to moment. Each unit's activation level is a function of its own previous activation as well as the inputs the unit receives over incoming connections. In turn, each unit sends output (a function of its activation) as a signal to other units over its outgoing connections. These connections are weighted (the signal sent over the connection is multiplied by a numerical weight) and unidirectional (signals pass in only one direction, conventionally indicated by an arrowhead, over each connection). However, a pair of connections may go in opposite directions between two units so that each can influence the other. Inputs arriving at a unit from separate units are simply summed.

Assume, for instance, that units 2 and 3 send connections to unit 1. The weight on the connection from unit 2 to unit 1 is symbolized as w_{12}, and that on the connection from unit 3 to 1 is w_{13}. The activation levels of units 2 and 3 are symbolized as a_2 and a_3. The activation of each of those units is multiplied by the corresponding connection weight, and all the incoming signals are summed by unit 1. In algebraic terms, the total input to unit 1 is $w_{12}a_2 + w_{13}a_3$. The activation of unit 1 at the next time point will be a function of that input value.

In contrast to the rapidly changing activation level of each unit, weights on connections change only slowly through the operation of the network's learning rule. These weights, therefore, are the repository of the network's long-term knowledge.

AUTOASSOCIATIVE CONNECTIONIST MEMORY

One specific type of connectionist network, an autoassociative memory, will be the focus of our discussion. A detailed discussion of the workings of an autoassociative memory can be found in Smith and DeCoster (1998). The important point for the present is the way such a network functions, which can conveniently be discussed as involving two phases. During the *learning phase*, many patterns are input to the units, many times each. After each pattern is presented, a specific learning rule is applied that slightly modifies all the connection weights. Weights are changed upward between pairs of units that are concurrently active in the given pattern, and downward between pairs of units that have different activation levels. Thus, connections are strengthened between units that tend to be coactive because they are included in similar patterns. (This is termed the Hebb rule for unsupervised learning.) Following an adequate amount of learning, the network is able to carry out pattern reconstruction. Suppose that a pattern similar to a previously seen pattern, or a subset of the units that make up a previously seen pattern, is input to the network. Activation flowing from the nodes included in that subset will flow along the strengthened connections and will ultimately activate the rest of the learned pattern. This amounts to reconstruction (not "retrieval") of the whole pattern from a partial or erroneous cue.

There are three key properties of the type of connectionist memory just described (Clark, 1993).

Incremental Learning, Not Discrete Representation Construction

In symbolic and localist connectionist models, meaningful structures have to be assembled at a discrete point in time from their component units. Initial learning (the creation of a representation) and change (modification of existing representation) are thus conceptually quite different. In distributed connectionist models, in contrast, representations are incrementally built up through experience, through weight changes as the network processes multiple input patterns. There is no discrete point at which a representation is constructed, and no distinction between learning and change (representation change is just more learning).

Distinct Format of Currently Active Representation versus Latent Knowledge

In symbolic and localist connectionist models, active and inactive representations have the same format and structure (i.e., a set of nodes connected by links). Retrieval amounts to searching for and finding the structure and activating it; the metaphor is a warehouse or file cabinet in which many representations sit passively until they are pulled out. Moreover, individual representations are discrete and distinct (like separate sheets of paper in the file cabinet), so one can be activated or changed without affecting any others. In distributed connectionist models, in contrast, the currently active representation is a pattern of unit activations. These activations change rapidly moment to moment. Latent or inactive knowledge is not represented in the same format (i.e., as an activation pattern) but is implicit in a set of learned network connections that allow activation patterns to be reconstructed from input cues. In this latent form, all representations are superposed in a single set of connection weights. Changing one representation will (in general) change all, although the amount of interference may vary depending on specific details such as the similarity of the patterns, the learning rule used, and the size of the network.

It may be difficult to envisage the access of information from memory in any way other than with the familiar metaphor of storage and retrieval. But the notion of reconstruction is very intuitive in other psychological contexts, such as the experience of affect. It makes no sense to ask questions like: where is my happiness (anger, surprise, etc.) stored when I am not feeling it? Obviously these experiences are not "stored" anywhere; instead, our minds have the ability to reproduce or reconstruct these states under appropriate circumstances (i.e., given appropriate cues). Consider knowledge representation in the same light. The representation of another person, the self, or a social group is not "stored" anywhere when it is not currently active; instead, our minds can reconstruct these representations when given appropriate cues.

Context Sensitivity and Flexibility of Representations

In symbolic and localist connectionist models, a concept is represented by a structure that essentially remains the same whether it is inactive (stored away in memory) or active (current focus of attention). If a version of a concept that is tuned to a specific context is needed, it must be constructed on line from two or more parent concepts (Kunda et al., 1990). Research suggests, however, that conceptual knowledge is pervasively context sensitive (Yeh & Barsalou, 2000). For example, in a sentence like "the bird walked across the barnyard," the concept of "bird" centers around "chicken" and similar exemplars, while in a suburban backyard context, "bird" would more likely mean something like "sparrow" (Barsalou, 1987). In distributed connectionist models, in contrast, because representations are reconstructed rather than retrieved, this type of flexibility and context sensitivity is automatically present. Cues that are present at the moment of reconstruction can tune and bias the pattern that is ultimately constructed to a contextually appropriate version of the concept (Clark, 1993).

As a demonstration of this point, Rumelhart, Smolensky, McClelland, and Hinton (1986) trained a network with the typical features of various types of rooms (living room, bedroom, and so forth). Presented with cues that clearly related to only one of the known room types (such as a bed), the network reactivated the entire known bedroom pattern. More important, when cues that typically relate to different rooms were presented (e.g., bed and sofa), the network did not decide arbitrarily between bedroom and living room, nor did it break down and give an error message about incompatible inputs. Instead, it combined compatible elements of the two knowledge structures to produce a concept something like a large, fancy bedroom (complete with floor lamp and fireplace). Memories virtually always involve the combination of multiple knowledge structures in the way suggested by this example. For instance, retrieval of an autobiographical memory may be influenced by general knowledge as well as by traces laid down on a specific occasion (Ross, 1989; Loftus, 1979). Or perceptions and reactions to a person who is a member of multiple categories, such as a male Pakistani engineer, may be influenced by knowledge relating to all of the categories.

This third property is the focus of this paper. The property states that connectionist representations involve the on-line reconstruction of concepts (represented as occurrent activation patterns) based on an underlying array of long-term representational resources (connection weights). Applied to the self as a concept, this property is very much in line with the statement by Turner, Oakes, Haslam, and McGarty (1994) that "the concept of the self as a separate mental structure does not seem necessary, because we can assume that any and all cognitive resources—long-term knowledge, implicit theories, . . . and so forth—are recruited, used, and deployed when necessary" (p. 459) to construct a self-representation. With that, we turn to a consideration of the flexible and context-sensitive social self from an underlying connectionist viewpoint.

RECONSTRUCTION OF THE SOCIAL SELF

From a connectionist viewpoint as just described, all conceptual knowledge is actively reconstructed rather than passively retrieved. In particular, this applies to self-knowledge or the representation of the self (Markus & Wurf, 1987). The central insight of the social identity and self-categorization theoretical tradition is that *knowledge about one's social groups is used in the construction of the self.* This is the basis for self-stereotyping—people's tendency to conform to group norms when group membership is salient (Spears, Doosje, & Ellemers, 1997; Turner, Hogg, Oakes, Reicher, & Wetherell, 1987). The reverse is certainly true as well (although it has received less conceptual emphasis): knowledge about the self is used in the construction of social group representations, in a kind of social projection (Krueger & Clement, 1997; Cadinu & Rothbart, 1996). This overall pattern has been described as involving a kind of "overlap" of self and group representations, but this term can be misleading. "Overlap"—as portrayed in Aron, Aron, and Smollan's (1992) IOS scale, for example—suggests that two independently existing objects share some parts. Instead, it seems better to stick with the ideas of superposition and reconstruction. Self and group representations are both constructed as needed, from a common pool of underlying knowledge that affects them both—just as the McClelland and Rumelhart room schema network can use its basic knowledge about what features go with what to reconstruct different types of bedrooms, living rooms, and so on.

What evidence do we have for the notion that self and group representations draw on common long-term knowledge resources (as stated by Turner et al., 1994)? I have developed such evidence in several studies using a response time paradigm. These studies show that people reporting on their own traits or other attributes are able to do so faster for self-attributes that match those of the person's ingroup—even though the ingroup is not explicitly part of the person's task. As an overview, the logic of the response time method is that

- *if* (a) self and ingroup representations draw on a common pool of underlying features (e.g., traits), and
- (b) while the person is attempting to make self-descriptiveness judgments, the ingroup representation is also activated (whether through a strong and permanent sense of group identification or through contextual activation of the specific group), then
- (c) features (e.g., traits) that are common to the self and ingroup will receive a "double dose" of activation (through their links to both self and group) and will therefore be associated with quicker and more accurate responses.

Several studies to date have confirmed the robustness of this effect and have shown that it relates as expected to independent measures of group identification. Our empirical studies (beginning with Smith & Henry, 1996) have used the following general paradigm, which we originally adapted from Aron, Aron, Tudor, and Nelson (1991). First, participants complete three questionnaires that list 90 traits, indicating the extent to which each trait describes the self, an ingroup, and the complementary outgroup. Participants next complete the response time task. Each of the traits in turn appears on a computer screen, and the participant presses a "me" or "not-me" key to indicate whether or not the trait is self-descriptive. The response times to make these decisions are analyzed based on whether the response is the same or different for self and the ingroup. The key prediction is a statistical interaction, with faster responses when the trait's relation to the self matches its relation to the ingroup (that is, when the trait describes both the self and in-group, or neither the self nor ingroup).

In Smith and Henry (1996), the groups used were liberal arts or engineering majors; for participants who were neither of those, the groups were Greek (i.e., fraternity or sorority member) or non-Greek. The results are shown in Figure 2.1.

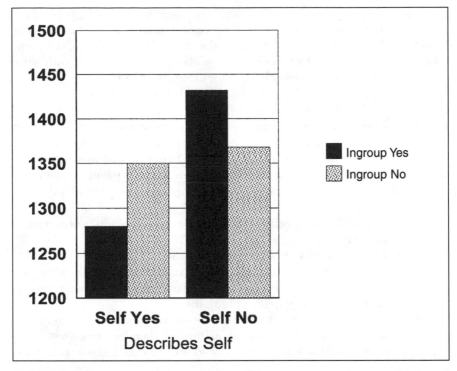

FIGURE 2.1. Response times (in msec) for self-descriptiveness judgments. (Replotted from data originally presented in E. R. Smith and S. Henry, *Personality and Social Psychology Bulletin*, vol. 22, no. 6, pp. 635–642. Reprinted by permission of Sage Publications, Inc.)

Note that self-descriptiveness responses to traits where self and ingroup matched were faster than responses for mismatching traits. Interestingly, neither match to the outgroup nor the distinctiveness of the trait (i.e., whether the trait was one on which ingroup and outgroup differed) affected response times.

We next tested the hypothesis that the effect should operate in the reverse direction. When participants answer questions about the ingroup, response times should be affected by the self-descriptiveness of the traits. In other words, not only the representation of the self but also of the ingroup is constructed on-line. This study was reported by Smith, Coats, and Walling (1999), and used Greek or non-Greek as groups (the vagaries of the participant pool meant that all participants were non-Greek). The results shown in Figure 2.2, for group-descriptiveness judgments, are essentially the same as those in the initial study of self-descriptiveness judgments. This process of using the self as a basis for assigning properties to an ingroup has also been studied by Otten (this volume) and her associates under the term "self-anchoring."

We next wanted to examine the generalizability of the effect beyond traits

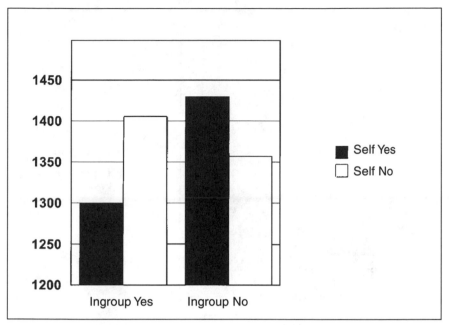

FIGURE 2.2. Response times (in msec) for ingroup descriptiveness judgments. (Replotted from data originally presented in E. R. Smith, S. Coates, and D. Walling, *Personality and Social Psychology Bulletin*, vol. 25, no. 7, pp. 873–882. Reprinted by permission of Sage Publications, Inc.)

as features of the self-representation. Our next study (Coats, Smith, Claypool, & Banner, 2000) had one condition using traits (replicating the Smith & Henry, 1996 study) and one condition using attitude objects. In the latter condition, participants simply indicated on the computer whether they liked or disliked the given object. Groups in this study were again Greek or non-Greek (and this time all participants were Greek).

Figure 2.3 shows the overall results collapsing across attitudes versus traits. The replication of the previous findings is obvious. In fact, the size of the match effect did not statistically differ between the attitudes and traits condition, although like/dislike responses to the attitude objects were quicker than me/not-me responses to the traits overall.

In this study we also computed the response time effect of matching versus mismatching one's ingroup on a per-subject basis, and correlated that implicit measure of group identification with several explicit measures. The correlation with the Social Identity measure of Brown, Condor, Mathew, Wade, and Williams (1986), which Jackson and Smith (1999) found to be one of the factorially purest measures of group identification, was $r = .34$ (p < .05). The correlation with the Avoidance measure of Smith, Murphy, and Coats (1999), an inversely scaled group identification measure conceptually deriving from an

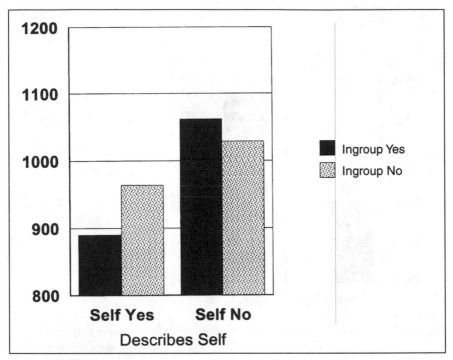

FIGURE 2.3. Response times (in msec) for self-descriptiveness judgments and like/dislike (attitude) judgments combined. (Replotted from data originally presented in S. Coats, E. R. Smith, H. M. Claypool, and M. J. Banner, *Journal of Experimental Social Psychology*, vol. 36, pp. 302–315. Copyright Academic Press, 2000)

application of attachment theory to group memberships, was $r = -.36$ (p < .05). And the correlation of the RT match effect with a measure of perceived self/ingroup similarity (the correlation between each subject's self and ingroup ratings, across the 90 traits or attitudes) was $r = .47$ (p < .001). Thus, it seems clear that participants who identified themselves more strongly as Greeks, or saw themselves as more similar to Greeks, showed larger RT effects of matching versus mismatching that ingroup when they made self-descriptiveness responses. These findings clearly implicate the mental linkage between self and ingroup—the conceptual representation of group identification—as part of the process that generates these RT findings.

It is worth noting that none of these findings are specific to groups. Close personal relationships as well as group identification have been conceptualized as involving an "overlap" between self and partner representations, although as noted earlier the notions of superposition and reconstruction are probably more apt than overlap. Aron et al. (1991) initially found this RT difference, with faster responses for self traits matching a close relationship partner than for those mismatching the partner. Smith, Coats, and Walling (1999) found the same RT difference when the computer timed responses for the relationship partner rather than the self, and showed that the RT difference calculated on a per-subject basis correlated with the IOS relationship closeness measure. Finally, Aron and Fraley (1999) found that the RT difference (when responses were given for self) correlates with the IOS, measures of love for the partner, and various "cognitive" indicators of relationship closeness. Moreover, the RT difference predicted relationship outcomes over time. In terms of our thinking, all these findings indicate that knowledge about a close relationship partner, as well as about the individual self and ingroup, also constitutes part of the overall pool out of which self-representations, partner representations, and ingroup representations are constructed.

THE RECONSTRUCTED SELF AND INTERGROUP RELATIONS

The notion of active, on-line reconstruction of the self incorporating relationship partners or groups has an almost infinite range of implications for social behavior. Some examples are as follows:

- Incorporation of a partner or group into the self has motivational implications: the partner or group's welfare will be psychologically equivalent to the person's own. This process forms a basis for altruism and self-sacrifice (Turner et al., 1987).
- Seeing oneself as a member of a group results in "self-stereotyping," increased conformity to group norms regarding behaviors, attitudes, and thoughts (Turner et al., 1987).
- Seeing oneself as linked to a group or partner also has affective implications, such as the well-known fact that we experience positive (or negative) affect when the group or partner attains good or bad outcomes (Cialdini et al., 1976; Tesser, 1988).

For this chapter, we will briefly consider the implications for intergroup relations. Incorporation of group membership into the self through the reconstruction process means that self-regulatory processes operate on behalf of the ingroup as well as for the individual self. Self-regulatory processes have important implications for both emotional experience and overt behavior. For example, consider the recent proposal (Higgins, 1998) that there are two regulatory systems aimed respectively at promotion (attaining positive outcomes; nurturance) and prevention (avoiding negative outcomes; security). Whether a person appraises an event or situation as a threat to the personal self or (when group membership is salient) as a threat to the ingroup, the prevention system will become active. Feelings of fear and anxiety, and corresponding motives to avoid or overcome the threat, will be elicited by the event. In fact, negative emotional reactions to outgroups triggered by group-relevant, self-regulatory processes may constitute the core of intergroup prejudice. This is the central theme of Intergroup Emotions Theory, which will be discussed in much more detail in a companion chapter (Mackie & Smith, this volume).

Consistent with this perspective, there is substantial preliminary evidence for the relevance of self-regulatory processes to intergroup relations. Foerster, Higgins, and Strack (2000) demonstrate that stereotypes of outgroups are important for self-regulation systems. Their studies show that people with high chronic activation of the prevention system show anxiety-related emotions and vigilance motivation in response to information that challenges outgroup stereotypes. Research by Shah, Brazy, and Higgins (in press) shows, similarly, that people with high chronic activation of the prevention system are likely to try to distance themselves from outgroup members in a situation allowing intergroup contact.

CONCLUSION

We have covered a lot of conceptual territory, from models of mental representation to the reconstructed social self to self-regulatory processes that operate with respect to relationship partners and social groups as well as the individual self. The notion of self-regulation also all but inevitably brings in an evolutionary perspective, thereby bringing intergroup relations within the compass of that perspective as well.

As several theorists have argued (Caporael, 1997; Caporael & Baron, 1997; Smith, Murphy, & Coats, 1999), self-regulatory processes are important not only at the level of the individual self (e.g., to attain food and avoid predators). In our species, relationships are equally as important for survival—relationships between mates, allies, and caregivers and children—so processes that regulate relationship closeness are also assumed to have a long evolutionary history that contributes importantly to their properties (Simpson & Kenrick, 1997). For example, this evolutionary emphasis can be found in attachment theory, which in Bowlby's original formulation (stressing the mother–infant bond) was heavily based on evolved mechanisms (Bowlby, 1982). The evolutionary emphasis is weaker in current work in social psychology on close relationships but is still evident in much work (e.g., Kirkpatrick, 1998).

Similarly, group memberships have been essential for survival; in the early evolutionary history of hominids, survival outside of the social group would have been impossible. Therefore, regulation of closeness to ingroups also has an evolutionary basis, as several theorists have noted (Caporael & Baron, 1997).

The key conclusion from this line of thinking is that the fundamental purpose of the psychological self-system is self-regulation—and this remains equally true when we consider the extended self that includes relationship partners and group memberships as well as the biological individual. In this broad perspective, intergroup phenomena (such as bias and prejudice against outgroups) are considered as outcomes of processes that are *essentially continuous* with individual-level emotional and self-regulatory processes. This integrative perspective affords many opportunities for innovative and integrative theoretical development (Mackie & Smith, 1998), illustrating the heuristic value of putting groups and relationships in a common framework and drawing on evolutionary and functional perspectives as well as new models of mental representation. Brewer (this volume) provides a nice example of integrative theorizing at these different levels.

To close with a frankly speculative suggestion: Consider the possibility that it is the operation of (extended) self-regulatory systems that determines and explains our subjective sense of self. In other words, the affective and motivational consequences of self-regulatory systems may be subjectively accessible cues that tell us what is (and what is not) incorporated within the self. Since self-regulatory systems (by the hypothesis of this chapter) operate at the individual, relational, and group levels, this process should operate in conceptually the same way at each level. Thus: (a) I know it's *my* foot because when someone steps on it, it hurts; (b) I know it's *my* partner because when someone pays her a compliment, I feel warm inside; (c) I know it's *my* group because when someone disrespects us, I feel angry. Further research needs to be conducted to examine this possibility, that self-regulation in this extended sense actually constitutes the subjective sense of self.

REFERENCES

Aron, A., Aron, E. N., & Smollan, D. (1992). Inclusion of Other in the Self Scale and the structure of interpersonal closeness. *Journal of Personality and Social Psychology, 63,* 596–612.

Aron, A., Aron, E. N., Tudor, M., & Nelson, G. (1991). Close relationships as including other in the self. *Journal of Personality and Social Psychology, 60,* 241–253.

Aron, A., & Fraley, B. (1999). Relationship closeness as including other in the self: Cognitive underpinnings and measures. *Social Cognition, 17,* 140–160.

Barsalou, L. (1987). The instability of graded structure: Implications for the nature of concepts. In U. Neisser (Ed.), *Concepts and conceptual development* (pp. 101–140).

Cambridge, UK: Cambridge University Press.

Bowlby, J. (1982). *Attachment and loss: Vol. 1. Attachment* (2nd ed.). New York: Basic Books.

Brooks, R. A. (1991). *Intelligence without reason.* MIT AI Lab Memo 1293.

Brown, R., Condor, S., Mathew, A., Wade, G., & Williams, J. (1986). Explaining intergroup differentiation in an industrial organization. *Journal of Occupational Psychology, 59,* 273–286.

Cadinu, M. R., & Rothbart, M. (1996). Self-anchoring and differentiation processes in the minimal group setting. *Journal of Personality and Social Psychology, 70,* 661–677.

Caporael, L. R. (1997). The evolution of truly social cognition: The core configurations model. *Personality and Social Psychology Review, 1,* 276–298.

Caporael, L. R., & Baron, R. M. (1997). Groups as the mind's natural environment. In J. Simpson & D. Kenrick (Eds.), *Evolutionary social psychology* (pp. 317–343). Mahwah, NJ: Erlbaum.

Cialdini, R. B., Borden, R. J., Thorne, A., Walker, M. R., Freeman, S., & Sloan, L. R. (1976). Basking in reflected glory: Three (football) field studies. *Journal of Personality and Social Psychology, 34,* 366–375.

Clark, A. (1993). *Associative engines: Connectionism, concepts, and representational change.* Cambridge, MA: MIT Press.

Coats, S., Smith, E. R., Claypool, H., & Banner, M. (2000). Overlapping mental representations of self and in-group: Response time evidence and its relationship with explicit measures of group identification. *Journal of Experimental Social Psychology, 36,* 302–315.

Elman, J. L., Bates, E. A., Johnson, M. H., Karmiloff-Smith, A., Parisi, D., & Plunkett, K. (1996). *Rethinking innateness.* Cambridge, MA: MIT Press.

Foerster, J., Higgins, E. T., & Strack, F. (2000). When stereotype disconfirmation is a personal threat: How prejudice and prevention focus moderate incongruency effects. *Social Cognition, 18,* 178–197.

Higgins, E. T. (1998). Promotion and prevention: Regulatory focus as a motivational principle. In M. P. Zanna (Ed.), *Advances in experimental social psychology* (Vol. 30, pp. 1–46). New York: Academic Press.

Jackson, J. W., & Smith, E. R. (1999). Conceptualizing social identity: A new framework and evidence for the impact of different dimensions. *Personality and Social Psychology Bulletin, 25,* 120–135.

Kirkpatrick, L. A. (1998). Evolution, pair-bonding, and reproductive strategies: A reconceptualization of adult attachment. In J. A. Simpson & W. F. Rholes (Eds.), *Attachment theory and close relationships* (pp. 353–393). New York: Guilford.

Krueger, J., & Clement, R. W. (1997). Estimates of social consensus by majorities and minorities: The case for social projection. *Personality and Social Psychology Review, 1,* 299–313.

Kunda, Z., Miller, D. T., & Claire, T. (1990). Combining social concepts: The role of causal reasoning. *Cognitive Science, 14,* 551–577.

Kunda, Z., & Thagard, P. (1996). Forming impressions from stereotypes, traits, and behaviors: A parallel-constraint-satisfaction theory. *Psychological Review, 103,* 284–308.

Loftus, E. F. (1979). *Eyewitness testimony.* Cambridge, MA: Harvard University Press.

Mackie, D. M., & Smith, E. R. (1998). Intergroup relations: Insights from a theoretically integrative approach. *Psychological Review, 105,* 499–529.

Markus, H., & Wurf, E. (1987). The dynamic self-concept: A social psychological perspective. *Annual Review of Psychology, 38,* 299–337.

McClelland, J. L., Rumelhart, D. E. (Eds.). (1986). *Parallel distributed processing* (Vol. 2). Cambridge, MA: MIT Press.

Read, S. J., & Miller, L. C. (Eds). (1998). *Connectionist models of social reasoning and social behavior.* Mahwah, NJ: Erlbaum.

Ross, M. (1989). Relation of implicit theories to the construction of personal histories. *Psychological Review, 96,* 341–357.

Rumelhart, D. E., Smolensky, P., McClelland, J. L., & Hinton, G. E. (1986). Schemata and sequential thought processes in PDP models. In J. L. McClelland & D. E. Rumelhart (Eds.), *Parallel distributed processing: Explorations in the microstructure of cognition* (Vol. 2, pp. 7–57). Cambridge, MA: MIT Press.

Shah, J. Y., Brazy, P. C., & Higgins, E. T. (in press). Considering the regulatory focus of intergroup bias. In D. M. Mackie & E. R. Smith (Eds.), *From prejudice to intergroup emotions: Differentiated reactions to social groups.* Philadelphia: Psychology Press.

Shultz, T. R., & Lepper, M. R. (1996). Cognitive dissonance reduction as constraint satisfaction. *Psychological Review, 103,* 219–240.

Simpson, J. A., & Kenrick, D. T. (Eds). (1997). *Evolutionary social psychology.* Mahwah, NJ: Erlbaum.

Smith, E. R. (1996). What do connectionism and social psychology offer each other? *Journal of Personality and Social Psychology, 70,* 893–912.

Smith, E. R. (1998). Mental representation and memory. In D. Gilbert, S. Fiske, & G. Lindzey (Eds.), *Handbook of social psychology* (4th ed., Vol. 1, pp. 391–445). New York: McGraw-Hill.

Smith, E. R., Coats, S., & Walling, D. (1999). Overlapping mental representations of self, in-group, and partner: Further response time evidence and a connectionist model. *Personality and Social Psychology Bulletin, 25*, 873–882.

Smith, E. R., & DeCoster, J. (1998). Knowledge acquisition, accessibility, and use in person perception and stereotyping: Simulation with a recurrent connectionist network. *Journal of Personality and Social Psychology, 74*, 21–35.

Smith, E. R., & Henry, S. (1996). An in-group becomes part of the self: Response time evidence. *Personality and Social Psychology Bulletin, 22*, 635–642.

Smith, E. R., Murphy, J., & Coats, S. (1999). Attachment to groups: Theory and measurement. *Journal of Personality and Social Psychology, 77*, 94–110.

Smith, E. R., & Semin, G. R. (2000). *The foundations of socially situated action: Socially situated cognition.* Unpublished manuscript, Purdue University, West Lafayette, IN.

Spears, R., Doosje, B., & Ellemers, N. (1997). Self-stereotyping in the face of threats to group status and distinctiveness: The role of group identification. *Personality and Social Psychology Bulletin, 23*, 538–553.

Tesser, A. (1988). Toward a self-evaluation maintenance model of social behavior. In L. Berkowitz (Ed.), *Advances in experimental social psychology, Vol. 21: Social psychological studies of the self: Perspectives and programs* (pp. 181–227). San Diego, CA: Academic Press.

Turner, J. C., Hogg, M. A., Oakes, P. J., Reicher, S. D., & Wetherell, M. S. (1987). *Rediscovering the social group: A self-categorization theory.* Oxford, UK: Blackwell.

Turner, J. C., Oakes, P. J., Haslam, S. A., & McGarty, C. (1994). Self and collective: Cognition and social context. *Personality and Social Psychology Bulletin, 20*, 454–463.

Yeh, W., & Barsalou, L. W. (2000). *The situated nature of concepts.* Unpublished manuscript, Emory University, Atlanta, GA.

3

Egocentrism and the Social Self

Anchoring (and Adjustment) in Self and Social Judgments

THOMAS GILOVICH

INTRODUCTION

*I*t is easy to feel as if one is sticking out like the proverbial sore thumb—when there is no one to talk to at a cocktail party; when one emerges from the lavatory and discovers a spot of water on one's trousers that looks indistinguishable from a quite different, and much more embarrassing, accident; or when one must dine alone at a restaurant. Many people, in fact, report that they make it a rule never to dine alone in public or go to a movie theater alone out of concern for how it will appear to others.

My colleagues and I have been conducting research that aims to sketch the phenomenology of being caught in such situations (Gilovich, Kruger, & Medvec, 2002; Gilovich, Medvec, & Savitsky, 2000; Gilovich & Savitsky, 1999; Savitsky,

Address for correspondence: Tom Gilovich, Psychology Department, Cornell University, Ithaca, NY 14853, USA. E-mail: tdgl@cornell.edu

Epley, N., & Gilovich, T., 2001). The most prominent finding of this program of research is that people consistently and substantially overestimate the extent to which they do indeed stand out in others' attention. People overestimate, in other words, the extent to which others notice, judge, and remember their actions and appearance. We have dubbed this phenomenon the "spotlight effect" after people's common conviction that the social spotlight shines more brightly upon them than it actually does.

THE SPOTLIGHT EFFECT: EMPIRICAL EVIDENCE

We have documented the existence of the spotlight effect in several ways. In one of the simplest demonstrations, individual participants were asked, upon their arrival at the experiment, to don a T-shirt featuring a picture of pop singer Barry Manilow (a figure of questionable repute among college students). The participant was then escorted, Mr. Manilow's face front and center, to another room in the laboratory and instructed to knock on the door. A second experimenter answered and ushered the participant into the room, where four to six other (normally-dressed) participants were seated filling out questionnaires. After a brief interchange, the second experimenter escorted the participant back out of the room and into the hallway. There, the participant was asked to estimate how many of those seated in the room could recall who was pictured on his/her shirt. As expected, participants overestimated the actual accuracy of the observers (by a factor of 2). The T-shirt wearers were noticed far less than they suspected. Subsequent experiments have demonstrated that the same effect is observed when participants are wearing a T-shirt featuring a person with whom they would be proud to be associated (Gilovich et al., 2000). The spotlight effect thus exists when people feel conscious of *any* aspects of themselves that might attract attention, not just those that are potentially embarrassing.

The spotlight effect also applies beyond people's judgments of the salience of their appearance. It applies to their behavior and performance as well. We have shown, for example, that people overestimate the salience of their own contributions to a group discussion (Gilovich et al., 2000). Here too, the spotlight effect applies both to moments of triumph and moments of embarrassment: participants overestimated how highly others would rate such things as the extent to which they advanced the discussion and the glaringness of their speech errors. In a further extension, we have shown that people overestimate the salience to others of their own physical absence. Participants who were removed from a portion of an experiment expected their absence to be more apparent to the other participants than it actually was (Savitsky, Gilovich, Berger, & Medvec, 2001). Once again, people expect others to notice them (even their absence) more than is actually the case.

Of course it is not simply the fear of being noticed by others when one is dining alone or has no one to talk to at a cocktail party that is so disturbing.

There is also the concern that, once spotted, others will be less than charitable in their evaluations. These concerns have likewise been found to be exaggerated (Epley, Savitsky, & Gilovich, in press; Savitsky et al., in press; Van Boven, Kamada, & Gilovich, 1999). We have demonstrated that individuals expect others to judge them more harshly after a failure—whether a social faux pas or an intellectual downfall—than others actually do. Participants who fail to perform well at solving anagrams or answering general knowledge questions, for instance, expect their faulty performance to garner more condemnation than it actually does, and expect observers to rate them more harshly on attributes such as intelligence and creativity than they actually do.

THE SPOTLIGHT EFFECT AND THE SOCIAL SELF

The existence of a pervasive spotlight effect has several implications for the theme of this volume, the social self. For instance, as numerous self theorists have long maintained, a person's sense of self is constructed in large measure by internalizing the perceived assessments of others (Cooley, 1902; Mead, 1934). Thus, according to such "looking glass self" models, an essential task of self-understanding is the accurate assessment of others' views of the self. That may not be an easy task. On one hand, each of us has a number of expectations, hopes, fears, and feelings about ourselves that can distort our perceptions of how we are seen by others (Holmes, 1968). On the other hand, a variety of interpersonal conventions and constraints lead others to give off signs that are something other than their true reactions to who we are and what we do (Higgins & Rholes, 1978; Manis, Cornell, & Moore, 1974; Newtson & Czerlinsky, 1974). In addition to these two powerful barriers to accurate self-understanding, the spotlight effect constitutes a third limitation on the fidelity of our understanding of what others think of us. An exaggerated sense of the extent to which others typically notice our actions can lead to unrealistic assessments of our general importance in the lives of others. In addition, a tendency to exaggerate the extremity of others' evaluations of us can lead to both overly extreme and unnecessarily variable views of the self. The existence of the spotlight effect, in other words, puts something of a limit on the accurate perception of the reflected self.

The spotlight effect is also richly connected to what many theorists regard as a key source of the fundamentally social nature of the self. In particular, it has been claimed that a sense of belonging with others is a fundamental human need (Baumeister & Leary, 1995). The importance of social connectedness is seen in how the ups and downs of a person's sense of inclusion are so tightly connected to the ups and downs of self-esteem (Leary, this volume). Its importance is also seen in the rather extreme cognitive, emotional, and behavioral reactions to social exclusion (Baumeister, Twenge, & Ciarocco, this volume; Tice, Twenge, & Schmeichel, this volume). Given the profound importance people attach to fitting in with others, it stands to reason that people would be exquisitely sensitive to the possibility of standing out and the prospect of being evaluated. One who is not highly attuned to the possibility of being judged negatively may run the risk of devastating isolation. Thus, it may well be that people have acquired a set of sensibilities such that they are more likely to overestimate rather than underestimate their own salience in the eyes of others, and to overestimate rather than underestimate the harshness of others' judgments. The argument could be made, then, that the spotlight effect is a quite functional adaptation that helps people avoid the level of ostracism and exclusion that is simply not tolerable.

Nevertheless, although the spotlight effect may bring such a benefit, the benefit is often paid at great cost. The costs are the needless worry and anxiety that result from an unwarranted fear of others' judgments. In extreme cases, in fact, the excessive concern about the likelihood of negative evaluations from others can lead to a host of debilitating social disorders such as speech anxiety (Savitsky & Gilovich, 2001; Stein, Walker, & Forde, 1996), shyness (Zimbardo, 1990), social phobia (Clark & Arkowitz, 1975; McEwan & Devins, 1983), and paranoia (Fenigstein & Vanable, 1992). More often, the tendency to exaggerate the harshness of others' likely judgments leads people to refrain from engaging in certain behaviors out of a misplaced concern over what others might think of them. One may refrain from speaking in public, from expressing one's true feelings, or from hosting a party—all because of an unnecessarily strong fear of how others would react if things did not go as well as one hoped. People's excessive fear of social censure often comes back to haunt them. Thus, research has documented that with hindsight the biggest regrets in people's lives tend to involve things they had not done but wished they had, rather than things they had done and wish they had not (Gilovich & Medvec, 1995).

THE SPOTLIGHT EFFECT AS INSUFFICIENT ADJUSTMENT

Excessive attentiveness to how one might fare in others' evaluation (Baumeister & Leary, 1995; Leary, this volume) might be considered a distal cause of the spotlight effect. Some would doubtless be tempted to put it in evolutionary terms: in our ancestral past, rejection by the group was tantamount to a death sentence as no individual could successfully go it alone. An acute sensitivity to anything that risked the sort of negative evaluation that might lead to exclusion thus facilitated survival. Whether or not such an account can ever be more than a sort of glib evolutionary theorizing that is all too common and all too untestable, it is important to understand more proximal determinants of the spotlight effect. What are the precise information-processing tendencies that give rise to this pervasive egocentric bias?

In our attempts to address this question, we have focused on the difficulty of getting beyond one's own phenomenological experience. To be sure, people are typically aware that others are less focused on them than they are on themselves. They know that although they may be consumed with the embarrassing T-shirt they are wearing, or with how it might look to be seen dining alone, others are likely to be less consumed with such incidents. They thus recognize that some adjustment from their own experience is necessary to capture how they appear in the eyes of others. Even so, it can be difficult to get beyond one's own perspective. The "adjustment" that one makes from the "anchor" of one's own phenomenology (Jacowitz & Kahneman, 1995), or the "correction" from an initial "characterization" (Gilbert, in press), tends to be insufficient. The net result is that estimates of how one appears to others are overly influenced by how one appears to oneself (Kenny & DePaulo, 1993).

We have obtained support for this anchoring and adjustment interpretation in a number of ways. In one of our "T-shirt" experiments, for example, some participants were given an opportunity to acclimate to wearing an embarrassing shirt prior to confronting their "audience." Others were not. Because the habituation period tended to decrease the extent to which participants were themselves focused on the shirt, their estimates began from a less powerful internal state—or lower "anchor"—and their predictions of the number of observers who had noticed them were diminished. Note that the objective nature of the stimulus was unchanged across conditions—it was, after all, the same shirt. But because participants' phenomenological experience of wearing the shirt had changed, so did their sense of being in the spotlight.

We have also found in virtually all of our studies in this program of research that participants' ratings of what they think of their own behavior tends to be more extreme than their ratings of what they think others will think of their behavior. Thus, participants appear to be adjusting from their own phenomenological experience. But they do so insufficiently, as their ratings of how they are seen by others overstate how they are actually seen.

This account of the spotlight effect is thus similar to a number of other prominent accounts of various biases in social information processing. Most well-known, perhaps, is Dan Gilbert's account of the "correspondence bias" in attribution, or the tendency for social observers to attribute behavior to an actor's dispositions even when the behavior was completely constrained by prevailing situational pressures (Gilbert, in press). According to Gilbert, observers initially characterize an actor in terms of the dispositions that correspond to how he or she behaved, whether the behavior was constrained or not. This initial characterization is then corrected to take into account any prevailing situational constraints. Because this latter step is an adjustment from the initial characterization, and because such adjustments are typically insufficient (Tversky & Kahneman, 1974), the net result is an overly dispositionist attributional calculus. Very similar accounts have been put forward by Justin Kruger to account for the frequently observed "above average" effect—and a less-frequently observed "below average" effect—in trait inference (Kruger, 1999), and by Boaz Keysar to explain various egocentric tendencies in language production and comprehension (Keysar & Barr, in press). Thus, the anchoring and adjustment account that my colleagues and I have offered for the spotlight effect appears to be in very good company.

DO ANCHORING EFFECTS RESULT FROM INSUFFICIENT ADJUSTMENT?

Although each of these accounts provides support for the other, each is threatened by recent research examining the psychological processes underlying anchoring and adjustment. This research suggests that the ubiquitous anchoring effects observed in the laboratory and in everyday life are not the result of insufficient adjustment. This, of course, has significant implications for an anchoring and insufficient adjustment interpretation of any phenomenon, be it the correspondence bias, the above average effect, egocentric language use, or the spotlight effect.

The basis of this revisionist account of anchoring effects is two-fold. First, 25 years of research on anchoring effects has failed to provide any direct evidence for explicit adjustment. Various process-tracing methodologies have not succeeded in uncovering evidence of adjustment, and a number of factors that ought to influence the magnitude of adjustment—such as cognitive load and incentives for accuracy—have been found to have no effect (Chapman & Johnson, in press). Second, a recent program of research by Thomas Mussweiler and Fritz Strack has shown instead that the anchoring effects observed in standard anchoring experiments are the product of the increased accessibility of anchor consistent information (Mussweiler & Strack, 1999, 2000; Strack & Mussweiler, 1997). In the standard anchoring experiment, a person is first asked one of two comparative questions (e.g., did Mozart die before or after the age of 30 [or 40])? The person is then asked to make a related absolute judgment: "How old was Mozart when he died?"

Mussweiler and Strack argued that the attempt to answer the initial comparative question (did Mozart live to the age of 30? [or 40?]) activates information consistent with the given anchor value. Because people evaluate hypotheses by attempting to confirm them (Klayman & Ha, 1987; Skov & Sherman, 1986), entertaining such a question generates evidence disproportionately consistent with the anchor. The absolute judgment is then biased by the ready availability of evidence recruited in this confirmatory search. As Mussweiler and Strack (1999) explained, there are two steps to their Selective Accessibility Model:

> . . . participants solve the comparative task by selectively generating semantic knowledge that is consistent with the notion that the target's value is equal to the anchor (the selectivity hypothesis). Generating such knowledge increases its subsequent accessibility, so that it is used to form the final absolute judgment (the accessibility hypothesis). (p. 138)

Mussweiler and Strack have cleverly employed a number of different experimental paradigms to collect evidence in support of their account. For example, they found that on a lexical decision task that followed right after the type of comparative question typically used in the anchoring literature, participants were faster at identifying anchor-consistent words than anchor-inconsistent words. Those who had just decided, for instance, whether the price of an average German car is higher or lower than 40,000 marks (high anchor) were faster at identifying words associated with expensive cars (e.g., Mercedes, BMW) than words associated with inexpensive cars (e.g., Volkswagen). The opposite was true for those who were first asked whether the price of an average German car is higher or lower than 20,000 marks (Mussweiler & Strack, 2000). Information consistent with an initial anchor value, in other words, is made more accessible by the mere consideration of that value.

Mussweiler and Strack's research has led to something of a consensus that "anchoring occurs because of biased retrieval of target features" and not because of insufficient adjustment (Chapman & Johnson, in press). Indeed, their research makes a persuasive case that the anchoring effects reported in the literature are just that—anchoring effects, not anchoring and (insufficient) adjustment effects. This much can be said, at least, for the anchoring effects observed in the standard anchoring paradigm.

ANCHORING EFFECTS WITH SELF-GENERATED ANCHORS

The standard anchoring paradigm is meant to capture the same psychological processes that are involved in everyday situations that might prompt the use of the anchoring and adjustment heuristic. But is it typically the case in everyday life that one is first confronted with a comparative question and then asked for an absolute estimate? Probably not. Consider, for example, how one might answer such questions as "What is the height of the Himalayan peak, K-2?" or "When was George Washington first elected President?" Few people know the answers to these questions. And if not, chances are they can nonetheless arrive at a reasonable approximation to the right answer by tinkering with a value they do know, but know is wrong. One might know, for example, that the height of Mt. Everest is 29,035 feet and therefore estimate that, as the world's second tallest mountain, K-2 is, say, 28,700. Or one might never have learned the date of the first U.S. presidential election but recognize it had to take place after 1776. Thus, 1784 might be given as a reasonable estimate. (The correct values are 28,250 for K-2's elevation and 1789 for Washington's election.)

Note that the psychology here is quite different from that in the typical anchoring paradigm. The typical anchoring paradigm suggests to participants a value they had not previously considered. Thus, it is sensible for them to ask themselves whether the true value is equal to this suggested value. In Mussweiler and Strack's (1999) words, "participants who are asked whether the target's value along the judgmental dimension is greater or smaller than the anchor value may generate the answer by testing the hypothesis that the target's value is equal to the anchor" (p. 138). This leads them to access information consistent with that hypothesis (Klayman & Ha, 1987; Skov & Sherman, 1986), and so their final judgment is assimilated to the provided anchor.

In the examples just given, however, the initial anchor value is one the person knows—without any reflection—to be wrong. There is thus no reason to consider whether "the target's value is equal to the anchor." One already knows it is not. One has selected it as something from which one needs to adjust. This implies a process of true adjustment, a process that corresponds with most people's intuitions of how they go about determining, say, when George Washington was first elected president or when the second Spanish explorer landed in the New World (i.e., some time after 1492).

Thus, the consensus that seems to be emerging that there is no adjustment in the anchoring and adjustment heuristic (Chapman & Johnson, in press; Mussweiler & Strack, 1999) may be premature. Such a conclusion appears to be apt with respect to anchoring effects observed in the standard anchoring paradigm. But for anchoring effects observed in many real-life contexts in which the anchors are self-generated, a process of true adjustment may be alive and well. In fact, my colleague Nick Epley and I have recently obtained evidence that people do indeed adjust from self-generated anchors (Epley & Gilovich, 2001).

In one study, we asked people to tell us the year Washington was first elected president and the year the second European explorer landed in the West Indies. As expected, almost none of the participants knew either answer so their responses were estimates, not recollections. We then asked them how they arrived at the dates they provided and tape-recorded their responses. Finally, we coded their responses for whether they mentioned either of the two obvious anchor values (1776 and 1492) and, critically, whether they mentioned adjusting from those values to reach their final answers. Eighty-nine percent of the respondents reported engaging in explicit adjustment in response to the European explorer question, and 64% reported adjusting in response to the question about Washington's election. In marked contrast, fewer than 15% reported anything resembling adjustment when asked how they arrived at their responses to questions used in the standard anchoring paradigm. Judging from what people report at least, a process of explicit adjustment from self-generated (but not experimenter-provided) anchors appears to be something in which people do indeed engage.

But can we judge from what people say? There are, of course, widespread doubts about how accurately people can report on their own mental processes (Nisbett & Wilson, 1977). We thus sought to obtain convergent evidence of a more convincing, experimental sort. The logic of our follow-up experiments was as follows: If people adjust from an initial anchor value, there must be some tentative, intermediate values that they assess before arriving at a final answer ("Could Washington have been elected in 1780? No, the war for independence was not yet over. Could it have been in 1785 . . . ?"). Anything that influences a person's tendency to agree with the propositions underlying these tentative questions should influence the extent to which he/she conforms to or deviates from the initial anchor. If one is, for whatever reason, particularly inclined to accept values, one should terminate the adjustment process more quickly and provide a final estimate closer to the original anchor value. If one is less accepting, in contrast, he/she should continue to adjust and arrive at a final estimate further from the anchor.

Accordingly, we employed a procedure based on the finding that people are more likely to accept propositions they encounter while nodding their heads up and down than when shaking them from side to side (Wells & Petty, 1980; see also Forster & Strack, 1996). We reasoned that asking participants to nod their heads while considering questions likely to elicit self-generated anchor values would make them more willing to accept their initial adjustment values and thus produce less adjustment from the initial anchor. Shaking their heads from side to side, in contrast, should make them more willing to reject their initial adjustment values and thus produce more adjustment from self-generated anchors. However, because nodding and shaking should not systematically influence the selective accessibility of anchor-consistent information, the direction of head movement should have no influence on people's answers to the sorts of questions asked in the standard anchoring paradigm.

This is just what we found (Epley & Gilovich, 2001, Studies 2 and 3). Participants who estimated, while nodding their heads, the year Washington was first elected president gave values that were closer to 1776 (M=1778) than those who answered while shaking their heads (M=1788). Participants who estimated, while nodding their heads, the year the second European explorer landed in the West Indies gave values closer to 1492 (M=1502) than those who answered while shaking their heads (M=1548). Note that these data are not simply the result of head nodding leading to lower estimates than head shaking because a complementary pattern of results was obtained on questions in which the adjustment called for was *downward* from the initial anchor value. For example, head nodding participants who estimated the boiling point of water atop Mt. Everest gave values closer to 212 degrees (M=189) than head shaking participants (M=141). In all of these cases, furthermore, the estimates made by participants who were told to keep their heads still fell in between those made by the head nodders and head shakers.

It is hard to see how this head movement manipulation would have such systematic effects if participants were not, in fact, adjusting from some initial anchor value. One cannot manipulate the magnitude of adjustment if no adjustment is taking place. In further support of this conclusion, note that head nodding and shaking did not have any influence on participants' responses to experimenter-provided anchoring questions. The psychological processes involved in answering questions that elicit self-generated anchors are different from those involved in answering questions that arise in the standard anchoring paradigm. The former involves a process of adjustment; the latter does not.

ARE ADJUSTMENTS FROM SELF-GENERATED ANCHORS TYPICALLY INSUFFICIENT?

According to the earliest theoretical statements on the subject, the anchoring and adjustment heuristic was thought to yield biased judgments because adjustments from anchor values were believed to be typically insufficient (Tversky & Kahneman, 1974). Empirical demonstrations of anchoring effects, however, were typically obtained in the standard anchoring paradigm which, as Mussweiler and Strack have convincingly shown, does not involve any process of adjustment. Inevitably, this leads to the question of whether the adjustments people *do* engage in are typically insufficient. Are adjustments from self-generated anchor values, in other words, typically insufficient? There is nothing in the existing literature to settle this question.

Thus, Nick Epley and I sought to examine the adequacy of people's adjustments from self-generated anchor values, and we found that they do indeed tend to be insufficient (Epley & Gilovich, 2002). We have obtained evidence for such a conclusion from several sources. In one study, for example, we asked people to estimate the year of the founding of the first English settlement in North America, Jamestown. Very few participants knew the correct answer (1607) and thus were required to venture a best guess. The key element of the study was a manipulation of whether the participants were likely to (self-) anchor on an earlier date and thus adjust upward, or on a later date and thus adjust downward. Specifically, in one condition participants were asked, "In what year do you think Jamestown, the first English settlement in the *New World* [italics added], was established?" The phrase "new world" was designed to trigger an association to Columbus and hence the date 1492. In the other condition, participants were asked, "In what year do you think Jamestown, the first English settlement in the *United States* [italics added], was founded?" The mention of "United States" was intended to trigger an association to the most salient date in U.S. Colonial history, 1776. A follow-up inquiry at the end of the study revealed that 84% of the participants did indeed anchor on the intended date.

And the manipulated anchor values both influenced participants' estimates and revealed that the adjustments made from these anchor values were typically insufficient. Those led to anchor on 1492 provided estimates that were earlier than the correct date (M=1577), whereas those led to anchor on 1776 provided estimates that were later than the correct date (M=1643). A follow-up study in which individuals were asked to estimate the number of U.S. states in 1840, after being led to (self-) generate an anchor value of either the original 13 states or the current 50 states, yielded similar results. Adjustments from self-generated anchors do indeed tend to be insufficient. Thus, the anchoring and adjustment heuristic, though doubtless a useful tool for arriving at serviceable answers to challenging problems, nonetheless leads to biased responses.

ANCHORING IN EGOCENTRIC SOCIAL JUDGMENTS

The demonstration that there are two kinds of anchoring effects—those observed when the anchor values are self-generated and those observed in the standard anchoring paradigm—is not a demonstration that one is "real," important, and present in everyday life, whereas the other is artificial, unimportant, and restricted to laboratory paradigms. Although it is true that the earlier exclusive reliance on the standard anchoring paradigm has limited psychologists' understanding of anchoring phenomena, what was learned from that paradigm clearly applies to at least some anchoring effects observed in everyday life. It is not unusual to be confronted with an initial value before making a given estimate, and on such instances the former influences the latter through the very selective accessibility effects that Mussweiler and Strack have so clearly and convincingly demonstrated in their experiments (Mussweiler & Strack, 1999, 2000; Strack & Mussweiler, 1997). Those who must estimate a fair selling price of a house, for example, often do so with prior knowledge of the asking price (Northcraft & Neale, 1987).

But it is also clear that many anchoring effects in everyday life are not like those observed in the standard anchoring paradigm. Gilbert (in press) has argued that "anchoring and adjustment describes the process by which the human mind does virtually all of its inferential work." "In this sense," he continues, "anchoring and adjustment is a fundamental description of mental life." Research by Mussweiler and Strack as well as others (see Chapman & Johnson, in press, for a review) might seem to call Gilbert's analysis into question. But examined carefully, the analysis has merit because so many anchor values are self-generated (and hence true adjustment processes are involved). As Nick Epley and I have shown, when trying to answer certain factual questions, often the first thing to come to mind—and the only thing to come to mind with certainty—is some ballpark value that one knows is not right and needs adjustment. As Kruger has shown, the first thing that comes to mind when estimating one's standing on an ability dimension is some gut feeling that one is good or bad at the task in question—a gut feeling that is then adjusted to take into account one's sense of how good others are at the task (Kruger, 1999). As Gilbert has shown, the first thing that comes to mind when making attributions about behavior is a characterization of the actor in line with the most salient characteristics embodied by the act—a characterization that is then adjusted to take into account prevailing situational inducements or constraints (Gilbert, in press). And as research on the spotlight effect has shown, the first thing that comes to mind when assessing how one looks to others is a gut feeling about how one feels oneself—a feeling that is then adjusted to take into account the abstract realization that one occupies a more prominent position in one's own universe than anyone else's (Gilovich et al., 2000). In each of these cases, the starting point for the person's judgment (i.e., the initial anchor) is self-generated. Thus, these basic tasks of self and social understanding—estimating one's salience in the eyes of others, estimating one's standing on a given ability dimension, forming causal attributions—conform to Gilbert's "fundamental description of mental life." They all involve a true process of adjustment. Thus, the anchoring and adjustment processes examined in this chapter are likely to have direct implications for the way people perceive themselves in social situations, the way they estimate others' reactions, and ultimately, the way their self-conceptions are constructed and maintained.

REFERENCES

Baumeister, R. F., & Leary, M. R. (1995). The need to belong: Desire for interpersonal attachments as a fundamental human motivation. *Psychological Bulletin, 117,* 497–529.

Chapman, G. B., & Johnson, E. J. (in press). Incorporating the irrelevant: Anchors in judgments of belief and value. In T. Gilovich, D. W. Griffin, & D. Kahneman (Eds.), *Heuristics and biases: The psychology of intuitive judgment.* New York: Cambridge University Press.

Clark, J. V., & Arkowitz, H. (1975). Social anxiety and self-evaluation of inter-personal performance. *Psychological Reports, 36,* 211–221.

Cooley, C. H. (1902). *Human nature and the social order.* New York: Scribner.

Epley, N., & Gilovich, T. (2002). *Are adjustments from self-generated anchors typically insufficient?* Manuscript in preparation, Cornell University, Ithaca, NY.

Epley, N., & Gilovich, T. (2001). Putting adjustment back in the anchoring and adjustment heuristic: An expansion of self-generated and experimenter-provided anchors. *Psychological Science, 12,* 391–396.

Epley, N., Savitsky, K., & Gilovich, T. (in press).

Empath neglect: Reconciling the spotlight effect and the correspondence bias. *Journal of Personality and Social Psychology.*

Fenigstein, A., & Vanable, P. A. (1992). Paranoia and self-consciousness. *Journal of Personality and Social Psychology, 62,* 129–138.

Forster, J., & Strack, F. (1996). Influence of overt head movements on memory for valenced words: A case of conceptual-motor compatibility. *Journal of Personality and Social Psychology, 71,* 421–430.

Gilbert, D. T. (in press). Inferential correction. In T. Gilovich, D. W. Griffin, & D. Kahneman (Eds.), *Heuristics and biases: The psychology of intuitive judgment.* New York: Cambridge University Press.

Gilovich, T., Kruger, J., & Medvec, V. H. (2002). The spotlight effect revisited: Overestimating the manifest variability in our actions and appearance. *Journal of Experimental Social Psychology, 31,* 93–99.

Gilovich, T., & Medvec, V. H. (1995). The experience of regret: What, when, and why. *Psychological Review, 102,* 379–395.

Gilovich, T., Medvec, V. H., & Savitsky, K. (2000). The spotlight effect in social judgment: An egocentric bias in estimates of the salience of one's own actions and appearance. *Journal of Personality and Social Psychology, 78*, 211–222.

Gilovich, T., & Savitsky, K. (1999). The spotlight effect and the illusion of transparency: Egocentric assessments of how we're seen by others. *Current Directions in Psychological Science, 8*, 165–168.

Higgins, E. T., & Rholes, W. S. (1978). Saying is believing: Effects of message modification on memory and liking for the person described. *Journal of Experimental Social Psychology, 14*, 363–378.

Holmes, D. S. (1968). Dimensions of projection. *Psychological Bulletin, 69*, 248–268.

Jacowitz, K. E., & Kahneman, D. (1995). Measures of anchoring in estimation tasks. *Personality and Social Psychology Bulletin, 21*, 1161–1166.

Kenny, D. A., & DePaulo, B. M. (1993). Do people know how others view them? An empirical and theoretical account. *Psychological Bulletin, 114*, 145–161.

Keysar, B., & Barr, D. J. (in press). Self anchoring in conversation: Why language users don't do what they should. In T. Gilovich, D. W. Griffin, & D. Kahneman (Eds.), *Heuristics and biases: The psychology of intuitive judgment*. Cambridge University Press.

Klayman, J. & Ha, Y. (1987). Confirmation, disconfirmation, and information in hypothesis testing. *Psychological Review, 94*, 211–228.

Kruger, J. (1999). Lake Wobegon be gone! The "below-average" effect and the egocentric nature of comparative ability judgments. *Journal of Personality and Social Psychology, 77*, 221–232.

Manis, M., Cornell, S. D., & Moore, J. C. (1974). Transmission of attitude-relevant information through a communication chain. *Journal of Personality and Social Psychology, 30*, 81–94.

McEwan, K. L., & Devins, G. M. (1983). Is increased arousal in social anxiety noticed by others? *Journal of Abnormal Psychology, 92*, 417–421.

Mead, G. H. (1934). *Mind, self, and society*. Chicago: University of Chicago Press.

Mussweiler, T., & Strack, F. (1999). Hypothesis-consistent testing and semantic priming in the anchoring paradigm: A selective accessibility model. *Journal of Experimental Social Psychology, 35*, 136–164.

Mussweiler, T., & Strack, F. (2000). The use of category and exemplar knowledge in the solution of anchoring tasks. *Journal of Personality and Social Psychology, 78*, 1038–1052.

Newtson, D., & Czerlinsky, T. (1974). Adjustment of attitude communications for contrasts by extreme audiences. *Journal of Personality and Social Psychology, 30*, 829–837.

Nisbett, R. E., & Wilson, T. D. (1977). Telling more than we can know: Verbal reports on mental processes. *Psychological Review, 84*, 231–259.

Northcraft, G. B., & Neale, M. A. (1987). Experts, amateurs, and real estate: An anchoring-and-adjustment perspective on property pricing decisions. *Organizational Behavior and Human Decision Processes, 39*, 84–97.

Savitsky, K., Epley, N., & Gilovich, T. (2001). Is it as bad as we fear? Overestimating the extremity of others' judgments. *Journal of Personality and Social Psychology, 81*, 44–56.

Savitsky, K., & Gilovich, T. (2001). *The illusion of transparency and the alleviation of speech anxiety*. Unpublished manuscript, Cornell University, Ithaca, NY.

Savitsky, K., Gilovich, T., Berger, G., & Medvec, V. H. (2001). *Is our absence as conspicuous as we think?: Overestimating the salience and impact of one's absence from a group*. Unpublished manuscript.

Skov, R. B., & Sherman, S. J. (1986). Information-gathering processes: Diagnosticity, hypothesis-confirmatory strategies, and perceived hypothesis confirmation. *Journal of Experimental Social Psychology, 22*, 93–121.

Stein, M. B., Walker, J. R., & Forde, D. R. (1996). Public-speaking fears in a community sample: Prevalence, impact on functioning, and diagnostic classification. *Archives of General Psychiatry, 53*, 169–174.

Strack, F., & Mussweiler, T. (1997). Explaining the enigmatic anchoring effect: Mechanisms of selective accessibility. *Journal of Personality and Social Psychology, 73*, 437–446.

Tversky, A., & Kahneman, D. (1974). Judgment under uncertainty: Heuristics and biases. *Science, 185*, 1124–1131

Van Boven, L. D., Kamada, A., & Gilovich, T.

(1999). The perceiver as perceived: Everyday intuitions about the correspondence bias. *Journal of Personality and Social Psychology, 77,* 1188–1199.

Wells, G. L., & Petty, R. E. (1980). The effects of overt head movements on persuasion: Compatibility and incompatibility of responses. *Basic and Applied Social Psychology, 1,* 219–230.

Zimbardo, P. G. (1990). *Shyness: What it is, what to do about it* (Rev. ed.). Reading, MA: Addison-Wesley.

4

Judgment Standards and the Social Self

A Shifting Standards Perspective

MONICA BIERNAT
SCOTT EIDELMAN
KATHLEEN FUEGEN

Introduction
The Shifting Standards Model
Shifting Standards and the Self
Some Relevant Research
Implications and Extensions
Summary

INTRODUCTION

When we judge other people and ourselves, we must rely on some implicit or explicit standard of comparison. Deciding that "I am bad at tennis" requires reference to some point of comparison, perhaps the tennis playing ability of similar others, or my tennis playing ability over time. Likewise, judging that a woman is "smart" requires that one compare her to some standard of intelligence. Only when our judgments are situated against some frame of reference can we make sense of what incompetence at tennis or intelligence might mean. This theme is not new to social psychology; indeed, the literature is replete with examples of the relativity and context-dependence of self- and other-judgment. Assessment of traits (Higgins & Stangor, 1988), abilities (Goethals & Darley, 1977), attitudes and opinions (Sherif & Hovland,

The research reported in this chapter was supported by NIMH grant # R01 MH48844 awarded to the first author.

1961), emotions (Schachter, 1959), and outcomes (Crosby, 1976), to list but a few examples, have all been shown to depend on standards invoked from situational or contextual cues.

Over the past decade, research in our laboratory has focused on the role of one particular type or source of judgment standard that is used to evaluate others. Specifically, work on the "shifting standards model" suggests that social stereotypes may serve as judgment standards against which members of stereotyped groups are evaluated (Biernat & Manis, 1994; Biernat, Manis, & Nelson, 1991; Biernat & Thompson, 2002). For example, the stereotypes that women have stronger verbal ability than men, and that men are more aggressive than women, may lead perceivers to judge the verbal ability and aggressiveness of individual women and men relative to within-gender standards. That is, standards shift as one evaluates members of different social categories on stereotyped dimensions. One purpose of this chapter is to provide a brief overview of the shifting standards model and its empirical support in the domain of other-judgments.

Less well-examined, however, is the role of stereotypes as judgment standards for evaluating the *self*. To what extent is the self evaluated with reference to social stereotypes? Two literatures seem relevant to this question. One is the large body of work on social comparison theory, which suggests that we compare ourselves with similar others (Festinger, 1954). Although Festinger's original paper was vague regarding the meaning of "similarity," more recent theorizing has suggested that similarity may be based on broad categories such as membership in demographic or social groups (Goethals & Darley, 1977; Major, Testa, & Bylsma, 1991; Wood, 1989). The second is the less extensive literature on self-stereotyping—the tendency to ascribe to oneself the attributes of one's group(s), and to see the self as a prototypical group member (Biernat, Vescio, & Green, 1996; Chiu, Hong, Lam, Fu, Tong, & Lee, 1998; Spears, Doosje, & Ellemers, 1997; Turner, 1987). Both of these literatures suggest that stereotypes of one's group may play a role in self-evaluation by serving as either interpretive (assimilative) or comparative (contrastive) frames of reference. A second major purpose of the present chapter is to describe how these two literatures, in combination with the shifting standards model, may provide new insights into how the self is evaluated with reference to important social groups. We begin by first considering the shifting standards model.

THE SHIFTING STANDARDS MODEL

The basic premise of the shifting standards model is that when we judge individual members of stereotyped groups on stereotype-relevant dimensions, we use *within-category* reference points or standards. For example, given stereotypes that men are better leaders than women, we are likely to judge the leadership competence of a particular woman relative to (lower) standards of competence *for women*, and the leadership competence of a particular man relative to (higher) standards of competence *for men*. The result is that evaluations of men and women on leadership competence may not be directly comparable, as their meaning is tied to different frames of reference: "Good" for a woman does not mean the same thing as "good" for a man — presumably it means "objectively less good" in this example.

A standard incorporates the average and range that is expected from members of a group on a particular dimension, and aids the judge in anchoring the endpoints of a subjective rating scale (e.g., "high" to "low" competence). Rating points are defined to reflect the expected distribution of category members on the dimension, with high numbers reserved for targets with the highest expected level of the attribute *among members of the category*. When groups are expected to differ (i.e., when a stereotype is held), endpoints are anchored differently for the contrasting groups (for related themes in other judgment models, see Parducci, 1963; Postman & Miller, 1945; Upshaw, 1962; Volkmann, 1951).

Evidence supporting the operation of stereotype-based standard shifts can be gleaned from comparisons between judgments that are made on *subjective* rating scales and those made on *objective* rating scales. The terms "subjective" and "objective" require some clarification. A "subjective scale" refers to any rating system in which the units of judgment have no ties to external reality. For example, Likert-type scales, semantic differentials, and many instruments that display trait judgments as continua (e.g., "very unathletic" to "very athletic") are subjective in the sense that their rating points can be differentially defined and adjusted (e.g., across time, across perceivers, across targets). Thus, subjective judgments are "slippery" as they do not connote a fixed meaning. On the other hand, an "objective scale" refers to an externally anchored, "common rule" scale consisting of judgment units that maintain a constant meaning across contexts and/or types of targets. For example, judging the wealth of a person in currency units would be an objective judgment, whereas rating the person on a "poor" to "rich" scale would be a subjective judgment. Objective scales used in our research have included standardized test scores or grades (to assess competence stereotypes), monetary or time judgments (to assess salary, effort, or worth), and rank orderings (which fit our conception of objectivity in that a ranking unit places a target in a readily interpretable position relative to a given frame of reference; see Biernat & Manis, 1994; Biernat et al., 1998). In short, objectivity refers not to an accurate or unchanging judgment, but rather to one whose meaning can be readily interpreted because of its common rule nature.

The key prediction of the shifting standards model is that objective or externally anchored judgments are more likely than subjective judgments to reveal the influence of stereotypes. That is, judgments of individual group members will generally be assimilated to group stereotypes when objective response scales are used, but will show less strong, null, or contrastive influences of stereotypes when subjective scales are used. This occurs because objective scales call forth an external frame of reference which then reveals or captures the available stereotype, whereas subjective scales can be differentially adjusted for different target categories (within-category frames of reference). In short, subjective scales may mask the operation of stereotypes because the response language can be defined in category-specific terms.

Evidence of Shifting Judgment Standards in the Evaluation of Others

We have now accumulated considerable evidence supporting the prediction that stereotyping effects will be more pronounced when targets are judged in objective (externally anchored) relative to subjective response language. In initial research, we examined the judgmental influences of accurate gender stereotypes—that men are taller, weigh more, and earn more money than women (Biernat et al., 1991). Participants judged the heights, weights, and incomes of a series of photographed women and men. Results clearly indicated that when judgments were made in "objective" or externally-anchored units (feet and inches, pounds, dollars earned), they were consistent with gender stereotypes, but when judgments were made in "subjective" units (short–tall, light–heavy, financially unsuccessful–successful), stereotyping effects were significantly reduced or reversed. This pattern is consistent with the notion that subjective judgments were based on within-category comparisons: Men and women might each be judged, subjectively, as "heavy" when *objectively*, the man might be perceived to weigh about 40 pounds more; the same women who were judged as earning $9,000 less per year than men were *subjectively* seen as more "financially successful" than these men.

We also have evidence of shifting judgment standards based on stereotypes of unknown, debated, or refuted accuracy as well. In one study, the stereotype that women are more verbally able than men led perceivers to judge individual women and men relative to within-sex judgment standards on this dimension (Biernat & Manis, 1994, Study 2). When verbal ability estimates were made in letter grades, women were judged more verbally able than men, but in subjective units, men were perceived as slightly, though not significantly, more verbally able than women (a null effect of stereotypes). Somewhat more complex findings emerged in a study of gender stereotypes regarding competence (Biernat & Manis, 1994, Study 1). When rating the quality of magazine articles in "objective" units (e.g., monetary worth), evidence of gender stereotyping was clear: Articles on feminine topics were judged better when written by a female than a male, whereas "masculine" articles were judged better when written by a male than a female. In subjective judgments, however, author sex had no impact on evaluations. That is, despite a greater perception of worth when an author's sex "matched" the article topic, this translated into equivalent subjective evaluations for the two authors (see also Biernat & Kobrynowicz, 1997, Study 1).

Other research has documented comparable effects with regard to racial stereotypes. Judgment standards for Black versus White Americans shift in the domains of verbal ability, athleticism, math skill, and job-related competence (Biernat & Kobrynowicz, 1997; Biernat & Manis, 1994; Kobrynowicz & Biernat, 1997). A field study of U.S. Army captains also provided evidence of gender-based shifting standards in judgments of leadership ability, suggesting that the model has relevance for real-world judgments of live targets (Biernat, Crandall, et al., 1998). Furthermore, we have demonstrated that if no group-relevant stereotype exists, judgment standards do not shift for members of different groups. For example, judgments of age and movie viewing frequency showed no evidence of shifting standards effects, as perceivers do not hold stereotypes that men and women differ on these dimensions (Biernat et al., 1991; Biernat & Manis, 1994).

SHIFTING STANDARDS AND THE SELF

Research on stereotype-based shifting standards in judging others has led us to the question of whether we use within-category standards in judgments of ourselves. Of course, there are many differences between self- and other-judgments, including the amount of knowledge available and the kinds of motivations that may be operative when judgments are made (Brown, 1986; Prentice, 1990). Nonetheless, our findings regarding other judgments may bear some resemblance to patterns of self-assessment as well.

Indeed, years of social comparison research, for example, suggest that we compare ourselves to *similar* others (Festinger, 1954; see also Goethals & Darley, 1977; Wood, 1989). Although Festinger's intended meaning of similarity was unclear, it's generally assumed that he referred to similarity in a rather restricted sense (i.e., similarity on characteristics related to an opinion or ability). However, more recent perspectives on social comparison offer a broader conceptualization of the construct. An influential review of the literature by Wood (1989) suggests that similarity may be defined by features as diffuse as shared group membership (e.g., gender category) and broad personality traits (Buunk & VanYperen, 1991; Crocker & Major, 1989; Miller, Turnbull, & McFarland, 1988; Tesser, 1988).

For example, Major and Testa (1989) found that women and men tend to make within-sex rather than cross-sex comparisons of their jobs and wages (see also Miller & Prentice, 1996). An earlier study also demonstrated that even when one could choose between an own-sex comparison other and an opposite sex "standard setter" on the performance dimension of interest, 97% of participants chose a same sex reference group member first (Zanna, Goethals, & Hill, 1975). Among possible explanations advanced for such comparisons are that people may 1) perceive themselves to be closer to others who are somehow similar even if on a dimension unrelated to the task at hand (Miller et al., 1988; Tesser, 1988), 2) make ingroup comparisons to protect self-esteem (Crocker & Major, 1989), 3) believe that targets similar with respect to unrelated attributes are potential competitors, and thereby relevant to one's outcomes, 4) believe attributes such as gender to be related to performance across a wide variety of domains, and 5) view some attributes (such as gender) as self-defining, even if unrelated to a given comparison dimension (see Miller et al., 1988; Wood, 1989).

The notion that individuals compare themselves to ingroup members is clearly related to the shifting standards model perspective that *others* are judged relative to within-group standards. Although the judgment target differs (self versus other), our goal in the research to be described here was to begin connecting these perspectives by documenting patterns of shifting standards in judgments of the self. Critical to building these connections is one other premise of the shifting standards model. The model suggests that within-group comparisons are made on *stereotyped* judgment dimensions. This idea is not an explicit part of social comparison theory, though one could argue that ingroup members are likely to be perceived as even more similar to the self on dimensions that (stereotypically) define the group.

This brings us to the literature on "self-stereotyping," which we also see as highly relevant to understanding how within-group judgment standards are used to evaluate the self. Although a number of studies pre-date the event, the term "self-stereotyping" was formally introduced as part of self-categorization theory, and defined as "the perceptual interchangeability or perceptual identity of oneself and others in the same group on relevant dimensions" (Turner, 1984, p. 528). Self-stereotyping represents the transformation of individual behavior into group behavior, presumably the intervening process that leads to phenomena such as ingroup bias (Spears et al., 1997). Turner and his colleagues suggested that the process of self-categorization provides the basis for self-stereotyping: "Self-categorization leads to a stereotypical self-perception and depersonalization, and adherence to and expression of ingroup normative behavior" (Turner, Hogg, Oakes, Reicher, & Wetherell, 1987, p. 102; see also Haslam, Oakes, Turner, & McGarty, 1996; Hogg & Turner, 1987).

Before explicitly drawing a connection to the shifting standards model, two issues relevant to the self-stereotyping literature deserve mention. One is that various motivational factors have proven important in understanding the strength of self-stereotyping effects. Specifically, those *highly identified* with their groups are more likely to self-stereotype (Turner et al., 1987), as are those experiencing some form of *threat* (Brewer, this volume, 1999; Burris & Jackson, 2000; Dion, 1975). The combination of high identification and threat are particularly likely to produce self-stereotyping effects (Spears et al., 1997;

Verkuyten & Nekuee, 1999). Motivational effects such as these have not yet been examined in research on the shifting standards model, but they may be particularly important when one moves from considering judgments of others to judgments of self.

The second issue concerns the measurement of self-stereotyping. A number of studies assess self-stereotyping through direct questions about similarity to the group (e.g., "I am similar to the average psychology student," Spears et al., 1997; see also Simon & Hamilton, 1994). Our own preference, however, is to do so by examining the extent to which individuals ascribe to themselves the attributes of their groups (e.g., Biernat et al., 1996; Brewer & Pickett, 1999; Dion, 1975). For example, Dion (1975) found that women self-stereotyped (by evaluating themselves more strongly on positive female stereotypic traits such as warmth and nurturance) following competitive failure against men. From our perspective, it will be important to examine not merely perceived similarity to the group, but rather the manner in which one evaluates the self on stereotyped traits.

The bottom line of the self-categorization and self-stereotyping literature is that to the extent that one categorizes oneself as a member of a group, attributes of the group should be taken on as part of the self. This suggests that self-evaluations on stereotyped dimensions should be *assimilated* to the group stereotype. However, if the group serves as a standard of comparison, as suggested in social comparison theory and the shifting standards model, one might also expect a *contrast* effect. A woman, for example, might self-stereotype by considering herself a warm and caring person. At the same time, *compared to women* she might see herself as less warm than she would had men been part of her reference group (see Biernat, Manis, & Kobrynowicz, 1997, for a discussion of simultaneous assimilation and contrast effects).

What may be key to understanding when each of these judgment outcomes occurs is a consideration of the response scale on which self-evaluations are assessed (subjective or common rule). This brings us back to one of the main methodological contributions of the shifting standards model—the evidence that judgments made on common rule or externally anchored response scales are more likely to reveal evidence of stereotyping effects, whereas subjective response scales reduce, mask, or reverse these effects.

In short, we are suggesting that to the extent that "self" is considered a member of a stereotyped group, and to the extent that comparison of self to ingroup others occurs, the processes previously outlined for stereotype-based judgment of *others* may also apply to the self. That is, the use of within-category judgment standards may lead to reductions of self-stereotyping effects on "subjective" compared to "objective" judgment scales: If women judge themselves relative to women, and men to men, subjective judgment scales will mask the female–male differentials in self-evaluation that occur on more common rule response scales. Such a pattern would link the shifting standards model with the literatures on social comparison and self-stereotyping by demonstrating that within-group comparison processes allow individuals to shift or adjust the meaning of subjective evaluative dimensions for judgments of both others and themselves, at the same time that "objective" judgments reveal assimilation to available stereotypes.

SOME RELEVANT RESEARCH

To date, we have conducted four studies that are relevant to the prediction of stereotype-based shifting standards in judgments of the self. Again, the hypothesis was that self-judgments on common rule scales (in the present studies, rankings or q-sorts) would show evidence of self-stereotyping, whereas self-judgments on response scales that allow for within-category comparisons (subjective scales) would dampen or reverse these self-stereotyping effects.

Furthermore, these studies allowed us to assess the effects of one situational factor on the tendency for shifting standards effects to emerge. This situational factor—the number of category members present in the judgment situation—is one that may influence the salience of that social categorization. Specifically, research suggests that an individual who is the sole representative of his/her group (a "solo") draws increased attention; this attention, in turn, leads perceivers to judge the solo more extremely—often, more stereotypically— than they otherwise would (Biernat & Vescio, 1993; Taylor & Fiske, 1978; Taylor, Fiske, Etcoff, & Ruderman, 1978). Furthermore, solos themselves tend to experience increased self-focus and the sense of being isolated and stereotyped on the basis of the relevant social category (Kanter, 1977; Pettigrew & Martin, 1987). Solo status may therefore have implications for stereotyping of both others and the self.

The first two relevant studies were conducted in a field setting that was briefly mentioned above. We examined gender stereotyping effects among U.S. Army captains attending a leadership training school (Biernat, Crandall, et al., 1998). Mixed-sex members of work groups ranked and rated each other and themselves on a highly gender-stereotyped dimension: leadership competence. Through no design of our own, some of the 12- to13-person work groups in this study included a solo woman, whereas others included two women (no groups included more than two women). This provided us with a first opportunity to examine the impact of gender status (one versus two women present) on judgments of leadership competence. The second set of studies, conducted in a laboratory setting, allowed us to examine self-stereotyping on the dimensions of both leadership and warmth, and incorporated solo-male groups into the design.

In general, we predicted that self-stereotyping effects—endorsing gender stereotypes as characteristics of the self—would be quite marked in rankings (the common rule rating scale). That is, men should judge themselves to be competent at leadership (but low in warmth) and women should judge themselves to be relatively less competent at leadership (but higher in warmth). At the same time, we expected subjective judgments to reduce these effects. Furthermore, we predicted that to the extent that solo status increases the salience of gender as a judgment cue, these effects would be most marked in the groups containing gender solos.

The Army Studies

Participants in these studies were U.S. Army Captains completing a 9-week course in leadership training at the Combined Arms and Services Staff School (CAS3) at Fort Leavenworth, Kansas. Study 1 included 100 Captains (89 men, 11 women) surveyed at 3 points in time, and Study 2 included 373 Captains (324 men, 49 women) surveyed at 2 points in time. Participants in these studies were assigned to 12- to 13-person work groups by Army personnel; these work groups (as part of Army policy) are intentionally created to reflect as much diversity as possible (in terms of gender, race, branch of service, etc.). Participants were asked to judge themselves and their groupmates in terms of overall effectiveness as leaders/commanders. In Study 1, these judgments were made in rankings and subjective ratings ("outstanding"–"needs much improvement") on the first day of classes, after 3 weeks, and again after 8 weeks in the course. In Study 2, the ranking procedure was replaced with a q-sort to allow for ties; judgments were made at day 2 of training and again after 2 weeks (see Biernat, Crandall, et al., 1998 for more details on the procedure).

For our purposes here, we are interested in how self-judgments were affected by gender and by the work group's gender composition (solo-woman or 2-women groups). In Study 1, self-judgments were standardized within scale type, and then regressed on a set of control variables (e.g., medals, badges, combat deployment, number of years of comissioned service, race). The residuals were then submitted to a Participant Sex × Time × Response Scale × Group Type (1 or 2 women) mixed-model ANOVA with time and response scale as within-subjects factors. The four-way interaction was reliable—$F(2,170) = 3.68, p < .05$, and is depicted in Figure 4.1 (see Biernat, Crandall, et al., 1998, Figure 3). Female participants' self-judgments were subtracted from male participants' self-judgments. Thus, differences above 0 reflect gendered self-stereotyping (men better leaders than women).

At Time 1, women *ranked* themselves as much lower in leadership competence than did men, but *ratings* revealed no gender differences. This pattern is consistent with the shifting standards model's prediction that subjective judgment scales *reduce* the appearance of stereotyping effects because they are based on within-category frames of reference. Men presumably compared themselves to men, and women compared themselves to women when subjective scales were available. At Times 2 and 3, only groups with solo women continued to

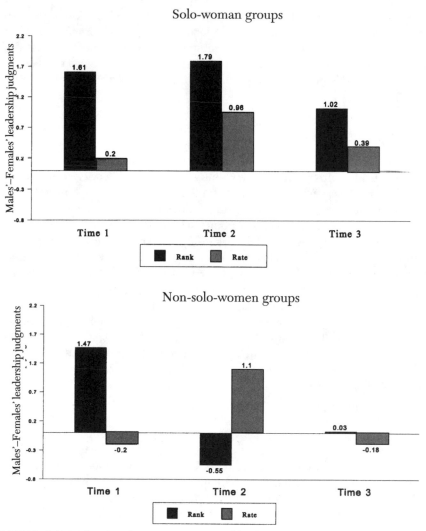

FIGURE 4.1. Male–Female Army captains' self-judgments of leadership competence by time and group type (top panel = solo-woman groups, bottom panel = non-solo women groups; adapted from Biernat, Crandall, et al., 1998).

show this pattern, suggesting that being the lone woman in a group may en-hance the likelihood that the use of within-category judgment standards will persist over time. In the groups that included two women, however, this pattern dissipated (with a strange reversal of the ranking-rating difference occurring at Time 2). Statistically speaking, looking only at groups containing solo women (top panel of Figure 4.1), the 3-way ANOVA revealed a main effect of sex—

$F(1,51) = 7.55, p < .01$; and a Sex × Scale interaction—$F(1,51) = 5.57, p < .01$. For these groups, the shifting standards pattern—greater sex differentiation on ranks than on ratings—was apparent at all three time points. However, for groups containing two women (bottom panel of Figure 3), the 3-way interaction was reliable—$F(2,68) = 9.59, p < .001$. Here, the shifting standards pattern appeared only at Time 1 ($p < .05$); at Time 2, the rank–rate difference was reliable but in the opposite direction predicted by the model ($p < .01$), and no sex effects were apparent at Time 3.

In Study 2, self-judgments were again standardized within scale-type and submitted to a Participant Sex × Race × Time × Response Scale × Group Type (1 or 2 women) ANOVA (no information on medals and badges was available in this study). Only the Participant Sex × Response Scale × Group Type interaction was reliable—$F(1,333) = 6.00, p < .05$—and is depicted in Figure 4.2 (see Biernat, Crandall, et al., 1998, Figure 6). Overall, groups containing a solo woman showed strong evidence of self-stereotyping in the predicted shifting standards pattern (the male–female difference was stronger using q-sorts than ratings—Sex × Response Scale $F(1,121) = 5.69, p < .05$. Groups including two women showed no evidence of self-stereotyping; men and women judged themselves equally competent as leaders. Both field studies supported our main hypotheses: Evidence of self-stereotyping was stronger on common rule (rankings, q-sorts) than subjective judgment scales, and this shifting self-standards effect was stronger (or in Study 2, only present) in groups containing a solo woman.

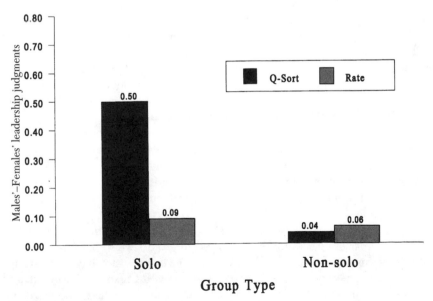

FIGURE 4.2. Male–Female Army captains' self-judgments of leadership competence by group type (adapted from Biernat, Crandall, et al., 1998).

The Small Group Studies

Given the importance of solo- versus non-solo group composition in the field studies, we decided to bring a similar research design into the controlled conditions of the laboratory (see Fuegen & Biernat, in press, for details). We created mixed-sex groups to work together on a group problem-solving task (the NASA Decision-Making Problem; Cammalleri, Hendrick, Pittman, Blout, & Prather, 1973). Members then judged themselves and each other on a series of dimensions, some of which were conceptualized as "masculine" or "competent" in nature (leadership ability, competence, influence) and some of which were conceptualized as "feminine" or "warm" in nature (ability to maintain group harmony, likability). This allowed us to separately examine gender-based self-stereotyping on masculine and feminine qualities. As in the Army field study, participants both ranked and rated themselves and their groupmates on these dimensions (the subjective rating scale used a 1/"very low" to 6/"very high" format).

Two types of groups were created to mirror those in the Army studies: Groups of 1 woman and 5 men (solo groups) and groups of 2 women and 4 men (non-solo groups). Nine groups of each type were run (for a full report of the data relevant to judgments of others, see Fuegen & Biernat, in press). After standardization within scale-type, self-judgments were submitted to a Participant Sex × Group Type × Response Scale × Judgment Dimension (competence/warmth) mixed-model ANOVA. To take into account the non-independence of participants, group was included as a nesting factor in this analysis. The 4-way interaction was marginally significant—$F(1,83) = 3.48, p < .07$. Decomposing this interaction, we found no effects on the masculine/competence dimension (all $ps > .25$). Instead, it was on the feminine/warmth dimension that evidence of self-stereotyping emerged, particularly on rankings and in solo-female groups—3-way interaction $F(1,83) = 2.80, p < .10$. This interaction is depicted in Figure 4.3. Here, male participants' self-judgments were subtracted from female participants' self-judgments such that differences above 0 reflect gender self-stereotyping (women more "warm" than men).

As can be seen in the figure, it was only in the solo-female groups that evidence of shifting self-standards was revealed. Women ranked themselves as warmer than men did in this group, but ratings significantly reduced this effect—Sex × Scale interaction $F(1,32) = 4.46, p < .05$. In the groups consisting of 2 women and 4 men, there was simply no evidence of self-stereotyping or a shifting standards effect ($F < 1$).

Thus far we have focused only on solo-female groups, but we wondered whether similar effects would be observed in groups where *men* had solo or minority status. We therefore collected data from two additional types of groups using the same method described above: Groups with 1 man and 5 women, and groups with 2 men and 4 women. Again, nine groups of each type were run through the NASA task and judgment procedure.

Self-judgments were again submitted to a Participant Sex × Group Type ×

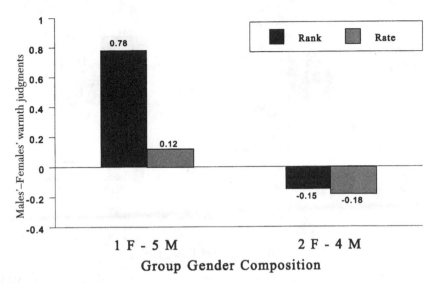

FIGURE 4.3. Females'–Males' self-judgments of warmth in solo-woman groups (1 F, 5 M) and non-solo groups (2 F, 4 M).

Response Scale × Judgment Dimension (competence/warmth) mixed-model ANOVA, with group included as a nesting factor. In this study, only the Sex × Group Type × Judgment Dimension interaction was reliable—$F(1,87) = 5.09, p < .05$—which led us to conduct separate ANOVAs for the "competence" and "warmth" dimensions. As in the female minority groups, self-judgments on the competence dimension showed no effects (all $ps .>25$), but evidence of self-stereotyping again emerged on the feminine/warmth dimension. The Sex × Group Type × Response Scale interaction was not reliable—$F(1,87) = 2.18, p < .15$; but the Sex × Scale interaction was—$F(1,87) = 4.99, p < .05$. Nonetheless, for comparison with the female minority group data, these self-judgments are depicted separately for each type of group in Figure 4.4. Again, difference scores above 0 reflect gendered self-stereotyping (women judging themselves more "warm" than men).

This figure indicates that rank ordering showed evidence of self-stereotyping in both group types—women judged themselves to be warmer than men did. Both groups also showed trends consistent with the shifting standards pattern—reductions of the self-stereotyping effect on subjective scales—but this reduction seemed to take different forms in the two group types. In non-solo groups, subjective judgments showed reductions of the self-stereotyping effect, though the Sex × Scale interaction was not significant ($F < 1$). *Solo* male groups actually showed a contrast effect, with men judging themselves subjectively more warm than women did—Sex × Scale interaction $F(1,36) = 5.25, p < .01$). This is our first strong documentation of a contrast effect: Because these solo groups may be particularly likely to prompt use of within-sex judgment standards, men

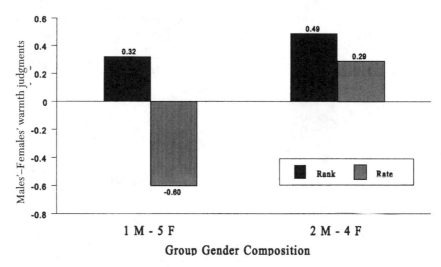

FIGURE 4.4. Females'–Males' self-judgments of warmth in solo-man groups (1 M, 5 F) and non-solo groups (2 M, 4 F).

subjectively viewed themselves as extremely warm (relative to women's self-judgments when they compared themselves to other women).

That self-stereotyping effects emerged only when men and women judged themselves on warmth but not on competence deserves further comment. It may have been that interpersonal warmth was the more relevant judgment dimension in the context of our laboratory studies. This warmth dimension—composed of the items "likeable" and "able to maintain group harmony"—seems to capture the qualities that are important in small group interactions of the sort we arranged in our lab. In contrast, because the Army setting emphasizes leadership and achievement, these stereotypically "masculine" dimensions may have been most relevant to self-perception. Others have also argued that context is a strong determinant of the dimensions on which individuals self-stereotype (see Hogg & Turner, 1987). Still, the relevance interpretation is speculative here, and more research on the issue would be valuable. Whatever the explanation, the findings regarding self-rated warmth are consistent with the notion that the tendency to self-stereotype, when it occurs, is more marked on objective than subjective response scales, and especially in groups where there is a solo member of one gender present.[1]

---

1. The reader will note that our predictions for solo-female and solo-male groups are identical. That is, when *either* gender has solo status, we predict stronger gender-based self-stereotyping effects. In an analysis that combined the four group types into solo groups (1 female, 5 males or 1 male, 5 females) and non-solo groups (2 females, 4 males or 2 males, 4 females), the Participant Solo × Solo Composition (yes or no) × Response Scale interaction on warmth ratings was reliable—$F(1,172) = 4.30$, $p < .05$—

IMPLICATIONS AND EXTENSIONS

We believe the research described here adds to our general understanding of how the self is evaluated with reference to important social groups. More specifically, our research suggests that the standards used in self-evaluation may shift based on one's group membership, and this shifting may be revealed through comparision of responses on subjective and externally anchored response scales. Stereotypes associated with a group may serve as a standard not just for judging others, but for judging the self as well. Our research also raises some important additional issues and considerations, to which we now turn.

When Will Patterns of Shifting Self-Standards Occur?

As indicated above, evidence for group-based shifting standards in evaluation of the self is likely to be restricted to (a) stereotyped dimensions (there must be a stereotype that differentiates groups in order for within-group standards to be necessary; see Biernat et al., 1991), (b) dimensions that are relevant to the situation (e.g., Hogg & Turner, 1987), and (c) context that make the relevant group categorization salient. For example, though Black and White Americans are stereotypically perceived as differing in athleticism, self-judgments of athleticism may only be group-based if the situation itself makes this dimension salient (a basketball game), but not if it does not (a business meeting).

Furthermore, the basketball game will prompt more within-group comparison for self-evaluation of athleticism when race is highly salient. In our research, we found that the presence of a solo group member was a cue that increased category salience, but other cues can easily be imagined as well. From a self-categorization theory perspective, for example, category salience is a function of the "meta-contrast ratio"—the within-category difference relative to the differences between categories in a given context (Turner, 1985). By this formulation, it is in "balanced" conditions—where there are roughly equal numbers of members from each category present—that the meta-contrast ratio is high (see Oakes, 1987). And category salience will be further increased to the extent that "normative fit" is high as well—the "perceived differences are consistent with the perceiver's background theories about the nature of distinctions between those groups" (Oakes & Reynolds, 1997, pp. 60–61). Thus, in our basketball game, the use of within-category standards to judge athleticism might be greatest when a highly accomplished Black team plays a less accomplished White team. Further work examining how other determinants of salience influence patterns of self-stereotyping is needed.

Along with cues to category salience, other "meta-informational cues" may

---

with solo groups showing a mean female–male difference of .29 in rankings and .00 in ratings, and non-solo groups showing no ranking–rating differences (mean female–male difference = .15 in rankings and .12 in ratings).

also affect the likelihood of making within-group comparisons (Abele & Petzold, 1998). For example, in studies involving judgments of other people (not the self), perceivers differentiated *between* members of two groups when information about them was presented in a mixed, alternating, fashion, but made *within*-group differentiations when information about one group was presented separately from information about the other. The former comparisons produced assimilation (e.g., nurses were judged more helpful than stockbrokers), but the latter produced contrast (stockbrokers were judged more helpful than nurses; Abele & Petzold, 1998, Study 1).

The analogy in our own work is that judgments on externally-anchored response scales require cross-group comparisons, producing assimilation effects, whereas judgements on subjective scales invite within-group comparisons, producing reduced assimilation or contrast. In this sense, the judgment scale itself may serve as a meta-informational cue as to which frame of reference should guide one's judgements.

It may be interesting to determine whether other contextual features—such as solo status—serve to heighten the impact of this cue. Because solos have no other ingroup members immediately present with whom to compare, the cross-category perspective prompted by a ranking or q-sort scale may intensify—hense the strong assimilative evidence of self-stereotyping we found on such scales in the solo groups. At the same time, to the extent that solo status makes one's category membership salient, the within-category perspective prompted by a subjective scale may be heightened as well. Only one piece of evidence from the present studies supported this later effect: Solo males showed strong contrast from the male stereotype of warmth in their subjective judgments (see Figure 4.4). In each of the other studies, however, subjective judgments did not markedly differ in solo and non-solo groups (see Figures 4.1, 4.2, and 4.3). Nonetheless, it seems plausible that in addition to making a category salient, some of the effect of solo status occurs by simple virtue of its informational value—especially in prompting a cross-category judgment perspective on objective response scales.

Motivation, Context, and Shifting Standards

The shifting standards model is largely cognitive in its emphasis, and to date, little work has focused on motivational factors that might enhance or reduce the tendency to use within-category standards for juding others and the self. Likely motivational candidates in this regard include self-esteem protection or enhancement, and needs for belongingness versus differentiation, among others.

Furthermore, our research to date has not considered two facts about social life that might bear on how comparison with our social groups influences the self-concept. First, people are often not afforded the luxury of choosing their social comparisons (Wheeler & Miyake, 1992). Circumstances may dictate with whom we compare, and because social comparisons are often spontaneous and unintentional, comparison information present in the environment may affect self-evaluation without deliberate awareness (e.g., see Baldwin & Holmes, 1987). Second, stereotypes of virtually all the groups we belong to have both positive and negative content, and at any given moment, we may be focused on either set of beliefs.

To illustrate, consider a simple study in which we oriented University of Kansas (KU) undergraduates toward either the positive or negative aspects of their group, and then examined their group and self-perceptions (Heckathorn & Biernat, 1996). Participants read a brief interview with an individual who highlighted either the positive or negative aspects of KU (e.g., KU students are either smart or concerned or immature and naive—all found to be stereotypic of this group in pretesting). They then judged the group and themselves on a series of other stereotyped traits, using subjective response scales.

Judgments of KU students as a group were assimilated to this valenced priming. Whether through persuasion or simple availability processes, negative priming led to negative group perceptions whereas positive primes led to positive group perceptions. At the same time, however, self-judgments were *contrasted* from the primes, a finding consistent with the use of the available group stereotype (manipulated to be positive or negative) as a comparison standard. It was as if participants said, "Compared to this negative group, I look pretty good" or "Compared to this positive group, I don't quite measure up!" Furthermore, these contrast effects were limited to self-judgments on stereotyped traits, but not on stereotype-irrelevant traits.

This research provides an example of how a shift in one's perspective of the group—in either a positive or negative direction—may produce an opposing pattern of self-stereotyping to the extent that the group is used as a referent for judging the self. In this case, circumstances forced particular images of the group upon participants, and they responded by shifting their perceptions of the group as a whole (at least temporarily) in the direction of these images and then adjusting their self-standing relative to it. These findings are consistent with the spirit of the shifting standards model, but they demonstrate the tendency to shift standards in a novel way—one that does not rely on the use of different response language to tap the shift. They also point to the ease with which self-standing on stereotyped dimensions can be moderated by contextual variation in the content of the group stereotype.

Returning to the theme of motivation, it also seems likely that egoistic or other concerns may affect the degree and direction in which self-perceptions shift in such circumstances, and also whether individuals eschew comparison with a given group in favor of comparison with a new one. For example, when faced with an upward comparison to a group member that speaks unfavorably to one's abilities, one might drop the relevant group identification in favor of an identity that enhances self-esteem or positive affect (Mussweiler, Gabriel, &

Bodenhausen, 2000). We simultaneously belong to many groups, and both situational factors and internal motivations may lead us to focus on any of their various (and often conflicting) stereotypes at any given point in time. In short, the opportunities for standards of self-judgment to shift based on group membership are great and varied, and research to date has only begun to examine the manner in which these standard shifts occur and the consequences they produce.

Assimilation and Contrast

Earlier in this chapter, we described the self-stereotyping literature as predicting assimilation to group stereotypes, and the social comparison literature as predicting contrast (to the extent that the stereotype serves as a standard). In our reading of self-categorization theory, the assimilation hypothesis seems central and invariable: Self-stereotyping, by definition, is the "perception of increased identity between the self and ingroup members and increased difference from outgroup members (on relevant dimensions)" (Oakes, Haslam, & Turner, 1994, p. 100).

However, when one conceptualizes group stereotypes as standards against which one compares the self, *contrast* may be the more frequent, but certainly not the only, judgment outcome. As our own research has indicated, self-stereotyping in terms of rankings (externally anchored scales) may reveal assimilation at the same time that subjective judgments reveal contrast. And in social comparison theory more generally, the individual may sometimes assimilate to the relevant comparison standard.

For example, though upward comparison is typically considered detrimental to the self (one feels worse by comparison to a highly favorable other), some research suggests that those comparing upward may also feel good about themselves. This may occur because the self is perceived as similar to the other (Wheeler, 1966), or because the other's achievement seems attainable for the self (Lockwood & Kunda, 1997; see also Buunk, Collins, Taylor, VanYperen, & Dakof, 1990; Collins, 1996). And although downward comparison is traditionally thought to be self-enhancing (one feels better by comparison to the worse-off other; Wills, 1981), it can have adverse consequences for the comparer to the extent that the other's failure is threatening to the self (Major et al., 1991; Taylor & Lobel, 1989).

In short, it is misleading to suggest that social comparison theory consistently predicts contrast effects, or that the use of group stereotypes as standards for judging the self will produce subjective shifts away from that point of reference. In fact, in most of the research described here, we found reduced assimilation effects, but not contrast, when individuals judged themselves on the subjective scales that allowed for within-group comparisons. Elsewhere we have suggested that assimilation to a standard is likely to the extent that the target—

the self in this case—is generally consistent with the stereotype, but not when a large discrepancy is perceived (Biernat, Vescio, & Manis, 1998). For example, when a fun-loving but highly studious young man joins a fraternity, his comparison to the group stereotype may produce assimilation on some dimensions (e.g., high sociability), but contrast on others (e.g., academic laziness). The whens and whys of assimilation and contrast effects in self-perception is another research area worthy of continued attention.

SUMMARY

The shifting standards model suggests that group stereotypes lead perceivers to judge others relative to within-group standards. Because the subjective language of most evaluations is "slippery" in nature, this means that judgments such as "good" or "tall" or "aggressive" may not mean the same thing when they are applied to members of contrasting social categories. At the same time, when judges are forced to take a cross-category perspective by virtue of judgment scales being tied to externally-anchored units or by a single rank-ordering being required, available stereotypes are revealed.

The goal of this chapter has been to suggest that similar effects emerge when it comes to judging the self. Both social comparison theory and self-categorization theory's consideration of self-stereotyping processes suggest that the self is routinely compared with ingroups and their attributes. An extension of the shifting standards model to the domain of self-judgment draws on these perspectives, and also offers some clarification about when self-stereotyping effects are most likely to occur. Specifically, such effects are most likely to be detected on stereotypes that are relevant to the immediate context and on relatively "objective" response scales, with contrast effects occasionally emerging on subjective scales. The research reported here further suggests that a situational factor that increases the salience of social categories—groups consisting of "solos"—may also increase the tendency for self-stereotyping and shifting standards effects to emerge. Consideration of other contextual and motivational factors that might enhance or diminish self-stereotyping tendencies is now needed.

REFERENCES

Abele, A. E., & Petzold, P. (1998). Pragmatical use of categorical information in impression formation. *Journal of Personality and Social Psychology, 75,* 347–358.

Baldwin, M. W., & Holmes, J. G. (1987). Salient private audiences and awareness of the self. *Journal of Personality and Social Psychology, 52,* 1087–1098.

Biernat, M., Crandall, C. S., Young, L. V., Kobrynowicz, D., & Halpin, S. M. (1998). All that you can be: Stereotyping of self and others in a military context. *Journal of Per-*

sonality and Social Psychology, 75, 301–317.

Biernat, M., & Kobrynowicz, D. (1997). Gender- and race-based standards of competence: Lower minimum standards but higher ability standards for devalued groups. *Journal of Personality and Social Psychology, 72,* 544–557.

Biernat, M., & Manis, M. (1994). Shifting standards and stereotype-based judgments. *Journal of Personality and Social Psychology, 66,* 5–20.

Biernat, M., Manis, M., & Kobrynowicz, D. (1997). Simultaneous assimilation and contrast effects in judgments of self and other. *Journal of Personality and Social Psychology, 73,* 254–269.

Biernat, M., Manis, M., & Nelson, T. E. (1991). Stereotypes and standards of judgment. *Journal of Personality and Social Psychology, 60,* 485–499.

Biernat, M., & Thompson, E. R. (2002). Shifting standards and contextual variation in stereotyping. In W. Stroebe & M. Hewstone (Eds.), *European Review of Social Psychology, Volume 12* (pp. 103–137). London: Wiley.

Biernat, M., & Vescio, T. K. (1993). Categorization and stereotyping: Effects of group context on memory and social judgment. *Journal of Experimental Social Psychology, 29,* 166–202.

Biernat, M., Vescio, T. K., & Green, M. L. (1996). Selective self-stereotyping. *Journal of Personality and Social Psychology, 71,* 1194–1209.

Biernat, M., Vescio, T. K., & Manis, M. (1998). Judging and behaving toward members of stereotyped groups: A shifting standards perspective. In C. Sedikides, J. Schopler, & C. A. Insko (Eds.), *Intergroup cognition and intergroup behavior* (pp. 151–175). Hillsdale, NJ: Erlbaum.

Brewer, M. B., & Pickett, C. L. (1999). Distinctiveness motives as a source of the social self. In T. R. Tyler, & R. M. Kramer (Eds.), *The psychology of the social self: Applied social research* (pp. 71–87). Mahwah, NJ: Erlbaum.

Brown, J. D. (1986). Evaluations of self and other: Self-enhancement biases in social judgments. *Social Cognition, 4,* 353–376.

Burris, C. T., & Jackson, L. M. (2000). Social identity and the true believer: Responses to threatened self-stereotypes among the intrinsically religious. *British Journal of Social Psychology, 39,* 257–278.

Buunk, B. P., Collins, R. L., Taylor, S. E., VanYperen, N. W., & Dakof, G. A. (1990). The affective consequences of social comparison: Either direction has its ups and downs. *Journal of Personality and Social Psychology, 59*(6), 1238–1249.

Buunk, B. P., & VanYperen, N. W. (1991). Referential comparisons, relational comparisons, and exchange orientation: Their relation to marital satisfaction. *Personality and Social Psychology Bulletin, 17,* 709–717.

Cammalleri, J. A., Hendrick, H. W., Pittman, W. C., Blout, H. D., & Prather, C. C. (1973). Effects of different leadership styles on group accuracy. *Journal of Applied Psychology, 57,* 32–37.

Chiu, C., Hong, Y., Lam, I. C., Fu, J. H., Tong, J. Y., & Lee, V. S. (1998). Stereotyping and self-presentation: Effects of gender stereotype activation. *Group Processes and Intergroup Relations, 1,* 81–96.

Collins, R. L. (1996). For better or worse: The impact of upward social comparison on self-evaluation. *Psychological Bulletin, 119,* 51–69.

Crocker, J., & Major, B. (1989). Social stigma and self-esteem: The self-protective properties of stigma. *Psychological Review, 96*(4), 608–630.

Crosby, F. (1976). A model of egotistical relative deprivation. *Psychological Review, 83,* 85–113.

Dion, K. L. (1975). Women's reactions to discrimination from members of the same or opposite sex. *Journal of Research in Personality, 9,* 294–306.

Festinger, L. (1954). A theory of social comparison processes. *Human Relations, 7,* 117–140.

Fuegen, K., & Biernat, M. (in press). Reexamining the effects of solo status for women and men. *Personality and Social Psychology Bulletin.*

Goethals, G. R., & Darley, J. M. (1977). Social comparison theory: An attributional approach. In J. M. Suls & R. L. Miller (Eds.), *Social comparison processes: Theoretical and empirical perspectives* (pp. 259–278). Washington, DC: Hemisphere.

Goldberg, P. (1968). Are women prejudiced against women? *Transaction, 5,* 28–30.

Haslam, S. A., Oakes, P. J., Turner, J. C., & McGarty, C. (1996). Social identity, self-categorization, and the perceived homogeneity of ingroups and outgroups: The interaction between social motivation and cognition. In R. M Sorrentino & E. T. Higgins (Eds.), *Handbook of motivation and cognition (Volume 3): The interpersonal context* (pp. 182–222). New York: Guilford.

Heckathorn, H., & Biernat, M. (1996). *Self-stereotyping.* Unpublished data, University of Kansas, Lawrence, KS.

Higgins, E. T., & Lurie, L. (1983). Context, categorization, and memory: The "change of standard" effect. *Cognitive Psychology, 15,* 525–547.

Hogg, M. A., & Turner, J. C. (1987). Intergroup behaviour, self-stereotyping, and the salience of social categories. *British Journal of Social Psychology, 26,* 325–340.

Kanter, R. M. (1977). *Men and women of the corporation.* New York: Basic Books.

Kobrynowicz, D., & Biernat, M. (1997). Decoding subjective evaluations: How stereotypes provide shifting standards. *Journal of Experimental Social Psychology, 33,* 579–601.

Lockwood, P., & Kunda, Z. (1997). Superstars and me: Predicting the impact of role models on the self. *Journal of Personality and Social Psychology, 73,* 91–103.

Major, B., & Testa, M. (1989). Social comparison processes and judgments of entitlement and satisfaction. *Journal of Experimental Social Psychology, 25,* 101–120.

Major, B., Testa, M., & Bylsma, W. H. (1991). Responses to upward and downward social comparisons: The impact of esteem-relevance and perceived control. In J. Suls & T. A. Wills (Eds.), *Social comparison: Contemporary theory and research* (pp. 237–260). Hillsdale, NJ: Erlbaum.

Miller, D. T., & Prentice, D. A. (1996). The construction of social norms and standards. In E. T. Higgins & A. W. Kruglanski (Eds.), *Social psychology: Handbook of basic principles* (pp. 799–829). New York: Guilford.

Miller, D. T., Turnbull, W., & McFarland, C. (1988). Particularistic and universalistic evaluation in the social comparison process. *Journal of Personality and Social Psychology, 55,* 908–917.

Mussweiler, T., Gabriel, S., & Bodenhausen, G. V. (2000). Shifting social identities as a strategy for deflecting threatening social comparisons. *Journal of Personality and Social Psychology, 79,* 398–409.

Oakes, P. J. (1987). The salience of social categories. In J. C. Turner, M. A. Hogg, P. J. Oakes, D. D. Reicher, & M. S. Wetherall (Eds.), *Rediscovering the social group: A self-categorization theory* (pp. 117–141). Oxford, UK: Blackwell.

Oakes, P. J., Haslam, S. A., & Turner, J. C. (1994). *Stereotyping and social reality.* Oxford, UK: Blackwell.

Oakes, P. J., & Reynolds, K. J. (1997). Asking the accuracy question: Is measurement the answer? In R. Spears, P. J. Oakes, N. Ellemers, & S. A. Haslam (Eds.), The social psychology of stereotyping and group life (pp. 51–71). Oxford, UK: Blackwell.

Parducci, A. (1963). Range-frequency compromise in judgment. *Psychological Monographs, 77* (2, no. 565).

Pettigrew, T. F., & Martin, J. (1987). Shaping the organizational context for Black American inclusion. *Journal of Social Issues, 43,* 41–78.

Postman, L., & Miller, G. A. (1945). Anchoring of temporal judgments. *American Journal of Psychology, 58,* 43–53.

Prentice, D. A. (1990). Familiarity and differences in self- and other-representations. *Journal of Personality and Social Psychology, 59,* 369–383.

Schachter, S. (1959). *The psychology of affiliation.* Palo Alto, CA: Stanford University Press.

Sherif, M., & Hovland, C. I. (1961). *Social judgment: Assimilation and contrast effects in communication and attitude change.* New Haven, CT: Yale University Press.

Simon, B., & Hamilton, D. L. (1994). Self-stereotyping and social context: The effects of relative in-group size and in-group status. *Journal of Personality and Social Psychology, 66,* 699–711.

Spears, R., Doosje, B., & Ellemers, N. (1997). Self-stereotyping in the face of threats to group status and distinctiveness: The role of group identification. *Personality and Social Psychology Bulletin, 23,* 538–553.

Swim, J., Borgida, E., Maruyama, G., & Myers, D. G. (1989). Joan McKay versus John McKay: Do gender stereotypes bias evaluations? *Psychological Bulletin, 105*, 409–429.

Taylor, S. E., & Fiske, S. T. (1978). Salience, attention, and attribution: Top-of-the-head phenomena. In L. Berkowitz (Ed.), *Advances in Experimental Social Psychology* (Vol. 11, pp. 249–288). New York: Academic Press.

Taylor, S. E., Fiske, S. T., Etcoff, N. L., & Ruderman, A. J. (1978). Categorical and contextual bases of person memory and stereotyping. *Journal of Personality and Social Psychology, 36*, 778–793.

Taylor, S. E., & Lobel, M. (1989). Social comparison activity under threat: Downward evaluation and upward contacts. *Psychological Review, 96*, 569–575.

Tesser, A. (1988). Toward a self-evaluation maintenance model of social behavior. *Advances in Experimental Social Psychology, 21*, 181–226.

Turner, J. C. (1984). Social identification and psychological group formation. In H. Tajfel (Ed.), *The social dimension: European developments in social psychology* (Vol. 2, pp. 518–538). Cambridge, UK: Cambridge University Press.

Turner, J. C. (1985). Social categorization and the self-concept: A social cognitive theory of group behavior. In E. J. Lawler (Ed.), *Advances in group processes: Theory and research* (Vol. 2). Greenwich, CT: JAI Press.

Turner, J. C. (1987). A self-categorization theory. In J. C. Turner, M. A. Hogg, P. J. Oakes, S. D. Reicher, & M. S. Wetherell (Eds.), *Rediscovering the social group: A self-categorization theory*. Oxford, UK: Blackwell.

Turner, J. C., Hogg, M. A., Oakes, P. J., Reicher, S. D., & Wetherell, M. (1987). *Rediscovering the Social Group: A self-categorization theory* (pp. 77–122). Oxford, UK: Blackwell.

Turner, J. C., & Oakes, P. J. (1989). Self-categorization theory and social influence. In P. B. Paulus (Ed.), *Psychology of group influence* (2nd ed., pp. 253–275). Hillsdale, NJ: Erlbaum.

Upshaw, H. S. (1962). Own attitude as an anchor in equal-appearing intervals. *Journal of Abnormal and Social Psychology, 64*, 85–96.

Verkuyten, M., & Nekuee, S. (1999). Ingroup bias: The effect of self-stereotyping, identification, and group threat. *Journal of Experimental Social Psychology, 29*, 411–418.

Volkmann, J. (1951). Scales of judgment and their implications for social psychology. In J. H. Rohrer & M. Sherif (Eds.), *Social psychology at the crossroads*. New York: Harper.

Wheeler, L. (1966). Motivation as a determinant of upward comparison. *Journal of Experimental Social Psychology, 2* (Suppl. 1), 27–31.

Wheeler, L., & Miyake, K. (1992). Social comparison in everyday life. *Journal of Personality and Social Psychology, 62*(5), 760–773.

Willis, T. A. (1981). Downward comparison principles in social psychology. *Psychological Bulletin, 90*, 245–271.

Wood, J. V. (1989). Theory and research concerning social comparisons of personal attributes. *Psychological Bulletin, 106*(2), 231–248.

Zanna, M. P., Goethals, G. R., & Hill, J. F. (1975). Evaluating a sex-related ability: Social comparison with similar others and standard setters. *Journal of Experimental Social Psychology, 11*, 86–93.

5

Affective Influences on Self-Perception and Self-Disclosure

JOSEPH P. FORGAS
STEPHANIE J. MOYLAN

INTRODUCTION

"Who am I?" Of all the questions investigated by psychologists, understanding the concept of the self remains one of the most difficult and intriguing. Philosophers and writers from Aristotle to William James

This work was supported by a Special Investigator award from the Australian Research Council, and the Research Prize by the Alexander von Humboldt Foundation, to Joseph P. Forgas. The contribution of Joseph Ciarrochi, Patrick Vargas, and Joan Webb to this project is gratefully acknowledged.

For further information on this research project, see also website at www.psy.unsw.edu.au/users/jforgas.htm

Address for correspondence: Joseph P. Forgas, School of Psychology, University of New South Wales, Sydney 2052, Australia. E-mail: jp.forgas@unsw.edu.au.

have pondered this question, and research on the self remains one of the most popular domains today (Sedikides & Brewer, 2001). How do human beings construct enduring representations of themselves as unique persons? The main contribution of contemporary research is to point out that the self is not some kind of stable, mysterious internal entity that is directly accessible and "knowable" by an individual (Bem, 1972; Hilgard, 1980; Sedikides, 1992). Rather, the self is a social construction that is created and maintained as a result of the same kinds of judgmental and inferential processes that we also use to make sense of the external world (see also Biernat & Eidelman; Kashima, Kashima & Clark; Leary; Smith, this volume). Just as social perception and social judgments are subject to various distortions and biases, so too constructing an image of ourselves can be influenced by a variety of affective and motivational factors (Sedikides, 1992, 1995). This chapter will review recent empirical evidence, including several studies from our laboratory, showing that fleeting, superficial mood states can have a highly predictable and significant influence on how people see themselves, the way they explain and interpret their own behaviors, and the way they disclose and communicate about themselves to others.

Discussing affective influences on the self is especially important in the context of a volume such as this, considering that the last two decades saw something like an "affective revolution" in psychological research. In fact, most of what we know about the influence of affective states on social thinking and behavior has been discovered since the early 1980s (see also Forgas, 2000, 2001). For the first time, we are making real progress toward providing empirical answers to the age-old questions about the relationship between the rational and the emotional aspects of human nature (Hilgard, 1980). Nowhere is the interaction between the objective and the subjective, the rational and the emotional sides of human beings more interesting than when it comes to understanding the nature of the self. The chapter will begin with a brief review of past theoretical and empirical ideas about the links between affect and the self, followed by a summary of some of the contemporary cognitive theories applicable to this issue, including the integrative Affect Infusion Model (AIM; Forgas, 1995). The second part of the chapter will discuss recent evidence for affective influences on the self, including a number of experiments carried out in our laboratory.

BACKGROUND

For much of the history of psychology, research on the self was considered as outside the realm of scientific inquiry. This absurd position was the direct consequence of radical behaviorist dogma that excluded the study of mental phenomena such as the self from the legitimate subject matter of psychology (Hilgard, 1980). Research on affect fared only slightly better. Within the behaviorist paradigm, emotion, if considered at all, was manipulated in animals through such crude devices as the delivery of electric shocks or food or drink deprivation. Affective responses were sometimes operationalized by counting the number of faecal boli that a rodent deposited while scurrying around its cage trying to escape electric shocks.

Early interest in the self owes far more to symbolic interactionist, and phenomenological theorizing. George Herbert Mead (1934) was among the first to suggest that the concept of self is a symbolic creation, and its existence is entirely dependent on human beings' unique ability to abstract and symbolize their interactive experiences. For Mead, the self was a social construct, the accumulated symbolic residue of interpersonal experiences that informed a person's unique sense of identity (see also Ickes, this volume). This idea also lies at the heart of the work by Charles Cooley, who discussed extensively the principles and functions of the "looking glass self." This evocative metaphor captures nicely the notion that the self is, in the last analysis, the sum total of our perceptions and interpretation of how other people see and respond to us. These ideas paved the way for subsequent empirical research by social psychologists on self-processes. Ned Jones and his colleagues in several ingenuous experiments examined how such a "looking glass self" might operate. They showed that social performances that meet with the approval of others are readily incorporated into our unique concept of the self, but people will reject as their own, behaviors that meet with social disapproval. Decisions about what is "me" and what is "not me" of course necessarily involve complex inferential judgmental processes and attributions, as Jones showed. In its most radical form, it was Bem (1972) who proposed the idea that the self is based on inferences derived from observed external behaviors in exactly the same way as are impressions about others. Although self-perception theory has perhaps gone too far in denying the importance of subjective experiences in the construction of the self, the principle that judgmental and inferential processes are involved has been firmly established.

Contemporary research on the self, and experiments exploring affective influence on self perception in particular, are all predicated on the assumption that self-judgments are governed by the same mechanisms, and are subject to the same kinds of biases and distortions as are judgments about other aspects of the social world (see also Gilovich, this volume). Indeed, affective influences on the self may be particularly salient and important because affective reactions often constitute the primary and determining response to information we receive about ourselves. Although all social perception can involve some degree of affectivity, judgments about the self are particularly prone to such influences. Most of us have the strongest emotional reactions to information that touches on our sense of the self (Trope, Ferguson, & Raghunanthan, 2001), and especially information that indicates interpersonal evaluation by others (Leary, 2000). In a similar vein, Zajonc (2000) argued that affect functions as the primary and often dominant force in determining people's responses to social situations, and nowhere should this influence be stronger than when it comes to evaluating the self.

There are several lines of empirical evidence that support this view. In a series of studies (Forgas, 1979, 1982), we have found that attitudes toward, and implicit cognitive representations about, common, recurring social interactions are largely determined by what these encounters mean for the self and how people *feel* about the personal consequences of these events. Affective reactions such as feelings of anxiety, confidence, intimacy, pleasure, or discomfort seem to be critical in defining the implicit structure and complexity of people's cognitive representations about their social encounters. Interestingly, the objective, descriptive features of social episodes play comparatively little role in mental representations—it is how we subjectively feel about them that matters. More recently, Niedenthal and Halberstadt (2000) also found that a wide variety of "stimuli can cohere as a category even when they have nothing in common other than the emotional responses they elicit" (p. 381). Similar conclusions were reached several decades ago by Pervin (1976), who argued that "what is striking is the extent to which situations are described in terms of affects (e.g. threatening, warm, interesting, dull, tense, calm, rejecting) and organized in terms of similarity of affects aroused by them" (p. 471). Thus, affective reactions to a wide variety of social events seem to be predominantly determined by how they are seen as affecting the self (Leary, 2000, this volume).

In addition, affect, once elicited, also has a dynamic influence on how social information – including information about the self—is selected, interpreted, processed, and remembered (Forgas, 2001). Such "affect infusion" effects were initially explained in terms of either psychodynamic or associationist principles. Psychoanalytic theories assumed that affect has a dynamic, invasive quality and can "take over" judgments unless adequate psychological resources are deployed to control these impulses. Conditioning and associationist theories provided an alternative account, suggesting that previously neutral concepts can become affectively loaded as a result of incidental associations with affect-eliciting stimuli. According to radical behaviorists such as Watson, all affective reactions acquired throughout life—including affective evaluations of the self—are the product of such a cumulative pattern of associations. The conditioning metaphor was specifically applied to social evaluations by Byrne and Clore (1970) and Clore and Byrne (1974), who suggested that affective states triggered by unrelated events can become "attached" to previously neutral responses. For example, an aversive environment can produce a negative affective reaction that can spontaneously become associated with previously neutral stimuli encountered in this setting (Clore & Byrne, 1974).

COGNITIVE MECHANISMS OF AFFECTIVE INFLUENCES ON THE SELF

Unlike earlier psychoanalytic or associationist explanations, contemporary cognitive theories focus on the information-processing mechanisms that allow affective states to influence both the content and the processes of thinking and judgments.

Memory Based Processes

The associative network model by Bower (1981) proposed that affect and cognition are integrally linked within an associative network of mental representations. An affective state should thus selectively and automatically prime related thoughts and ideas that are more likely to be used in constructive cognitive tasks—for example, tasks that involve the perception and evaluation of the self. In several experiments, Bower (1981) found that self-related thinking is indeed subject to such an affect-congruent bias. For example, people who were induced to feel good (or bad) were likely to selectively remember positive (or negative) details of their childhood and their activities during the preceding weeks. Clearly, their perception and evaluation of themselves was biased by their selective recall of affect-congruent information.

However, subsequent research showed that such affect priming is subject to important boundary conditions (Bower & Forgas, 2001; Eich & Macauley, 2000; Forgas, 1995a). Affect congruity is more likely when the affective state is strong, salient and self-relevant, and when the task involves the constructive generation and elaboration of information rather than the simple reproduction of stored details. Thus, *constructive processing* may be defined as thinking that requires the active selection, elaboration, and transformation of the available stimulus information, based on the use of previous knowledge structures, leading to the creation of new judgments from the combination of stored information and new stimulus details. Thus, mood effects are most reliably found when the stimulus information is rich, complex and involving as is typically the case with self-related judgments (Forgas, 1994, 1999a, 1999b; Sedikides, 1995). According to Fiedler (1991, 2000), affect infusion also depends on the nature of the task; tasks that require simply recognizing a stimulus or retrieving a pre-structured response involve no constructive thinking and show little affect infusion. Thus, affect priming crucially depends on the kind of information-processing strategy people employ in a particular task.

Misattribution Mechanisms

In an alternative theory, Schwarz and Clore (1983) argued that "rather than computing a judgment on the basis of recalled features of a target, individuals may . . . ask themselves: 'How do I feel about it? [and] in doing so, they may mistake feelings due to a pre-existing state as a reaction to the target" (Schwarz, 1990, p. 529). This "how-do-I-feel-about-it" heuristic suggests that affect influences self-related judgments because of an inferential error: people misread their prevailing affective states as informative of their evaluations of themselves. This theory is similar to earlier conditioning models by Clore and Byrne (1974) who also posited an incidental link between affect and unrelated responses. However, the misattribution model has little to say about how information other than affect will be used, if at all. In a sense, this is a theory of non-judgment or aborted judgment rather than a theory of judgment. And as Martin (2000) observed, the informational value of affect, even if used, is itself dependent on the situational context that qualifies its meaning. Research now suggests that people only seem to rely on affect as a heuristic cue when they are unfamiliar with the task, have no prior evaluations to fall back on, their personal involvement is low, and have insufficient cognitive resources or motivation to compute a more thorough response (Forgas, in press). Self-related judgments are rarely like this. Although people may rely on the affect-as-information heuristic when talking to a stranger doing a telephone survey (Schwarz & Clore, 1983), or when responding to a street survey (Forgas & Moylan, 1987), it is unlikely that their enduring sense of self would be based on such superficial, unreliable, and truncated judgmental strategies. As most judgments about the self involve some degree of elaboration and processing, affect priming rather than misattribution are the mechanisms most likely to be involved in producing affect infusion.

Affect and Processing Strategies

Both the memory and the misattribution theories focus on the informational role of affect. In addition to such informational effects (influencing *what* people think), affect may also influence the *process* of thinking, that is, *how* people think about themselves (Clark & Isen, 1982; Forgas, 2000, 2001). Early evidence suggested that positive affect promotes less effortful and more superficial processing strategies, whereas negative affect seemed to trigger a more effortful, systematic, analytic, and vigilant processing style (Clark & Isen, 1982). More recent studies showed, however, that positive affect also produces some processing advantages, facilitating more creative, open, flexible, and inclusive thinking styles (Bless, 2000; Fiedler, 2000). The main consequence of positive and negative affect is thus not simply an increase or decrease in processing effort. Rather, positive affect seems to promote a more assimilative, schema-based processing style, whereas negative affect produces a more accommodative, externally-focussed thinking strategy (Bless, 2000; Fiedler, 2000; Higgins, 2001).

Toward an Integration: The Affect Infusion Model

A comprehensive explanation of affect infusion effects needs to specify the circumstances that promote or inhibit affect congruence and should also define the conditions that promote affect priming, or the misattribution mechanisms. A recent integrative theory, the Affect Infusion Model (Forgas, 1995a; in press) sought to accomplish this task by predicting that affect infusion should only occur in circumstances that promote an open, constructive processing style (Fiedler, 1991; Forgas, 1992b, 1995b). Constructive processing involves the active elaboration of the available stimulus details and the use of memory-based information in this process. The AIM thus assumes that (a) the extent and nature of affect infusion should be dependent on the kind of processing strategy that is used, and (b) that all things being equal, people should use the least effortful and simplest processing strategy capable of producing a response. As this model has been adequately described elsewhere, only a brief overview will be included here (Forgas, 1992a, 1995a, in press).

The AIM identifies four alternative processing strategies: *direct access, motivated, heuristic,* and *substantive* processing. These four strategies differ in terms of two basic dimensions: the degree of *effort* exerted in seeking a solution, and the degree of *openness* and constructiveness of the information search strategy. The combination of these two processing features—quantity (effort) and quality (openness)—produces four distinct processing styles (Fiedler, 2001): *substantive processing* (high effort/open, constructive), *motivated processing* (high effort/closed), *heuristic processing* (low effort/open, constructive), and *direct access processing* (low effort/closed). The first two of these strategies, direct access and motivated processing, involve highly targeted and predetermined patterns of information search and selection, strategies that limit the scope for incidental affect infusion. According to the model, mood congruence and affect infusion are only likely when constructive processing is used, such as substantive or heuristic processing (see also Fiedler, 1991, 2001).

The AIM also specifies a range of contextual variables related to the *task,* the *person,* and the *situation* that jointly influence processing choices. For example, greater personal relevance and reduced task familiarity, complexity, and typicality should recruit more substantive processing. Situational features that impact on processing style include social norms, public scrutiny, and social influence by others (e.g., Forgas, 1990). An important feature of the AIM is that it recognizes that affect itself can also influence processing choices. The key prediction of the AIM is the *absence* of affect infusion when direct access or motivated processing is used, and the *presence* of affect infusion during heuristic and substantive processing. The implications of this model have now been supported in a number of the experiments dealing with self-related judgments and communication, considered below.

AFFECTIVE INFLUENCES ON SELF-JUDGMENTS

As we have seen above, there are good theoretical reasons to assume that fluctuating affective states play an important role in influencing how people think and communicate about themselves. The self represents a particularly complex and elaborate cognitive schema that includes an extremely rich array of information accumulated throughout a lifetime about our successes and failures, positive and negative experiences. In terms of the theoretical framework outlined above, affective states should have a particularly strong influence on self-related judgments whenever constructive, substantive processing is adopted (Forgas, 1995a, 2001; Sedikides, 1995).

Affective Influences on Interpreting Our Behaviors

Perhaps the most fundamental judgment we make about ourselves in everyday life is the way we interpret our ongoing social behaviours. As the meaning of social actions is often inherently ambiguous and equivocal (Heider, 1958), mood may selectively influence the interpretations we place on our own behaviors due to affect-priming effects. This prediction was first tested by inducing happy or sad affect in participants who were then shown a videotape of their own social interactions with a partner from the previous day (Forgas, Bower, & Krantz, 1984). Participants were asked to make a series of rapid, on-line judgments evaluating the observed behaviors of themselves as well as their partners. There were significant affective distortions on these judgments. Happy people identified significantly more positive, skilled and fewer negative, unskilled behaviors both in themselves and in their partners than did sad subjects. In contrast, observers who received no mood manipulation showed no such differences. These results establish that affect can have a fundamental influence on how people evaluate their own interpersonal behaviors, even when objective, videotaped evidence is readily available.

These effects seem to occur because affect-priming influences the kinds of interpretations, constructs, and associations that people rely on as they interpret intrinsically complex and indeterminate social behaviors. For example, the same smile that may be seen as "friendly" in a good mood could be judged as "awkward" or "condescending" when the observer experiences negative affect. Talking about a recent trip may be seen as "friendly" or "poised" by a person in a good mood but might appear "boring" or "pretentious" when the observer is in a bad mood.

Affective Influences on Self-Related Judgments

Much of the existing research suggests such a fundamental affect-congruent pattern: positive affect improves, and negative affect impairs the way we see ourselves (Nasby, 1994, 1996). However, as predicted by the Affect Infusion Model (Forgas, 1995a), these effects are not universal: they are most marked in circumstances that require people to adopt an open, constructive, and substantive processing style, such as attribution judgments requiring inferences. Despite the strong roots of the attribution paradigm in Heider's (1958) phenomenological work, the role of affect in inferential judgments about the self has received little previous attention. In several studies, we asked participants who were feeling happy, sad, or neutral (after receiving bogus feedback about test performance or viewing films) to make attributions for the success or failure outcomes of themselves and others in typical life situations (job performance, financial success, etc.) (Forgas, Bower, & Moylan, 1990). Results showed that happy persons made more lenient, positive attributions, crediting success to themselves and blaming failure on external causes. Sad participants in turn used a more negative, self-blaming attributional strategy, emphasizing their own responsibility for negative outcomes, but failing to take credit for positive results (Forgas et al., 1990, Exp. 1). (See Figure 5.1.)

We found that these effects prevailed even in more realistic and personally relevant judgmental tasks, such as when students were asked to explain their

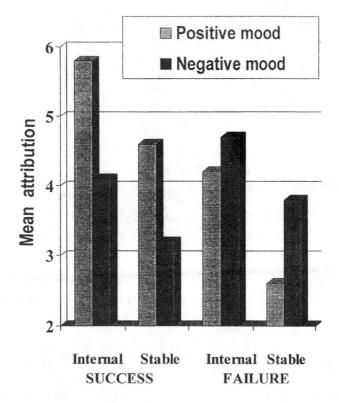

FIGURE 5.1. The effects of positive and negative mood on attributions to internal and stable causes for success and failure in an exam. Happy persons claim credit for success (make more internal and stable attributions) but reject blame for failure (make more external and unstable attributions). Persons in negative mood in turn take less credit for success and blame themselves more for failing. (Data based on Forgas, Bower, & Moylan, 1990).

actual good or bad performance on a recent exam (Forgas et al., 1990). Results showed a significant mood-congruent influence on these real-life achievement attributions. Those in a negative mood blamed themselves more when failing and took less credit for their successes, whereas those in a positive mood were inclined to claim credit for success but refused to accept responsibility for their failures (Forgas et al., 1990). These results are interesting because they suggest that greater access to positive memories in a good mood, and negative memories in a bad mood, are likely to have a wide-ranging influence on how the self is viewed even in more elaborate inferential tasks.

In order to further establish the ecological validity of this phenomenon, an additional series of experiments investigated mood effects on how people perceive and interpret a critical aspect of their self: their real-life initimate relationships (Forgas, Levinger, & Moylan, 1994). Personal relationships are a critical component of how the self is constructed, a link that has been well recognized ever since the pioneering theories of Mead (1934) as well as Charles Cooley. Affective influences on how significant others are viewed and evaluated are likely to have important consequences for our self-concept and self-evaluations. Two experiments found a significant mood-congruent influence on such judgments: happy persons felt content and satisfied with their relationships and partners, but sad persons felt more dissatisfied with this critical domain of their lives. Intuitively one might predict a decline in such mood effects as the longevity and familiarity of a relationship increases. In terms of the AIM, however, we predicted and found undiminished mood effects on judgments even in long-term relationships of many years' standing. Since long-term relationships provide partners with an even richer and more varied range of both positive and negative experiences, mood can continue to play a critical role in selectively priming the kinds of details happy and sad people selectively recall and base their judgments on (Forgas et al., 1994).

Affective Influences on Blaming the Self

The way people think about and explain their responsibility for personal conflicts in their relationships also has important consequences for their self-concept. In a series of experiments, we assessed affective influences on the way blame for relationship conflicts is assigned to the self and the partner in real-life relationships (Forgas, 1994). Participants were induced to feel good or bad by first reading about happy or sad stories (the mood induction), before making causal explanations for recent happy and conflict events in their current intimate relationships (Forgas, 1994, Exp. 1). Results supported the affect infusion hypothesis, with more self-deprecatory explanations by sad subjects than by happy subjects. In the next study, attributions for simple versus complex relationship conflicts were compared using people who just saw happy, sad, or neutral movies as subjects in an unobtrusive field experiment (Forgas, 1994, Exp. 2).

In a non-obvious pattern, sad persons saw themselves as more responsible and identified more internal, stable, and global causes for conflicts than did happy subjects. Surprisingly, these mood effects were much greater on explanations for serious rather than simple conflicts. A laboratory experiment measuring processing latencies confirmed these results (Forgas, 1994, Exp. 3): even with these highly realistic real-life judgments, greater mood effects were always associated with longer processing times, as suggested by the Affect Infusion Model (Forgas, 1995a). (See Figure 5.2.) These results show that affect is likely to infuse highly involving self-related judgments, as long as some degree of open, constructive thinking is required to perform the task. Further, and paradoxically, these effects are likely to be magnified when the task is particularly demanding and requires more extensive thinking. Thus, explaining difficult, intractable self-related problems in our lives may be even more influenced by temporary moods than are snap judgments about simple, unproblematic issues (Forgas, 1994). In contrast, self-related responses that can be produced using either direct access or motivated processing strategies tend to be more impervious to affective influences. However, these effects are also subject to a range of moderating influences, as the next section will show.

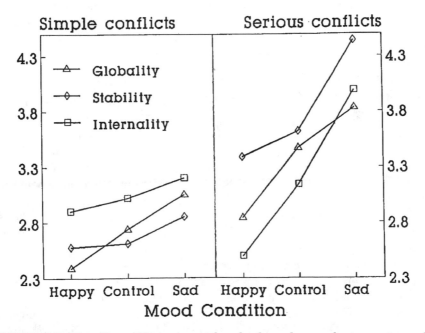

FIGURE 5.2. The effects of happy, control, and sad mood on attributions to internal, stable, and global causes for simple and serious relationship conflicts; the effects of both positive and negative mood are significantly greater on attributions for serious rather than simple conflicts, as predicted by the AIM. (Data based on Forgas, 1994.)

MODERATING INFLUENCES

The Role of Task Features

The nature of the self-judgment required appears to significantly moderate mood effects on self-judgments, according to Nasby (1994). In this study, participants were induced into a happy, neutral, or sad mood through the Velten (1968) procedure, and were then asked to make judgments about a series of trait adjectives that required either an affirmative response ("yes," applies to me) or a negative response ("no," does not apply to me). Later, their recall memory for the trait adjectives rated was tested. Happy persons remembered more positive, and sad persons remembered more negative, self-traits, suggesting a clear mood-congruent recall pattern. However, this only occurred when the judgment required an affirmative response. This result seems due to the different processing strategies that affirmative and non-affirmative trait judgments recruit, as suggested by the AIM. Rejecting a trait as not applicable to the self is likely to be a simple, short, and direct process that requires little elaborate processing. Affectively primed information is thus less likely to be incidentally used. In contrast, affirming that a trait actually applies to the self is likely to recruit more elaborate thinking, and it is in the course of such elaborate processing that affect is most likely to impact on how the information is interpreted and integrated into the existing self-concept.

What Aspect of the Self is Being Judged?

Affective influences on the self-concept also depend on what aspect of the self is being judged. In an interesting series of studies, Sedikides (1995) found that central and peripheral aspects of the self may be differentially sensitive to affect infusion. Central self-conceptions are directly accessible, are more in the focus of awareness, and are more regularly rehearsed and used than are peripheral aspects of the self (Markus, 1977; Sedikides, 1995). Thus, judgments about the "central" self require less on-line elaboration, allowing less scope for affect to infuse these ready-formed judgments. This "differential sensitivity" hypothesis was supported in an elegant series of experiments by Sedikides (1995). Participants were put into a happy, neutral, or sad mood using a guided imagery mood induction, and then rated themselves on a number of behaviors related to their central and peripheral traits as assessed previously. Affect had little influence on judgments related to central traits but had a significant mood-congruent influence on judgments related to peripheral traits. Later experiments showed that reduced certainty and the more extensive, elaborate processing required when making peripheral judgments were indeed responsible for the greater mood effects on these responses (Sedikides, 1995, Exp. 2 and 3). The process mediation of this effect, as also predicted by the Affect Infusion Model (Forgas, 1995a), was further confirmed when it was found that encouraging people to think more extensively about peripheral self-conceptions (paradoxically) further increased rather than decreased the influence of affect on these judgments.

Self-Esteem as a Moderator of Affective Influences

A number of individual difference variables such as self-esteem also appear to moderate the effects of mood on self-related judgments (Baumeister, 1998; Rusting, 2001). Low-self-esteem persons generally have less certain and stable self-conceptions. Affect may thus have a greater influence on self-judgments by low rather than high-self-esteem individuals. Such a link was demonstrated by Brown and Mankowski (1993) who used the Velten (1968) procedure or music to induce good or bad mood and asked participants to rate themselves on a number of adjectives. Induced mood had a significant mood-congruent influence on the self-judgments of low-self-esteem persons but had a much less clear-cut effect on ratings by high-self-esteem individuals.

Another series of studies by Smith and Petty (1995) also confirmed this pattern. These authors induced happy and sad mood in high- and low-self-esteem participants who were then asked to report on three memories from their school years. Mood had a significant influence on both the quantity and quality of responses by the low- but not by the high-self-esteem group. It appears that people with high self-esteem have a more stable and certain self-concept and seem to respond to self-related questions by directly accessing this stable knowledge, a process that does not allow the incidental infusion of affect into judgments. Low-self-esteem people, in turn, may engage in more open and elaborate processing when thinking about themselves, and their current mood may thus influence the outcome (Sedikides, 1995). Affect intensity may be another individual difference moderator of mood congruency effects (Rusting, 2001). Recent work suggests that mood congruency effects may indeed be stronger among high affect intensity participants (Haddock, Zanna, & Esses, 1994) and among people who score higher on measures assessing openness to feelings as a personality trait (Ciarrochi & Forgas, 2000).

MOTIVATIONAL EFFECTS: ELIMINATION AND REVERSAL OF AFFECT CONGRUENCE IN SELF-JUDGMENTS

The Affect Infusion Model also predicts that affect-congruent outcomes may be eliminated or reversed when people have reason to adopt a motivated processing style directed at a mood-incongruent outcome. There is indeed evidence for such opposite, affect-incongruent outcomes in circumstances that trigger more motivated processing strategies, as shown for example in a study by Cervone, Kopp, Schaumann, and Scott (1994). These authors induced either a sad or neutral mood in their participants and then asked them to evaluate either their own *performance* on a task. Alternatively, subjects had to indicate the minimum *standard* of performance that they would have to attain in order to be satisfied with themselves. Straight performance ratings showed a clear mood-congruent pattern: sad participants expressed lower evaluations of the same level of performance than did neutral participants. However, mood had the opposite, paradoxical effect on judgments about performance standards: sad participants now endorsed higher personal standards than did neutral mood participants. One explanation for this interesting finding is that negative mood may have primed more negative performance expectations in both groups. When the question asked for performance standards, however, those in a negative mood may have nominated higher expected standards as defensive strategy to justify their expected failure, in a process somewhat similar to self-handicapping attributions (see also Hirt & McCrea; Rhodewalt & Tragakis, this volume).

Motivated Mood Management and Self-Related Judgments

The moderating influence of motivated processing strategies is further illustrated in an experiment by Sedikides (1994). In this study, participants were induced to feel good, neutral, or bad using guided imagery procedures and were then asked to write an extended series of self-descriptive statements. Early responses showed a clear mood-congruent effect, as sad mood participants described themselves in more negative and happy participants in more positive terms than did controls. However, with the passage of time, negative self-judgments were spontaneously reversed, suggesting something like a spontaneous, automatic mood management strategy (Figure 5.3). This motivated "mood management" hypothesis was further investigated in a recent series of experiments (Forgas, Ciarrochi, & Moylan, 2000). We also found that negative mood effects on self-descriptions were spontaneously reversed over time. These motivated mood management processes also seem to be closely linked to individual differences such as self-esteem. People who score high on self-esteem were able to spontaneously eliminate the negativity of their self-judgments very rapidly, while low self-esteem individuals continued to persevere with negative self descriptions to the end of the task.

Mood and Motivated Decisions Affecting the Self

Affect itself may be crucial in triggering motivated processing in self-relevant tasks. Several studies suggest that people will engage in targeted information search and retrieval to alleviate dysphoria. Motivated processing may also influence the way people go about choosing interaction partners for various activities, a common and important judgmental task in everyday life. Schachter (1959) was among the first to show that anxious or frightened people prefer the company of others, and particularly of those in a similar predicament to themselves,

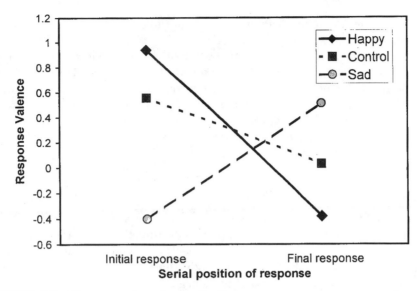

FIGURE 5.3. Changes in the valence of self-descriptive responses over time for respondents who received positive, neutral, and negative mood induction; initially mood-congruent responses were spontaneously reversed and became mood-incongruent by the end of the task for both experimental groups. (Data based on Forgas, Ciarrochi, & Moylan, 2000.)

in an apparent effort to control negative affect by seeking self-relevant comparisons about an impending noxious event. Other evidence also suggests that people prefer to interact with partners who are in a matching rather than different mood (Locke & Horowitz, 1990).

In a series of experiments, we investigated mood effects on self-relevant partner choices. Happy or sad persons were asked to select a partner either for themselves or for another person. As expected, the combination of sad mood and a self-relevant task led to a highly motivated processing strategy: these people selectively looked for and found a rewarding companion, while in all other conditions task-competent partners were chosen (Forgas, 1989). In the self-related task, sad individuals also selectively recalled diagnostic information about rewarding partners later on (Forgas, 1991, Exp. 1). In later work, descriptions about potential partners were provided on a series of information cards (Forgas, 1991, Exp. 2), or on a computer file, allowing the step-by-step recording of each person's decision path and reaction latencies (Forgas, 1991, Exp. 3). Sad persons making a self-relevant choice again selectively searched for and found rewarding partners, reaching their decision faster, but studied motivationally relevant details at greater length and remembered them better later on. As predicted by the AIM, there was no evidence for affect infusion in any of these motivated judgments. Instead of focusing on affect-related information, judges looked for and used information most relevant to servicing their motivational objective—in this instance, mood repair.

Interestingly, self-focussed attention alone can also reduce mood effects. In several ingenuous experiments, Berkowitz, Jaffee, Jo, and Troccoli (2000) found that judgments were affectively congruent when the subjects' attention was directed away from themselves, presumably because of the relatively automatic influence of the affective state, but displayed an affective incongruence after the subjects had attended to their feelings, as self-directed attention apparently induced a controlled, motivated processing strategy.

Positive Affect as a Resource

Positive affect may also serve motivational functions as a resource that allows people to more effectively deal with potentially threatening information about themselves (Trope et al., 2001). The prospect of accepting negative feedback about ourselves often elicits powerful motivational conflicts, as we need to assess the immediate emotional cost of damaging information against the long-term benefits of gaining useful diagnostic feedback about ourselves. Studies by Trope et al. (2001) confirmed that temporary mood influences the relative weight people assign to the emotional costs versus the informational benefits to the self when receiving negative feedback. People in a positive mood were more likely to voluntarily expose themselves to threatening but diagnostic information. It seems that positive affect functioned as a buffer, enabling people to better handle the emotional costs of negative self-related information. Over the longer term, positive mood can thus play an important role in facilitating the process of acquiring diagnostic self-knowledge. However, this effect is not unconditional. It is important for the negative feedback to be seen as diagnostic and useful before people will willingly undergo the emotional cost of acquiring it (Trope et al., 2001). These effects may also have important real-life consequences. Trope and his colleagues also found that people in a positive mood not only selectively sought, but also processed in greater detail and remembered better, negatively valenced arguments about health risks than did people in a negative mood.

In summary, the evidence thus suggests a complex picture; affect seems to have a strong mood-congruent influence on many self-related attitudes and judgments, but only when some degree of open and constructive processing is required and there are no motivational forces to override affect congruence. Low self-esteem, judgments related to peripheral rather than central self-conceptions, and ratings that require elaborate rather than simple processing all seem to promote affect infusion into self-judgments. In addition to its dynamic influence on self-judgments, affect may also play an important role in the structure and organization of the self-concept (Niedenthal & Halberstadt, 2000). One interesting example comes from the work of DeSteno and Salovey (1997). These investigators found that in a neutral mood, participants structured their self-conceptions around the descriptive dimensions of achievement and affiliation. However, participants who experienced positive or negative affect organized their self-conceptions in terms of the positive or negative valence of their self-representations. In other words, affect may also function as a key organizing dimension of the self, likely to reduce the complexity of self-conceptions and structure of the self-concept whenever intense affective states are experienced.

AFFECTIVE INFLUENCES ON COMMUNICATING ABOUT THE SELF: SELF-DISCLOSURE

Affective states may influence not only the privately constructed self-concept, but also the way people publicly communicate about and disclose information about themselves. Self-disclosure is one of the most important communicative tasks people undertake in everyday life. The ability to disclose intimate information about ourselves is an essential skill in the maintenance and development of rewarding intimate relationships, and is also critical to mental health and social adjustment (Forgas, 1985). Inappropriate self-disclosure can lead to adverse evaluations by others and, ultimately, relationship breakdown and social isolation. Do temporary mood states influence people's self-disclosure strategies? Several lines of evidence suggest that the answer is likely to be "yes."

Recent research suggests that affect has an influence on verbal communication in a variety of strategic interpersonal tasks that are characterised by psychological ambiguity. For example, we have found that positive mood tends to prime a more confident, direct requesting style, and negative mood leads to more cautious, polite requests (Forgas, 1999a, 1999b). (See Figure 5.4.) Further, these mood effects on requesting seem to be much stronger when the request situation was more demanding and difficult, and thus required more extensive, substantive processing. Affective states also influenced the latency of making a request in a realistic encounter: those in a negative mood were more hesitant and delayed making their requests much longer than did control, or happy, persons. Further, affective states were found to play an important role in elaborately planned interpersonal encounters such as bargaining and negotiating encounters (Forgas, 1998a). People in a positive mood develop more positive and optimistic attitudes about the bargaining task, and formulate and use more optimistic, cooperative, and integrative negotiating strategies. These findings suggest that even slight changes in affective state will influence the way people interpret communication situations, the goals they set for themselves, and the way they communicate information about themselves.

In a series of recent experiments, we explored the effects of induced mood on self-disclosure strategies (Forgas, 2001b). Affective state was induced by exposing people to positively or negatively valenced videotapes. Subsequently,

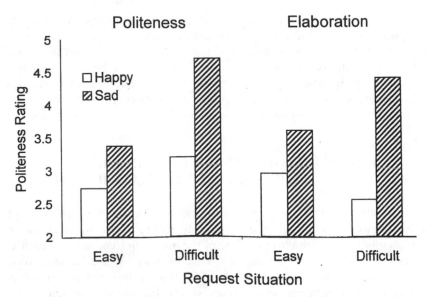

FIGURE 5.4. The effects of happy and sad mood on the politeness and elaboration of requests used in easy or difficult interpersonal situations. Positive mood produces more direct, less polite, and less elaborate requests, and these mood effects are significantly greater when the situation is difficult and requires more extensive processing. (Data based on Forgas, 1999a.)

in an allegedly unrelated experiment, they were asked to indicate the order in which they would feel comfortable disclosing increasingly intimate information about themselves to a person they have just met, selected from a list of topics pre-rated for interpersonal intimacy. Results indicated a small but significant tendency for people in a positive mood to select more intimate disclosure topics than did people in a negative mood.

Of course, these effects occurred in a highly artificial, simulated context. In order to extend the ecological validity of the results, in a subsequent experiment participants were asked to interact with another person in a neighboring room through a computer keyboard, as if they were exchanging e-mails. In fact, there was no other person; the computer was pre-programmed to respond in ways that indicated either consistently high or low levels of self-disclosure or showed a gradually increasing pattern of self-disclosure intimacy. This procedure allowed us to investigate not only the overall intimacy of self-disclosure as a function of mood but also the effects of various partner disclosure patterns.

Results again showed that mood had an influence on self-disclosure intimacy, but these effects were also dependent on the behavior of the partner. Individuals induced to feel good generally responded with more intimate disclosure but only when the partner was also disclosing either consistently or increasingly intimate information (Figure 5.5). Positive mood did not increase the intimacy of self-disclosure when the partner was not disclosing. People in a positive mood also disclosed significantly more positive rather than negative information about themselves, and formed more positive impressions of the partner than did people in a negative mood, consistent with the overall mood-congruent pattern also found in other interpersonal tasks (Forgas, 2001).

Why do these effects occur? When people face an uncertain and unpredictable social encounter, such as a task involving self-disclosure, they need to rely on open, constructive processing in order to formulate their plans to guide their interpersonal behaviors. In other words, they must go beyond the information given and rely on their available thoughts and memories to construct a response. Affect can selectively prime more affect-congruent thoughts and associations, and these ideas should ultimately influence the level of intimacy in

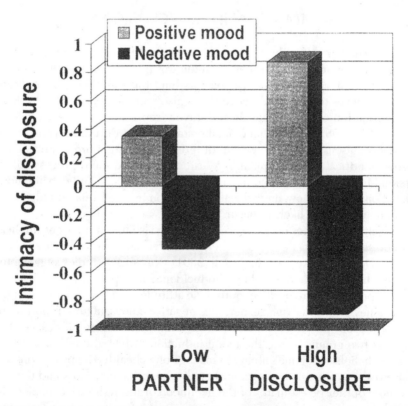

FIGURE 5.5. The effects of positive and negative mood on self-disclosure: positive mood increases and negative mood decreases the intimacy of self-disclosure, and these effects are significantly greater when the partner is high disclosing rather than low disclosing (unpublished data).

self-disclosure. Happy persons seem to disclose more because they assess the likelihood of a positive, accepting response and reciprocal disclosure more optimistically. However, these mood effects rapidly disappear when the interaction partner does not appear to match disclosure intimacy. Self-disclosure is a risky interpersonal strategy, because revealing too much about ourselves may give away intimate information at too early a stage and may also be seen as socially inappropriate. Whether we undertake such a risky move depends on a constructive assessment of the situation; it is at this stage that affect may play a role, influencing the way intrinsically ambiguous social situations are interpreted as either benign or dangerous. The very same mechanisms also seem to influence the way people formulate risky interpersonal requests, the way they respond to approaches by others, and the way they plan and execute negotiations (Forgas, 1998b, 1998c, 1999a, 1999b).

SUMMARY AND CONCLUSIONS

The evidence reviewed in this chapter shows that mild everyday affective states can have a highly significant influence on the way people perceive themselves, the way they interpret their own behaviors, and the way they communicate about themselves to others. Affective states also seem to play a critical role in how information about the self is cognitively represented and categorized (Forgas, 1979; 1982; Niedenthal & Halberstadt, 2000). Further, several of the experiments discussed here show that different information processing strategies play a critical role in explaining these effects. The multi-process Affect Infusion Model (Forgas, 1995a) in particular offers a simple and parsimonious explanation of when, how, and why affect infusion into self-related judgments and communication is likely to occur.

Affective influences on self-perception may also have important implications for such applied domains as health-related cognitions and behaviors (Salovey, Detweiler, Steward, & Bedell, 2001). Numerous studies suggest, for example, that happy moods reduce the incidence of reported physical symptoms and promote more positive, optimistic attitudes and beliefs about health-related issues. Individuals who experience negative moods, in turn, report more and more severe physical symptoms, even when there are no differences between the two groups before the mood induction. Affect also influences attitudes and beliefs about one's ability to manage one's health. Happy persons see themselves as more able to carry out health-promoting behaviors and tend to form more optimistic estimates of the likelihood of future health events. Individual difference variables such as optimism, affect intensity, anxiety, hope, and affect regulation skills appear to mediate many of these effects (Salovey et al., 2001).

These affect infusion effects influence not only self-related attitudes and judgments but also impact on strategic interpersonal behaviors such as self-disclosure. Several of the experiments described here found that affect can influence the way people monitor and interpret their social encounters, the way they formulate and respond to requests, the way they plan and execute strategic negotiations, and the way they communicate intimate information about themselves (Forgas, 1998a, 1998b, 1999a, 1999b). In contrast, as predicted by the AIM, affect infusion tends to be absent whenever a social cognitive task can be performed using a simple, well-rehearsed direct access strategy or a highly motivated strategy. In these conditions, there is little need, and little opportunity for incidentally primed affect-congruent information to infuse information processing (Fiedler, 1991; Forgas, 1995a, in press). Several of the experiments reviewed here also show that affect infusion occurs not only in the laboratory but also in many real-life situations (Forgas, 1994).

In summary, this chapter emphasized the important role that affective states can play in the way people think and communicate about themselves. The Affect Infusion Model offers a multi-process explanation of the conditions likely to facilitate or inhibit such affect infusion effects. The self is one of the most complex and most affectively loaded schema we possess. Undoubtedly a great deal more research is needed before we can fully understand the multiple influences that affect has on self-related thinking and behavior. This chapter could do little more than report some initial findings and, hopefully, stimulate further interest in this intriguing area of research.

REFERENCES

Baumeister, R. F. (1998). The self. In D. T. Gilbert, S. T. Fiske, & G. Lindzey (Eds.), *The handbook of social psychology* (pp. 680–740). New York: Oxford University Press.

Bem, D. (1972). Self perception theory. In L. Berkowitz (Ed.). *Advances in experimental social psychology* (pp. 201–234). New York: Academic Press.

Berkowitz, L., Jaffee, S., Jo, E., & Troccoli, B. T. (2000). On the correction of feeling-induced judgmental biases. In J. P. Forgas (Ed.), *Feeling and thinking: The role of affect in social cognition.* (pp. 131–152). New York: Cambridge University Press.

Bless, H. (2000). The interplay of affect and cognition: The mediating role of general knowledge structures. In J. P. Forgas (Ed.), *Feeling and thinking: The role of affect in social cognition* (pp. 201–222). New York: Cambridge University Press.

Bower, G. H. (1981). Mood and memory.

American.Psychologist, 36, 129–148.

Bower, G. H., & Forgas, J. P. (2001). Mood and social memory. In J. P. Forgas (Ed.), *The handbook of affect and social cognition* (pp. 95–120). Mahwah, NJ: Erlbaum.

Brown, J. D., & Mankowski, T. A. (1993). Self-esteem, mood, and self-evaluation: Changes in the mood and the way you see you. *Journal of Personality and Social Psychology, 64,* 421–430.

Byrne, D., & Clore, G. L. (1970). A reinforcement model of evaluation responses. *Personality: An International Journal, 1,* 103–128.

Cervone, D., Kopp, D. A., Schaumann, L., & Scott, W. D. (1994). Mood, self-efficacy, and performance standards: Lower moods induce higher standards for performance. *Journal of Personality and Social Psychology, 67,* 499–512.

Ciarrochi, J. V., & Forgas, J. P. (1999). On being tense yet tolerant: The paradoxical effects of trait anxiety and aversive mood on intergroup judgments. *Group Dynamics: Theory, Research and Practice, 3,* 227–238.

Ciarrochi, J. V., & Forgas, J. P. (2000) The pleasure of possessions: Affect and consumer judgments. *European Journal of Social Psychology, 30,* 631–649.

Clark, M. S., & Isen, A. M. (1982). Towards understanding the relationship between feeling states and social behavior. In A. H. Hastorf & A. M. Isen (Eds.), *Cognitive social psychology* (pp. 73–108). New York: Elsevier–North Holland.

Clore, G. L., & Byrne, D. (1974). The reinforcement affect model of attraction. In T. L. Huston (Ed.), *Foundations of interpersonal attraction* (pp. 143–170). New York: Academic Press.

DeSteno, D. A., & Salovey, P. (1997). The effects of mood on the structure of the self-concept. *Cognition and Emotion, 11,* 351–372.

Eich, E., & Macauley, D. (2000). Fundamental factors in mood-dependent memory. In J. P. Forgas (Ed.), *Feeling and thinking: The role of affect in social cognition* (pp. 109–130). New York: Cambridge University Press.

Fiedler, K. (1991). On the task, the measures and the mood in research on affect and social cognition. In J. P. Forgas (Ed.), *Emotion and social judgments* (pp. 83–104). Oxford, UK: Pergamon Press.

Fiedler, K. (2000). Towards an integrative account of affect and cognition phenomena using the BIAS computer algorithm. In J. P. Forgas (Ed.), *Feeling and thinking: The role of affect in social cognition* (pp. 223–252). New York: Cambridge University Press.

Fiedler, K., & Forgas, J. P. (1988). (Eds.). *Affect, cognition, and social behavior: New evidence and integrative attempts* (pp. 44–62). Toronto, Canada: Hogrefe.

Forgas, J. P. (1979). *Social episodes: The study of interaction routines.* London: Academic Press.

Forgas, J. P. (1982). Episode cognition: Internal representations of interaction routines. In L. Berkowitz (Ed.), *Advances in experimental social psychology* (Vol. 15, pp. 59–100). New York: Academic Press.

Forgas, J. P. (1985). *Interpersonal behaviour: The psychology of social interaction.* Oxford, UK, and Sydney, Australia: Pergamon Press.

Forgas, J. P. (1989). Mood effects on decision-making strategies. *Australian Journal of Psychology, 41,* 197–214.

Forgas, J. P. (1990). Affective influences on individual and group judgments. *European Journal of Social Psychology, 20,* 441–453.

Forgas, J. P. (1991). Mood effects on partner choice: Role of affect in social decisions. *Journal of Personality and Social Psychology, 61,* 708–720.

Forgas, J. P. (1992a). Affect in social judgments and decisions: A multi-process model. In M. Zanna (Ed.), *Advances in experimental social psychology* (Vol. 25, pp. 227–275). New York: Academic Press.

Forgas, J. P. (1992b). On bad mood and peculiar people: Affect and person typicality in impression formation. *Journal of Personality and Social Psychology, 62,* 863–875.

Forgas, J. P. (1994). Sad and guilty? Affective influences on the explanation of conflict episodes. *Journal of Personality and Social Psychology, 66,* 56–68.

Forgas, J. P. (1995a). Mood and judgment: The affect infusion model (AIM). *Psychological Bulletin, 117*(1), 39–66.

Forgas, J. P. (1995b). Strange couples: Mood effects on judgments and memory about prototypical and atypical targets. *Personality and Social Psychology Bulletin, 21,* 747–765.

Forgas, J. P. (1998a). On feeling good and getting your way: Mood effects on negotiation strategies and outcomes. *Journal of Personality and Social Psychology, 74,* 565–577.

Forgas, J. P. (1998b). Asking nicely? Mood effects on responding to more or less polite requests. *Personality and Social Psychology Bulletin, 24,* 173–185.

Forgas, J. P. (1998c). Happy and mistaken? Mood effects on the fundamental attribution error. *Journal of Personality and Social Psychology, 75,* 318–331.

Forgas, J. P. (1999a). On feeling good and being rude: Affective influences on language use and request formulations. *Journal of Personality and Social Psychology, 76,* 928–939

Forgas, J. P. (1999b). Feeling and speaking: Mood effects on verbal communication strategies. *Personality and Social Psychology Bulletin, 25,* 850–863.

Forgas, J. P. (Ed.). (2000). *Feeling and thinking: The role of affect in social cognition.* New York: Cambridge University Press.

Forgas, J. P. (Ed.). (2001a). *The handbook of affect and social cognition.* Mahwah, NJ: Erlbaum.

Forgas, J. P. (2001b). *Affective influence on self-disclosure strategies.* Unpublished manuscript, University of New South Wales, Sydney, Australia.

Forgas, J. P. (in press). Feeling and doing: Affective influences on social cognition and behavior. *Psychological Inquiry.*

Forgas, J. P., Bower, G. H., & Krantz, S. (1984). The influence of mood on perceptions of social interactions. *Journal of Experimental Social Psychology, 20,* 497–513.

Forgas, J. P., Bower, G. H., & Moylan, S. J. (1990). Praise or blame? Affective influences on attributions for achievement. *Journal of Personality and Social Psychology, 59,* 809–818.

Forgas, J. P., Ciarrochi, J. V., & Moylan, S. J. (2000). Subjective experience and mood regulation: The role of information processing strategies. In H. Bless & J. P. Forgas (Eds.), *The message within: The role of subjective experience in social cognition* (pp. 197–222). Philadelphia: Psychology Press.

Forgas, J. P., Levinger, G., & Moylan, S. (1994). Feeling good and feeling close: Mood effects on the perception of intimate relationships. *Personal Relationships, 2,* 165–184.

Forgas, J. P., & Moylan, S. J. (1987). After the movies: The effects of transient mood states on social judgments. *Personality and Social Psychology Bulletin, 13,* 478–489.

Haddock, G., Zanna, M. P., & Esses, V. (1994). Mood and the expression of intergroup attitudes: The moderating role of affect intensity. *European Journal of Social Psychology, 24,* 189–205.

Heider, F. (1958). *The psychology of interpersonal relations.* New York: Wiley.

Higgins, E. T. (2001). Promotion and prevention experiences: Relating emotions to nonemotional motivational states. In J. P. Forgas (Ed.), *The handbook of affect and social cognition* (pp. 241–270). Mahwah, NJ: Erlbaum.

Hilgard, E. R. (1980). The trilogy of mind: Cognition, affection, and conation. *Journal of the History of the Behavioral Sciences, 16,* 107–117.

Leary, M. (2000). Interpersonal emotions, social cognition, and self-relevant thought. In J. P. Forgas (Ed.), *Feeling and thinking: The role of affect in social cognition* (pp. 188–212). New York: Cambridge University Press.

Locke, K. D., & Horowitz, L. M. (1990). Satisfaction in interpersonal interactions as a function of similarity in level of dysphoria. *Journal of Personality and Social Psychology, 58,* 823–831.

Mackie, D. M., & Worth, L. T. (1989). Processing deficits and the mediation of positive affect in persuasion. *Journal of Personality and Social Psychology, 57,* 27–40.

Markus, H. (1977). Self-schemata and processing information about the self. *Journal of Personality and Social Psychology, 35,* 63–78.

Martin, L. (2000). Moods don't convey information: Moods in context do. In J. P. Forgas (Ed.), *Feeling and thinking: The role of affect in social cognition* (pp. 153–177). New York: Cambridge University Press.

Mead, G. H. (1934). *Mind, self and society.* Chicago: University of Chicago Press.

Nasby, W. (1994). Moderators of mood-congruent encoding: Self-/other-reference and affirmative/nonaffirmative judgement. *Cognition and Emotion, 8,* 259–278.

Nasby, W. (1996). Moderators of mood-congruent encoding and judgment: Evidence that elated and depressed moods implicate distinct processes. *Cognition and Emotion, 10,* 361–377.

Niedenthal, P., & Halberstadt, J. (2000). Grounding categories in emotional response. In J. P. Forgas (Ed.), *Feeling and thinking: The role of affect in social cognition* (pp. 357–386). New York: Cambridge University Press.

Pervin, L. A. (1976). A free-response description approach to the analysis of person-situation interaction. *Journal of Personality and Social Psychology, 34,* 465–474.

Rusting, C. (2001). Personality as a mediator of affective influences on social cognition. In J. P. Forgas (Ed.), *The handbook of affect and social cognition* (pp. 371–391). Mahwah, NJ: Erlbaum.

Salovey, P., Detweiler, J. B., Steward, W. T., & Bedell, B. T. (2001). Affect and health-relevant cognition. In J. Forgas (Ed.), *Handbook of affect and social cognition* (pp. 344–370). Mahwah, NJ: Erlbaum.

Schachter, S. (1959). *The psychology of affiliation*. Stanford, CA: Stanford University Press.

Schwarz, N. (1990). Feelings as information: Informational and motivational functions of affective states. In E. T. Higgins & R. Sorrentino (Eds.), *Handbook of motivation and cognition: Foundations of social behaviour* (Vol. 2, pp. 527–561). New York: Guilford.

Schwarz, N., & Clore, G. L. (1983). Mood, misattribution and judgments of well being: Informative and directive functions of affective states. *Journal of Personality and Social Psychology, 45*, 513–523.

Sedikides, C. (1992). Changes in the valence of self as a function of mood. *Review of Personality and Social Psychology, 14*, 271–311.

Sedikides, C. (1994). Incongruent effects of sad mood on self-conception valence: Its a matter of time. *European Journal of Social Psychology, 24*, 161–172.

Sedikides, C. (1995). Central and peripheral self-conceptions are differentially influenced by mood: Tests of the differential sensitivity hypothesis. *Journal of Personality and Social Psychology, 69*(4), 759–777.

Sedikides, C., & Brewer, M. B. (Eds.). (2001). *Individual self, relational self, collective self.* Philadelphia: Psychology Press.

Smith, S. M., & Petty, R. E. (1995). Personality moderators of mood congruency effects on cognition: The role of self-esteem and negative mood regulation. *Journal of Personality and Social Psychology, 68*, 1092–1107.

Trope, Y., Ferguson, M., & Raghunanthan, R. (2001). Mood as a resource in processing self-revalant information. In J. P. Forgas (Ed.), *The handbook of affect and social cognition* (pp. 256–274). Mahwah, NJ: Erlbaum.

Velten, E. (1968). A laboratory task for induction of mood states. *Advances in Behavior Research and Therapy, 6*, 473–482.

Zajonc, R. B. (2000). Feeling and thinking: Closing the debate over the independence of affect. In J. P. Forgas (Ed.), *Feeling and thinking: The role of affect in social cognition* (pp. 31–58). New York: Cambridge University Press.

6

Positioning Self-Handicapping within the Self-Zoo
Just What Kind of Animal Are We Dealing With?

EDWARD R. HIRT
SEAN M. McCREA

INTRODUCTION

*I*n his famous 1980 *American Psychologist* paper, Greenwald likened the self (or ego) to a totalitarian regime, emphasizing how the self attempts to protect itself from threatening information. As with totalitarian political systems that use thought control and propaganda devices to suppress dissension

---

Address for correspondence: Edward R. Hirt, Department of Psychology, Indiana University, Bloomington, IN 47405, USA. E-mail: ehirt@indiana.edu

and maintain social order, Greenwald discussed parallel biases that exist within the self system to revise and distort our personal history in ways that reflect favorably on the self. Indeed, work on such phenomena as the self-serving bias (Bradley, 1978), biased assimilation of evidence (Lord, Ross, & Lepper, 1979), and motivated skepticism (Ditto & Lopez, 1992) has illustrated various different ways in which people selectively process and interpret information to minimize its threat to the self. Positive information about the self (or information that verifies cherished beliefs or attitudes) is readily accepted as valid, whereas negative information about the self (or information that challenges our belief or attitudes) is scrutinized and ultimately dismissed as invalid or inapplicable.

More recently, there has been a proliferation of other self-protective strategies that one uses when confronted with potentially threatening feedback about one's abilities or characteristics. Steele's (1988) theory of self-affirmation has demonstrated how people can compensate for threatening negative feedback in a self-relevant performance domain by affirming themselves on important core values or on other unrelated but highly self-relevant performance domains. According to Steele, self-affirmation reestablishes "the perception of global self-integrity" (Steele, 1988, p. 290) so that the feelings of adequacy and self-worth are maintained in spite of threats to an important self-aspect. Indeed, Steele and his colleagues (Steele & Liu, 1981, 1983) have demonstrated that the opportunity to self-affirm following counterattitudinal behavior (under high choice conditions in the standard induced compliance paradigm) eliminated the need to engage in dissonance-reducing attitude change.

Tesser's self-evaluation maintenance (SEM) model (Tesser, 1988) posits two alternative mechanisms whereby individuals can protect or enhance self-esteem when performing a task in situations where consensus information is available. When the domain is high in personal relevance, people engage in a comparison process. A negative social comparison to a close other is particularly threatening and leads to compensatory changes in the perceived relevance of the performance domain (Tesser & Campbell, 1980), the perceived closeness to the other (Pleban & Tesser, 1981), or even attempts to sabotage the other's performance to ensure favorable social comparison (Tesser & Smith, 1980). When the domain is low in personal relevance, people engage in a reflection process. Here, one can enhance self-esteem by noting a close association to a successful other. Thus, to derive positive benefit from another's success, one may try to enhance the perceived closeness of the other in order to bask in his/her reflected glory (Cialdini et al., 1976).

THE "SELF-ZOO"

It is clear that social psychology has identified many ways in which people work to protect the self in the face of ego threats. However, do each of these different self-protective mechanisms have independent psychological effects, or can we integrate or organize them in some coherent way? Recently, Tesser, Martin, and Cornell (1996) have noted that a number of different self-theories share the assumption that behavior is motivated by a desire to maintain a positive self-evaluation. Indeed, the proliferation of different self-protective mechanisms (self-affirmation, self-evaluation maintenance, etc.), ostensibly serving the same underlying motive, has been labeled the "self-zoo." Each theory may have its own set of antecedents or "triggers," but they appear to be alternative avenues to achieving the same basic goal.

If these various members of the self-zoo share the same fundamental goal of preserving self-esteem, Tesser et al. (1996) argued that they might be able to be used interchangeably to accomplish that desired end state (of goal fulfillment). Lewin's (1935) classic work on goal tension demonstrated that goals have the property of "equifinality." That is, activities that satisfy the same underlying goal are substitutable for one another. Extending this logic to the self domain, if two different mechanisms are satisfying the same higher-order goal of self-esteem maintenance, Tesser et al. predicted that engaging in one such mechanism should substitute for engaging in another. Thus, an individual who has the opportunity to self-affirm should be less likely to change his/her attitudes in a dissonance situation than individuals who have not had the opportunity to self-affirm. Conversely, if two mechanisms are satisfying different goals, then engaging in one should not affect engaging in the second.

Indeed, as we alluded to earlier, Steele's early work (Steele & Liu, 1981, 1983) has illustrated that self-affirmation can effectively substitute for dissonance-induced attitude change. Using a similar paradigm, work by Tesser and Cornell (1991, Studies 2 and 3) demonstrated that SEM processes (e.g., writing an essay about a time you outperformed a close other on a high relevance domain) can effectively substitute for dissonance reduction. Tesser and Cornell (Tesser & Cornell, 1991; Cornell & Tesser, 1994) have also shown that self-affirmation and SEM processes can effectively substitute for each other. From this evidence, it appears that these are just alternative mechanisms that achieve the same higher level goal—namely, to maintain global self-esteem.

WHAT ABOUT SELF-HANDICAPPING?

It is tempting at this point to speculate that other members of the self-zoo share the same underlying goal and would similarly substitute for one another. For several years, our research has focused on the self-protective mechanism of self-handicapping. Self-handicapping is a self-protective strategy whereby individuals erect an impediment to success in order to control attributions following a performance (see Rhodewalt & Tragakis, this volume). For example, a person may go out drinking before a big test or skip practice the week before an important athletic contest. As originally formulated by Berglas and Jones (1978), self-handicapping relies upon the attributional principles of discounting and augmenting (Kelley, 1973). Ability can be augmented as the cause of success but discounted as the cause of failure due to the presence of an inhibitory causal factor (the handicap). Thus, the self-handicapper is protected from the possible negative consequences of an upcoming performance.

A good deal of research has explored the underlying motivation(s) behind self-handicapping. In its original formulation (Jones & Berglas, 1978), self-handicapping was thought to be motivated solely by a need to protect global self-esteem. This motivation has been shown to be enhanced by anticipated threats to self-esteem (Snyder & Smith, 1982) or manipulations such as noncontingent success feedback (Berglas & Jones, 1978) or public self-focus (Hirt, McCrea, & Kimble, 2000) that create uncertainty about one's ability. Although other researchers have disputed this claim and argued that self-presentational or impression-management concerns may motivate self-handicapping (Arkin & Baumgardner, 1985; Kolditz & Arkin, 1982), it is important to note that self-handicapping has been shown to occur in situations where self-presentational concerns are minimized (e.g., Rhodewalt & Fairfield, 1991).

Moreover, recent research has found direct support for the notion that self-handicapping preserves overall self-esteem. If self-handicapping serves to maintain global self-esteem, then the self-handicapper should show evidence of augmenting self-attributions of ability following success and discounting self-attributions of ability following failure. Furthermore, these attributions should allow the individual to maintain global self-esteem in the event of failure (self-protection) as well as enhance global self-esteem in the event of success (self-enhancement). Work by Rhodewalt and his colleagues (Rhodewalt & Hill, 1995; Rhodewalt, Morf, Hazlett, & Fairfield, 1991) has demonstrated that individuals who self-handicapped maintained high levels of self-esteem following failure (but see Isleib, Vuchinich, & Tucker, 1988, for a notable exception). In contrast, individuals who did not self-handicap in these studies (or did not have a self-handicap available to them) reported lower self-esteem following failure. Moreover, these studies demonstrated that the preservation of self-esteem by self-handicappers was mediated by their (discounted) performance attributions. Regression-based path analyses revealed that the effects of self-handicapping on self-esteem were mediated by ability attributions, supporting the original Jones and Berglas (1978) conceptionalization. Thus, self-handicapping appears to serve the self-protective function of preserving self-esteem in the face of poor performance.

Evidence for self-enhancement following success has been more equivocal. Rhodewalt et al. (1991) found no evidence of augmentation following self-handicapping. However, a recent study by Feick and Rhodewalt (1997) found evidence of both more extreme ability attributions as well as elevated self-esteem following success in a naturalistic setting. Moreover, these results were obtained for both high- and low-self-esteem individuals, unlike previous research (Rhodewalt et al., 1991; Tice, 1991). Feick and Rhodewalt (1997) argued that this may be the consequence of performing the study in a field (i.e., classroom) setting outside the laboratory, where self-presentational motives may be less active. In any event, these results provide strong support for the notion that self-handicapping preserves (or enhances) global self-esteem.

Given these findings, it seems likely that self-handicapping, like these other members in the "self-zoo," shares the same underlying goal of maintaining positive self-regard. Thus, one would expect that self-handicapping, self-affirmation, and SEM processes should effectively substitute for one another. The focus of our current program of research (and this chapter) is to investigate these questions concerning the fundamental motivation of self-handicapping as well as its substitutability for other self-protective mechanisms. In this endeavor, we hope to examine how self-handicapping fits in with the other members of the self-zoo.

WHY SELF-HANDICAP?

As we began this line of inquiry, an important issue to consider is why someone would opt to self-handicap when alternative mechanisms exist that serve the same underlying motive. Indeed, as Baumeister and Scher (1988) noted, self-handicapping appears to be a costly strategy that involves a significant tradeoff in the service of protecting global self-esteem. By self-handicapping, the individual increases the likelihood of task failure. Moreover, research investigating observer reactions to self-handicapping (Hirt, McCrea, & Boris, 2001; Luginbuhl & Palmer, 1991; Rhodewalt, Sanbonmatsu, Tschanz, Feick, & Waller, 1995) has demonstrated that self-handicappers incur substantial interpersonal costs: Observers do not like self-handicappers as well as they like non-self-handicappers, and do not wish to have them as friends, roommates, and study partners (Boris & Hirt, 1994; Luginbuhl & Palmer, 1991). Observers also rate self-handicappers lower on a number of characterological dimensions, including motivation level and concern about performance. Indeed, Luginbuhl and Palmer (1991) concluded that "coupled with the somewhat negative attributions about personal qualities, self-handicapping may be quite a poor tradeoff and may be more self-defeating than previously assumed" (p. 661). Moreover, given the importance of maintaining social acceptance and feelings of belongingness for self-esteem (see Leary, this volume), trading off these key social needs in the service of maintaining perceptions of competence and ability would appear to be a highly counterproductive strategy. It would seem likely that individuals would opt for a less costly strategy (if one were available) if it could effectively substitute for self-handicapping and achieve the same underlying goal. Given that in most real-world situations outside of the constraints of a controlled laboratory setting individuals have a plethora of options from which to choose to maintain a positive sense of self, one might question why someone would ever choose to self-handicap over other self-protective strategies.

We believe that self-handicapping may not be a strategy whose sole goal is to preserve global self-esteem. Instead, we argue that self-handicapping is also directed at protecting much more specific beliefs of ability. That is, by self-handicapping, an individual is able to maintain the belief that he/she has high ability in an important domain despite poor objective performance. Alternative forms of self-protection such as self-affirmation and SEM processes like basking in reflected glory (Cialdini et al., 1976) may maintain global feelings of self-worth and self-esteem in the face of a self-threat (such as an upcoming performance in an important domain), but they do not allow the individual to protect the desired belief that he/she has ability in that domain.

This point is perhaps best illustrated by example. You are an athlete preparing for a big track meet against a rival school. You know your team needs you to do well to win this meet, but there is some tough competition and you are uncertain about how well you will do. If you self-handicap, you could maintain the belief that you have the requisite ability to do well in track even if you perform poorly. However, if instead you self-affirm by telling yourself you are still a good student or a good friend, you may feel better (i.e., global self-esteem is preserved) but you still have not addressed your specific self-doubt about your ability in track!

Importantly, we are not arguing that self-handicapping does not also protect global self-esteem. There is sufficient evidence from the work of Rhodewalt and his colleagues (Feick & Rhodewalt, 1997; Rhodewalt & Hill, 1995; Rhodewalt et al., 1991; see also Rhodewalt & Tragakis, this volume) to support this proposition. However, we propose that protecting global self-esteem is an additional benefit accrued from the use of self-handicapping. What makes self-handicapping unique among the "self-zoo" is that self-handicapping first and foremost protects self-conceptions of ability and competence in a specific important domain. Thus, our perspective is not incompatible with but is instead complementary to the past work demonstrating that self-handicappers can and do protect global self-esteem by the use of this strategy.

STUDY 1: THE ROLE OF ABILITY RATINGS (McCREA & HIRT, 2001)

This first study (McCrea & Hirt, 2001) was designed to investigate the question about the fundamental motivation underlying self-handicapping. Although past research has demonstrated that self-handicapping participants discount the role of ability after a failure (e.g., Berglas & Jones, 1978; Mayerson & Rhodewalt, 1988) and (at least sometimes) augment ability attributions after success (e.g.,

Feick & Rhodewalt, 1997), no study had determined whether self-handicapping actually preserves ratings of ability in a domain subsequent to performance feedback. To date, research has not addressed whether self-handicapping is only intended as a protection of global self-esteem or can also protect specific self-conceptions of ability.

We attempted to address this issue by examining the consequences of self-handicapping in a naturalistic setting (cf. Feick & Rhodewalt, 1997). Participants were 158 students enrolled in an introductory psychology course. In an earlier mass testing, participants had completed several individual difference measures, most notably the Rosenberg (1965) Self-Esteem Inventory and Jones and Rhodewalt's (1982) Self-Handicapping Scale (SHS), given that many previous studies (Hirt, Deppe, & Gordon, 1991, 2000; Rhodewalt & Hill, 1995; Rhodewalt et al., 1991) have found that individuals scoring high on the SHS are more likely to engage in self-handicapping behaviors.

The second session took place after the participants had taken at least one exam in the course, and occurred approximately three to six days prior to the next exam. As part of a survey assessing feelings about and satisfaction with the introductory psychology sequence, participants were asked to report, among other things, their last test score (to serve as a baseline estimate of performance) as well as several indices of the amount of preparation they had done or planned to do for the upcoming exam (i.e., time spent studying, class attendance, textbook reading, and note taking). These measures were combined to form a single index of claims of poor preparation, since effort withdrawal has been one of the most frequently assessed measures of self-handicapping (Harris & Snyder, 1986; Hirt et al., 1991, 2000). Participants also completed a stress inventory, which asked them to check any of 45 common types of stress they might have experienced during the past few weeks (e.g., "roommate difficulties," "concerns about future," "working too many hours"; cf. Hirt et al., 1991). For those items checked, participants were asked to rate the severity of the stressor on a scale from one (somewhat severe) to three (extremely severe). This measure constituted a second assessment of claimed handicapping, albeit one that has a less direct connection to task performance.

Approximately a week after the participants had completed their next exam, participants returned and reported their actual performance on the exam. Participants also made attributions regarding their test performance and completed a series of measures assessing their posttest mood and self-esteem (cf. Feick & Rhodewalt, 1997). Finally, participants provided beliefs of their abilities in a variety of domains. These items were adapted from Pelham and Swann's (1989) Self-Attributes Questionnaire (SAQ) and asked participants to rank their ability, relative to other college students of the same age, in academics, social competence, athletics, artistic/musical creativity, and, most relevant, psychology.

As expected, high-self-handicapping (HSH) individuals claimed more self-handicaps than did low-self-handicapping (LSH) individuals. In particular, HSH males claimed to have put forth less preparation for the exam than all the other groups. HSH males and females reported greater stress than their LSH counterparts. These patterns are consistent with previous work (Hirt et al., 1991), which has demonstrated that only HSH males engage in more active or behavioral forms of self-handicapping (e.g., effort withdrawal), whereas both HSH males and females will claim external handicaps (e.g., stress).

We expected HSH individuals who claimed self-handicaps to receive significantly lower grades on the exam. Furthermore, we expected claims of behavioral self-handicaps (given their more obvious relation to actual performance on the exam) to correlate more strongly with performance than claims of stress. Indeed, HSH individuals scored significantly lower on the second exam, scoring almost a full letter grade lower (71%) than their LSH counterparts (79%). Moreover, regression analyses revealed that claims of poor preparation did mediate the effects of SHS score on test performance. However, claims of stress did not significantly predict test outcome. Thus, it appears that claims of poor preparation may indeed reflect real differences in behavioral self-handicapping, given that they mediated the effects of trait self-handicapping on test outcome.

Consistent with Feick and Rhodewalt (1997), we predicted a significant interaction between claimed handicaps and test outcome such that students would make lower ability attributions for failure (discount) the greater the amount of claimed handicaps, but would make more extreme ability attributions for success (augment) the greater the amount of claimed handicaps. The results indicated that students attributed failure less to ability the greater the amount of claimed behavioral handicapping, but attributed success more to ability the greater the amount of claimed behavioral handicapping. Thus, evidence for both augmenting and discounting was obtained for ability attributions. Interestingly, again, no effects were obtained for claims of stress. As was the case with test outcome, it appears that claims of behavioral handicaps were critical for ability attributions, whereas self-reported stress was not.

In addition, consistent with Feick and Rhodewalt (1997) and Rhodewalt and Hill (1995), we expected HSH individuals to maintain global self-esteem despite objectively poor performance. Our results indicated that both measures of claimed handicapping predicted posttest self-esteem. Importantly, there were no interactions by test outcome, indicating that self-esteem was higher for both success and failure students the greater the amount of claimed handicapping. Thus, both forms of handicapping had a buffering effect on global self-esteem following the test. Moreover, consistent with Feick and Rhodewalt (1997), we found that ability attributions mediated the effects of claimed handicaps on posttest self-esteem.

Thus, to this point, we replicated the results obtained by Rhodewalt and his colleagues illustrating that self-handicapping preserves global self-esteem. However, we also expected HSH individuals who fail, particularly those who made claims of behavioral self-handicapping, to maintain high ratings of their specific ability in psychology (at a level comparable to those who did well), indicating that the self-handicapping strategy had been effective in maintaining specific ability beliefs despite failure. On our measure of ratings of psychology ability, we found that HSH men rated themselves significantly higher in psychology ability than did the other groups, despite the fact that they performed quite poorly on the exam. Claims of poor preparation also significantly predicted ratings of psychology ability. Finally, paralleling the effects obtained on the posttest self-esteem measure, the results indicated that ability attributions mediated the effects of the individual differences and claims of poor preparation on these ability ratings. Interestingly, these effects were not obtained on any of the other ability rating items; thus, it appears that self-handicapping serves to maintain perceptions of competence in a specific domain (psychology ability) rather than more general perceptions of academic ability or global perceptions of self-worth across a wide variety of domains. For HSH males, perceptions of high ability were maintained despite poor performance, for they could blame their lackluster performance on their poor preparatory behavior (i.e., claimed behavioral handicapping).

Our results suggest that both global self-esteem and specific conceptions of ability are maintained by self-handicapping. A final question addressed in this study was the causal sequence of these two effects—was it the case that these changes in specific ability beliefs mediated changes in global self-esteem or were these specific ability beliefs simply a consequence of changes in global feelings of self-esteem? Path analyses performed on the data indicated that changes in specific ability ratings mediated changes in global self-esteem, but global self-esteem did not mediate changes in psychology ability ratings (see Figure 6.1). Thus, our findings suggest that the goal of preserving specific ability assessments may be primary for self-handicappers, which may explain why an individual might choose to self-handicap despite the myriad of other options available in the "self-zoo" that can maintain positive self-regard in the face of poor objective performance. It is precisely self-handicapping's ability to preserve an individual's belief in his/her inherent ability in a specific domain that may make it unique from alternative self-protective mechanisms.

FIGURE 6.1. Study 1: Path diagram depicting the causal relationships among the variables.

STUDY 2: THE SUBSTITUTABILITY QUESTION (McCREA, 1999)

The results of McCrea and Hirt (2001) suggest that by self-handicapping, an individual not only is able to maintain positive self-regard in the face of poor objective performance but is also able to maintain the belief that he/she has high levels of ability in that domain. Moreover, our data provide some suggestive evidence that the maintenance of ability beliefs may supercede concerns with preserving global self-esteem. Indeed, it may be this additional benefit that separates self-handicapping from alternative mechanisms that preserve global self-esteem, such as self-affirmation (Steele, 1988).

We then are arguing that self-handicapping serves multiple goals. Nonetheless, the evidence concerning the relative prominence of these goals is speculative at best. One could question, for example, whether global self-esteem is still the primary goal of self-handicapping, with the benefit of maintaining perceptions of ability secondary, or whether it is the other way around. To more directly address this question, we followed the avenue employed by Tesser and his colleagues (Tesser & Cornell, 1991; Tesser, Martin, & Cornell, 1996) to examine the potential substitutability of alternative self-protective mechanisms for self-handicapping. Specifically, in this first line of inquiry, we focused on the substitutability of self-affirmation for self-handicapping. If indeed self-handicapping is primarily motivated by the goal of preserving self-esteem, we might expect that the opportunity to self-affirm on an important dimension should eliminate the need to self-handicap in a threatening evaluative situation. If, however, a self-affirmation opportunity failed to substitute for self-handicapping, it would provide support for the notion that preserving global self-esteem may not be the primary goal served by self-handicapping.

We began this research with the question: Are all affirmations created equal? Generally, within the self-affirmation literature, little attention is given to the specific domain of the affirmation so long as it addresses a valued and self-relevant domain. Our research (McCrea & Hirt, 2001) would seem to imply that self-affirmation would only substitute for self-handicapping if the affirmation reinforced beliefs about competence in the threatened domain. Thus, in this experiment, we tested this notion by varying the domain of the affirmation opportunity: some participants were given the opportunity to affirm themselves in an unrelated (but self-relevant) domain, whereas other participants were given the opportunity to affirm themselves in the same (i.e., the threatened) domain. The substitutability hypothesis would predict that both affirmation conditions should significantly reduce self-handicapping (relative to a no-affirmation control group), whereas McCrea and Hirt would predict that only the same domain affirmation should reduce (and effectively substitute for) self-handicapping.

Participants reported for an experiment ostensibly comparing different kinds of intelligence tests and were told they would be taking both a verbal and

nonverbal intelligence test (McCrea, 1999). All participants were first introduced to a standard verbal intelligence test modeled after the Miller Analogies
Test. Participants were given 15 difficult analogies to solve in 5 minutes (using
a multiple choice format). All participants then received noncontingent success
feedback that they performed quite well (12/15 correct, in the 90th percentile)
on the test. Participants were then told they would be taking a second, nonverbal test. The experimenter emphasized that we would be comparing their performance on the two tests but that our expectations were that they would perform equally well on the upcoming nonverbal test. Participants were then
introduced to the Conditions subtest of Cattell and Cattell's (1961) Culture-
Fair Intelligence Test (CFIT). The experimenter extolled the virtues of this
test, emphasizing how it eliminated racial and ethnic biases that exist with other
intelligence tests. Participants were introduced to sample items, which were
again moderate to very difficult in order to increase uncertainty about performance (and encourage self-handicapping).

Prior to taking the test, participants were told that they would have the
opportunity to practice these sorts of problems. Consistent with our previous
work (Hirt et al., 1991, 2000), participants were told either that (1) practice has
been shown to significantly improve the test's ability to assess your true level of
ability (Practice Matters condition) or (2) practice has been shown to have no
reliable effect on test performance (Practice Doesn't Matter condition). The
Practice Matters condition informs participants that by not practicing, individuals
may receive a score that is lower than their true level of ability, and thus sets up
practice effort withdrawal as a potential self-handicap in the event of poor test
performance. The Practice Doesn't Matter condition serves as a control or no-
handicap condition from which we can compare participants' natural inclina-
tions to practice even when practicing has no ostensible effect on the diagnosticity
of the test. Our past research has demonstrated that HSH individuals show
significantly less practice effort than their LSH counterparts in the Practice
Matters condition, whereas no differences are found in the Practice Doesn't
Matter condition, a finding we interpret as reflecting self-handicapping. Thus,
the key condition in our experiment is the amount of practice effort displayed
in the Practice Matters condition.

Participants were then told that the experimenter needed a few minutes to
prepare the CFIT materials and that they would participate in a second unrelated experiment in the interim time. Participants were told that this second
study was interested in examining people's writing about significant events in
their lives. Passing reference was given to Jamie Pennebaker's work illustrating
the therapeutic value of being able to write about personal events. Participants
were randomly assigned to one of the three affirmation conditions: (a) a related
affirmation, in which they wrote about a time when they performed exceptionally well in the academic domain; (b) an unrelated affirmation, in which they
wrote about a time when they performed exceptionally well in an important

nonacademic domain (e.g., a date, an interview, etc.); or (c) a control/no affirmation condition, in which they wrote about the events of yesterday. Participants were given 10 minutes to complete the essay writing task.

After completing the essay writing task, participants were given the opportunity to practice items from the CFIT practice test for up to 10 minutes prior to taking the actual (timed) test. Participants were told they could practice for as much or as little of that time as they liked. After they decided to finish practicing, the computer would begin the actual test and they would have 5 minutes to complete it. Both time spent practicing and number of practice problems solved were measured, and a composite measure of practice effort was created by combining the two. Finally, following completion of the actual test, participants were given the option of looking at the answer key and scoring their test themselves or not. Thus, interest in obtaining feedback about their test score served as an additional dependent variable (cf. Koch & Hirt, 2000).

The results in the control condition nicely paralleled our previous findings: HSH participants practiced significantly less than LSH participants only in the Practice Matters condition, displaying great practice effort withdrawal when it could serve as a viable excuse for poor performance. Moreover, HSH participants in the control condition were relatively uninterested in obtaining feedback about their test performance unless they had previously handicapped in the Practice Matters (handicap present) condition. In the unrelated affirmation condition, we observed a significant reversal of the results obtained in the control condition. HSH participants were now practicing more than LSH participants in the Practice Matters condition, showing no evidence of self-handicapping following the unrelated affirmation condition. Overall, HSH participants were also more willing to obtain feedback about their test performance in this condition. Thus, these findings seem to suggest that engaging in the unrelated affirmation effectively substituted for self-handicapping, consistent with the substitutability hypothesis.

Unfortunately, the results obtained in the related affirmation condition were not so readily interpretable. According to both the substitutability hypothesis and the McCrea and Hirt (2001) ability preservation hypothesis, affirmation in the same domain should eliminate the need to self-handicap. In this condition, no significant differences in practice effort were found between HSH and LSH individuals; indeed, both groups tended to show moderately low practice effort (see Figure 6.2).

Initially, we were perplexed by this surprising finding. Nonetheless, a careful reexamination of the literature on self-affirmation introduced a potential explanation for the null effects in the related affirmation condition. When individuals are asked to think about a time when they performed quite well in the past in a threatened domain, two possible reactions could result: (1) individuals could be inspired by their past success and use it as motivation to perform well, or (2) individuals' past success could serve as a standard of comparison which only increases anxiety about being able to match that earlier standard in the current

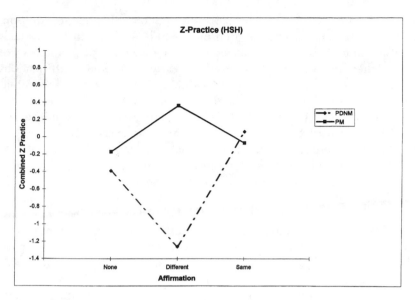

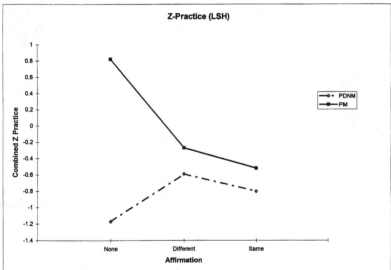

FIGURE 6.2. Study 2: Standardized practice scores as a function of affirmation condition, practice instructions, and level of self-handicapping. PM = practice matters condition; PDNM = practice does not matter condition.

performance situation. Our theorizing focused exclusively on the former possibility, seeing the past success as an inspiration; however, work by many authors, most notably the recent work by Lockwood and Kunda (1997), has pointed to the fact that another's success can deflate an individual as well as inspire him/her. Indeed, within the dissonance and hypocrisy literature, many studies

(Aronson, Blanton, & Cooper, 1995; Blanton, Cooper, Skurnick, & Aronson, 1997; Stone, Weigand, Cooper, & Aronson, 1996) have shown that individuals avoid affirmations in the same domain precisely because the affirmations serve to remind them of their past transgression. Clearly, same-domain affirmations could have either effect under certain conditions. What features of the situation determine which effect of same-domain affirmations will predominate? Lockwood and Kunda (1997) argued that it is the perceived attainability of the success that plays a critical role: if we perceive that past success as attainable, it can motivate and inspire us. If we perceive that past success as unattainable, it will deflate us and only increase the anxiety associated with the current threat.

An examination of the related affirmations generated by participants in our study illustrated tremendous variability. Some individuals wrote about recent events of academic success (e.g., I aced the final in my biology course last semester to get one of the only A's in the class), whereas others wrote about events in the distant past (elementary school, high school). Work by Fritz Strack, Norbert Schwarz, and their colleagues (Strack, Schwarz, & Gschneidinger, 1985) has shown that recall of events from the recent past leads to affective assimilation, whereas recall of events from the distant past leads to affective contrast effects. We recoded the same domain essays in terms of the time frame of the events and found that the more recent events tended to have a more inspirational effect, whereas the distant past events tended to have a more deflating effect. These results clearly illustrated the need to exert greater control over the time frame participants use in writing their affirmations, particularly in the related domain.

Despite these procedural issues, there still remains the issue of why the unrelated affirmation manipulation was successful in substituting for self-handicapping in the present study. The substitutability hypothesis posits that self-affirmation is an alternative mechanism for maintaining global self-esteem and thus reaffirms the integrity of the individual despite the current self-threat. McCrea and Hirt's (2001) results suggested that preservation of global self-esteem is not the primary goal of self-handicapping, and thus an unrelated affirmation should not be able to satisfy that goal and should not substitute for self-handicapping. Indeed, an important question that needed to be addressed was exactly what effects were these affirmation manipulations having so that we could then demonstrate how these changes mediate their ability to substitute for self-handicapping.

STUDY 3: WHAT DO THESE AFFIRMATIONS REALLY DO? (McCREA & HIRT, 2000)

To address this question, we took a step back and conducted another experiment (McCrea & Hirt, 2000) in which we assigned participants to one of the three affirmation conditions (in the same experimental context of comparing

verbal and nonverbal tests of intelligence). All affirmations required participants to recall recent events of past success (in either an unrelated or related
domain) to enhance the assimilative effect of the manipulation. In this study,
instead of measuring self-handicapping (i.e., practice behavior), we gave participants a series of measures following the affirmation manipulation to assess
changes in several potential mediators, most notably affect, self-esteem, and
expectations about the upcoming nonverbal exam. The results of this investigation provided some very interesting results. First, we found no evidence that
self-affirmation improved participants' global self-esteem. We measured several types of self-esteem using both traditional self-report measures (Fleming
and Courtney's, 1984, scale, which includes global, social, and academic self-
esteem subscales) as well as more implicit measures (reaction times to global,
social, or academic self-esteem related words on a me/not me task; cf. Markus,
1977), and found no effects of the affirmation manipulations on any of these
measures. In fact, the most notable effects observed occurred on measures of
anxiety and evaluative concern. On a self-report measure of evaluative concern
with poor performance, a measure that in our previous work (Hirt, McCrea, &
Kimble, 2000) had served as a mediator for self-handicapping, we found that
HSH showed a significant decrease in concern in the related affirmation condition relative to the control–no affirmation condition. The unrelated affirmation
condition did not differ reliably from either of these other two conditions (see
Figure 6.3). Similarly, on the reaction time measure (me/not me task) to anxiety
related words (e.g., secure, anxious), HSH were significantly slower in their

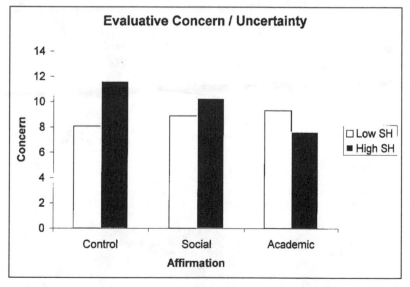

FIGURE 6.3. Study 3: Mean level of evaluative concern/uncertainty as a function of
affirmation condition and level of self-handicapping.

reaction times (RTs) to negative anxiety-related words in the related affirmation condition, suggesting that these constructs were less accessible following this type of affirmation. No effects were observed of the unrelated affirmation condition on these anxiety-related words (see Figure 6.4). In fact, the only ef-

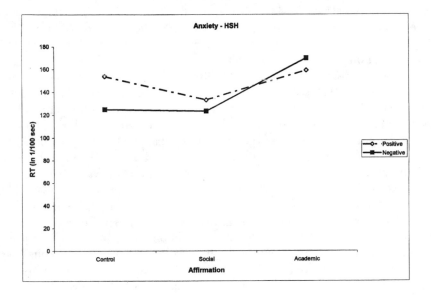

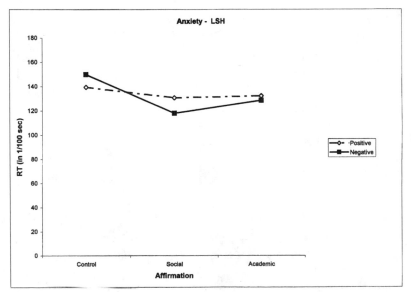

FIGURE 6.4. Study 3: Mean reaction time to anxiety-related words as a function of affirmation condition, word valence, and level of self-handicapping.

fects detectable in this study resulting from the unrelated affirmation manipulation was a modest increase in positive affect.

On the surface, the results of this study appear to conflict with the results of McCrea (1999), which found effects of only the unrelated affirmation condition on self-handicapping. In this study, the crucial mediator of self-handicapping from our earlier work (Hirt et al., 2000)—heightened evaluative concern—was affected only by the related affirmation manipulation and not the unrelated affirmation condition, a finding that is consistent with the ability preservation hypothesis proposed by McCrea and Hirt (2001). Moreover, it seems disturbing that neither affirmation manipulation showed any evidence of affecting self-esteem, when the entire edifice of the substitutability hypothesis appears to hinge on the belief that these manipulations all work to maintain global self-esteem and positive self-regard.

We have several responses to these concerns. First, the change made to our related affirmation manipulation (focusing on recent events) appears to have alleviated the variability in its effects; the related affirmation served to motivate and inspire, resulting in reduced evaluative concern and anxiety, as opposed to serving as a troubling standard of comparison. Thus, it is our strong belief that if we reran the McCrea (1999) study, both the unrelated and related affirmation conditions would result in significant decreases in self-handicapping. However, if this were to be the case, that means that both affirmations could successfully substitute for self-handicapping, despite the fact that neither actually had an effect on global self-esteem. Instead, the only consistent effect that both of these affirmation manipulations shared was to increase participants' level of positive affect. What does this mean for the substitutability hypothesis? Interestingly, Tesser (2000) recently argued that the mechanism by which all of these self-protective mechanisms work is affect. Affect has been implicated in dissonance (e.g., Cooper & Fazio, 1984), SEM (Tesser, Pilkington, & McIntosh, 1989), and self-affirmation processes (Koole, Smeets, van Knippenberg, & Dijksterhuis, 1999), as well as a range of other self-related judgments and behaviors (cf. Forgas, this volume). Moreover, it appears that the affect derived from these alternative sources must be misattributed to serve as a resource for self-regulation. Studies that have used blatant affect manipulations or have enhanced participants' awareness of the source of their affect (cf. Schwarz & Clore, 1983) have been shown to negate these substitution effects (Arndt, 1999). Thus, it may be that we need to revise the substitutability hypothesis somewhat to denote more specifically that it is the maintenance of positive affect, affect that may or may not translate directly into feelings of positive self-regard (at least as evidenced on traditional measures of self-esteem), that seems to mediate the effectiveness of these different self-protective mechanisms.

IMPLICATIONS FOR UNDERSTANDING THE GOALS OF SELF-PROTECTIVE MECHANISMS

If indeed it is simply the maintenance of positive affect that is the individual's overarching goal in the use of these self-protective mechanisms, it stands to reason that simple manipulations of affect (using the traditional misattribution paradigms) should likewise substitute for these various self-protective mechanisms. Work by Trope and his colleagues (Trope & Pomerantz, 1998) has demonstrated that positive mood serves as a resource in individual's processing of potentially threatening performance feedback, suggesting less defensive and self-protective behavior resulting from a mood induction procedure. Similar findings have been obtained showing that positive mood reduces dissonance reduction processes (Simon, Greenberg, & Brehm, 1995).

But does this then imply that modulating affect is the primary goal of these different self-protective mechanisms? We believe that the answer to this question lies in a consideration of the short-term versus long-term consequences of the self-protective behavior (see also Rhodewalt & Tragakis, this volume). The studies to date have clearly focused on the short-term implications of these different self-protective mechanisms: Do these actions effectively reduce the self-threat in the immediate situation? The answer to this question appears to be "Yes," in that these alternative mechanisms maintain the individual's positive affect, enabling him/her to cope better with the immediate self-threat. The affect seems to serve as a resource by which individuals can trivialize (Simon et al., 1995) or reduce the perceived importance of the current threat (Hull, 1999), alleviating the need to engage in additional defensive or self-protective behaviors. These goals may be satisfied more effectively by alternatives that are unrelated to the source of the current threat or discrepancy, as these compensatory forms of sustaining positive affect reduce the salience of the current discrepancy far better than more direct (e.g., same-domain) forms of self-protection.

However, one can certainly argue that these short-term "fixes" may be temporary and may not be as effective in terms of the long-term reduction of the self-threat as more direct forms of self-protection. Harking back to our earlier example, an individual who self-handicaps prior to an important track meet may temporarily take solace in the fact that he/she is competent in other important domains of life, but this may not reduce the threat presented by later meets or in other situations that may reinstate the original threat or discrepancy. It may be that a more direct approach, addressing the threat within the same domain, carries with it more short-term costs (in terms of maintaining the salience of the original threat and discrepancy) but is more beneficial in the long-term in permanently reducing the magnitude of the threat. But would participants if given the choice to engage in more direct (related) or indirect (unrelated) self-protective alternatives prefer one over the other? When the focus is on the short-term, we would expect that individuals would opt for the indirect forms of self-protection, which avoid the pain of directly dealing with the immediate discrepancy (as several studies in the dissonance literature have shown, cf. Blanton et al., 1997; Stone, 1999); however, when participants are aware that they will be reminded of the current threat in the future (e.g., accountability or future interaction situations), one might expect a shift to a more direct form of self-protection to effectively deal with the discrepancy once and for all. Individual differences in self-esteem (cf. Steele, Spencer, & Lynch, 1993) or consideration of future consequences (Strathman, Gleicher, Boninger, & Edwards, 1994) may also moderate these preferences for direct versus indirect forms of self-protection.

SELF-HANDICAPPING AND THE SOCIAL SELF

In addition, there exists an interesting paradox in the use of a strategy like self-handicapping rather than other forms of impression management and self-protection. As we mentioned earlier, self-handicapping involves a considerable tradeoff between belongingness and social acceptance needs in the service of maintaining perceptions of competence and ability. Given the importance of these needs to maintaining positive self-esteem (Leary, this volume), an important question remains concerning how self-handicappers are able to sustain a positive sense of self while compromising these critical needs. To examine this question, we believe a shift toward a more interpersonal research perspective will be necessary (cf. Ickes, this volume). To date, the research examining the interpersonal consequences of self-handicapping (Hirt et al., 2001; Luginbuhl & Palmer, 1991; Rhodewalt et al., 1995) has focused on the reactions of strangers to hypothetical scenarios depicting the self-handicapping behavior of an individual. In these impoverished situations, it may be very easy for individuals to be critical of the self-defeating behavior of these people. However, in real-world interpersonal relationships, we may be far more forgiving of these actions in our friends or acquaintances and may attribute a different set of underlying motivations to these behaviors. Thus, an interesting question for future research concerns whether self-handicappers place relatively less importance on these motivations, are unaware of the negative reactions of others, or whether they satisfy these belongingness needs by surrounding themselves with sympathetic individuals who accept or perhaps even enable their self-defeating behavior. We know very little about the social worlds of these self-handicappers and how they construct their social selves. It is precisely these sorts of questions that our future research hopes to address.

In sum, our research to date has illustrated that self-handicapping may indeed be a unique self-animal among the members of the "self-zoo" because of its many benefits and costs. The use of self-handicapping strategies over other, less destructive, self-protection strategies, and the preference for certain types of self-handicaps, may be a result of the interplay of these multiple motives.

REFERENCES

Arkin, R. M., & Baumgardner, A. H. (1985). Self-handicapping. In J. H. Harvey & G. W. Weary (Eds.), *Attribution: Basic issues and applications* (pp. 169–202). New York: Academic Press.

Arndt, J. (1999). *The role of physiological arousal in the threat and defense of self-esteem.* Unpublished manuscript, University of Missouri-Columbia.

Aronson, J., Blanton, H., & Cooper, J. (1995). From dissonance to disidentification: Selectivity in the self-affirmation process. *Journal of Personality and Social Psychology, 68,* 986–996.

Baumeister, R. F., & Scher, S. J. (1988). Self-defeating behavior patterns among normal individuals: Review and analysis of common self-destructive tendencies. *Psychological Bulletin, 104,* 3–22.

Berglas, S., & Jones, E. E. (1978). Drug choice as a self-handicapping strategy in response to noncontingent success. *Journal of Personality and Social Psychology, 36,* 405–417.

Blanton, H., Cooper, J., Skurnick, I., & Aronson, J. (1997). When bad things happen to good feedback: Exacerbating the need for self-justification with self-affirmation. *Personality and Social Psychology Bulletin, 23,* 684–692.

Boris, H. I., & Hirt, E. R. (1994, May). *Audience reaction to self-handicapping.* Paper presented at the meeting of the Midwestern Psychological Association, Chicago, IL.

Bradley, G. W. (1978). Self-serving biases in the attribution process: A reexamination of the fact or fiction question. *Journal of Personality and Social Psychology, 36,* 56–71.

Cattell, R. B., & Cattell, A. K. S. (1961). *Test of "g": Culture fair intelligence test.* Champaign, IL: The Institute for Personality and Ability Testing.

Cialdini, R. B., Borden, R. J., Thorne, A., Walker, M. R., Freeman, S., & Sloan, L. R. (1976). Basking in reflected glory: Three (football) field studies. *Journal of Personal-*

ity and Social Psychology, 39, 366–375.

Cooper, J., & Fazio, R. H. (1984). A new look at dissonance theory. In L. Berkowitz (Ed.), *Advances in Experimental Social Psychology* (Vol. 17, pp. 229–267). New York: Academic Press.

Cornell, D. P., & Tesser, A. (1994). *On the confluence of self-processes: II. SEM affects self-affirmation.* Unpublished manuscript, University of Georgia, Athens.

Ditto, P. H., & Lopez, D. F. (1992). Motivated skepticism: Use of differential decision criteria for preferred and nonpreferred conclusions. *Journal of Personality and Social Psychology, 63,* 568–584.

Feick, D. L., & Rhodewalt, F. (1997). The double-edged sword of self-handicapping: Discounting, augmentation, and the protection and enhancement of self-esteem. *Motivation and Emotion, 21,* 147–163.

Fleming, J. S., & Courtney, B. E. (1984). The dimensionality of self-esteem: II. Hierarchical facet model for revised measurement scales. *Journal of Personality and Social Psychology, 46,* 404–421.

Greenwald, A. G. (1980). The totalitarian ego: Fabrication and revision of personal history. *American Psychologist, 35,* 603–618.

Harris, R. N., & Snyder, C. R. (1986). The role of uncertain self-esteem in self-handicapping. *Journal of Personality and Social Psychology, 51,* 451–458.

Hirt, E. R., Deppe, R. K., & Gordon, L. J. (1991). Self-reported versus behavioral self-handicapping: Empirical evidence for a theoretical distinction. *Journal of Personality and Social Psychology, 61,* 981–991.

Hirt, E. R., McCrea, S. M., & Boris, H. I. (2001). *Audience reaction in self-handicapping: A matter of who sees what in whom.* Manuscript submitted for publication, Indiana University, Bloomington.

Hirt, E. R., McCrea, S. M., & Kimble, C. E. (2000). Public self-focus and sex differences in behavioral self-handicapping: Does increasing self-threat still make it "just a man's game?" *Personality and Social Psychology Bulletin, 26,* 1131–1141.

Hull, J. G. (1999). *A dynamic theory of personality and self.* Unpublished manuscript, Dartmouth University, Hanover, NH.

Isleib, R. A., Vuchinich, R. E., & Tucker, J. A. (1988). Performance attributions and changes in self-esteem following self-handicapping with alcohol consumption. *Journal of Social and Clinical Psychology, 6,* 88–103.

Jones, E. E., & Berglas, S. (1978). Control of attributions about the self through self-handicapping strategies: The appeal of alcohol and the role of underachievement. *Personality and Social Psychology Bulletin, 4,* 200–206.

Jones, E. E., & Rhodewalt, F. (1982). *Self-Handicapping Scale.* Unpublished scale, Princeton University, Princeton, NJ and University of Utah, Salt Lake City.

Kelley, H. H. (1973). The processes of causal attribution. *American Psychologist, 28,* 107–128.

Koch, K. A., & Hirt, E. R. (2000, May). *The effects of self-handicapping on the selection of positive and negative feedback.* Paper presented at the meeting of the Midwestern Psychological Association, Chicago, IL.

Kolditz, T. A., & Arkin, R. M. (1982). An impression management interpretation of the self-handicapping strategy. *Journal of Personality and Social Psychology, 43,* 492–502.

Koole, S. L., Smeets, K., van Knippenberg, A., & Dijksterhuis, A. (1999). The cessation of rumination through self-affirmation. *Journal of Personality and Social Psychology, 77,* 111–125.

Leary, M. R., & Shepperd, J. A. (1986). Behavioral self-handicaps vs. self-reported handicaps: A conceptual note. *Journal of Personality and Social Psychology, 51,* 1265–1268.

Lewin, K. (1935). *A dynamic theory of personality: Selected papers* (D. E. Adams & K. E. Zener, Trans.). New York: McGraw-Hill.

Lockwood, P., & Kunda, Z. (1997). Superstars and me: Predicting the impact of role models on the self. *Journal of Personality and Social Psychology, 73,* 91–103.

Lord, C. G., Ross, L., & Lepper, M. (1979). Biased assimilation and attitude polarization:

The effects of prior theories on subsequently considered evidence. *Journal of Personality and Social Psychology, 37,* 2098–2109.

Luginbuhl, J., & Palmer, R. (1991). Impression management aspects of self-handicapping: Positive and negative effects. *Personality and Social Psychology Bulletin, 17,* 655–662.

Markus, H. (1977). Self-schemata and processing information about the self. *Journal of Personality and Social Psychology, 35,* 63–78.

Mayerson, N. H., & Rhodewalt, F. (1988). The role of self-protective attributions in the experience of pain. *Journal of Social and Clinical Psychology, 6,* 203–218.

McCrea, S. M. (1999). *Self-handicapping as a self-evaluation maintenance strategy: Substituting for self-sabotage.* Unpublished manuscript, Indiana University, Bloomington.

McCrea, S. M., & Hirt, E. R. (2000, May). *Relatedness and self-affirmation effectiveness: Determining the goal of self-handicapping.* Paper presented at the meeting of the Midwestern Psychological Association, Chicago, IL.

McCrea, S. M., & Hirt, E. R. (2001). The role of ability judgments in self-handicapping. *Personality and Social Psychology Bulletin, 27,* 1378–1389.

Pelham, B. W., & Swann, W. B. (1989). From self-conceptions to self-worth: On the sources and structure of global self-esteem. *Journal or Personality and Social Psychology, 57,* 672–680.

Pleban, R., & Tesser, A. (1981). The effects of relevance and quality of another's performance on interpersonal closeness. *Social Psychology Quarterly, 44,* 278–285.

Rhodewalt, F., & Davison, J. (1986). Self-handicapping and subsequent performance: Role of outcome valence and attributional ambiguity. *Basic and Applied Social Psychology, 7,* 307–323.

Rhodewalt, F., & Fairfield, M. (1991). Claimed self-handicaps and the self-handicapper: Reduction in intended effort to performance. *Journal of Research in Personality, 25,* 402–417.

Rhodewalt, F., & Hill, S. K. (1995). Self-handicapping in the classroom: The effects of claimed self-handicaps on responses to academic failure. *Basic and Applied Social Psychology, 16,* 397–416.

Rhodewalt, F., Morf, C., Hazlett, S., & Fairfield, M.. (1991). Self-handicapping: The role of discounting and augmentation in the preservation of self-esteem. *Journal of Personality and Social Psychology, 61,* 122–131.

Rhodewalt, F., Sanbonmatsu, D. M., Tschanz, B., Feick, D. L., & Waller, A. (1995). Self-handicapping and interpersonal trade-offs: The effects of claimed self-handicaps on observers' performance evaluations and feedback. *Personality and Social Psychology Bulletin, 21,* 1042–1050.

Rosenberg, M. (1965). *Society and adolescent self-image.* Princeton, NJ: Princeton University Press.

Schwarz, N., & Clore, G. L. (1983). Mood, misattribution, and judgments of well-being: Informative and directive functions of affective states. *Journal of Personality and Social Psychology, 45,* 513–523.

Simon, L., Greenberg, J., & Brehm, J. (1995). Trivialization: The forgotten mode of dissonance reduction. *Journal of Personality and Social Psychology, 68,* 247–260.

Snyder, C. R. (1990). Self-handicapping processes and sequelae: On taking a psychological dive. In R. L. Higgins, C. R. Snyder, & S. Berglas (Eds.), *Self-handicapping: The paradox that isn't* (pp. 107–150). New York: Plenum Press.

Snyder, C. R., & Smith, T. W. (1982). Symptoms as self-handicapping strategies: The virtues of old wine in a new bottle. In G. Weary & H. L. Mirels (Eds.), *Integrations of clinical and social psychology* (pp. 104–127). New York: Oxford University Press.

Steele, C. M. (1988). The psychology of self-affirmation: Sustaining the integrity of self. In L. Berkowitz (Ed.), *Advances in experimental social psychology* (Vol. 21, pp. 261–302). New York: Academic Press.

Steele, C. M., & Liu, T. J. (1981). Making the dissonance act unreflective of the self: Dissonance avoidance and the expectancy of a value affirming response. *Personality and Social Psychology Bulletin, 7,* 393–397.

Steele, C. M., & Liu, T. J. (1983). Dissonance processes as self-affirmation. *Journal of Per-*

sonality and Social Psychology, 45, 5–19.

Steele, C. M., Spencer, S. J., & Lynch, M.. (1993). Self-image resilience and dissonance: The role of affirmational resources. *Journal of Personality and Social Psychology, 64,* 885–896.

Stone, J. (1999). What exactly have I done?: The role of self-attribute accessibility in dissonance. In E. Harmon-Jones & J. Mills (Eds.), *Cognitive dissonance: Progress on a pivotal theory in social psychology* (pp. 175–200). Washington, DC: American Pyschological Association.

Stone, J., Wiegand, A. W., Cooper, J., & Aronson, J. (1996). When exemplification fails: Hypocrisy and the motive of self-integrity. *Journal of Personality and Social Psychology, 72,* 54–65.

Strack, F., Schwarz, N., & Gschneidinger, E. (1985). Happiness and reminiscing: The role of time perspective, mood, and mode of thinking. *Journal of Personality and Social Psychology, 49,* 1460–1469.

Strathman, A., Gleicher, F., Boninger, D. S., & Edwards, C. S. (1994). The consideration of future consequences: Weighing immediate and distant outcomes of behavior. *Journal of Personality and Social Psychology, 66,* 742–752.

Tesser, A. (1988). Toward a self-evaluation maintenance model of social behavior. In L. Berkowitz (Ed.), *Advances in experimental social psychology* (Vol. 21, pp. 181–228). New York: Academic Press.

Tesser, A. (2000). On the confluence of self-esteem maintenance mechanisms. *Personality and Social Psychology Review, 4,* 290–299.

Tesser, A., & Campbell, J. (1980). Self-definition: The impact of the relative performance and similarity of others. *Social Psychology Quarterly, 43,* 341–347.

Tesser, A., & Cornell, D. P. (1991). On the confluence of self-processes. *Journal of Experimental Social Psychology, 27,* 501–526.

Tesser, A., Martin, L. L., & Cornell, D. P. (1996). On the substitutability of self-protective mechanisms. In P. M. Gollwitzer & J. A. Bargh (Eds.), *The psychology of action: Linking cognition and motivation to behavior* (pp. 48–68). New York: Guilford.

Tesser, A., Pilkington, C., & McIntosh, W.

(1989). Self-evaluation maintenance and the mediational role of emotion: The perception of friends and strangers. *Journal of Personality and Social Psychology, 57,* 442–456.

Tesser, A., & Smith, J. (1980). Some effects of friendship and task relevance on helping: You don't always help the one you like. *Journal of Experimental Social Psychology, 16,* 582–590.

Tice, D. M. (1991). Esteem protection or enhancement?: Self-handicapping motives and attributions differ by trait self-esteem. *Journal of Personality and Social Psychology, 60,* 711–725.

Trope, Y., & Pomerantz, R. E. (1998). Resolving conflicts among self-evaluative motives: Positive experiences as a resource for overcoming defensiveness. *Motivation and Emotion, 22,* 53–72.

7

Self-Handicapping and the Social Self
The Cost and Rewards of Interpersonal Self-Construction

FREDERICK RHODEWALT
MICHAEL W. TRAGAKIS

INTRODUCTION

O f all of the universal life tasks confronting us as individuals, the construction and maintenance of our self-concepts is probably the most involving and certainly the most enduring. Personality theorists (Erikson, 1959; Rogers, 1961), development psychologists (Harter, 1990), and social psychologists (Higgins, 1996) have all characterized and investigated from their disciplinary perspectives the processes involved in this endeavor. Collectively they conclude that the self is learned through experience, and the bulk of this experience is embedded in the individual's social context and relationships. The self is inherently social. In this chapter we focus on the strategies that people employ as they undertake the task of self-concept construction and maintenance and examine the consequences of these strategies for self-understanding and future behavior. In particular, we use our theorizing and research on self-

Address for correspondence: Frederick Rhodewalt, Department of Psychology, Univeristy of Utah, 390 S. 1530 East, Rm 502, Salt Lake City, UT 84112-0250, USA. E-mail: fred.rhodewalt@psych.utah.edu

handicapping behavior to illustrate the more general point that often the activity of self-concept construction and maintenance is at odds with the goal of clear and accurate self-understanding. The chapter will conclude by extending our analysis of self-handicapping to other areas of strategic social self-construction and identity maintenance.

The concept of *self-handicapping* was first introduced by Edward E. Jones and Steven Berglas (1978). Their basic observation was that people often create, or at least claim obstacles to successful performances when they harbor doubts about their ability to be successful and when failure would confirm that the ability is lacking. According to Jones and Berglas, the person who procrastinates and fails to prepare adequately for a sales presentation or who gets drunk the night before taking the college entrance exams is manipulating in a self-serving way the attributions that one may draw about the actor's ability or competency. Inadequate preparation and inebriation decrease the likelihood of a successful sales presentation or a high SAT score, but they also protect the belief that one has the ability to do well. Jones and Berglas (1978) argued that the self-handicapper is capitalizing on the attributional principles of *discounting* and *augmentation* (Kelley, 1972). That is, conclusions about lack of ability are discounted, or downplayed, because the handicap offers an equally plausible explanation for the rejection or failure. In the unlikely event of success, attributions to ability are augmented, or accorded greater causal importance, because the good performance happened despite the handicap. The self-handicapper then is willing to trade the increased likelihood of failure for the opportunity to protect a desired self-image. It is important to point out that the self-handicapper is willing to accept the label of procrastinator or drunkard in order to preserve a more central label of competence and worthiness. The label implied by the handicap is almost always to a quality that is external to the individual or is believed to be modifiable, while the attribute that is being protected is believed to be fixed and unmodifiable, a point to which we will return momentarily.

Self-handicapping embraces several more general assumptions running through social psychological treatments of the self. First, self-handicapping recognizes that people apply the attributional logic used in the perception of others to understand the meaning of their own behaviors with regard to self-definition (Bem, 1972; Weiner, 1985). That is, people come to understand who they are—which dispositions, talents, competencies, and vulnerabilities they possess—through the same inferential processes used in the perception of others. Although there are many examples and discussions of the differences between self-attribution and other attribution (Jones & Nisbett, 1971), it is clear that self-attributional principles and processes are the engine that powers self-concept formation and maintenance.

Second, on most occasions, self-handicapping is played out in the social arena. Self-handicappers attempt to guide others' perceptions of their abilities or talents. Although there has been some debate in the self-handicapping literature about whether self-handicapping is motivated by self-deceptive or self-presentational concerns (Arkin & Oleson, 1998; Kolditz & Arkin, 1982), we take the position that social feedback and social regard are part and parcel of self-understanding. The presence of an audience intensifies self-handicapping motivations because protecting the self in the eyes of others is essential to protecting the self in one's own mind.

Nonetheless, self-handicapping falls within the broader domain of strategic self-presentation because it is "designed to elicit or shape others' attributions of the actor's dispositions" (Jones & Berglas, 1978) and thus it demonstrates a third general theme found in most contemporary writings on the self. Self-handicapping illustrates the more general idea that people actively attempt to manipulate social reactions to, and the interpretations of their behavior to produce a specific image of the self. Self-handicapping stretches the analogy of the individual as a naive scientist or psychologist. Perhaps the metaphor of self-handicappers as lawyers or solicitors would be more apt in that they often try to marshal the best case (or defense) for their desired self-conceptions. More generally, individuals actively shape their self-understanding through self-serving causal analysis of their own behavior. They attribute positive outcomes to the self while looking to the situation and circumstances to deflect responsibility for negative outcomes (Miller & Ross, 1975; Weary, 1978). They selectively react to social comparisons and manipulate their interpersonal relationships so as to maintain valued self-conceptions (Morf & Rhodewalt, 1993; Tesser, 1988, 2000). Further, they strategically self-present and directly manipulate others' impressions of them through a variety of self-presentation tactics (Arkin, 1981; Jones & Pittman, 1982; Swann, 1983, 1985). We will consider the active role played by the individual in eliciting and shaping self-relevant social feedback. For the moment, we simply wish to highlight that individuals are active constructors rather than passive observers of reactions to, and interpretations of social feedback about the self. Self-handicapping is one tool employed in this activity (see Hirt & McCrea, this volume).

THE SELF-HANDICAPPING PROCESS

Since its introduction in 1978, self-handicapping has generated a great deal of research interest (see Arkin & Oleson, 1998; Higgins, Snyder, & Berglas, 1990 for reviews). This work falls into four main categories: the antecedents of self-handicapping, the varieties of self-handicapping strategies, the consequences of the use of such strategies, and individual differences in the tendency to employ self-handicapping strategies. Collectively this work describes what we have termed the self-handicapping process (Rhodewalt & Tragakis, in press) which is depicted in Figure 7.1. As one can see in Figure 7.1, our model of self-handicapping is recursive in the sense that the consequences of self-handicapping

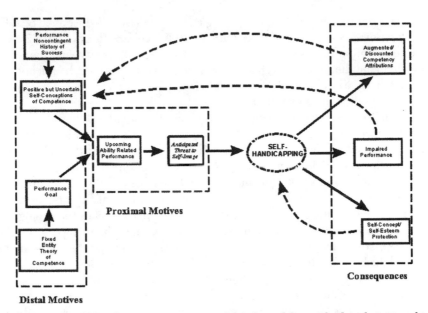

FIGURE 7.1. Self-handicapping process model (adapted from Rhodewalt & Tragakis, in press).

feed back into the model and reinforce self-handicapping acts while maintaining or, perhaps, exacerbating antecedent motives and concerns. We will focus on research pertinent to the antecedents and consequences components of the model because they are the elements of the process most closely related to self-understanding. Of course, some of the antecedent factors are stable characteristics of the person, so our discussion will necessarily include consideration of individual differences in the tendency to self-handicap where appropriate. The reader interested in research on modes of self-handicapping is directed to Arkin and Baumgardner (1985), Hirt, Deppe, and Gordon (1991), Leary and Shepperd (1986), and Rhodewalt and Tragakis (in press) for discussions.

Antecedents of Self-Handicapping Behavior

Distal motives. In their original theoretical statement, Jones and Berglas (1978) contended that self-handicapping is motivated by a desire to protect a positive but insecurely held competency image. We agree with this proposition but suggest that it is only a part of a more complex set of precipitating elements in the self-handicapping cycle. We think it is most useful to conceive of self-handicapping as deriving from the combined influence of two classes of motives, which we have labeled proximal and distal. Proximal motives are those elements and concerns in the immediate situation that trigger episodes of self-handicapping behavior. For example, the importance of an outcome for the person's self-concept and self-esteem would be a proximal factor. Distal motives are those characteristics of the person stemming from past personal experiences and learning that would engender a proclivity to self-handicap as opposed to some other performance strategy. Again, the recursive nature of the model blurs the proximal/distal distinction because in many instances proximal influences may more greatly affect some people than others, reflecting the interplay between short-term and long-term motives. In addition, we will argue that the consequences of self-handicapping feedback on these motivational states to influence subsequent acts of self-handicapping.

As illustrated in Figure 7.1, distal motives have two sources. The first source is the motivational set described by Jones and Berglas (1978) stemming from a unique history of experiences upon which the sense of competency is based. For example, two executives may wish to believe that they possess brilliant business acumen but differ in the past experiences that would support such a claim. One executive may have had a history of very cunning business decisions and a clear grasp of how she arrived at those decisions. The other executive may have also made a number of decisions that worked out well for his company. These successful decisions also imply ability, but the person is uncertain that other factors such as good fortune were not involved. In Jones and Berglas' (1978) terminology, this latter person has had a history of response non-contingent success feedback while the former has had a history of response contingent success feedback. Thus, one distal contributor to acts of self-handicapping is a positive but insecure sense of self.

Berglas and Jones (1978) tested this idea more formally by proposing that people who have had a positive but capricious reinforcement history with respect to some desired attribute are motivated to self-handicap when called upon to provide evidence of that attribute or competency. They demonstrated this hypothesis in a classic experiment that participants believed was a study of the effects of various drugs on intellectual performance. Participants were told that they would be taking two equivalent forms of an IQ test. The first test was to be taken under optimal conditions, and the second was to be taken after the participant had chosen and ingested either a drug that was thought to improve performance or a drug that was thought to interfere with performance. Drug choice was the main dependent measure.

All participants received feedback that they had done exceptionally well. For half of the participants, this feedback was response contingent in that there was a correct answer for each item on the test so that these participants had a clear idea of what they did to do well. For the other half of the participants, the success feedback was response non-contingent, meaning that there was no correct answer and thus no connection between their behavior and the feedback they received. These non-contingent feedback success participants were told that their test results indicated that they were very intelligent, but they had no idea what they did to do well on the test. They were then asked to replicate their success on the second test, but first they had to select the drug they wanted to be administered before taking the test. The major finding was that those participants who were uncertain of why they achieved the initial success (non-contingent success feedback) showed a clear preference for self-handicapping while those who were confident of their ability (contingent success feedback) did not.

These findings have been replicated many times with different modes of self-handicapping and for different abilities. They clearly demonstrate the importance of the distal motive of wanting to maintain a desired but insecurely anchored self-conception. These fragile self-images, in turn, stem from capricious reinforcement experiences.

Although Jones and Berglas documented one antecedent of the self-handicapping motive, there seems to be a piece missing from the puzzle. Why self-handicap when there are a number of other responses available? When one's competency is on the line, why not respond with increased effort or more rigorous preparation? It appears obvious from the observer's perspective that self-handicapping is ultimately self-defeating and that other responses might be more adaptive. There is little doubt that concerns about competency motivate self-handicapping behavior, but there must be more to story.

This question has been approached in our laboratory by building on the seminal thinking of Carol Dweck and her colleagues (Dweck, 1999; Dweck & Leggett, 1988; Elliot & Dweck, 1988). Although Dweck's interest is with mastery oriented versus helpless behaviors in achievement contexts, we believe her framework extends to an understanding of self-handicapping behavior. Dweck contends that people differ in their beliefs or personal theories about the causes of ability and competency. "Fixed-entity" theorists believe that ability is a fixed trait. Whatever one's capacity, it is relatively fixed and unmodifiable. In contrast, "incremental" theorists assume that ability can be cultivated through learning, that one's capacities are malleable. It is probably more accurate to say that most people entertain both theories and differ in the extent to which they favor one over the other as the predominant explanation for ability.

According to Dweck, "fixed-entity" and "incremental" self-theories are associated with different goals in achievement contexts. The "fixed-entity" theorist pursues performance goals, that is, goals of receiving positive feedback and outcomes such as a high grade or praise from the teacher. The "incremental" theorist, in contrast, pursues learning goals characterized by learning something new or improving upon an existing skill. Our hypothesis was that the combination of a "fixed-entity" view of competency and the pursuit of performance goals would also promote the tendency to self-handicap when the individual anticipated negative feedback about the "fixed-entity." Consider two students who are uncertain about their intelligence and who are also facing an important test of that intelligence. For the "incremental theorist/learning goal" student, this is clearly an unsettling situation. The evaluation is important, and the outcome is uncertain. However, the meaning of that outcome while potentially disappointing is not damning. A negative evaluation signals that more training and preparation are required before the student can move on. Now consider the "fixed-entity theorist/performance goal" student facing the same challenge. Failure for this student does not mean that more preparation is required. Rather it signals that ability is lacking; this is a devastating message because, according to the fixed-entity view, there is not much one can do to remedy the deficit. Thus, when situations require the demonstration of a certain competence, the performance goals and focus on ability of those who hold fixed theories of competence may also motivate self-protective, self-handicapping tactics.

More formally, our model proposes that the use of self-handicapping strategies is the product of two learning histories (Rhodewalt, 1994). First, the self-handicapper has had a set of socialization experiences that instill the belief that competency is fixed and can only be demonstrated rather than improved. Second, this person possesses ability self-conceptions that are based on a causally ambiguous and shaky history of success. Thus, self-handicappers enter many evaluative situations with the goal of demonstrating an ability of which they are uncertain. It is the confluence of these two learning histories and the more immediate performance demands that set the stage for self-handicapping. Evaluative situations that pose the threat of negative feedback about the self are to be avoided because their implications are so damaging. In these contexts, people will embrace self-handicaps because the trade-off of increased risk of failure for the protection of an ability self-conception seems like a bargain.

Support for this part of our model comes from a correlational study (Rhodewalt, 1994) in which theories of ability and goals were assessed in a group of individuals who had also completed the Self-Handicapping Scale (SHS; Jones & Rhodewalt, 1982). The SHS is a face valid, self-report measure of people's tendencies to make excuses and use self-handicaps. Theories of ability were measured in several ways. Participants responded to a set of open-ended questions such as "What does it mean to be intelligent (athletic, socially skilled)?", "What does it mean to be unintelligent (unathletic, not socially skilled)?", and "What could one do, if anything, to become more intelligent (athletic, socially skilled)?". They then read a vignette about a bright and accomplished college student who had been accepted to medical school. They rated the person in the vignette for intelligence and then apportioned 100 points among possible causes of her academic achievement including the factors "innate intelligence," "effort," and "privileged background." Finally, participants completed a measure of goals in school (Nichols, 1984), which assessed both performance and learning goals. Both measures of naive theory assessment revealed that self-handicappers held fixed-entity theories of ability to a greater extent than did non-self-handicappers. Also, as hypothesized, self-handicapping was also associated with performance goals in academic settings.

Although more research is required, the results of this investigation suggest that one set of distal contributors to the tendency to self-handicap is the person's belief that one's abilities are relatively fixed and stable. Consequently one can only display behavioral evidence of the ability. The other distal contributor is a lack of confidence or certainty that one actually possesses a desired ability. It is the confluence of these two belief systems that draws the individual to self-handicapping behavior.

Before leaving our discussion of distal causes of self-handicapping there is one additional point of note. The model treats self-theories and goals as one independent influence on self-handicapping separate from the influence of a non-contingent learning history and positive but uncertain self-conceptions. These two influences may be more related than they appear on the surface. They may connect at a developmental level that involves understanding of the contingencies between behavior and outcomes. Jones and Berglas (1978) argued that the self-handicapper simply does not understand the connection between past success and personal attributes. We suggest that the same sort of ambiguous understanding of ability is more compatible with a fixed-entity view than it is with an incremental view of competency. That is, an incremental theory implies an understanding of the contingencies among effort, practice, preparation, and performance. A fixed-entity view of ability requires less attention to contextual and motivational influences on performance. Future research may reveal that the same developmental experiences that contribute to a positive but confused self-image also foster fixed-entity beliefs about the characteristics of that self-image.

Proximal motives. There are a number of eliciting conditions for specific acts of self-handicapping. The Berglas and Jones (1978) experiment described previously illustrates a major proximal precipitator of self-handicapping. Specifically, episodes of self-handicapping are triggered by being called upon to exhibit the valued attribute or competency. It is the fear that one cannot produce evidence of a competence, skill, ability, or attribute that elicits acts of self-handicapping. The self-handicapper is relatively comfortable until called upon to perform. Snyder and Smith (1982) have argued more broadly that self-handicapping is a response to anticipated threats to the self. Thus, self-handicaps can be used to hide feelings of inferiority as well as to protect a shaky self-concept. While some may object to this characterization of self-handicapping (Berglas, 1988), it does capture the wide array of research findings in the literature. Clearly, having a desired self-conception debunked by a poor performance is a threat to the self.

A second issue that we include in our discussion of proximal motivations concerns the self-deception versus self-presentation aspects of self-handicapping. In fact, Berglas and Jones (1978) raised the possibility that people self-handicap in order to protect their images in the eyes of others rather than to deceive themselves. Berglas and Jones attempted to address this question by varying whether the experimenter would know of the participant's choice to self-handicap. Whether or not the experimenter was allegedly aware of the self-handicap did not make a difference, leading Berglas and Jones to conclude that self-handicapping was for self-protection. Others (see Kolditz & Arkin, 1982) have produced evidence that self-presentational concerns can increase the likelihood of self-handicapping. Rhodewalt and Fairfield (1991) found that self-handicappers who anticipated doing poorly on an IQ test stated that they were not going to try on the upcoming test (and actually withdrew effort), even when these claims of intended effort were ostensibly anonymous and could serve no self-presentational purpose. As we noted previously, our reading of the literature leads us to conclude that self-handicappers are as concerned about their self-concept in their own eyes as they are concerned about how they appear to others.

Consequences of Self-Handicapping

The right side of Figure 7.1 illustrates the hypothesized direct effects of self-handicapping. According to Jones and Berglas (1978), people self-handicap to create the opportunity to discount failure and augment success with regard to self-perceived competency. Thus, self-handicapping should ultimately protect or enhance those self-images. Self-handicappers are also interested in protecting their public reputations as competent individuals. Does self-handicapping accomplish these self-protective and self-presentational objectives? We have examined these questions in both laboratory (Rhodewalt, Morf, Hazlett, & Fairfield, 1991; Rhodewalt, Sanbonmatsu, Feick, Tschanz, & Waller, 1995) and naturalistic investigations (Feick & Rhodewalt, 1998; Rhodewalt & Hill, 1995; see also McCrea & Hirt, in press) and found that in the short-term the answer is "yes"—self-handicapping in most instances accomplishes these hypothesized outcomes.

Discounting and augmentation. With regard to self-attributional processes, there is considerable evidence that self-handicappers discount ability attributions after failure and some evidence that they augment after success. To illustrate this point, Rhodewalt et al. (1991, Study 1), preselected participants based on high and low scores on the Self-Handicapping Scale and high and low scores on self-esteem. Participants were given non-contingent success feedback on an intelligence test and then took a second form of the test in the presence of a handicap (ostensibly distracting background music). Half of the participants learned that they had again performed well on the second intelligence test and half learned that they had performed poorly. Most participants discounted the implications of failure by reporting that the failing test performance indicated little about their ability. Only low self-handicappers who were also low in self-esteem failed to take advantage of the attributional benefits of the handicap. In contrast, participants were more reticent to interpret a successful performance in the presence of a handicap as evidence for augmented ability. Only high self-handicappers who were high in self-esteem made such self-aggrandizing ability attributions (see Tice, 1991, for a similar finding).

Evidence of discounting and augmentation also comes from naturalistic studies of self-handicapping (Feick & Rhodewalt, 1998; Rhodewalt & Hill, 1995). In these "classroom studies" we examined not only who self-handicaps but also the role these handicaps play in reactions to academic feedback. The procedure was similar in both investigations. At the beginning of the academic term, students reported their expected class performance and were assessed for individual differences in self-handicapping (SHS) and self-esteem. Prior to the first exam they reported any "handicaps" they were undergoing that might affect their performance on the upcoming exam. As expected, high SHS students claimed more handicaps than did low SHS students. When the graded exams were returned to the students, they were asked to make attributions for their performance and to report their state self-esteem at that moment. We categorized students' performances by comparing their grades on the exam with their grade expectations reported at the beginning of the term. Students were grouped into those who performed worse than they expected (failure), equal to their expectations (expected success) or better than their expectations (unexpected success). The test performance attributions as a function of whether or not the student had claimed handicaps prior to the test and test outcome from the Feick and Rhodewalt study are displayed in Figure 7.2. There is clear evidence for discounting and augmentation. Student's who failed claimed significantly higher ability if they had previously handicapped than if they had not. In fact, the ability attributions of failing self-handicappers were not different from the ability attributions of students who had performed up to their expectations—clear evidence of discounting. Students who performed better than they expected claimed augmented ability if they achieved this success in the presence of a handicap. These students reported levels of ability that were significantly higher than students who had performed unexpectedly well but who had not handicapped. Rhodewalt and Hill (1995) examined only reactions to failure and found the same pattern of discounting. Collectively these studies provide clear support for the attributional component of the model.

Self-esteem and self-concept. There is also evidence that self-handicapping moderates the effects of failure and success on self-esteem. In the laboratory, Rhodewalt et al. (1991, Study 2) led students to believe that they had performed well on an intelligence test and then administered a second form of the same test. Half of the students received feedback that they continued to be successful on the second test and half received feedback that they were now failing. Independent of this feedback was the presence or absence of an experi-

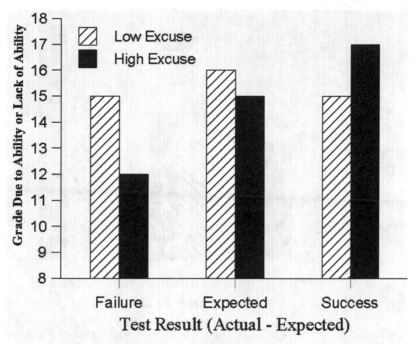

FIGURE 7.2. Ability attributions as a function of test performance and amount of self-handicapping (Feick & Rhodewalt, 1998).

menter-imposed handicap. Those students who failed but had a handicap reported levels of ability and self-esteem equal to those who succeeded on both tests. In contrast, students who failed and did not have a handicap concluded that they had low ability and displayed lowered self-esteem.

This study found no evidence of self-enhancement when participants were successful and handicapping. However, we have found evidence for the esteem-enhancing effects of self-handicapping following good performances in other studies. Recall that Rhodewalt et al. (1991, Study 1) found that participants who were both high scorers on the SHS and high in self-esteem employed self-handicaps for self-enhancement. Figure 7.3 displays the effects of self-handicapping and test outcome on self-esteem in the Feick and Rhodewalt (1998) field study. It is evident in the figure that claimed handicaps buffered self-esteem from the effects of failure and enhanced self-esteem after success. The self-esteem of self-handicappers who failed is not significantly different from successful students and significantly higher than failing nonself-handicappers. Students who were unexpectedly successful and who handicapped displayed elevated self-esteem in line with their augmented ability attributions. In fact, mediation analyses indicated that the test performance by self-handicapping interaction on posttest self-esteem was mediated by the ability attributions stu-

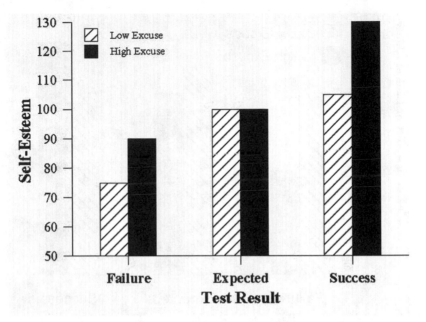

FIGURE 7.3. Self-esteem as a function of test performance and amount of self-handicapping (Feick & Rhodewalt, 1998).

dents offered for their performances. More recent research by McCrea and Hirt (in press) finds that specific competencies are buffered from the effects of failure and augmented by success when the individual self-handicaps.

These findings return us to the question of motives. Specifically, are self-handicappers mainly concerned with self-protection or self-enhancement? Some findings suggest that self-handicapping for the opportunity to augment anticipated success is limited to high self-esteem individuals (Rhodewalt et al., 1991; Tice, 1991). Our reading of the research suggests that most acts of self-handicapping are primarily in the service of self-concept protection. Although it is true that certain individuals—particularly high self-esteem, high self-handicappers—are quick to understand and accept augmented ability attributions, self-enhancement is unlikely to be the primary reason for their self-handicapping behavior. These individuals self-handicap only when they are uncertain about their ability. If self-enhancement was the goal of self-handicapping for high self-esteem individuals, then one would observe self-handicapping among individuals who are certain of their ability. There is no evidence to support this argument.

Self-presentational outcomes. There is a small but consistent literature that examines the self-presentational utility of self-handicapping (Luginbuhl &

Palmer, 1991; Rhodewalt et al., 1995; Smith & Strube, 1994). This work asks how self-handicappers are perceived by others. These studies uniformly find that observers give self-handicappers the attributional benefit of the doubt by discounting attributions to ability (or lack thereof) following poor performance. It is also clear, however, that observers do not like self-handicappers. Along this line, we found that observers will evaluate the same objective performance more negatively when it is produced by a self-handicapping person than when it is produced by a non-self-handicapping person (Rhodewalt et al., 1995). It is as if the evaluator recognizes the handicap and does not feel concerned about softening the feedback. This finding highlights one of the recursive aspects of our model by suggesting that the act of self-handicapping may engender more threatening feedback than one would otherwise normally encounter.

Self-handicapping and performance. The final outcome category is actual performance and achievement. Researchers have only begun to examine the effects of creating or claiming obstacles on task engagement and performance outcomes. For example, in one study in our laboratory, we (Rhodewalt & Fairfield, 1991) asked students to state privately how hard they were going to try at an upcoming test of intelligence (lack of effort being a claimed self-handicap). Unknown to the students, we had manipulated the difficulty of a set of practice items so that half of the students expected to do well and half expected to do poorly. Students who were suspicious that they would not do well on the IQ test *claimed* prior to taking it that they did not intend to put forth as much effort as did students who expected to do well. All students were then administered the same test. What is striking about this experiment is that students who made the claim of low intended effort actually performed significantly worse on the math test than did students who did not make the claim. Given that the test was the same for everyone, we assume that stating that they were not going to try led them to try less hard, which accounted for their poorer performance. Surely, the relation between the mode of self-handicap and performance is complex and warrants additional research.

A second way of addressing the self-handicapping and performance question is to examine the long-term effects of self-handicapping. To the extent that an individual chronically self-handicaps, one would expect that there would be deleterious effects on achievement and accomplishment. We have evidence suggesting that this is true. We created an index of overachievement/underachievement by using students' SAT/ACT scores as a measure of aptitude and their GPAs as a measure of achievement (Rhodewalt & Saltzman reported in Rhodewalt, 1990). In samples from two different universities, the overachievement/underachievement index correlated negatively with scores on the SHS. That is, the more a student was a chronic self-handicapper as evidenced by his/her SHS score, the less likely his/her grades were as high as what would be expected from his/her SAT/ACT scores.

Zuckerman, Kieffer, and Knee (1998) provided a follow-up examination of the relation between chronic self-handicapping and academic performance. In two studies these researchers found that individual differences in self-handicapping as measured by the SHS were related to lower academic performance as indexed by GPA. Moreover, the negative relation between the SAT/ACT scores and GPA was independent of verbal and quantitative SAT and level of self-esteem. Zuckerman et al. (1998) also measured study habits and found that poor exam preparation seemed to drive the relationship between individual difference in the tendency to use self-handicaps and poor performance.

Self-Handicapping, Future Behavior, and the Uncertain Self

Our model and supporting research paints a portrait of self-handicappers as individuals who believe that characteristics and competencies are fixed and immutable. They also possess competency self-conceptions that are positive but about which they are uncertain and insecure. Thus, when they anticipate the possibility of negative feedback that would question or challenge their desired self-views, they act in ways that invite failure but reduce its threat to the desired sense of self. We have also seen that self-handicapping permits the discounting of failure and the augmentation of success and, thus, serves to protect and enhance the self. These are the short-term immediate "benefits" of self-handicapping.

However, the model depicted in Figure 7.1 is recursive in that the effects of self-handicapping feed back and influence earlier elements in the model. That is, the figure depicts acts of self-handicapping and their immediate effects as influencing self-understanding and subsequent behavior. What are those effects?

With regard to behavior, self-handicapping should foster future acts of self-handicapping. This is because the "short-term" results of specific episodes of self-handicapping are positive and should reinforce the idea that self-handicapping is an effective strategy. Numerous studies have shown that self-handicapping buffers one's self-esteem from the effects of failure and allows one to discount the role of lack of ability in producing that failure. While self-handicapping might look self-defeating and counterproductive to the observer, from the perspective of the self-handicapper, it works.

There are other recursive influences that would perpetuate the self-handicapping cycle. For example, audiences understand the attributional logic of self-handicapping and are willing to give the self-handicapper the benefit of the doubt in the event of poor performance. At the same time they are willing to provide the self-handicapper with harsh feedback about the quality of the self-handicapper's performance. Audiences then are coconspirators in perpetuating self-handicapping behavior because they allow the actor to protect a desired image but also are more likely to confront the individual with threatening feedback.

Finally, and we believe most important, self-handicapping should perpetuate uncertainty about the self. At its essence, self-handicapping operates by creating what Snyder and Wicklund (1981) termed "attribute ambiguity." Snyder and Wicklund defined attribute ambiguity as a strategy for enhancing personal control. In their view, actors are at times interested in avoiding dispositional attributions because having their behaviors attributed to underlying characteristics would be constraining. Research on self-handicapping reveals that attribute ambiguity can also be called to the service of protecting a sense of competency when threatening feedback is anticipated. Self-handicapping thus reflects an explicit attempt to create and benefit from attribute ambiguity. Nonetheless, the veil of attribute ambiguity can only sustain the self-handicapper's uncertainty about the attribute in question. In sum, the recursive properties of the model contribute to maintaining a positive but insecure self-concept and, thus, guarantee subsequent acts of self-handicapping.

SELF-SOLICITATION AND THE DISCOUNTED SELF

That people actively manipulate their social worlds to control feedback about the self is well-established. Jones and Pittman (1982), Swann (1983, 1985), and Tesser (1988, 2000) among others have detailed the interpersonal strategies that people use to shape others' views of them. Self-handicapping is one such strategy, but we think it is particularly instructive because it provides a unique window for understanding some of the paradoxical aspects of social construction and maintenance of the self. We contend that people are often insecure about their competencies and characteristics and, as a consequence, try to solicit social feedback that supports these desired conceptions. They seek confirmation by actively manipulating the attributions that can be drawn from their behavior through a variety of self-presentation strategies. We further submit that most strategic attempts to manipulate feedback about the self generate attribute ambiguity, either explicitly or implicitly, and thus undermine the possibility of secure self-understanding. The ultimate consequence of this cycle is that the individual must remain engaged in the quest for self-confirmation through social interaction.

One point that emerges from the self-handicapping literature is the critical importance of certainty or clarity of the self-concept in strategic interpersonal behavior. Others have also argued that the clarity or confidence with which people hold self-views guides their interaction goals (Campbell, 1990; Kernis, 1993; Swann & Schroeder, 1995). For example, Michael Kernis and his colleagues (Kernis, 1993; Kernis, Cornell, Sun, Berry, & Harlow, 1993) have asserted that high but unstable self-esteem individuals pursue the goal of gaining more stable and secure views of the self through their interpersonal contacts. Not surprisingly, they report that high but unstable self-esteem individuals are more likely to self-handicap than are stable, high self-esteem people.

The importance of self-concept confidence or clarity has also been a focus of Swann's extensive research on self-verification processes (Swann, 1983, 1985). According to Swann, people orchestrate their social worlds in an attempt to verify confidently held self-views because consensus about the self bolsters the predictability and controllability of the social environment. Individuals seek self-confirming feedback (e.g., Swann, Wenzlaff, Krull, & Pelham, 1992), target self-confirming interaction partners (e.g., Swann, Hixon, & de la Ronde, 1992), as well as act in ways to bring others' impressions in line with self-views (e.g., Swann & Ely, 1984), all in the service of verifying their self-beliefs. Self-verification processes have been demonstrated with both positive and negative self-conceptions; people with high self-esteem have been found to seek positive self-confirmatory information, whereas individuals with low self-esteem will actually seek negative confirmations of self (Geisler & Swann, 1999; Swann et al., 1992).

Most important to the present discussion is Swann's claim that the propensity to self-verify varies as a function of how well the self is known. For self-beliefs that are confidently held, Swann and colleagues have found that individuals are especially likely to seek self-verification. In contrast, for less confidently held self-conceptions people seek self-enhancement (Swann, Griffin, Predmore, & Gaines, 1987). Thus, for individuals who are unsure of themselves, their self-presentational behavior involves "wishful thinking" in that they hope to acquire evidence that they are who they would like to be. Swann includes strategic self-presentation, self-handicapping, self-affirmation, and self-monitoring among the list of possible tactics available for individuals who must confront feedback that challenges these "hoped for" self-views (Swann & Schroeder, 1995).

We suggest that the insecure individual enters social interactions with the goal of *self-solicitation*. Whereas self-verification involves interacting with others so that they come to see you as you see yourself, self-solicitation involves seeking social feedback that enables you to maintain or protect desired or "hoped for" self-images. Self-solicitation then encompasses a set of interaction strategies that constrain others so that they provide feedback that supports the precarious self-view. As evidenced by our self-handicapping studies, such strategies do accomplish this goal. However, this attributional manipulation can cause other interpretive ambiguities for the self-solicitor. Foremost is the possible awareness that the feedback was not unsolicited. At some level, self-solicitors have to be concerned about the hand their manipulations played in eliciting and shaping the feedback they received. The active role of the individual in setting the social stage serves as a discounting cue for interpreting the feedback with regard to the self. That is, the causal implications of self-solicitation itself point to self-discounting.

Take the obvious example of defensive reassurance seeking, common in depressed individuals (see Joiner, Katz, & Lew, 1999). Reassurance seeking involves the strategic solicitation of self-enhancing feedback by individuals who have doubts about their competence and worth. Queries such as, "Don't you love me anymore?" or "Do you think I'm funny?" would fall under this category of attempts to be enhanced by others. Depressed individuals have been found to seek reassurance to excess, which results in impaired relationships and negative evaluations by others (Joiner, Metalsky, Katz, & Beach, 1999). If an individual who seeks to self-enhance by seeking reassurance from others is successful, there is the nagging question of whether the positive response would have occurred without the solicitation. Attributions to ability or worth must be discounted in this scenario. On the other hand, if the reassurance-seeking individual is rebuffed and receives negative feedback from others, attributions to low worth or competence are augmented because negative feedback also implies rejection of the individual.

The example of self-handicapping is more complex; not only does the self-handicap serve as an additional possible cause of one's outcomes, but the self as initiator of the handicap must also be factored into judgments about competency. One can imagine the paradoxical problem of being aware of the strategic creation of an impediment to success. Even when the self is protected in the short-term, the self-handicapper has to wonder about whether the ability would have been confirmed had he/she not employed the handicap. Thus, the gains afforded by the implementation of a self-handicap may be undermined by attributions to self-influence on the outcomes or feedback.

More broadly, we are proposing that self-handicapping and other defensive, strategic manipulations of social feedback are cases of "self-discounting." Ironically, the tools that uncertain individuals use to maintain and protect desired self-conceptions are often the implements that sustain their uncertainty. Self-solicitors become caught in an unending cycle of interpersonal self-knowledge and self-esteem regulation (Morf & Rhodewalt, in press). They must be suspicious of any self-relevant feedback that they had a hand in producing. So they return to the interpersonal arena in an attempt to manufacture additional evidence that they are who they wish to be. Such are the vagaries of the social self.

REFERENCES

Arkin, R. M. (1981). Self-presentation styles. In J. Tedeschi (Ed.), *Impression management and social psychological research* (pp. 311–333). San Diego, CA: Academic Press.

Arkin, R. M., & Oleson, K. C. (1998). Self-handicapping. In J. Darley & J. Cooper (Eds.), *Attribution and social interaction: The legacy of Edward E. Jones* (pp. 313–348). Washington, DC: American Psychological Association.

Arkin, R. M., & Baumgardner, A. H. (1985). Self-handicapping. In J. Harvey & G. Weary (Eds.), *Attribution: Basic Issues and Applications* (pp. 169–202). New York: Academic Press.

Bem, D. J. (1972). Self-perception theory. In L. Berkowitz (Ed.), *Advances in experimental social psychology* (Vol. 6, pp. 1–62). New York: Academic Press.

Berglas, S. (1988). The three faces of self-handicapping: Protective self-presentation, a strategy for self-esteem enhancement, and a character disorder. In R. Hogan (Ed.), *Perspectives in personality* (Vol. 1, pp. 235–270). Greenwich, CT: JAI Press.

Berglas, S., & Jones, E. E. (1978). Drug choice as a self-handicapping strategy in response to non-contingent success. *Journal of Personality and Social Psychology, 36*, 405–417.

Campbell, J. (1990). Self-esteem and clarity of the self-concept. *Journal of Personality and Social Psychology, 59*, 538–549.

Dweck, C. S. (1999). *Self-theories: Their role in motivation, personality and development.* Philadelphia: Psychology Press.

Dweck, C. S., & Leggett, E. L. (1988). A social-cognitive approach to motivation and personality. *Psychological Review, 95*, 256–273.

Elliot, E. S., & Dweck, C. S. (1988). Goals: An approach to motivation and achievement. *Journal of Personality and Social Psychology, 54*, 5–12.

Erikson, E. (1959). *Identity and the life cycle.* New York: International Universities Press.

Feick, D. L., & Rhodewalt, F. (1998). The double-edged sword of self-handicapping: Discounting, augmentation, and the protection and enhancement of self-esteem. *Motivation and Emotion, 21*, 147–163.

Geisler, R. B., & Swann, W. B. (1999). Striving for confirmation: The role of self-verification in depression. In T. Joiner & J. C. Coyne (Eds.), *The interactional nature of depression: Advances in interactional approaches* (pp. 189–217). Washington, DC: American Psychological Association.

Harter, S. (1990). Cause, correlates, and the fundamental role of global self-worth: A life-span perspective. In R. Sternberg & J. Kolligian (Eds.), *Curiosity, imagination, and play: On the development of spontaneous*

motivational processes (pp. 67–97). New Haven, CT: Yale University Press.

Higgins, E. T. (1996). The "self-digest": Self-knowledge serving self-regulatory functions. *Journal of Personality and Social Psychology, 71*, 1062–1083.

Higgins, R., Snyder, C. R., & Berglas, S. (1990). *Self-handicapping: The paradox that isn't.* New York: Plenum Press.

Hirt, E. R., Deppe, R. K., & Gordon, L. J. (1991). Self-reported versus behavioral self-handicapping: Empirical evidence for a theoretical distinction. *Journal of Personality and Social Psychology, 61*, 981–991.

Joiner, T. E., Jr., Katz, J., & Lew, A. (1999). Harbingers of depressotypic reassurance seeking: Negative life events, increased anxiety, and decreased self-esteem. *Personality and Social Psychology Bulletin, 25*, 630–637.

Joiner, T. E., Jr., Metalsky, G. I., Katz, J., & Beach, S. R. H. (1999). Depression and excessive reassurance seeking. *Psychological Inquiry, 10*, 269–278.

Jones, E. E., & Berglas, S. (1978). Control of attributions about the self through self-handicapping strategies: The appeal of alcohol and the role of underachievement. *Personality and Social Psychology Bulletin, 4*, 200–206.

Jones, E. E., & Nisbett, R. M. (1971). The actor and the observer: Divergent perception of the causes of behavior. In E. E. Jones, D. E. Kanouse, H. H. Kelley, R. E. Nisbett, S. Valins, & B. Weiner (Eds.), *Attribution: Perceiving the causes of behavior* (pp. 79–94). Morristown, NJ: General Learning Press.

Jones, E. E., & Pittman, T. (1982). Toward a general theory of strategic self-presentation. In J. Suls (Ed.), *Psychological perspectives on the self* (pp. 231–262). Hillsdale, NJ: Erlbaum.

Jones, E. E., & Rhodewalt, F. (1982). *The Self-Handicapping Scale.* Unpublished scale, Princeton University, Princeton, NJ and University of Utah, Salt Lake City.

Kelley, H. H. (1972). Attribution in social interaction. In E. E. Jones, D. F. Kanouse, H. H. Kelley, R. E. Nisbett, S. Valins, & B. Weiner (Eds.), *Attribution: Perceiving the causes of behavior* (pp. 1–26). Morristown, NJ: General Learning Press.

Kernis, M. H. (1993). The roles of stability and

level of self-esteem in psychological functioning. In R. Baumeister (Ed.), *Self-esteem: The puzzle of low self-regard* (pp. 167–182). New York: Plenum Press.

Kernis, M. H., Cornell, D. P., Sun, C. R., Berry, A., & Harlow, T. (1993). There's more to self-esteem than whether it's high or low: The importance of self-esteem stability. *Journal of Personality and Social Psychology, 65*, 1190–1204.

Kolditz, T. A., & Arkin, R. M. (1982). An impression management interpretation of the self-handicapping strategy. *Journal of Personality and Social Psychology, 43*, 492–502.

Leary, M. R., & Shepperd, J. A. (1986). Behavioral self-handicaps versus self-reported handicaps: A conceptual note. *Journal of Personality and Social Psychology, 51*, 1265–1268.

Luginbuhl, J., & Palmer, R. (1991). Impression management aspects of self-handicapping: Positive and negative effects. *Personality and Social Psychology Bulletin, 17*, 655–662.

McCrea, S. M., & Hirt, E. R. (in press). The role of ability judgments in self-handicapping. *Personality and Social Psychology Bulletin*.

Miller, D. T., & Ross, M. (1975). Self-serving biases in the attribution of causality: Fact or fiction? *Psychological Bulletin, 82*, 213–225.

Morf, C. C., & Rhodewalt, F. (1993). Narcissism and self-evaluation maintenance: Explorations in object relations. *Personality and Social Psychology Bulletin, 19*, 668–676.

Morf, C. C., & Rhodewalt, F. (in press). Unraveling the paradoxes of narcissism: A dynamic self-regulatory processing model. *Psychological Inquiry*.

Nichols, J. G. (1984). Achievement motivation: Conceptions of ability, subjective experience, task choice, and performance. *Psychological Review, 91*, 328–346.

Rhodewalt, F. (1990). Self-handicappers: Individual differences in the preference for anticipatory self-protective acts. In R. Higgins, C. R. Snyder, & S. Berglas (Eds.), *Self-handicapping: The paradox that isn't* (pp. 69–106). New York: Plenum Press.

Rhodewalt, F. (1994). Conceptions of ability, achievement goals and individual differences in self-handicapping behavior: On the application of implicit theories. *Journal of Personality, 62*, 67–85.

Rhodewalt, F., & Fairfield, M. (1991). Claimed self-handicaps and the self-handicapper: The relation of reduction in intended effort to performance. *Journal of Research in Personality, 25*, 402–417.

Rhodewalt, F., & Hill, S. K. (1995). Self-handicapping in the classroom: The effects of claimed self-handicaps in responses to academic failure. *Basic and Applied Social Psychology, 16*, 397–416.

Rhodewalt, F., Morf, C., Hazlett, S., & Fairfield, M. (1991). Self-handicapping: The role of discounting and augmentation in the preservation of self-esteem. *Journal of Personality and Social Psychology, 61*, 121–131.

Rhodewalt, F., Sanbonmatsu, D., Feick, D., Tschanz, B., & Waller, A. (1995). Self-handicapping and interpersonal trade-offs: The effects of claimed self-handicaps on observers' performance evaluations and feedback. *Personality and Social Psychology Bulletin, 21*, 1042–1050.

Rhodewalt, F., & Tragakis, M. (in press). Self-handicapping and school: On academic self-concept and self-protective behavior. In J. Aronson & D. Cordova (Eds.), *Improving academic achievement: Impact of psychological factors*. New York: Academic Press.

Rogers, C. R. (1961). *On becoming a person*. Boston: Houghton Mifflin.

Smith, D. S., & Strube, M. J. (1991). Self-protective tendencies as moderators of self-handicapping impressions. *Basic and Applied Social Psychology, 12*, 63–80.

Snyder, C. R., & Smith, T. W. (1982). Symptoms as self-handicapping strategies: The virtues of old wine in a new bottle. In G. Weary & H. L. Mirels (Eds.), *Integration of clinical and social psychology* (pp. 104–127). New York: Oxford University Press.

Snyder, M. L., & Wicklund. (1981). Attribute ambiguity. In J. H. Harvey, W. Ickes, & R. F. Kidd (Eds.), *New directs in attribution research* (Vol. 3, pp. 197–221). Hillsdale, NJ: Erlbaum.

Swann, W. B. (1983). Self-verification: Bringing social reality into harmony with the self. In J. Suls & A. Greenwald (Eds.), *Psychological perspectives on the self* (Vol. 2, pp. 33–66). Hillsdale, NJ: Erlbaum.

Swann, W. B. (1985). The self as architect of

social reality. In B. Schlenker (Ed.), *The self and social life* (pp. 100–125). New York: McGraw-Hill.

Swann, W. B., & Ely, R. (1984). The battle of wills: Self-verification versus behavioral confirmation. *Journal of Personality and Social Psychology, 46,* 1287–1302.

Swann, W. B., Griffin, J. J., Predmore, S. C., & Gaines, B. (1987). The cognitive-affective crossfire: When self-consistency confronts self-enhancement. *Journal of Personality and Social Psychology, 52,* 881–889.

Swann, W. B., Hixon, J. G., & de la Ronde, C. (1992). Embracing the bitter "truth": Negative self-concepts and marital commitment. *Psychological Science, 3,* 118–121.

Swann, W. B., & Schroeder, D. G. (1995). The search for beauty and truth: A framework for understanding reactions to evaluations. *Personality and Social Psychology Bulletin, 21,* 1307–1318.

Swann, W. B., Wenzlaff, R., Krull, D., & Pelham, B. (1992). Allure of negative feedback: Self-verification strivings among depressed persons. *Journal of Abnormal Psychology, 101,* 293–306.

Tesser, A. (1988). Toward a self-evaluation maintenance model of social behavior. In L. Berkowitz (Ed.), *Advances in experimental social psychology* (Vol. 21, pp. 181–227). New York: Academic Press.

Tesser, A. (2000). On the confluence of self-esteem maintenance mechanisms. *Personality and Social Psychology Review, 4,* 290–299.

Tice, D. (1991). Esteem protection or enhancement?: Self-handicapping motives and attributions differ by trait self-esteem. *Journal of Personality and Social Psychology, 60,* 711–725.

Weary, G. B. (1978). Self-serving biases in the attribution process: A re-examination of the fact or fiction question. *Journal of Personality and Social Psychology, 36,* 56–71.

Weiner, B. (1985). An attributional theory of achievement motivation and emotion. *Psychological Review, 92,* 548–573.

Zuckerman, M., Kieffer, S., & Knee, C. R. (1998). Consequences of self-handicapping: Effects on coping, academic performance, and adjustment. *Journal of Personality and Social Psychology, 74,* 1619–1628.

PART II

INTERPERSONAL AND RELATIONAL ASPECTS OF THE SELF

8

The Interpersonal Basis of Self-Esteem
Death, Devaluation, or Deference?

MARK LEARY

INTRODUCTION

*T*heorists have recognized for many years that self-esteem is strongly affected by how people believe they are perceived and evaluated by others (Cooley, 1902; James, 1890), but the source of the relationship between interpersonal appraisals and self-esteem has been a matter of debate. In part, the controversy stems from the fact that self-esteem has traditionally been conceptualized as a personal self-evaluation, making it difficult to explain precisely why people's private self-views should be so heavily influenced by what other people think of them.

For example, James' (1890) well-known formula describing self-esteem as the ratio of one's successes to one's pretensions conceptualizes self-esteem as an individual's private assessment of how well he/she is doing in domains that

---

I wish to thank Catherine Cottrell, Jennifer Saltzman, Richard Bednarski, and Misha Phillips for their work on the unpublished research that is described in this chapter.

Address for correspondence: Mark R. Leary, Department of Psychology, Wake Forest University, Box 7778, Reynolds Station, Winston-Salem, NC 27109, USA. E-mail: leary@wfu.edu

are personally important. When self-esteem attracted the attention of humanistic psychologists in the middle of the twentieth century, self-esteem became tied to inner authenticity. For example, Rogers (1959) proposed that true self-esteem arises when people live congruently with their deepest "organismic" values. This view was echoed more recently by Deci and Ryan (1985) who distinguished between true self-esteem (which arises when people behave autonomously in ways that are consistent with their intrinsic or core self) and contingent self-esteem (which depends on the person meeting certain social standards or expectations). Bednar, Wells, and Peterson (1989) offered a similar perspective when they suggested that true self-esteem results when people cope effectively with psychological threats and does not fundamentally depend on approbation from others. These and other intrapersonal perspectives do not deny that self-esteem is sometimes affected by other people's evaluations of the individual but view the effects of interpersonal evaluations on self-esteem as reflecting either a secondary source of self-evaluative information or an unhealthy reliance on the approval of other people.

In contrast to these intrapersonal perspectives, other theorists have conceptualized self-esteem in explicitly interpersonal terms, arguing that the self is an inherently social construction that arises in the context of interpersonal relations (Cooley, 1902; Mead, 1934). If we begin with the assumption that the self is inherently social, it is then easy to explain why people's feelings about themselves are strongly influenced by how they believe others evaluate them.

Theorists have conceptualized the interpersonal nature of self-esteem in a variety of ways, three of which are germane to this chapter. Specifically, this chapter offers critical reviews of three interpersonal perspectives on self-esteem—terror management theory, sociometer theory, and dominance theory. A brief overview of each theory will be offered, existing evidence reviewed, and new, often unpublished data relevant to each theory presented. The chapter will conclude with an attempt to integrate the insights of these three perspectives regarding the interpersonal nature of self-esteem.

TERROR MANAGEMENT THEORY

Terror management theory (TMT; Greenberg, Pyszczynski, & Solomon, 1986; Solomon, Greenberg, & Pyszczynski, 1991) offers an intriguing, albeit controversial perspective on self-esteem based on the work of Becker (1971, 1973). According to the theory, the continual possibility of experiencing painful and tragic events (death being the ultimate such occurrence) is a constant source of anxiety. To minimize the perpetual terror that results from awareness of one's fragility and mortality in a dangerous and unpredictable world, people adopt views of themselves and of the world that attenuate their fears.

Central to this anxiety-buffering process are individuals' beliefs that they meet the social standards by which people are judged to be worthwhile and valuable. All cultures specify what it means to be a "good" person and promise either symbolic or literal immortality to those who meet standards of goodness. During development, children learn to associate meeting cultural standards with parental support, thereby establishing a link between living up to cultural standards (and the accompanying experience of self-esteem) and a sense of personal security. Self-esteem has an interpersonal basis, according to TMT, because social approval typically reflects the degree to which one is meeting cultural standards.

Studies have supported many key predictions of TMT, particularly the notion that people endorse cultural standards more strongly when death is salient to them. Because cultural standards provide the basis for self-esteem and felt security, people punish those who violate such standards when mortality is salient (Greenberg et al., 1990; Greenberg, Simon, Pyszczynski, Solomon, & Chatel, 1992; Rosenblatt, Greenberg, Solomon, Pyszcynski, & Lyon, 1989). Furthermore, evidence supports the proposition that events that raise self-esteem lower anxiety, not only about death but about other threatening events as well (Greenberg, Solomon, et al., 1992).

Self-Esteem and Anxiety about Death

One untested implication of TMT is that people with low trait self-esteem should be more anxious about death than people with high self-esteem. People with high self-esteem should presumably be buffered against fear of death because meeting cultural standards (and the consequent feelings of self-esteem) is associated with security. In contrast, people with low self-esteem should worry more about death because they are less likely to believe they have met the cultural standards that promise safety, if not immortality.

This prediction stands in contrast to an equally plausible position, however, namely that people with low self-esteem are *less* afraid of dying than those with high self-esteem. Research shows that low self-esteem and self-blame are risk factors for suicide (Maris, 1981; Neuringer, 1974), suggesting that people with low self-esteem may be less worried about dying than people who value themselves highly. One should be more worried about losing something the more valued it is, and this should be true whether it is a personal possession or one's own life. One study that examined the relationship between self-esteem and fear of death found none (Feifel & Nagy, 1981), which led us to explore the relationship between self-esteem and fear of death more closely.

Participants completed the Revised Death Anxiety Scale (RDAS; Thorsen & Powell, 1992), which assesses four sources of death anxiety: no longer existing, helplessness, concerns about what happens after death, and pain. They also completed two measures of trait self-esteem—the self-regard subscale of the Self-Rating Scale (Fleming & Courtney, 1984) and the self-feelings adjectives

TABLE 8.1. Correlations between Trait Self-Esteem and
Subscales of the RDAS

RDAS Subscale	Alpha	Self-Feelings	Self-Regard
Nonexistence	.92	−.11	−.14
Loss of control	.58	−.18°	−.20°
After-death events	.66	−.11	−.18°
Pain	.71	−.20°	−.28°°
Total RDAS Score	.90	−.17°	−.22°

Note. °p < .05; °°p < .01; Cronbach's alpha coefficient was .87 for the self-feelings measure and .80 for the self-regard scale.

identified by McFarland and Ross (1982) (e.g., competent, inadequate, confident, worthless)—and a measure of anxiety.

Table 8.1 presents correlations between the two self-esteem measures and the four subscales of the RDAS. As can be seen, both self-esteem measures correlated weakly with fears involving loss of control and pain, and with the total RDAS score. In addition, the self-regard scale correlated weakly with concerns about what will happen after death.

Because research shows that trait self-esteem is related to anxiety (Barlow, 1988), these correlations may be due to participants' anxiety rather than their self-esteem. To test this possibility, partial correlations were calculated between the two self-esteem measures and the RDAS scores while controlling for anxiety. All partial correlations were nonsignificant ($-.14 < rs < .11$). In contrast, when self-esteem was partialed out of the relationship between anxiety and death-related fears, all correlations remained statistically significant, $rs > .17$. The partial correlations suggest that the correlations between self-esteem and death anxiety may be an artifact of the relationship between self-esteem and anxiety. Persons low in self-esteem worry more about nearly everything, including death.

Although trait self-esteem was negatively related to certain sources of death anxiety (as TMT predicts), self-esteem was not related to fears about nonexistence, which TMT suggests should show the strongest relationship to self-esteem. As Solomon, Greenberg, and Pyszczynski (1991) stated, "whenever we refer to the terror of death, we do not mean the intense fear of death per se, but rather of death as *absolute annihilation*" (p. 96, italics in original). Yet, no relationship between self-esteem and fear of nonexistence was found.

Self-Esteem and Domains of Death Anxiety

Although the RDAS has demonstrated reliability and validity as a measure of death anxiety (Thorsen & Powell, 1992), we wondered whether its subscales tap all of the major reasons that people fear death. For example, many people fear dying because they are distressed about leaving loved ones or about the bereavement of those they leave behind (Fiefel & Nagy, 1981), but the RDAS does not include interpersonal concerns such as these. If the relationship between self-esteem and death anxiety is mediated by fears not included on the RDAS, we might not detect the correlation that TMT predicts.

To broadly sample fears about death, 76 undergraduate students were asked to write down the primary reason they were bothered by thoughts of their own deaths. Two researchers sorted respondents' answers, identifying six distinct categories of death-related fears: uncertainty about what will happen after death, separation from loved ones, unfulfilled goals, the distress of other people, nonexistence, and painful dying. A questionnaire based on these categories was then administered to 122 participants, who rated the degree to which each of the six factors bother them when they think about their own death: (a) uncertainty about what, if anything, will happen to you after you die, (b) being separated from the friends and family you leave behind, (c) the things you haven't done and the goals you haven't reached, (d) how upset and distressed other people will feel about your death, (e) the fact that you will no longer exist, and (f) the pain you may experience while dying. Participants also rated how they generally feel about themselves on self-feelings and anxiety items (McFarland & Ross, 1982), and completed the self-regard subscale of the Self-Rating Scale (Fleming & Courtney, 1984).

Correlations between self-esteem and fears of death are shown in Table 8.2. Self-esteem was consistently related only to concerns regarding uncertainty about what will happen after death. Neither self-esteem measure correlated with concerns about nonexistence—the aspect of death specifically implicated by TMT. Overall, the multiple correlation between each of the measures of self-esteem and the set of six death fears was only .18 for self-feelings and .22 for self-regard. Clearly, trait self-esteem accounts for relatively little variance in anxiety about death.

Because the measures of self-esteem and anxiety correlated highly ($-.58 < rs < -.70$), we again calculated the partial correlation between each self-esteem measure and the six facets of death anxiety while partialing out general anxiety

TABLE 8.2. Correlations between Trait Self-Esteem and Domains of Death Anxiety

Domain of Death Anxiety	Self-Feelings	Self-Regard
Uncertainty about what happens after death	−.17°	−.18°
Being separated from loved ones	−.06	−.04
Things not done; goals not reached	−.03	−.11
Other people's distress	−.08	−.06
No longer existing	−.09	−.13
Possible pain while dying	−.08	−.12
Overall	−.09	.01

Note. °$p < .05$

scores. With anxiety removed, none of the correlations in Table 8.2 remained statistically significant. In contrast, removing self-esteem had virtually no effect on the magnitude of the correlations between anxiety and fear of uncertainty. As in the earlier study, self-esteem showed only weak relationships to fears of death, and partial correlations suggested that these relationships were attributable to anxiety rather than self-esteem per se.

Trait Self-Esteem and Reactions to Mortality Salience

TMT suggests that high self-esteem people should be less affected by thinking about death than low self-esteem people because self-esteem buffers them against death-related anxiety. To test this prediction, participants completed two measures of trait self-esteem, then reported to an experiment several weeks later where they were randomly assigned to write one of three essays. In the mortality-salient condition, participants were instructed to write an essay about their own death, imagining "what it will be like when you die. Think about how you will feel, what you will think, what you will experience as you are dying." In the rejection-salient condition, participants were asked to write about being rejected by someone they care about: "Imagine what it will be like to be rejected by a romantic partner, close friend, or family member, or ostracized by a group." Participants in the control condition wrote about what it will be like to retire after many years of working. After writing the essay, participants rated their anxiety on eight items (e.g., worried, safe, secure).

The sum of participants' anxiety ratings were analyzed with hierarchical multiple regression analyses that used essay condition (dummy-coded), pretest self-esteem scores, and their interaction as predictors. Both of the self-esteem measures yielded identical results—a significant main effect of self-esteem (showing that self-esteem predicted anxiety) and a nearly-significant ($p < .06$) interaction of essay condition by self-esteem. The nature of this interaction can be seen by examining the correlations between self-esteem and anxiety separately for each essay condition in Table 8.3. Scores on the self-esteem measures were not significantly correlated with anxiety when participants wrote about death or retirement. However, self-esteem scores and anxiety were inversely correlated ($rs > -.73$) when participants wrote about rejection, suggesting that

TABLE 8.3. Correlations between Trait Self-Esteem and Anxiety in Each Experimental Condition

	Essay Condition		
	Control	Death	Rejection
Self-Feelings	.02	−.19	−.73°
Self-Regard	−.08	−.30	−.78°

Note. °$p < .001$

trait self-esteem moderated reactions to imagined rejection, a finding consistent with the idea that self-esteem monitors social acceptance and rejection (Leary & Downs, 1995). Although it is possible that the experimental manipulation was not strong enough to induce anxiety about death, the essay-writing paradigm has demonstrated terror-management effects in many previous studies (e.g., Greenberg et al., 1990). Furthermore, parallel instructions to write about rejection had different effects depending on participants' self-esteem.

Self-Esteem and Death Concerns After Ego-Threat

The results of the three studies just described showed a negligible relationship between self-esteem and fear of death. Furthermore, when correlations were obtained, they tended to involve uncertainty or coping rather than fears of nonexistence, and were mediated by anxiety.

If high self-esteem buffers people against death-related anxiety, events that threaten self-esteem should increase concerns about death (because the esteem-based anxiety buffer is compromised), whereas events that increase self-esteem should lower them. Along these lines, Greenberg, Solomon, et al. (1992) found that participants who received positive feedback about themselves expressed less anxiety about watching a videotape of death-related scenes (such as an autopsy and an electrocution) than participants who received neutral feedback.

In a study that examined this hypothesis using a real threat to self-esteem, 122 students were tested on the day that they received grades on a midterm exam in a psychology course. After the instructor distributed students' scored tests, a questionnaire booklet was distributed. Participants were led to imagine vividly two positive and two negative events: their own death, graduating from college, rejection by another person, and receiving an honor or award. (The order of these four situations was counterbalanced.) After imagining each situation, participants rated how the hypothetical situation made them feel. Participants also indicated the score they had expected to obtain on the exam and the minimum score with which they would have been satisfied, and completed a measure of state self-esteem.

Correlations between self-esteem and feelings after imagining death, rejection, and graduation were all nonsignificant ($-.08 < rs < -.11$). Only feelings about being honored correlated with self-esteem ($r = -.20, p < .05$). (Perhaps persons with lower self-esteem are less accustomed to being honored and, thus, experience more positive affect in such situations.) Again, no support was obtained for a link between self-esteem and death-related anxiety.

To test the possibility that self-esteem and feelings about death are related only in the face of an esteem-threatening event, two indices of success versus failure were calculated. One involved the difference between the score participants expected on the exam and the score they obtained, and the other involved the difference between the minimum score with which participants would have been satisfied and the score they earned. In both cases, a positive difference reflected subjective failure, whereas a negative difference indicated subjective success. Both indices correlated highly with self-feelings ($r = -.39$ with the expected–obtained difference; $r = -.60$ with minimum-obtained difference), but neither index of subjective success-failure correlated with anxiety after imagining one's death. Thus, this study obtained no evidence of a link between self-esteem and feelings about death either in general or after contemplating one's own death. Further, subjective failure on the test was also unrelated to death anxiety.

Summary and Critique

Taken together, these four studies provide little support for a relationship between self-esteem and fear of death. A few negative correlations between self-esteem and death-related anxiety were obtained, but the effects involved fears stemming from uncertainty, loss of control, and pain rather than from death per se. Furthermore, the magnitude of the relationships were small, and analyses suggested that they were mediated by anxiety. In brief, the failure to obtain notable negative correlations between self-esteem and anxiety about death fails to support the hypothesis that high self-esteem buffers people against fears of death. Although each of the studies reported here has shortcomings, the failure to detect the predicted effect across four different studies using different methods and measures provides converging evidence that high self-esteem neither attenuates nor increases the fear of dying. Furthermore, the fact that all studies showed self-esteem to be related to other measures makes it unlikely that the null findings resulted from problems with the methods or measures used. It is also noteworthy that other research has failed to support the prediction that thinking about mortality leads people to bolster their self-esteem (Sowards, Moniz, & Harris, 1991). I wish to stress that these data are relevant only to the self-esteem hypothesis of TMT and do not in any way disconfirm other aspects of the theory. As noted, considerable research has supported the effects of mortality salience on judgments of people who violate cultural standards.

SOCIOMETER THEORY

Sociometer theory (Leary, 1999; Leary & Baumeister, 2000; Leary & Downs, 1995) offers an alternative interpersonal explanation of self-esteem, proposing that self-esteem responds to other people's evaluations because the self-esteem system monitors the degree to which other people accept versus reject the individual. According to sociometer theory, the system monitors the social environment for cues indicating low or declining relational evaluation (e.g., disinterest, dislike, rejection) and warns the individual via lowered self-esteem when such cues are detected. Thus, events that lower self-esteem do so because they indicate low or declining acceptance. Furthermore, the theory suggests that people are not motivated to increase their self-esteem per se as has been typically assumed (see, for example, Hirt & McCrea, this volume), but rather seek to increase their relational value and social acceptance. Self-esteem is simply the meter they use to gauge their success in doing so.

A great deal of existing research is consistent with sociometer theory. For example, self-esteem responds strongly to social acceptance and rejection, public events affect self-esteem more strongly than private events (presumably because public events have greater implications for acceptance and rejection), the primary dimensions of self-esteem reflect attributes that are relevant to one's relational value, the importance people place on various dimensions of self-esteem is based on the importance that they think significant others place on them, and individual differences in self-esteem are related to the degree to which people believe that they are accepted versus rejected by other people (for a review, see Leary & Baumeister, 2000).

Acceptance, Rejection, and State Self-Esteem

Interpersonal rejection has profound effects on people's thoughts, emotions, and behavior (see Baumeister et al., this volume; Tice et al., this volume.) Our own research shows that individuals' feelings about themselves vary systematically as a function of even minor changes in other people's appraisals of them. Leary, Tambor, Terdal, and Downs (1995, Study 3) gave participants bogus feedback indicating that they were either included or excluded as members of a laboratory group and that their membership was based either on a random selection or a vote of the other group members. Participants who thought they were excluded on the basis of a group vote subsequently showed notably lower state self-esteem than the other conditions. A second study (Leary et al., 1995, Study 4) conceptually replicated this finding by showing that participants who believed that another individual was ambivalent about interacting with them had lower state self-esteem than those who thought the other person wanted to interact with them.

Leary, Haupt, Strausser, and Chokel (1998, Study 4) provided participants with ongoing bogus feedback from another individual and measured state self-esteem "online" by having participants move a computer mouse to indicate how they were feeling about themselves in real time. State self-esteem increased as a function of feedback that connoted social acceptance and declined as a function of feedback that connoted rejection. In fact, 77% of the reliable variance in state self-esteem could be accounted for by the degree to which the interpersonal feedback connoted acceptance versus rejection. Interestingly, the relationship between rejection–acceptance feedback and state self-esteem was not strictly linear, taking an ogival function that flattened at the bottom and top of the curve. This ogival pattern, which was replicated in three other studies (Leary et al., 1998), suggests that self-esteem is most responsive to acceptance–rejection feedback in the middle range and less so at the extremes.

In another study (Leary et al., 1995, Study 2), participants wrote essays about a recent occasion on which they felt accepted or rejected, then answered questions regarding how excluded they felt in the situation and how they had felt about themselves at the time. Results showed that the more excluded that participants felt in the situation, the worse they felt about themselves. Ratings of perceived exclusion correlated very highly (between -.68 and -.92, depending on condition) with state self-esteem.

Esteem-Threatening Events

From the standpoint of sociometer theory, events that threaten self-esteem have their effects not because they challenge some private sense of self but rather because they raise the specter of relational devaluation and rejection. Leary et al. (1995, Study 1) provided direct evidence that events that lower self-esteem are those that people assume might lead others to reject them. Participants were given a list of behaviors that varied in social desirability, such as "I donated blood," "I lost my temper," and "I cheated on my boyfriend or girlfriend." They went through the list once and indicated how they thought other people would react toward them if they performed each behavior (1 = many people would reject or avoid me; 5 = many people would accept or include me). Later, they went through the list again and indicated on bipolar adjective scales how they would personally feel about themselves (e.g., good–bad, valuable–worthless) if they performed each behavior. The canonical correlation between participants' ratings of others' reactions vis-a-vis social inclusion–exclusion and their feelings about themselves was .70, and the order of the two sets of ratings was virtually identical. These data suggest that how people feel about themselves (i.e., their state self-esteem) after behaving in particular ways is a function of how they think others will react.

Individual Differences in Trait Self-Esteem

Sociometer theory predicts that individual differences in trait self-esteem should be predicted by how accepted people generally feel they are (Leary & Baumeister, 2000). In essence, trait self-esteem may be conceptualized as the resting position of the sociometer in the absence of explicit social feedback. In support of this idea, Leary et al. (1995, Study 5) found that two separate measures of trait self-esteem each correlated in excess of .50 with the degree to which respondents felt that other people valued and accepted them (see also Leary, Cottrell, & Phillips, in press). In an experimental study, Haupt and Leary

(1997) showed that people with low self-esteem assume that other people whom they have not yet met will be more likely to reject them than people with high self-esteem.

MacDonald, Saltzman, and Leary (2001) had participants complete a measure of trait self-esteem, rate themselves in three domains (competence, appearance, social skill), and indicate how important each domain was for social approval or disapproval. In all three domains, participants who rated themselves positively and who believed that the domain was important in affecting social approval or disapproval had higher self-esteem than those who did not believe the domain was important in influencing approval and acceptance. Thus, trait self-esteem was a function of believing that one possessed attributes that lead to approval and acceptance by other people.

Summary and Critique

In general, support for sociometer theory is quite strong. Not only have studies designed to test the theory's predictions generally supported it, but the theory has been able to explain and integrate much of the existing literature on self-esteem (Leary & Baumeister, 2000). Although there seems little doubt that self-esteem is exquisitely sensitive to events that connote relational devaluation and that people act as if they use self-esteem to gauge their social acceptability, the question may be raised of whether self-esteem is "only" a sociometer. Is self-esteem affected only by events with real or imagined implications for acceptance and rejection, or do other things influence self-esteem as well? When people appear to be motivated to protect or enhance their self-esteem, are they always actually seeking to increase social acceptance or avoid rejection? Although the strong version of sociometer theory maintains that all self-esteem phenomena are based on acceptance and rejection (or, possibly, are the result of such processes that have become functionally autonomous), we should be open to the possibility that self-esteem may serve other interpersonal functions (Kirkpatrick & Ellis, 2001).

DOMINANCE THEORY

An often overlooked interpersonal perspective on self-esteem is offered by dominance theory (Barkow, 1975a, 1975b, 1980). Like sociometer theory, dominance theory assumes that self-esteem monitors aspects of the social environment. However, whereas sociometer theory conceptualizes self-esteem as a monitor of relational value, dominance theory suggests that the self-esteem system evolved to monitor dominance (Barkow, 1980). According to Barkow (1975a, p. 557), "natural selection transformed primate social dominance into human self-esteem. . . . " Because dominance was associated with increased reproductive success in the ancestral environment, systems evolved to monitor one's social standing and to motivate behaviors that increase one's dominance. According to the theory, self-esteem reflects the amount of attention, deference, and respect that one receives from other people. Although the dominance hypothesis has not attracted much research attention, evidence shows that perceptions of one's social influence and dominance correlate moderately with self-esteem as the theory predicts (Hamilton, 1971; Heaven, 1986; Raskin, Novacek, & Hogan, 1991).

Deconfounding Dominance and Acceptance

One difficulty in assessing the dominance hypothesis involves the fact that dominance and acceptance are typically confounded in everyday life. In general, people who are deferred to and selected for positions of leadership are likely to feel more accepted than those who are never dominant or influential within their social groups. At the same time, people who feel accepted and valued may feel dominant and influential because they exercise referent power based on their likeability.

To disentangle the natural confound between acceptance and dominance, we devised an experimental paradigm in which participants received independent feedback regarding the degree to which other people desired them as a member and as a leader of a group (Studies 1 & 2, Leary et al., 2001). After participants completed a background questionnaire, copies of their answers were ostensibly given to four other participants. Thus, each participant received what he/she believed were copies of one another's personal information questionnaires in order to judge each person's membership and leadership qualities.

Each participant then rated the other four participants by allotting eight "membership points" to indicate the degree to which he/she desired each other participant as a member of the group. Participants were told to divide these eight points among the other four people in any proportion they desired. Similarly, each participant was given eight "leadership points" that were to be assigned to the other four people to indicate the degree to which the participant desired each other participant as a leader of the group.

When the ratings were completed, the researcher ostensibly calculated the total membership and leadership points that each participant received and gave the participants false feedback regarding the number of membership and leadership points that they had been awarded by the other participants. Although each participant logically could receive between 0 points (if none of the other participants gave the person any points) and 32 points (if all of the four other participants gave the person the maximum of 8 points), participants received between 2 and 14 points to make the feedback plausible. The feedback form showed the points that all five group members ostensibly received, thereby allowing them to easily understand their relative standings on the membership and leadership dimensions. Each participant received either a low or high number of points on both the membership and leadership ratings, and we then used five different measures to assess participants' feelings about themselves.

As expected, high membership feedback not only made participants feel accepted but also made them feel influential, and high leadership feedback not only increased perceptions of dominance and influence but also led participants to feel accepted. Given that the two feedback manipulations affected perceptions of both acceptance and dominance, it is not surprising that the measures of self-esteem revealed significant effects of both membership and leadership feedback.

Partialing out participants' ratings of how accepted they felt eliminated the membership effect, and partialing out how influential they felt eliminated the leadership effect. But, in each case, the other effect remained significant, suggesting that neither perceived acceptance nor perceived dominance uniquely accounted for the effects. Thus, these results provide support for both sociometer and dominance theories, although the membership (i.e., acceptance) feedback showed stronger independent effects than the leadership (i.e., dominance) feedback.

Dominance and Trait Self-Esteem

If self-esteem reflects perceived dominance as dominance theory maintains, individual differences in self-esteem should be strongly related to perceptions of dominance and influence, and research supports this hypothesis (Hamilton, 1971; Heaven, 1986; Raskin et al., 1991). However, again, the natural confound between perceived dominance and perceived acceptance makes it necessary to partial out perceived acceptance in order to discern the unique relationship between perceived dominance and self-esteem.

In a study designed to test predictions of dominance theory and sociometer theory regarding the basis of trait self-esteem (Study 3, Leary et al., 2001), 180 undergraduate students completed multiple measures of perceived dominance, perceived acceptance, and trait self-esteem. Results showed that both perceived dominance and perceived acceptance accounted for unique variance in trait self-esteem, but that perceived acceptance consistently accounted for substantially more variance in self-esteem than perceived dominance. Whereas perceived acceptance accounted for between 9% and 21% of the unique variance in trait self-esteem (depending on the analysis), perceived dominance accounted for between 0% and 5% of the unique variance. (Together, perceived acceptance and perceived dominance accounted for between 40% and 50% of the variance in trait self-esteem.) In addition, whereas the degree to which participants felt valued by particular people in their lives consistently predicted trait self-esteem, the degree to which participants thought those individuals perceived them as influential and dominant was unrelated to their self-esteem.

Summary and Critique

Overall, the data suggest that perceived dominance may account for unique variance in self-esteem as dominance theory predicts. Even with perceived acceptance partialed out, perceived dominance predicted both state and trait self-esteem. If dominance theory has a weakness, it is that it does not capture the full range of situations that affect self-esteem. Although dominance is by no means unimportant in interpersonal relations, human groups are characterized less by dominance hierarchies than the nonhuman primates that provided the model for the theory. Human self-esteem appears to be affected by many events that do not involve dominance. Thus, it seems unlikely that dominance tells the entire story of self-esteem.

CONCLUSIONS

Despite their differences, terror management, sociometer, and dominance theories concur that self-esteem is inherently tied to interpersonal processes and, thus, is understandably affected by interpersonal events, other people's appraisals, and the individual's perceptions of his/her personal characteristics. Of the three, terror management theory's perspective on self-esteem has the least support. As noted earlier, this does not suggest that people's concerns about their deaths do not have profound effects on their perceptions of other people and themselves, but rather that self-esteem per se does not seem to be uniquely connected to death anxiety or serve as a special buffer against it (except in as much as it is related to anxiety more generally). In the one head-to-head test against sociometer theory, self-esteem was related to anxiety involved with thinking about rejection but not about death.

Dominance theory fares somewhat better. Unique variance in state self-esteem can be predicted by one's perceived dominance in a particular context, and trait self-esteem is related to one's general sense of being dominant and influential. Even so, head-to-head competition continually showed that self-esteem was more strongly related to perceived acceptance than dominance, thus suggesting that acceptance may be more central to self-esteem than dominance.

The original statements of sociometer and dominance theory (e.g., Barkow, 1975a, 1980; Leary & Downs, 1995) suggest two different interpersonal bases for self-esteem—one involving acceptance and the other involving dominance. To the extent that being accepted and being dominant both lead to beneficial outcomes, it is certainly possible that self-esteem serves to monitor and respond to interpersonal outcomes vis-a-vis both acceptance and dominance. In fact, taking the evolutionary perspectives advanced by both Barkow (1975a) and Leary and Downs (1995; see also Kirkpatrick & Ellis, 2001), one could see how both acceptance and dominance would have increased individuals' chances of survival and reproduction in the ancestral environment, possibly leading to psychological mechanisms that track these important outcomes.

However, the effects of acceptance and dominance on self-esteem might be mediated by a single process. Perhaps self-esteem monitors not acceptance or dominance per se but rather the individual's *social value* to other people. The important consideration may not be whether the person is accepted or dominant, but rather whether he/she is regarded as a valued group member or relational partner (friend, mate, coalition member, or whatever). People may be relationally valued for many reasons. They may be friendly and likeable, thereby engendering affection and acceptance based on their social desirability. Alternatively, they may emerge as central, dominant members of a social group, thereby making themselves valued by virtue of their leadership ability, strength, influence, or effectiveness. People may also be valued because they are competent at important tasks, or because they promote cooperation and cohesiveness among group members. In each instance, the individual would be relationally valued by other people, albeit for different reasons. Perhaps sociometer theory and dominance theory converge in a common process for monitoring relational value.

Along these lines, Leary and Baumeister (2000) suggested that "self-esteem serves as a subjective monitor of one's relational evaluation—the degree to which other people regard their relationships with the individual to be valuable, important, or close" (p. 9). Importantly, relational value may go beyond considerations other than simply whether the individual is liked and accepted but that nonetheless make the person eligible for desired social outcomes. Believing that one possesses attributes that lead one to be valued by others will result in higher self-esteem than believing that one does not possess such attributes (or, worse, believing that one's characteristics are likely to lead to relational devaluation).

At this point, the choice between a model that posits two distinct processes (acceptance and dominance) versus a single process that subsumes social acceptance and dominance (relational value) is a matter of preference. The one-process model has the benefit of parsimony to recommend it, but future research is needed to determine whether the effects of both acceptance and dominance on self-esteem are mediated by an individual's perception of his/her relational value.

REFERENCES

Barkow, J. H. (1975a). Prestige and culture: A biosocial interpretation. *Current Anthropology, 16,* 553–562.

Barkow, J. H. (1975b). Reply. *Current Anthropology, 16,* 569–571.

Barkow, J. H. (1980). Pretige and self-esteem: A biosocial interpretation. In D. R. Omark, F. F. Strayer, & D. G. Freedman (Eds.), *Dominance relations: An ethological view of human conflict and social interaction* (pp.

319–332). New York: Garland STPM Press.

Barlow, D. H. (1988). *Anxiety and its disorders: The nature and treatment of anxiety and panic*. New York: Guilford.

Becker, E. (1971). *The birth and death of meaning*. New York: Free Press.

Becker, E. (1973). *The denial of death*. New York: Free Press.

Bednar, R. L., Wells, M. G., & Peterson, S. R. (1989). *Self-esteem: Paradoxes and innovations in clinical theory and practice*. Washington, DC: American Psychological Association.

Cooley, C. H. (1902). *Human nature and the social order*. New York: Scribner.

Deci, E. L., & Ryan, R. M. (1995). Human autonomy: The basis for true self-esteem. In M. H. Kernis (Ed.), *Efficacy, agency, and self-esteem* (pp. 31–49). New York: Plenum Press.

Feifel, H., & Branscomb, A. B. (1973). Who's afraid of death? *Journal of Abnormal Psychology, 81*, 82–88.

Feifel, H., & Nagy, V. T. (1981). Another look at fear of death. *Journal of Consulting and Clinical Psychology, 49*, 278–286.

Fleming, J. S., & Courtney, B. E. (1984). The dimensionality of self-esteem: II. Hierarchical facet model for revised measurement scales. *Journal of Personality and Social Psychology, 46*, 404–421.

Greenberg, J., Pysczynski, T., & Solomon, S. (1986). The causes and consequences of a need for self-esteem: A terror management theory. In R. F. Baumeister (Ed.), *Public self and private self* (pp. 189–212). New York: Springer-Verlag.

Greenberg, J., Pyszczynski, T., Solomon, S., Rosenblatt, A., Veeder, M., Kirkland, S., et al. (1990). Evidence for terror management theory II: The effects of mortality salience on reactions to those who threaten or bolster the cultural worldview. *Journal of Personality and Social Psychology, 58*, 308–318.

Greenberg, J., Simon, L., Pyszczynski, T., Solomon, S., & Chatel, D. (1992). Terror management and tolerance: Does mortality salience always intensify negative reactions to others who threaten one's worldview? *Journal of Personality and Social Psychology, 63*, 212–220.

Greenberg, J., Solomon, S., Pyszczynski, T., Rosenblatt, A., Burling, J., Lyon, D., et al. (1992). Why do people need self-esteem? Converging evidence that self-esteem serves an anxiety-buffering function. *Journal of Personality and Social Psychology, 63*, 913–922.

Hamilton, D. L. (1971). A comparative study of five methods of assessing self-esteem, dominance, and dogmatism. *Educational and Psychological Measurement, 31*, 441–452.

Haupt, A., & Leary, M. R. (1997). The appeal of worthless groups: Moderating effects of trait self-esteem. *Group Dynamics: Theory, Research, and Practice, 1*, 124–132.

Heaven, P. C. (1986). Authoritarianism, directiveness, and self-esteem revisited: A cross-cultural analysis. *Personality and Individual Differences, 7*, 225–228.

James, W. (1890). *Principles of psychology*. New York: Dover.

Kirkpatrick, L. A., & Ellis, B. J. (2001). Evolutionary perspectives on self-evaluation and self-esteem. In M. Clark & G. Fletcher (Eds.), *The Blackwell handbook of social psychology, Vol. 2: Interpersonal processes* (pp. 411–436). Oxford, UK: Blackwell.

Leary, M. R. (1999). The social and psychological importance of self-esteem. In R. M. Kowalski & M. R. Leary (Eds.), *The social psychology of emotional and behavioral problems: Interfaces of social and clinical psychology* (pp. 197–221). Washington, DC: American Psychological Association.

Leary, M. R., & Baumeister, R. F. (2000). The nature and function of self-esteem: Sociometer theory. In M. Zanna (Ed.), *Advances in experimental social psychology* (Vol. 32, pp. 1–62). San Diego, CA: Academic Press.

Leary, M. R., Cottrell, C. A., & Phillips, M. (in press). Deconfounding the effects of dominance and social acceptance on self-esteem. *Journal of Personality and Social Psychology*.

Leary, M. R., & Downs, D. L. (1995). Interpersonal functions of the self-esteem motive: The self-esteem system as a sociometer. In M. Kernis (Ed.), *Efficacy, agency, and self-esteem* (pp. 123–144). New York: Plenum Press.

Leary, M. R., Haupt, A., Strausser, K., & Chokel, J. (1998). Calibrating the sociometer: The relationship between interpersonal appraisals and state self-esteem. *Journal of Per-*

sonality and Social Psychology, 74, 1290–1299.

Leary, M. R., Tambor, E. S., Terdal, S. K., & Downs, D. L. (1995). Self-esteem as an interpersonal monitor: The sociometer hypothesis. *Journal of Personality and Social Psychology, 68*, 518–530.

MacDonald, G., Saltzman, J. L., & Leary. M. R. (2001). *Social approval and self-esteem: When a person succeeds in a forest, but nobody is there to approve.* Manuscript submitted for publication, Wake Forest University, Winston-Salem, NC.

McFarland, C., & Ross, M. (1982). Impact of causal attributions on affective reactions to success and failure. *Journal of Personality and Social Psychology, 43*, 937–946.

Maris, R. (1981). *Pathways to suicide: A survey of self-destructive behavior.* Baltimore: Johns Hopkins University Press.

McFarland, C., & Ross, M. (1982). Impact of causal attributions on affective reactions to success and failure. *Journal of Personality and Social Psychology, 43*, 937–946.

Mead, G. H. (1934). *Mind, self, and society.* Chicago: University of Chicago Press.

Neuringer, C. (1974). Attitudes toward self in suicidal individuals. *Life-Threatening Behavior, 4*, 96–106.

Raskin, R., Novacek, J., & Hogan, R. (1991). Narcissistic self-esteem management. *Journal of Personality and Social Psychology, 60*, 911–918.

Rogers, C. (1959). A theory of therapy, personality, and interpersonal relationships, as developed in the client-centered framework. In S. Koch (Ed.), *Psychology: A study of a science* (Vol. 3, pp. 184–256). New York: McGraw-Hill.

Rosenblatt, A., Greenberg, J., Solomon, S., Pyszczynski, T., & Lyon, D. (1989). Evidence for terror management I: The effects of mortality salience on reaction to those who violate and uphold cultural values. *Journal of Personality and Social Psychology, 57*, 681–690.

Solomon, S., Greenberg, J., & Pyszczynski, T. (1991). A terror management theory of social behavior: The psychological functions of self-esteem. *Advances in experimental social psychology, 24*, 93–159.

Sowards, B. A., Moniz, A. J., & Harris, M. J. (1991). Self-esteem and bolstering: Testing major assumptions of terror management theory. *Representative Research in Social Psychology, 19*, 95–106.

Thorsen, J. A., & Powell, F. C. (1992). A revised death anxiety scale. *Death Studies, 16*, 507–521.

9

The Inner World of Rejection
Effects of Social Exclusion on Emotion, Cognition, and Self-Regulation

ROY F. BAUMEISTER
JEAN M. TWENGE
NATALIE CIAROCCO

INTRODUCTION

One of the most basic and powerful human motivations is the need to belong, which impels people to form and maintain social connections with other people (Baumeister & Leary, 1995; Leary, this volume). The need to belong appears to involve both regular, non-aversive interactions with other people and a context of ongoing mutual concern extending into the future. The social self is a tool for satisfying this need, and its characteristics are shaped and oriented to facilitate that task, among other motives (Brewer & Pickett, this volume).

Not everyone can easily satisfy this need. Sociologists have long recog-

Address for correspondence: Roy F. Baumeister, Department of Psychology, Case Western Reserve University, 10900 Euclid Avenue, Cleveland, OH 44106-7123, USA. E-mail: rfb2@po.cwru.edu

nized that as modern societies emerged, the stable and close network of relationships that characterized traditional social life (such as in farming villages) was weakened (see Kashima, Kashima, & Clark, this volume). Even in large modern cities, where there would seem to be an inexhaustible supply of potential partners for interaction and relationship, many people report being lonely and socially isolated. Even people who do form strong ties to others periodically find them broken when their partners die, move away, or simply reject them.

The consequences of being rejected or excluded by other people can be severe and catastrophic. Medical research suggests that mortality from nearly all physical diseases is higher among people who are single and/or lack a network of close relationships than among people who have close relationships (Lynch, 1979). Mental illness is likewise significantly higher among people who are alone (Baumeister & Leary, 1995). Suicide rates are higher among people who are alone than among those with a network of relationships (Durkheim, 1897/1963), and suicide is especially likely among people who have recently lost close relationships (Baumeister, 1990; Hendin, 1982). Across American society, Twenge (2000) has documented significant correlations between rates of social pathology and rates of social isolation, and indeed a rise in the divorce rate appears to have more impact on antisocial or destructive behavior than does change in the main economic indicators. These broad statistical relationships have been complemented in recent years by a series of vivid news stories in which school pupils (and others) who felt socially excluded resorted to violent attacks on their fellows.

These patterns raise two significant questions for research. First, what are the behavioral effects of being excluded from social groups? Second, what are the inner processes that may mediate and explain the behavioral ones? In recent years, we have conducted a series of studies to address these questions. The purpose of this chapter is to summarize what we have found to answer the second question, about the inner processes. We will offer only a brief summary of what we have found with regard to the first question.

OUR RESEARCH APPROACH

The research on which this chapter is based consisted of a series of laboratory experiments. Social exclusion was manipulated in two ways. In one procedure, which we have named the "group rejection" procedure, we invited a group of participants (typically college students) to take part in a group discussion in order to get acquainted. They were then separated into individual rooms. Each was told that the next part of the study would involve working in pairs, and each was asked to select two people from the group with whom he/she would most like to work (see also Tice, Twenge, & Schmeichel, this volume).

The experimenter then returned to visit each participant. By random assignment, each was told one of two stories, both of which led to the conclusion that the participant would have to work alone during the next phase. Half the participants were told that every other person in the group chose to work with them. The others were told that no one chose to work with them. If elaboration was needed, the experimenter explained that the design for the study involved having each person work with one person who chose him/her and one person who did not, and so the unanimity of selection rendered this impossible. Thus, in a nutshell, each person was told that he/she would have to work alone—but for a crucially different reason. Half believed it was because they were rejected by everyone, whereas the others were chosen by everyone. In this way, we sought to assess the consequences of social rejection.

The other procedure involved running participants individually. The participant was first given a personality inventory. The experimenter then took the completed response sheet away and returned later, ostensibly with the results from that test. To establish credibility, the experimenter gave each participant accurate feedback about his/her score on introversion and extraversion. Following this, however, the experimenter gave bogus feedback about future social relations, by random assignment. In the crucial ("future alone") condition, participants were told that people with their personality profile had been found to end up alone in life. The experimenter said that people with that profile often have a good network of social relations while they are in their twenties, because this is the age at which people are constantly forming new ties, but as they get older these relationships drift apart and are not replaced with new ones. As a result, the person is likely to spend more and more time alone as he/she gets older.

Several control groups have been used in different studies. In one ("future belonging"), the experimenter said simply that the participant was likely to be surrounded by a good social network "of people who care about you" throughout life. In another, no forecast about the future was made at all.

In yet another ("misfortune control") group, people were told that they were likely to be accident prone later in life, which would entail having many mishaps that would lead to broken bones and other injuries. This last control group is important because it involves an aversive prediction—but not one that affects belongingness. We thought it possible that the "future alone" manipulation might have negative effects, not because of social exclusion per se but simply because participants are led to expect bad things will happen to them. If so, then the misfortune control should produce similar effects.

Our research has shown a series of behavioral consequences of these manipulations. First and foremost, social exclusion appears to produce a sharp increase in antisocial behavior (Twenge, Baumeister, Tice, & Stucke, 2001). Excluded people become more aggressive in criticizing and harming others—especially people who insulted or provoked them, but also people who have been neutral toward them. The increased aggressiveness is not limited to the

people who have rejected them but extends toward almost anyone they encounter. The only exception is that excluded people are no different from others in reciprocating positive treatment by others. The antisocial patterns extend
beyond aggression to encompass cheating on a test (by disregarding instructions to quit when the time elapses) and by adopting an antagonistic rather than
a cooperative style of interaction toward new partners.

On the other hand, prosocial behavior also appears to be reduced by social
exclusion (Twenge, Ciarocco, & Baumeister, 2002). Excluded people are less
likely to help in response to a request from others. Indeed, in one study using
the group manipulation the experimenter asked the participant for a favor, and
we reasoned that people who had just been rejected by a group would be especially receptive to a request for help from a different and high-status person.
That would be a rational, adaptive response, after all: if people do not like you,
it would seemingly behoove you to make friends with a new, high-status person
in order to establish a possible new relationship. But we found the opposite: the
rejected people were extremely unhelpful. In another study, excluded people
donated less money than others to the campus Student Emergency Fund.

Self-defeating behavior has also been found to increase following social
exclusion. To be sure, we did not find deliberately self-destructive behavior,
consistent with the vast majority of research findings (see Baumeister & Scher,
1988, or Baumeister, 1997, for review). Most self-defeating behavior involves
performing acts that are simply ill-advised and will tend to produce destructive
outcomes, even though the person may be seeking positive outcomes. (For example, people do not smoke cigarettes or take drugs in order to destroy their
health, but they do so out of a quest for pleasure, even though the destructive
outcomes do often follow.) We have found that socially excluded people tend to
take foolish, statistically unwise risks, as well as make a variety of unhealthy and
potentially harmful choices (Twenge, Catanese, & Baumeister, in press).

It is important to note that all these effects seem specific to social exclusion. The misfortune control group generally behaves more like the accepted
than the excluded participants. Thus, it is not simply receiving bad news about
one's future that causes these effects. Rather, there appears to be something
special and powerful about social exclusion, and it produces a variety of patho-
logical or undesirable behaviors.

EMOTION

When we embarked on this research, our theory was rather straightforward.
We predicted that social exclusion would produce emotional distress, and the
emotions would produce a variety of behavioral consequences. Our reasoning
seemed fairly secure, for past work has linked social exclusion to assorted emotional reactions. A review by Baumeister and Tice (1990) concluded that social

exclusion is the most common and well-supported cause of anxiety. Leary, Springer, Negel, Ansell, and Evans (1998) have shown that "hurt feelings" are principally linked to the perception that one has been rejected by others or, at least, that others do not value the relationship and may therefore leave it. In short, we seemed on solid ground in predicting that emotion would play a major, central role in determining the effects of social exclusion.

Our studies with social exclusion have repeatedly failed to find that emotion plays any role at all. Across the studies described above, we used an assortment of measures of emotion. The failure of emotion to show up in our results has been dramatic and multifaceted.

First, there was no significant effect on emotion at all in many of our studies. That is, the socially excluded people did not differ from the others in their reports of emotional state. To be sure, some studies did find significant differences in emotion between accepted and rejected individuals, although the effect was usually small.

Second, when there was a significant effect, it tended to follow the pattern that socially accepted people reported positive emotions, whereas the excluded (future alone) and misfortune control participants reported neutral ones. Thus, the emotions of the misfortune control (accident prone) people were the same as those of the excluded ones, even though their behavior was different. The implication is that all bad news may have a depressing effect on emotion—but this does not resemble the behavioral effects, on which the future accident prone manipulation produced effects quite different from the future alone manipulation.

Third, even when we did find a significant effect on emotion, it was very small and hence unlikely to explain the behavior. The behavioral effects of our manipulations have consistently been very large, often one and one-half standard deviations, whereas the differences on emotion (if there were any at all) were less than a third of a standard deviation. In other words, our manipulations of social exclusion produced very large effects on behavior but tiny effects on emotion.

Fourth, the literal meaning of the responses by the socially excluded participants has not indicated distress. Even when differences on emotion emerged, they typically indicated that the excluded person felt neutral or as if numb. The socially accepted people felt somewhat positive, which is not surprising given that they had just been told that everyone they just met in the group had rated them favorably. In some studies we used a one-item measure on which people rated their emotional state from very bad (1) to very good (7). The mean response by the excluded people was 4.0, which is precisely in the middle. Some participants made spontaneous comments to underscore that interpretation. For example, when the experimenter told one participant that he should fill out this questionnaire "to see how you're feeling," the participant said, "I'm not feeling much of anything right now."

Fifth, and most important, mediation analyses have consistently failed to show that emotion plays any role linking the manipulation to the behavior. Following statistical procedures outlined by Baron and Kenny (1986), we tested for mediation by computing partial correlations among the variables. These procedures required a series of analyses to meet certain criteria in order to permit the conclusion that one variable mediates between the other two. We have never met any of the criteria for mediation in any study.

Hence the conclusion that emotional distress mediates between social exclusion and the behavioral outcomes must be rejected. To be sure, it is possible that there is some form of unconscious emotional response that our measures have failed to detect or that people are aggressively regulating their emotional states in order to prevent distress from emerging. Such possibilities are difficult to rule out. But it is quite clear that participants do not respond to our manipulations of social exclusion with any kind of emotional distress (or any emotion at all) that can be found with an assortment of standard measures.

COGNITION

If emotion is not responsible for the effects of social exclusion, what is? Our line of inquiry turned next from emotion to cognitive processes. That is, we began to examine whether social exclusion produced significant changes in how people thought and processed information. Many of these studies have indeed found that an experience of social exclusion causes a significant impairment in people's ability to think (Baumeister, Twenge, & Nuss, in press).

In one study, we gave people a standard IQ test after exposing them to the manipulation of false feedback about their future. The people who had been told they would end up alone in life scored significantly lower than others, even though they had been randomly assigned to receive that false feedback. Thus, the forecast of future aloneness caused people to become less intelligent for at least a brief period of time.

The reading comprehension tests from the Graduate Record Examination (a standard test given to college seniors who hope to continue to graduate school, used to assess their intellectual capabilities) furnished materials for additional studies. This test is useful because the person must read a passage, comprehend it, store it into memory (encoding), and then summon the memory to answer questions about it. Social exclusion appeared to have the strongest effects on people's ability to retrieve the memory and use the information as a basis for thinking and reasoning. Thus, the excluded people did not perform any worse than other participants on a simple version of the test that asked direct questions about the reading passage. They did however perform worse than others when the questions challenged them to use the information they had learned in the passage.

Also, in one study we varied the timing of the manipulations and the debriefing (which informs the person that the social exclusion manipulation was bogus, thereby removing its effects). In a crucial condition, we had people read the passage after receiving the social exclusion manipulation, and then we debriefed them prior to the memory test. In that procedure, the excluded people performed just fine and no worse than anyone else. This finding suggests that social exclusion does not impair the mind's ability to encode new information. After all, if social exclusion caused people to be unable to process incoming information, they would not have been able to recall and use it later (after the debriefing). Obviously the information was stored in their memory in a usable form, even though the encoding was done right after the stressful experience of social exclusion.

In contrast, when the memory part of the task came after the social exclusion, people's performance was substantially impaired. These findings permitted two interpretations. One is that exclusion affects memory retrieval but not encoding. The other is that it affects reasoning rather than the memory process. The latter might be more appropriate, because the reading comprehension test questions required the person to think rather than simply remember.

Other studies have pointed toward the latter conclusion—that reasoning, rather than memory, is impaired. In one study, we gave a standard memory exercise of learning and recalling nonsense syllables, and socially excluded people performed as well as everyone else. Thus, the simple memory processes appeared to remain intact and unaffected by social exclusion. In contrast, excluded people showed significantly lower performance than others on logic and reasoning problems, using problems of the logic section of the Graduate Record Examination.

Taken together, these results suggest that social exclusion affects the highest levels of cognitive processing, while the lower and simpler processes remain largely intact. Socially excluded people can continue to understand new, incoming information and store it into memory. They can also retrieve this new information (or previously learned information) and read it back. What they cannot do is think and reason. This impairment includes a deficit in their capacity to use newly learned information as a basis for new thinking.

Clearly there is ample room for further research. Recent studies in other laboratories have found abundant links between cognitive processes and group identification. For example, people assimilate their self-concepts and their impressions of their ingroups, such that it becomes cognitively difficult to recognize traits present in the self but lacking in the ingroup (e.g., Mackie & Smith, this volume; Otten, this volume; Wright, Aron, & Tropp, this volume). People who identify strongly with their group will show attitude change upon witnessing counter-attitudinal behavior by an ingroup member (Cooper & Hogg, this volume), suggesting that they may experience a vicarious version of cognitive dissonance. All of these point toward remarkable, if subtle links between the cognitive processes of the self and one's feeling of belonging to a group. It is therefore not surprising that when the self is abruptly thrust out from a social network, its cognitive functioning is disrupted. The link between inner processes and interpersonal connection may be far stronger than many theorists have assumed.

TIME PERSPECTIVE

Another form of cognitive impairment involves the processing of time. A variety of altered psychological states produce distortions in the perception of time. We have found that socially excluded people seem to lose their habitual orientation in time.

In one study we simply asked people to estimate the duration of an interval. In essence, this procedure involves having the participant watch the experimenter click a stopwatch on, and then off (without letting the participant see the face of the stopwatch), and then the participant is asked to estimate how long the interval was. We found that people who had experienced the group rejection manipulation significantly overestimated the interval. Thus, if the actual interval was 40 seconds, their mean estimate was over a minute (63 seconds). The people in the group acceptance condition were quite accurate, in contrast, giving a mean estimate of 42 seconds for a 40-second interval.

This pattern of distortion suggests that time drags slowly for the socially excluded person. Indeed, research on suicidal people (from which we adapted this procedure) has found that suicidal people show similar distortions of substantially overestimating time intervals (Baumeister, 1990). In contrast, when people are happily involved in some fascinating, fulfilling activity, they tend to have the opposite experience that they lose track of time and are surprised at how much has gone by (e.g., Csikszentmihalyi, 1990).

Thus, excluded people show some of the same temporal disorientation that is associated with the presuicidal state. Recalling that the presuicidal state also contains a lack of orientation toward the future, we sought to investigate future orientation among excluded people. For this study, we used only a relatively simple manipulation. We asked people how they would advise a friend who was deciding between two job offers. The first job had a good starting salary but relatively poor prospects for long-term career advancement. The other had better long-term prospects but a lower starting salary. Among the accepted participants, there was an almost unanimous (94%) preference for the latter option, involving the better long-term prospects despite the short-term sacrifice. This future orientation was significantly reduced among the rejected participants, however, with only 73% of them making that choice. Thus, social exclusion significantly reduced the willingness to accept a short-term sacrifice for the sake of a long-term gain.

Sacrificing immediate gain for the sake of better long-term benefits is one hallmark of the ability to delay gratification (Mischel, 1974, 1996). Therefore, one could interpret the results of the advice study in terms of an impairment of the capacity to delay gratification. That capacity is generally regarded as involving self-regulation and self-control (Mischel, 1996), and so these findings raised the possibility that the effects of social exclusion include an impairment of self-regulation. We therefore investigated that possibility, as the next section will describe.

SELF-REGULATION

The capacity of the self to regulate its own behavior is one of the most important and adaptive features of the human psyche (e.g., Baumeister, Heatherton, & Tice, 1994; Higgins, 1996). In essence, it enables the self to override responses that would normally occur and to substitute other responses in their place, thereby greatly increasing the adaptive flexibility of human behavior.

Research on self-regulation suggests that it operates by means of a limited resource, akin to energy or strength (Baumeister, Bratslavsky, Muraven, & Tice, 1998; Baumeister, Muraven, & Tice, 2000; Muraven, Tice, & Baumeister, 1998). When this resource is depleted, people are less able to regulate their behavior effectively.

In the present context, we wanted to learn whether an experience of social exclusion would impair self-regulation, so we borrowed procedures that have been used by Muraven (1998) to measure capacity to regulate behavior. After the manipulation of social exclusion, people were instructed to consume as much as possible of a bad-tasting beverage. The beverage consisted of unsweetened Kool-Aid (an artificial fruit-flavored drink that, with copious amounts of sugar, is popular among small children) dissolved in equal parts water and vinegar. The drink was to be consumed in one-ounce units, and the experimenter offered the participant a small cash incentive to back up the general exhortation to drink as much as possible.

Sure enough, the rejected participants drank significantly less than the accepted ones. Thus, an experience of social exclusion seemed to impair the capacity to make oneself do something that one did not want to do. Self-regulation thus appears to be impaired following exclusion.

Several other findings point toward self-regulatory impairments. As already noted, the delay of gratification study (on advising the friend between the two job offers) could be interpreted as a sign of impaired self-regulation. The ability to resist short-term temptations in order to secure long-term benefits is one of the hallmarks of self-regulation, and so impairments of that ability can be taken as a sign of lowered capacity.

The self-defeating patterns we described earlier in the chapter also may reflect impaired self-regulation. For many people, dieting is the most familiar challenge for self-control, and in one study we measured how many fattening chocolate chip cookies people ate. Rejected participants ate significantly more (indeed, nearly twice as many) as accepted participants. Thus, the ability to restrain one's urge to eat fattening junk food was reduced among people who had been socially excluded.

In another study, people had to make a series of choices between healthy, beneficial options and relatively unhealthy, self-indulgent ones. For example, the experimenter said she needed a measure of the person's pulse rate, and she said she could take either a resting pulse or a measure after a minute of jogging in place—adding that the jogging measure was a much more reliable index of health status. Accepted participants chose the healthy approach, but the excluded ones favored the easier and lazier approach of the resting pulse. Likewise, when offered a choice between a high-fat candy bar and a low-fat, healthy snack bar, the excluded people chose the unhealthy option more frequently than the accepted ones.

Even the lottery choice findings noted above may indicate impaired self-regulation. As we described earlier, that study presented participants with a choice between a high-risk, high-payoff option and a play-it-safe option, and we set up the outcome matrix deliberately to ensure that the play-it-safe option was objectively and statistically the optimal choice. Sure enough, the accepted people favored the play-it-safe option (as did the misfortune control subjects). But the excluded (future alone) participants favored the long shot option, indicative of foolish risk-taking. Although such risk-seeking behavior can be explained in several ways, an earlier investigation by Leith and Baumeister (1996) concluded that impaired self-regulation was a crucial mediator. People choose the high-risk option when they fail to think through the various options, including both their outcomes and their probabilities. Hence, the preference of excluded people for risky behaviors may be one further sign of impaired self-regulation.

CONCLUSION

Our studies have begun to paint an intriguing picture of the effects of social exclusion, and it is not the picture we had in mind when we began this work. Several conclusions can be suggested.

First, overt signs of emotional distress are conspicuous by their absence. Social exclusion does not appear to produce strong, immediate emotional reactions, at least by the procedures we have used in our laboratory studies. Even when we have found signs of emotional distress, they have been unrelated to the strong and consistent behavioral effects we have found. Moreover, the effects we have found suggest more an emotional numbness than actual distress.

Second, we have found evidence of impairment of the higher cognitive functions, even though the simpler ones seem to remain intact. People can encode and retrieve information effectively despite a recent experience of social exclusion. Reasoning and logic are another matter, however, and we have found multiple signs that social exclusion produces at least a short-term impairment in the ability to analyze, think, and reason.

Third, the normal orientation in time appears to become distorted in the wake of social exclusion. Rejected people show the pattern of being stuck in the present. Time moves very slowly for them, in the sense that they overestimate how much time has passed—precisely the opposite pattern that is seen among people who are engrossed in what they are doing. Also, one finding suggested that the ability to delay gratification in favor of long-term future benefits was impaired among socially excluded people.

Fourth, the capacity to self-regulate also shows signs of impairment in the aftermath of social exclusion. Self-regulation depends on the ability to override one's initial responses, a capacity that is diminished in "excluded" people.

One may speculate that these various findings are interrelated, although we have no direct evidence of that. Still, it is plausible that the distorted perception of time contributes to the impaired self-regulation. Someone who is immersed in the present moment may be less willing to sacrifice the present for long-term gain or to accept an immediate outcome that is less than optimal. Although we regard it as unlikely that the self-regulation findings can be entirely reduced to altered time perception, they may have some relevance.

Meanwhile, the impaired self-regulation could be relevant to the cognitive impairments. The cognitive decrements have repeatedly been found on the tasks that require the person to use the mind in an effortful manner, such as by making oneself think about a problem and engage in reasoning. The more automatic cognitive processes, such as encoding information that one reads, appear to operate satisfactorily despite social rejection. Self-regulation is linked to the controlled processes involved in effortful analysis and logical reasoning (see Baumeister,1998, on executive function), and so it is possible that the depletion of the self-regulatory resources explains (or helps explain) the cognitive decrements.

It seems quite likely that self-regulation is involved in the behavioral effects of social exclusion. We have already said that the self-defeating behaviors we observed following social exclusion may involve failures at self-regulation. The antisocial behaviors may also be mediated by impaired self-regulation. By that interpretation, people frequently have selfish and antisocial impulses, but they restrain these and override them in order to perform socially desirable actions. If social exclusion undercuts the ability to self-regulate, then people would become more willing to indulge their selfish and antisocial impulses rather than restrain them. The increases in aggression and cheating, and the more selfish and uncooperative approaches to the "prisoner's dilemma" (a game widely used to examine whether people choose prosocial or antagonistic strategies), may thus be based on failures to regulate the self.

What about the lack of emotion? As we said, social exclusion appears to produce a state more aptly described as numb and empty than as filled with emotional distress. One possible explanation is that social rejection is in fact acutely upsetting, but when it arises, our research participants (and presumably others outside the laboratory as well) respond by stifling their emotional mechanism. Being numb might be preferable to feeling pain, anxiety, and sadness, and so people shut down quickly when confronted with the distressing experience of social rejection.

By that interpretation, socially rejected people may be engaging in affect regulation at the time we measure their responses. Their first priority is to avoid feeling the distress and anxiety that would come from facing up to their excluded status. These efforts deplete the self of its resources that would otherwise be used for self-regulation and volition. Put more simply, they can succeed in feeling numb, but at a cost. The cost involves depleted resources and hence an impairment in other self-regulatory and cognitive functions.

One theme that runs through many of our findings, despite the lack of direct evidence, is passivity. Social exclusion may make people more passive. The depletion of the self's resources would certainly predict this, as would any attempt to shift to a lower level of meaning so as to avoid emotional distress and self-awareness (Baumeister, 1991).

The passivity hypothesis would explain one seemingly contradictory finding that has emerged from research on ostracism. Williams, Cheung, and Choi (2000) found that people who were exposed to a laboratory manipulation of ostracism were subsequently more willing to conform to an erroneous group opinion, using the kind of procedure that Asch (1956) developed to study conformity. Williams et al. interpreted their finding as indicating that ostracized people became highly motivated to perform prosocial acts so as to establish good social relations with other people. As we said, we had initially sought such an adaptive pattern of response, but most of our findings point in the opposite direction, away from prosocial and toward an increase in antisocial behavior. One possible reconciliation for these seemingly contrary conclusions is that excluded people simply become more passive. Hence, they are less likely to restrain their aggressive impulses, but are also more willing to go along with what everyone else in a group is saying rather than think for themselves and assert the truth as they see it. Although the passivity hypothesis is speculative, it deserves further investigation.

In sum, the experience of social exclusion makes people stupid, selfish, impulsive, and emotionally numb. These findings suggest that many of the defining features of the civilized human being—including intelligent, rational thought, self-control, prosocial concern for others, and future orientation—are dependent on feeling integrated into the social matrix. The human being may be a social being to an even greater extent than has hitherto been appreciated.

REFERENCES

Asch, S. E. (1956). Studies of independence and conformity: A minority of one against a unanimous majority. *Psychological Monographs, 70* (Whole No. 417).

Baron, R., & Kenny, D. A. (1986). The moderator–mediator variable distinction in social psychological research: Conceptual, strategic, and statistical considerations. *Journal of Personality and Social Psychology, 51,* 1173–1182.

Baumeister, R. F. (1990). Suicide as escape from self. *Psychological Review, 97,* 90–113.

Baumeister, R. F. (1991). *Escaping the self: Alcoholism, spirituality, masochism, and other flights from the burden of selfhood.* New York: Basic Books.

Baumeister, R. F. (1997). Esteem threat, self-regulatory breakdown, and emotional distress as factors in self-defeating behavior. *Review of General Psychology, 1,* 145–174.

Baumeister, R. F. (1998). The self. In D. T. Gilbert, S. T. Fiske, & G. Lindzey (Eds.), *The handbook of social psychology* (4th ed., Vol.1, pp. 680–739). New York: McGraw-Hill.

Baumeister, R. F., Bratslavsky, E., Muraven, M., & Tice, D. M. (1998). Ego depletion: Is the active self a limited resource? *Journal of Personality and Social Psychology, 74,* 1252–1265.

Baumeister, R .F., Heatherton, T. F., & Tice, D. M. (1994). *Losing control: How and why people fail at self-regulation.* San Diego, CA: Academic Press.

Baumeister, R. F., & Leary, M. R. (1995). The need to belong: Desire for interpersonal attachments as a fundamental human motivation. *Psychological Bulletin, 117,* 497–529.

Baumeister, R. F., Muraven, M., & Tice, D. M. (2000). Ego depletion: A resource model of volition, self-regulation, and controlled processing. *Social Cognition, 18,* 130–150.

Baumeister, R. F., & Scher, S. J. (1988). Self-defeating behavior patterns among normal individuals: Review and analysis of common

self-destructive tendencies. *Psychological Bulletin, 104,* 3–22.

Baumeister, R. F., & Tice, D. M. (1990). Anxiety and social exclusion. *Journal of Social and Clinical Psychology, 9,* 165–195.

Baumeister, R. F., Twenge, J. M., & Nuss, C. (in press). Effects of social exclusion on cognitive processes: Anticipated aloneness reduces intelligent thought. *Journal of Personality and Social Psychology.*

Csikszentmihalyi, M. (1990). *Flow: The psychology of optimal experience.* New York: Harper & Row.

Durkheim, E. (1963). *Suicide.* New York: Free Press. (Original work published 1897)

Hendin, H. (1982). *Suicide in America.* New York: Norton.

Higgins, E. T. (1996). The "self digest": Self-knowledge serving self-regulatory functions. *Journal of Personality & Social Psychology, 71,* 1062–1083.

Leary, M. R., Springer, C., Negel, L., Ansell, E., & Evans, K. (1998). The causes, phenomenology, and consequences of hurt feelings. *Journal of Personality & Social Psychology, 74,* 1225–1237.

Leith, K. P., & Baumeister, R. F. (1996). Why do bad moods increase self-defeating behavior? Emotion, risk taking, and self-regulation. *Journal of Personality and Social Psychology, 71,* 1250–1267.

Lynch, J. J. (1979). *The broken heart: The medical consequences of loneliness.* New York: Basic Books.

Mischel, W. (1974). Processes in delay of gratification. In L. Berkowitz (Ed.), *Advances in experimental social psychology* (Vol. 7, pp. 249–292). San Diego, CA: Academic Press.

Mischel, W. (1996). From good intentions to willpower. In P. Gollwitzer & J. Bargh (Eds.), *The psychology of action* (pp. 197–218). New York: Guilford.

Muraven, M. (1998). Mechanism of self-control failure: Motivation and limited resources

(Doctoral dissertation, Case Western Reserve University, 1998). *Dissertation Abstracts International, 59,* 2487.

Muraven, M., Tice, D. M., & Baumeister, R. F. (1998). Self-control as a limited resource: Regulatory depletion patterns. *Journal of Personality and Social Psychology, 74,* 774–789.

Twenge, J. M. (2000). The age of anxiety? The birth cohort change in anxiety and neuroticism, 1952–1993. *Journal of Personality and Social Psychology, 79,* 1007–1021.

Twenge, J. M., Baumeister, R. F., Tice, D. M., & Stucke, T. S. (2001). If you can't join them, beat them: The effects of social exclusion on aggressive behavior. *Journal of Personality and Social Psychology, 81,* 1058–1069.

Twenge, J. M., Catanese, K. R., & Baumeister, R. F. (in press). Social exclusion causes self-defeating behavior. *Journal of Personality and Social Psychology.*

Twenge, J. M., Ciarocco, N. J., & Baumeister, R. F. (2002). *Help! I need somebody: Effects of social exclusion on prosocial behavior.* Unpublished manuscript.

Williams, K. D., Cheung, C. K., & Choi, W. (2000). Cyberostracism: Effects of being ignored over the Internet. *Journal of Personality & Social Psychology, 79,* 748–762.

10

Threatened Selves

The Effects of Social Exclusion on Prosocial and Antisocial Behavior

DIANNE M. TICE
JEAN M. TWENGE
BRANDON J. SCHMEICHEL

SOCIAL EXCLUSION AND PROSOCIAL AND ANTISOCIAL BEHAVIOR

During the 1990s, a series of violent incidents at American schools took the lives of a series of schoolchildren. The murderers were themselves pupils in the schools, and the common thread seemed to be that they felt themselves to be rejected by their peers. In some cases, a romantic rejection appeared to be the precipitating incident, whereas others felt chronically left out by the dominant cliques. These incidents created the impression that social rejection can be a stimulus that leads to violent, antisocial behavior.

The link between social exclusion and antisocial behavior is suggested by data more systematic than vivid news stories. The data suggest that people whose sense of self involves an isolated self are more antisocial than people who have a more social self (a self in which others may be included and where they feel included by others). Many violent young people are men who feel that their families and peer groups have rejected them (Garbarino, 1999). The majority of violent crimes are committed by young men who are single and who often lack other social ties. Indeed, the likelihood of committing a crime drops sig-

The preparation for this manuscript was supported by a grant from the National Institutes of Mental Health MH-57039.

Address for correspondence: Dianne Tice, Dept. of Psychology, Case Western Reserve University, 10900 Euclid Avenue, Cleveland, OH 44106-7123, USA. E-mail: dxt2@po.cwru.edu

nificantly when a man marries, and it rises again if he gets a divorce (Sampson & Laub, 1990, 1993; cf. Wright & Wright, 1992), suggesting that a social self can be a significant buffer against antisocial behaviors. Sometimes these unattached young men band together to form a club or gang, and these are often some of the most violent organizations in civil society (e.g., Jankowski, 1991). At the broadest level, homicide rates across society as a whole correlate well with statistics that measure social integration, such as marriage and divorce rates (Lester, 1994).

The link between antisocial behavior and social exclusion is familiar to developmental psychologists. Children who are rejected by their peers are more likely than other children to threaten and physically attack others, as well as being more disruptive in class and other settings (Newcomb, Bukowski, & Pattee, 1993). Bullies tend to have fewer friends than other children and to be less liked and accepted by them (Coie, 1990).

Yet the developmental research raises an important question about the direction of causality. Does the aggression cause the social rejection, or vice versa? Many experts believe that the aggression is the cause: children do not like aggressive children, and so they reject them. Although this is quite plausible and may be an important part of the story, our work has been concerned with the opposite possibility, namely that social exclusion and rejection contribute to causing violent, aggressive, and antisocial behavior.

The effects of social exclusion can be seen in the broader context of the human motivation to form social bonds with other people. Baumeister and Leary (1995) have argued that the human "need to belong" is one of the most powerful and pervasive motivations. According to their analysis, it consists of two components. The first is the motivation to have frequent interactions with other people, especially interactions that are either pleasant or neutral (as opposed to aversive, conflictual interactions). The second component involves an overarching structure of relatedness, in which the persons experience mutual concern and caring for each other's welfare. People find both the interactions and the relationship structure appealing and to some extent satisfying, but the need to belong is not fully satisfied unless both components are present. In other words, people want to have frequent interactions with someone with whom they have an ongoing relationship (see Leary, this volume).

If the need to belong is indeed a basic and powerful motivation, then social exclusion is a direct blockage that thwarts this motivation. To feel rejected or excluded is thus to experience a frustration of something one earnestly desires. On that basis, one could well predict that socially excluded people will exhibit a variety of signs of disturbance. It may be quite difficult to be indifferent to having one's most powerful needs and desires thwarted (see Brewer, this volume).

Then again, one could in principle make the opposite prediction — namely, that social exclusion would produce a shift toward more prosocial behavior. This line of reasoning would emphasize the notion of adaptation. If you have been rejected by a friend or a group, and your need to belong has therefore been frustrated, the adaptive response would be to redouble your efforts to secure social acceptance. Prosocial behavior, including cooperation, friendliness, generosity, and helpfulness, would seemingly be the best strategy for obtaining such acceptance. This line of reasoning follows a standard pattern in motivation, in which people respond to a goal blockage by finding an alternate path to reach that goal.

Thus, it is reasonable to think that social exclusion should ideally elicit ever more adaptive efforts to behave in a prosocial manner so as to be accepted by others. Why, then, might we predict the opposite? We had two lines of reasoning. First, we thought that social exclusion and rejection might produce strong negative emotions, and these in turn could lead to antisocial behavior. It is well known that anger can promote aggression, and indeed aggression has been linked to a variety of unpleasant emotional states (Berkowitz, 1989). Social exclusion has been shown to cause anxiety along with a variety of other negative emotions (Baumeister & Tice, 1990), and anxiety too tends to produce an assortment of undesirable rather than adaptive behaviors. Our first line of reasoning therefore emphasized emotional states as mediating between social exclusion and antisocial behavior (see Mackie, this volume, for a related view on intergroup exclusion).

The second line of reasoning starts with a somewhat darker view of human nature. By this view, people generally have a broad assortment of antisocial and selfish motivations, which they normally keep in check. Freud (1930) proposed that a civilized society is only made possible by virtue of a system of inner psychological restraints that prevent people from acting on their aggressive and other antisocial impulses. Recent work has confirmed that positive, prosocial outcomes are strongly linked to effective self-control (e.g., Gottfredson & Hirschi, 1990; Tangney & Baumeister, 2001).

Aggressive and antisocial behavior would thus constitute a regular, recurrent possibility, and it is only prevented by means of the system of inner controls. In essence, the person must learn to sacrifice the quest for immediate satisfaction of all impulses in order to live together with others in an equitable social group. We reasoned that these controls may depend on feeling that one belongs to the group, because that feeling would make the sacrifices seem worth while, and feelings of belonging to the group may be essential to experience a social self. Social exclusion would however undermine the feeling of belonging (almost by definition)—and, with it, the motivation to restrain oneself from acting on selfish, antisocial impulses. In essence, social exclusion sets free the antisocial impulses that were always there (see Baumeister, Twenge, & Ciarocco, this volume), perhaps by reducing the social component of the self.

The two lines of reasoning are not mutually exclusive. Negative affect is well established as having the power to weaken self-regulation and inner restraints (Baumeister, Heatherton, & Tice, 1994). There are probably multiple ways in which emotional distress impairs self-control (e.g., Tice, Bratslavsky, & Baumeister, in press). Negative affect could thus contribute to undermining the inner controls, thereby allowing the antisocial behavior to emerge.

Research Manipulations of Social Exclusion

The research on which this presentation is based has relied chiefly on labora-tory experiments (see Ickes, this volume). Social exclusion has been manipu-lated in two ways. In one procedure, we invite a group of participants (typically college students) to take part in a group discussion in order to get acquainted. They are then separated into individual rooms. Each is told that the next part of the study will involve working in pairs, and each is asked to select two people from the group with whom he or she would most like to work.

The experimenter then returns to visit each participant. By random as-signment, each is told one of two stories, both of which lead to the conclusion that the participant will have to work alone during the next phase. Half the participants are told that every other person in the group chose to work with them. The others are told that no one chose to work with them. If elaboration is needed, the experimenter explains that the design for the study involved having each person work with one person who chose him/her and one person who did not, and so the unanimity of selection renders this impossible. Hence each per-son is told that he or she will have to work alone—but the reason is crucially different. Half believe it is because they were rejected by everyone, whereas the others were chosen by everyone. In this way, we seek to assess the conse-quences of social rejection.

The other procedure (called the future status procedure) involves running participants individually. The participant is first given a personality inventory. The experimenter takes the completed response sheet away and returns later, ostensibly with the results from that test. To establish credibility, the experi-menter gives each participant accurate feedback about his or her score on in-troversion and extraversion. Following this, however, the experimenter gives bogus feedback about future social relations, by random assignment. In the crucial ("future alone") condition, participants are told that people with their personality profile have been found to end up alone in life. The experimenter says that people with that profile often have a good network of social relations while they are in their twenties, because this is the age at which people are constantly forming new ties, but as they get older these relationships drift apart and are not replaced with new ones. As a result, the person is likely to spend more and more time alone as he or she gets older.

Several control groups have been used in different studies. In one ("future belonging"), the experimenter says simply that the participant is likely to be surrounded by a good social network "of people who care about you" through-out life. In another, no forecast about the future is made at all.

In yet another ("misfortune control") group, people are told that they are likely to be accident prone later in life, which will entail having many mishaps that will lead to broken bones and other injuries. This last control group is important because it involves an aversive prediction—but not one that affects belongingness. We thought it possible that the "future alone" manipulation might have negative effects, not because of social exclusion per se, but simply because participants are led to expect bad things will happen to them. If so, then the misfortune control should produce similar effects.

Social Exclusion and Aggression

Using the manipulations described in the previous section, we sought to examine effects of social exclusion on a variety of prosocial and antisocial behaviors. Our first series of studies examined aggression. The central hypothesis was that social exclusion would increase aggression (Twenge, Baumeister, Tice, & Stucke, 2001).

One form of aggression consists of giving a bad evaluation to someone, especially in a context in which that person suffer adverse consequences of the bad evaluation. Specifically, we told participants that the other person was applying for a position as a research assistant in the psychology department and so we wanted evaluations from research participants that would aid in the department's decision as to who would be the best person to hire. In that context, a bad evaluation would presumably damage the person's chances of obtaining the job he or she desired. The procedure of using bad, damaging evaluations as a form of aggression has been used in prior studies of aggression (e.g., Kulik & Brown, 1979; Ohbuchi, Kameda, & Agarie, 1989; O'Neal & Taylor, 1989; for a review, see Baron & Richardson, 1994, pp. 64–66).

Our first experiment scheduled participants in same-sex pairs of strangers. They were put into separate rooms and asked to fill out a long questionnaire, which was presented as a measure of personality. They were also instructed to write a brief essay expressing their opinion on abortion. The experimenter then took the questionnaire away (ostensibly for scoring) and took the essay away (ostensibly to let the other participant evaluate it). The participant was given an essay to read and was led to believe it had been written by the other participant just as that participant wrote one. In fact, the essay given to each participant was a standard one that the experimenter had prepared and used for all participants. The only adjustment was that the experimenter had two essays, one on each side of the issue, and each participant was given the essay advocating the position opposite to his or her own. In that way, each participant was led to believe that the other participant held the view opposed to his or her own (and thus was a dissimilar person). The participant was asked to evaluate the essay.

The future status procedure was then administered. Most participants received bogus feedback about their responses to the questionnaire, and the feedback included saying that in the future they would be either alone much of the time, or generally embedded in a rich social network, or prone to accidents and injuries. There was also a no-feedback control group.

After this manipulation, the experimenter pretended to exchange the essay evaluations. In reality these were standard evaluations. Almost everyone received a bad evaluation. It consisted of low numerical ratings on all the dimensions (organization, writing style, etc.), and in the space for comments added the handwritten summary "one of the worst essays I've read!" There was however one "positive control" condition in which people received no feedback about their future and then received a favorable evaluation of their essay.

Following this, the participant was told that the other person had applied for a position as research assistant and was asked to evaluate that person. This constituted the measure of aggression. Thus, all participants were provoked by the other person by means of an insulting evaluation, and this evaluation came on the heels of the feedback about the participant's future status. The target of aggression was not involved in the social exclusion manipulation in any way, however.

The results of this study suggested that social exclusion can increase aggressive tendencies. People who received the future alone manipulation were significantly more critical of the other person than participants in any other condition. In absolute terms, the future alone participants gave very negative evaluations (with a mean of 26 on a 100-point scale), whereas the other negative feedback conditions had means around the midpoint of 50. The positive control condition was the only one in which participants gave favorable evaluations, with a mean rating of 78 out of a maximum 100 possible.

Thus, excluded people gave more negative ratings than people in any other condition, even though most participants received an identical provocation from the person who became the target of their aggression. Accepted and accident prone people did not attack the other person with anywhere near the intensity that the excluded people used. Social exclusion also produced significantly more aggression than the provocation (i.e., receiving a bad evaluation of one's essay) alone. Because of the importance of that conclusion, we conducted a replication of those two cells alone, and it confirmed that social exclusion plus provocation elicits higher aggression than the same provocation without any exclusion.

These first two studies thus showed that an experience of social exclusion —even one that simply forecasts being alone many years in the future—is sufficient to increase aggression under some circumstances. Specifically, the circumstances included a significant provocation. One might therefore interpret these findings by saying that social exclusion potentiates an aggressive response to provocation. These findings are already important, but they raised the question of whether social exclusion would also increase aggression toward someone who had not provoked and insulted the excluded person.

Our third experiment therefore examined the effects of social exclusion on aggression toward someone who praises rather than insults the participant. The procedure was almost identical to the first study, with one important change: Nearly everyone received a positive, praising evaluation of his or her essay, consisting of favorable numerical ratings and a handwritten comment "A very good essay!" The only exception was that we included a replication of the future alone/ negative evaluation condition from the first experiment.

This study did not find that social exclusion led to any increase in aggression toward the praising person. All participants who received positive evaluations on their essays gave the other person (who had praised them) very positive ratings in connection with the job application. These did not show any variation as a function of the future status manipulation. In other words, the people who were told they would end up alone in life were just as favorable and friendly toward the other person as the people who were told they would have many friends or would be accident prone. In fact, the mean ratings in these conditions were nearly identical.

The only exception was the condition in which people received the insulting, negative evaluation of their essay. This condition replicated the finding of the first experiment and showed a very negative, aggressive evaluation.

The implication of these studies is that social exclusion can potentiate aggressive responses to a provocation, but it does not appear to produce an aggressive tendency toward someone who is kind and friendly. Excluded people seem to respond well to those who treat them favorably, even if they become extra nasty toward others who offend them (Twenge et al., 2001).

To increase generality, we conducted a fourth experiment with quite different procedures. We used the group rejection manipulation (in which each person learns that everyone, or no one, in the group wanted to work with him or her). We also used a more standard measure of aggression than the negative job evaluation. Specifically, following Bushman and Baumeister (1998), we gave people the opportunity to deliver blasts of aversive, stressful noise to the other participant. This was done ostensibly as part of a reaction time competition. People were told that they would have to respond as fast as possible, and whichever of the two participants was slower would receive a blast of noise. Each person was permitted to set the intensity and duration of noise that would be delivered to the other person if the other person was slower.

The opponent in the reaction time task (who was thus also the target of aggression) was explicitly presented as someone who was not part of the group who had accepted or rejected the participant. Rather, the experimenter said that since the participant could not continue in the group experiment, the participant would do an entirely different experiment with different people. The participant did write an essay on abortion and receive a negative evaluation from the other person, thus constituting a provocation. Participants did not however see or evaluate any essay by that person, which would help eliminate any possibility that perceived dissimilarity would contribute to the aggressive behavior.

The fourth experiment provided valuable converging evidence. Rejected participants were significantly more aggressive than accepted ones. Again, the target of the aggression was someone who had provoked the participant by means of the negative essay evaluation (but was not involved in the social exclusion). Thus, using these different procedures, it was again found that social exclusion could potentiate aggressive responses to provocation.

At this point we felt rather secure in concluding that social exclusion produces an increase in aggression toward someone who insults and provokes the person but does not lead to aggression toward a friendly, praising person. One large question remained: What about neutral persons? That is, excluded people are aggressive toward their enemies and friendly toward their friends, but which is the exception? This question seemed important because it would indicate the scope of generality of the findings. One possibility was that excluded people would simply have a chip on their shoulder and would respond with hostility toward someone who provoked them but would be perfectly friendly toward everyone else. The other, darker possibility was that excluded people would be aggressive toward almost everyone, only making exceptions for someone who was explicitly nice to them.

Our fifth and final aggression experiment examined this by dispensing with the aggressive provocation. In other respects, the procedure was the same as in the fourth experiment. It used the group rejection manipulation and the noise-blast procedure for measuring aggression. The only change was to eliminate the essay writing and evaluation procedure. That way, the opponent in the noise-blast game was a neutral, seemingly innocent person who had not presented as either friend or enemy.

The results of this study pointed toward the darker, more disturbing conclusion. Rejected participants were significantly more aggressive than accepted participants toward the neutral partner.

The conclusion from our aggression studies is that social exclusion does cause an increase in aggression. Excluded people were more aggressive than others toward someone who provoked them and toward neutral, innocent persons. The increase in aggression was large in every study, and in several of them it was double the traditional criterion (.80 standard deviations) for a large effect size. Their hostility was thus not limited to the people who had excluded them or even to new people who provoked and insulted them. The only exception was that excluded people were not aggressive toward a new person who treated them in a friendly, praising manner. Also, the results were not simply a matter of bad feedback producing aggression, because the people who received the unpleasant feedback that their futures would contain accidents and injuries were no more aggressive than the people who received positive feedback. Apparently there is something special and distinctly upsetting about social exclusion.

We did not find that emotion mediated these results. The five studies used a variety of measures of emotion. The effects on emotion were very small and in some cases not even significant. The future misfortune condition tended to produce mood and emotion ratings that were the same as the future alone manipulation, even though the behavioral effects were quite different. Careful mediation analyses (following procedures outlined by Baron & Kenny, 1986) consistently contradicted the hypothesis that emotional distress mediated the aggression. Thus, social exclusion did not make people clearly or visibly upset, but it did make them clearly aggressive (see Forgas, this volume, for an extended discussion of affect and self-perception).

Other Antisocial Behaviors

Next, we sought to investigate whether social exclusion would produce a broader range of antisocial behaviors, in addition to aggression. Our first study examined test-taking behavior. We reasoned that college students would be quite familiar with procedures for fair and honest testing, and so we gave them an opportunity to cheat. Specifically, each participant was told to take a test in private. The experimenter set a timer and told the participant to stop when the timer bell rang. Crucially, however, she said that she would be elsewhere in the laboratory and unable to hear the timer ring, and so it was up to the participant to stop working when the bell rang. She said that the participant should leave the room and come find her as soon as the bell rang. This afforded an opportunity for the participant to continue working past the bell, thereby gaining an unfair advantage. In reality, the experimenter sat outside the testing room and was able to hear the bell. She started a stopwatch when the bell went off and measured how long it was after that that the participant came out of the room to get her. This constituted the measure of cheating. The cheating measure followed the future status manipulation of social exclusion.

The results indicated that social exclusion made people more willing to break the rules and disobey instructions (to their own advantage). Participants who received the future alone manipulation worked significantly longer than all other participants on the test. The future accepted people did not differ significantly from the misfortune control condition, and so the results were not simply due to hearing any unpleasant forecast about one's future. Rather, it was specifically learning that one would end up alone in life that appeared to make people more willing to take illicit extra time on the exam.

Next, we examined antisocial and prosocial behavior on the prisoner's dilemma game. In a pair of studies, people played ten trials of this game. They were led to believe they were playing against another person, but actually they played with the computer following a preprogrammed plan. The game requires each person to choose between a cooperative and an antagonistic response. The cooperative response produces a good outcome if both players use it, but it leaves one open to be exploited and defeated by the other. The antagonistic response protects one against exploitation and can potentially bring the largest reward (if one uses it when the other person makes the cooperative move), but if both players use the antagonistic move, they both end up losing. Put another way, mutual cooperation produces a good result, unilateral cooperation produces a big loss (while the unilateral antagonistic move produces a big gain), and mutual antagonism produces a poor result for both. The game has been widely used to examine whether people choose cooperative, prosocial strategies or selfish, antagonistic strategies.

We found that social exclusion produced significant shifts toward the antagonistic responses. People who received the future alone manipulation made significantly (and substantially) fewer cooperative responses than people who received either the future accepted or the misfortune control manipulation.

The two studies we ran differed as to how the computerized opponent behaved on the first trial. In one study, the computerized opponent started off with an antagonistic move. After that, the computerized opponent was programmed to follow a tit-for-tat strategy, which meant that its response on each trial would be whatever the participant had done on the preceding trial. The only exceptions were that the computerized opponent was programmed to give antagonistic responses on trials 5 and 9, regardless of what the participant had done previously. This was done to prevent the game from being simply an endless cycle of mutual cooperation. In this study, the effects were huge (nearly two standard deviations). Socially accepted participants made antagonistic responses on about four of the ten trials, whereas socially excluded ones did so on eight out of ten.

The second study changed the opening move of the computerized opponent, because we thought that the high degree of antagonism in the previous study might have been due to the antagonistic response by the computerized opponent on the first move. Therefore we had the computerized opponent start off with a cooperative move. Although overall there was a shift toward greater cooperation than what we found in the previous study, the results still showed a very large increase in antisocial behavior caused by social exclusion. Socially excluded (future alone) participants gave on average more than twice as many antagonistic responses as the socially accepted ones.

Thus, social exclusion appears to cause an increase in a variety of antisocial behaviors, and not just aggression. Excluded people were more willing than others to cheat on a test and make antagonistic, uncooperative moves on a mixed-motive game. Moreover, as in the aggression studies, emotional distress failed to mediate the results.

Prosocial Behavior

We have also conducted some studies examining prosocial behavior. Doing good deeds has long been recognized as a way of making oneself appealing to others, and so it would seemingly be an adaptive and rational strategy for an excluded person to adopt so as to gain social acceptance. Good deeds also help overcome bad moods (Cialdini, Darby, & Vincent, 1973; Manucia, Baumann, & Cialdini, 1984), and so if people feel bad after being socially excluded they might seek to cheer themselves up by helping others or performing prosocial acts. However, our previous findings with aggression and antisocial behavior led us to doubt that social exclusion would in fact produce such a desirable outcome, and we predicted that excluded people would become no more (and possibly less) willing to perform prosocial acts.

In a first study, we administered the group rejection manipulation. When the experimenter told the participant that he or she could not continue as part of the group study (because everyone, or no one, had chosen to work with the participant), the experimenter said that the participant could therefore leave at once — but, alternatively, the experimenter needed some pilot data for future studies and would appreciate it if the participant would be willing to do one, two, or three brief experiments in the remaining time. The measure was how many of these the participant volunteered to do. We thought this request would be especially appealing to the socially excluded individuals, because it presented the opportunity to do a favor for a high-status person (the experimenter) and thus might enable the participant to make a very desirable friend — which would presumably help offset the impact of having been rejected by everyone in the group of peers.

Contrary to that hope, we did not find any rise in willingness to help among the excluded participants. Indeed, they became less willing to help. Nearly all the rejected participants refused to do any of the additional procedures, and the mean of 0.3 out of three favors reflects a very negative and minimal response to the request for favors. In contrast, the socially accepted participants were much more generous with their time, consenting to do an average of nearly two (1.7) out of the maximum three additional studies.

Those findings suggested that social exclusion made people less willing to give help in response to a direct request for a favor. An alternative explanation was simply that the excluded people wanted to escape from the situation as fast as possible. Hence we conducted a second study that did not involve any difference in time. In this study, we gave each participant a series of coins as an ostensible reward for performance on an initial task. The purpose was simply to ensure that each person had some money. Then came the social exclusion manipulation. Last, when it was time for the participant to leave, the experimenter invited the participant to make a donation to the Student Emergency Fund, which helps students in financial need when they face personal crises. The donations were ostensibly anonymous.

Once again, social exclusion reduced prosocial behavior. Future alone participants donated significantly less money to the good cause than did participants in the other conditions.

CONCLUSION

The results of these studies suggest that social exclusion produces a significant shift toward antisocial behavior and away from prosocial behavior. Socially excluded participants became more aggressive toward other people generally, only making an exception for someone new who treated them nicely. They were more willing than others to cheat on an examination by disobeying the instructions about when to stop. They were less cooperative and more self-serving and antagonistic on a prisoner's dilemma game. They were less willing to offer help in response to a request for a favor, and they were less generous in response to a request for cash donations.

The main surprise in these findings was the lack of mediation by emotional distress. Socially excluded people did not report feeling bad. Rather, their emotional self-reports consistently depicted neutral, emotionless states. Moreover, their self-reported emotions did not mediate any of the behavioral effects.

The lack of emotional mediation suggests that the antisocial effects of social exclusion should be understood as the release of pre-existing impulses. It may be that people frequently have selfish, antisocial impulses, but they restrain these because of their commitment to the social community. When they feel excluded from the social community, however, they cease to see any reason to restrain themselves, and so they become more willing to act in antisocial ways. Having a social self involves (among other things) feeling included by others and including others in one's sense of self. The social self may thus be useful in reducing anitsocial behavior.

REFERENCES

Baron, R., & Kenny, D. A. (1986). The moderator-mediator variable distinction in social psychological research: Conceptual, strategic, and statistical considerations. *Journal of Personality and Social Psychology, 51*, 1173–1182.

Baron, R. A., & Richardson, D. R. (1994). *Human Aggression* (2nd ed.). New York: Plenum Press.

Baumeister, R. F., Heatherton, T. F., & Tice, D. M. (1994). *Losing control: How and why people fail at self-regulation.* San Diego, CA: Academic Press.

Baumeister, R. F., & Leary, M. R. (1995). The need to belong: Desire for interpersonal attachments as a fundamental human motivation. *Psychological Bulletin, 117*, 497–529.

Baumeister, R. F., & Tice, D. M. (1990). Anxiety and social exclusion. *Journal of Social and Clinical Psychology, 9*, 165–195.

Berkowitz, L. (1989). Frustration-aggression hypothesis: Examination and reformulation. *Psychological Bulletin, 106*, 59–73.

Bushman, B. J., & Baumeister, R. F. (1998). Threatened egotism, narcissism, self-esteem, and direct and displaced aggression: Does self-love or self-hate lead to violence? *Journal of Personality and Social Psychology, 75*, 219–229.

Cialdini, R. B., Darby, B. L., & Vincent, J. E. (1973). Transgressions and altruism: A case for hedonism. *Journal of Experimental Social Psychology, 9*, 502–516.

Coie, J. D. (1990). Toward a theory of peer rejection. In S. R. Asher & J. D. Coie (Eds.), *Peer rejection in childhood* (pp. 365–401). New York: Cambridge University Press.

Freud, S. (1930). *Civilization and its discontents* (J. Riviere, Trans.). London: Hogarth Press.

Garbarino, J. (1999). *Lost boys: Why our sons turn violent and how we can save them.* San Francisco: Jossey-Bass.

Gottfredson, M. R., & Hirschi, T. (1990). *A general theory of crime.* Stanford, CA: Stanford University Press.

Ickes, W. (1993). Empathic accuracy. *Journal of Personality, 61,* 587–610.

Jankowski, M. S. (1991). *Islands in the street: Gangs and American urban society.* Berkeley, CA: University of California Press.

Kulik, J. A., & Brown, R.(1979). Frustration, attribution of blame, and aggression. *Journal of Experimental Social Psychology, 15,* 183–194.

Lester, D. (1994). Time-series analysis of the murder and homicide rates in the USA. *Perceptual and Motor Skills, 79,* 862.

Malloy, T. E., & Albright, L. (1990). Interpersonal perception in a social context. *Journal of Personality and Social Psychology, 58,* 419–428.

Manucia, G. K., Baumann, D. J., & Cialdini, R. B. (1984). Mood influence on helping: Direct effects or side effects? *Journal of Personality and Social Psychology, 46,* 357–364.

Newcomb, A. F., Bukowski, W. M., & Pattee, L. (1993). Children's peer relations: A meta-analytic review of popular, rejected, neglected, controversial, and average sociometric status. *Psychological Bulletin, 113,* 99–128.

Ohbuchi, K., Kameda, M., & Agarie, N. (1989). Apology as aggression control: Its role in mediating appraisal of and response to harm. *Journal of Personality and Social Psychology, 56,* 219–227.

O'Neal, E. C., & Taylor, S. L. (1989). Status of the provoker, opportunity to retaliate, and interest in video violence. *Aggressive Behavior, 15,* 171–180.

Sampson, R. J., & Laub, J. H. (1990). Crime and deviance over the life course: The salience of adult social bonds. *American Sociological Review, 55,* 609–627.

Sampson, R. J., & Laub, J. H. (1993). *Crime in the making: Pathways and turning points through life.* Cambridge, MA: Harvard University Press.

Tangney, J. P., & Baumeister, R. F. (2001). *The Self-Control Scale.* Manuscript in preparation.

Tice, D. M., Bratslavsky, E., & Baumeister, R. F. (2001). Emotional distress regulation takes precedence over impulse control: If you feel bad, do it! *Journal of Personality and Social Psychology, 80,* 53–67.

Twenge, J. M., Baumeister, R. F., Tice, D. M., & Stucke, T. S. (2001). If you can't join them, beat them: The effects of social exclusion on aggressive behavior. *Journal of Personality and Social Psychology, 81,* 1058–1069.

Wright, K. N., & Wright, K. E. (1992). Does getting married reduce the likelihood of criminality? A review of the literature. *Federal Probation, 56,* 50–56.

11

The Social Self and the Social Other

Actor–Observer Asymmetries in Making Sense of Behavior

BERTRAM F. MALLE

INTRODUCTION

*H*uman social life poses a puzzle. More than any other species, humans develop a high degree of self–other differentiation, such as in their goals, beliefs, and habits. At the same time, their complex social relations demand a high degree of self–other coordination, particularly during ongoing social interactions. What solves the puzzle of simultaneous differentiation and coordination is human social cognition, which forges integrative representations of self and other in social situations. This integration is made possible in part by the *folk theory of mind and behavior*, which provides a common conceptual framework for the interpretation of information about self and other, centered on such concepts as agency, intentionality, belief, and desire (Barresi & Moore, 1996; Heider, 1958; Malle, in press; Malle & Knobe, 1997a). The social self—the self as represented in social interactions—is therefore conceptualized like any other social agent. Despite this shared conceptual framework, however, information access and perhaps even information processing about self and other are distinct. This chapter examines asymmetries in people's access and use of information about themselves and others within the bounds of the shared conceptual framework of mind and behavior.

In social psychology, the discussion of self–other (or actor–observer) asymmetries typically focuses on a single asymmetry—that between behavior explanations by actors, who are said to be using more "situation causes," and observers, who are said to be using more "person causes" (for a review see Watson, 1982). But that is far too simple a picture. The studies reported here show that social interactants face a variety of actor–observer asymmetries—in the events they attend to, the events they try to explain, and in the specific ways they explain those events.

Overview

Because actor–observer asymmetries arise within the bounds of the shared folk-conceptual framework of mind and behavior, I discuss both the bounding elements of this framework and the way actors and observers acquire and use information interpreted within this framework. A first level of analysis concerns the events actors and observers attend to in social interactions—events that people classify by means of two folk distinctions: between intentional and unintentional events and between observable and unobservable events. Heeding this same classification, I examine at a second level of analysis which events people wonder about and try to explain. A third level of analysis concerns the specific ways people explain behavior. Here I rely on a model of behavior explanation that considers the folk-conceptual distinctions people themselves use when explaining behavior, distinctions that take us significantly beyond the classic attribution dichotomy of person/situation causes. Throughout I argue that the asymmetries at all three levels can be understood as reflections of two fundamental determinants of cognition in social settings: epistemic access and motivational relevance.

ACTOR–OBSERVER ASYMMETRIES IN ATTENTION TO BEHAVIORAL EVENTS

Social interactions are taxing on people's attention. Interactants must process what others are saying and doing, infer what they are feeling and thinking, and predict impending actions. All the while, they must plan their own utterances, monitor their actions, and confront the vast inner landscape of their thoughts, feelings, and bodily states. How people regulate attention to this complex pattern of behavioral events[1] has been largely unexplored. In a recent series of

---

1. With the term *behavioral event* I refer, broadly, to behaviors as well as mental states, such as greeting, crying, thinking, feeling, but not to traits or stable attitudes.

studies we examined one aspect of this regulation during social interaction: how people distribute attention to various behavioral events in self and other and build up representations of these events (Malle & Pearce, 2001).

Some indications in the literature suggested that there would be actor–observer asymmetries in the kinds of behavioral events to which people attend. Jones and Nisbett (1972) argued that observers have access to the other person's behavior but little access to the other's internal states; actors, by contrast, have difficulty monitoring their own behavior but no difficulty accessing their own internal states. Indirect evidence for this proposition comes from studies by Sheldon and Johnson (1993), who asked people to estimate which of several objects they usually think about when speaking with another person. The two most frequently chosen objects of attention in conversation were people's own thoughts and feelings and the other person's appearance. Similarly, people's long-term memory representations of self contain more private aspects (e.g., thoughts and feelings) than public aspects (e.g., actions and appearance), whereas representations of others contain more public aspects than private aspects (Andersen, Glassman, & Gold, 1998; Prentice, 1990). People find it especially difficult to accurately track their own observable behaviors (Gosling, John, Craik, & Robins, 1998). For example, while actors are acutely aware of their own emotional states, they cannot easily observe their own facial expressions, leading them to overestimate their face's expressiveness and their interaction partner's ability to infer emotional states from those expressions (Barr & Kleck, 1995; Gilovich, Savitzky, & Medvec, 1998). Conversely, observers find it difficult to reliably infer others' internal states, as seen for example in their limited empathic accuracy (Ickes, 1993).

None of these findings assessed attention during social interactions, so we set out to do so systematically and using a firm theoretical foundation. First, we introduced a classification of behavioral events based on two central folk distinctions—intentionality and observability—that have been discussed in isolation in the literature (e.g., Andersen, 1984; Funder & Dobroth, 1987; Heider, 1958; White, 1991). According to this classification, behavioral events can be either *intentional* or *unintentional*, and they can be *publicly observable* or *unobservable*. By crossing these distinctions, four event types result (see Figure 11.1), which can be labeled as follows: (1) *actions* (observable and intentional; e.g., asking for a favor, greeting), (2) *mere behaviors* (observable and uninten-

	Intentional	Unintentional
Observable	actions	mere behaviors
Unobservable	intentional thoughts	experiences

FIGURE 11.1. Folk classification of behavioral events.

tional; e.g., shivering, crying), (3) *intentional thoughts* (unobservable and intentional; e.g., searching for things to say, imagining a vacation in Bali), and (4) *experiences* (unobservable and unintentional; e.g., being nervous, feeling angry).

As the second piece of theory, we identified two factors that are known to govern attention allocation in general (e.g., Fiske & Taylor, 1991; Posner, 1980) and are particularly important to social interaction: *epistemic access* and *motivational relevance*. To turn one's attention to a particular behavioral event one needs to have access to it—that is, become aware of it taking place (through introspection, perception, or at least inference). Moreover, attention to an event increases if the perceiver considers it relevant (i.e., informative, helpful) for processing or coordinating the ongoing interaction (e.g., Jones & Thibaut, 1958; Wyer, Srull, Gordon, & Hartwick, 1982). Using these two attention-allocating factors as well as the above classification of behavioral events, we formulated two main hypotheses regarding the behavioral events actors and observers attend to during social interaction.

Hypothesis 1

Actors have greater epistemic access to their own unobservable events than to their own observable events, because actors are constantly presented with their stream of consciousness but cannot easily monitor their own facial expressions, gestures, or posture (Bull, 1987; DePaulo, 1992; Gilovich, this volume). Observers obviously have greater access to other people's observable than unobservable (i.e., mental) events. We therefore hypothesized that, in interaction, people attend to observable events more as observers than as actors, whereas they attend to unobservable events more as actors than as observers ("observability gap").

Hypothesis 2

For observers, the perceived relevance of intentional events is greater than that of unintentional events, because intentional events define the main business of an encounter (Goffman, 1974); because they are directed at the other and thereby demand a response; and because they have powerful effects on the other's emotions and moral evaluations (Shaver, 1985). By contrast, for actors the perceived relevance of unintentional events is greater than that of intentional events, because unintentional events are not controlled and must therefore be observed and understood, whereas the execution of intentional events frequently relies on automatic programs (Norman & Shallice, 1986). We therefore hypothesized that, in interaction, people attend as observers to more intentional events than as actors, and they attend as actors to more unintentional events than as observers ("intentionality gap").

The Studies

To test these hypotheses, we developed an experimental paradigm in which pairs of participants had a conversation and, immediately afterward, were asked to report in writing everything "that was going on" with their partner (on one page) and with themselves (on another page), in counterbalanced order. The reports were then coded for references to behavioral events (verb phrases that referred to actions, mere behaviors, intentional thoughts, or experiences) and were classified according to their intentionality and observability (κ = .80–.92), using a coding scheme in the public domain (http://darkwing.uoregon.edu/~interact/bevd.html). In Study 1, we found strong support for both actor–observer gaps. Of approximately 8 events reported per page, actors reported 2.2 more unobservable events than did observers, and observers reported 2.2 more observable events than did actors, $F(1,57)$ = 79.4, p < .001, η^2 = 58%. (These means represent the actual interaction effect, computed after removing main effects; see Rosnow & Rosenthal, 1989.) Second, actors reported 0.8 more unintentional events than did observers, and observers reported 0.8 more intentional events than did actors, $F(1,57)$ = 13.6, p < .001, η^2 = 19%.

We interpreted these results as supporting the hypothesized asymmetries in attention during interaction, even though strictly speaking the measure assesses people's mental models of the interaction immediately afterward (which is the only measure for attention during social interaction currently available; e.g., Frable, Blackstone, & Scherbaum, 1990; Smart & Wegner, 1999). But we secured our interpretation against several alternative explanations. First, varying instructions (e.g., asking participants to report about their own and their partner's "behavior" or "experiences") had little biasing effect on people's overall reporting rates and did not interact with the actor–observer gaps, ensuring that participants were not merely constructing events on the spot. Second, we also examined "intrusive events"—behavioral events that were reported about the other person on the actor page and about the self on the observer page. Because intrusive events were obviously not offered in compliance with instructions, they should be free of demand characteristics and of strategic reporting. Among these intrusive events, too, both asymmetries replicated.

In two subsequent studies we explored factors that might close the two actor–observer gaps in attention (Malle & Pearce, 2001, Studies 2 and 3). First, we examined intimacy and found that among intimates the observability gap was cut in half and the intentionality gap disappeared. Second, making the conversation highly personal among strangers had no impact on either gap. Third, empathy instructions slightly reduced the observability gap but left the intentionality gap intact. The documented actor–observer differences in attention to events (especially the observability gap) thus vary somewhat but appear to be fairly resistant to change, although more research is necessary to determine just how resistant it is.

ACTOR–OBSERVER ASYMMETRIES IN WHICH BEHAVIORAL EVENTS PEOPLE EXPLAIN

Given that there are actor–observer asymmetries for both intentionality and observability in the events people attend to, one would expect parallel asymmetries in the events people wonder about and try to explain. Moreover, these asymmetries should be derivable from principles similar to the ones that applied to the domain of attention. That is what we examined in an earlier series of studies (Malle & Knobe, 1997b). Specifically, we posited that for an event to elicit a wondering-why (and, under most circumstances, an explanation), three conditions must be met: there must be *epistemic access* (people must be aware of the event to wonder about it), *nonunderstanding* (people must not already have an explanation for the event), and *relevance* (people must find it useful and important to generate an explanation for the event). From these three conditions we derived two hypotheses parallel to the ones for attention (see Malle & Knobe, 1997b, pp. 289–290).

First, actors have less access to their own observable events than to their own unobservable events (e.g., sensations, thoughts, feelings). Observers, on the other hand, have less access to other people's unobservable events than to their observable events. People cannot wonder about events they don't have access to, so we predicted that actors would tend to wonder more often about unobservable than observable events, while observers would tend to wonder more about observable than unobservable events. Second, actors are rarely in a state of nonunderstanding with respect to their intentional behaviors because they typically know, or at least believe they know, why they performed those behaviors; thus, they are unlikely to wonder about intentional behaviors. Observers, on the other hand, may find both intentional and unintentional events equally difficult to understand, but intentional ones will more often be relevant, because intentional events are socially consequential and highly diagnostic of a person's desires, beliefs, abilities, and character (Jones & Davis, 1965; Malle & Knobe, 1997a). Therefore, we predicted that actors would tend to wonder more about unintentional than intentional events, while observers would tend to wonder more about intentional than unintentional events.

We confirmed both predictions in two studies. In one, participants kept thought protocols of spontaneous wonderings during the day and described them in more detail in the evening. In the other study, wonderings were extracted from three twentieth-century novels. The events people wondered about were classified into the four event categories, using a coding scheme in the public domain (http://darkwing.uoregon.edu/~interact/bev.html). In these two studies, actors wondered about more unobservable events (67%) than observable events (33%), whereas observers wondered about more observable events (74%) than unobservable events (26%). Actors also wondered about more unintentional events (63%) than intentional events (27%), whereas observers wondered about more intentional events (67%) than unintentional events (33%).

As a next step, we examined actual explanations. We drew a distinction between explanations that are directed to oneself (in private thought) and explanations that are directed to a partner (in communication). Because explanations to oneself answer one's own wonderings, they should show the same pattern of explained events as do wonderings. Two studies that coded explanations from memory protocols and diaries confirmed this prediction and hence replicated both actor–observer asymmetries. By contrast, explanations to others in communication answer the partners' wonderings, which come from the observer perspective. Actors should therefore explain behavioral events about which observers wonder, namely, intentional and observable ones. Two studies using thought protocols and taped conversations confirmed this prediction, showing that during communication both actors and observers explain more observable and intentional behavioral events. Thus, the social self adapts to the social other by using a cognitive tool (i.e., behavior explanations) for pragmatic, interactive purposes.

But this adaptation appears limited. By shifting away from explaining unobservable and unintentional events, actors answer observers' (their partners') wonderings but fail to explain the very events that observers normally have little access to, namely, unobservable (mental) events. And these are precisely the events that observers would like to know about (Andersen, 1984). It appears, then, that actors widen the gap between self and other. Or do they?

To clarify this issue, we must draw a distinction between the event that is explained and the content of the explanation. Even though actors explain their own actions to their communication partners more often than they explain their own mental states, the content of these action explanations may refer to mental states—the *reasons* for which the actor decided to act (Malle, 1999). This way, observers receive information about mental states, but not through an explanation of those mental states but by way of reference to them in the content of actors' explanations. To support this claim we ought to move from exploring *which* behaviors people explain to exploring *how* they explain them.

ACTOR–OBSERVER ASYMMETRIES IN HOW PEOPLE EXPLAIN BEHAVIOR

After assessing actor–observer asymmetries at the level of which behavioral events people attend to and which events they wonder about and explain, I now examine actor–observer asymmetries at the level of how people explain behavior. This is where classic attribution models have proposed an asymmetry between person and situation causes. But the phenomena at issue are more complex. There are indeed actor–observer asymmetries in the ways people explain behavior, but these asymmetries cannot be reduced to a person–situation dichotomy, because people do not conceptualize their folk explanations of behavior merely in terms of this dichotomy (Buss, 1978; Malle, 1999; Malle, Knobe, O'Laughlin, Pearce, & Nelson, 2000; McClure & Hilton, 1997; Read, 1987; White, 1991). Rather, people distinguish between intentional and unintentional behavior (Malle & Knobe, 1997a) and apply different models of causality to each class of behavior, resulting in numerous distinct modes of explanation (Malle, 1999, 2001; Malle et al., 2000). To adequately investigate actor–observer asymmetries in explanation we must therefore identify the modes of explanation that people themselves distinguish. Then we can ask anew to what extent actors and observers differ in their use of these explanatory modes.

Modes of Behavior Explanation

People's explanations of behavioral events are centered on the folk concept of intentionality (Malle, 1999, 2001), which yields four modes of explanation (see Figure 11.2). When explaining unintentional events people use only one mode— that of causes. Cause explanations depict the factors that "mechanically" brought about the unintentional event, that is, without the agent's control and typically without the agent's awareness. These cause explanations can be analyzed within the classic person–situation framework (even though some adjustments are necessary to separate traits from other person causes).

The primary mode of explaining intentional behavior refers to the *reasons* the agent had for acting (Audi, 1993; Buss, 1978; Davidson, 1963; Locke & Pennington, 1978; Malle, 1999; Read, 1987). Reasons are seen as representational mental states (desires, beliefs, valuings) that the agent combines in a (sometimes rudimentary) process of reasoning, which leads up to an intention and, if all goes well, to the intended action. To assume, as people do, that agents form an intention in light of their reasons is to assume that agents have at least dim awareness of their reasons for acting (*subjectivity assumption*) and that the reasons provide rational support for the intended action (*rationality assumption*). Suppose someone asks, "Why did Ian work 70 hours last week?" The conversation partner's explanation will likely cite one (or several) of Ian's reasons, such

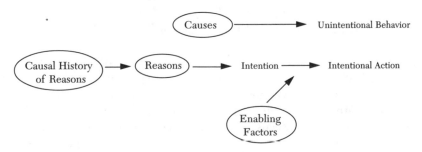

FIGURE 11.2. Four modes of behavior explanation.

as "he wanted to impress his new boss," "to get overtime pay," "he knew that the project was due," or "he was going on vacation the week after." What these explanations have in common is that they cite contents of mental states that (in the explainer's eyes) the agent considered when deciding to work for 70 hours, and they meet the subjectivity and rationality assumptions. That is, explainers assume that the agent was subjectively aware of his reasons and that they provided rational grounds for forming his intention to act. These assumptions of subjectivity and rationality are the defining characteristics of reason explanations and differentiate them from all other behavior explanations. (For further discussion and evidence of these two folk assumptions, see Malle, 1999; Malle et al., 2000; Mele, 1992; Searle, 1983.)

Even though reasons are the default mode by which people explain intentional actions, under some conditions they use alternate modes of explaining intentional behavior. One of these modes refers to the *causal history of reasons*, which are factors that lie in the background of reason and clarify how these reasons came about. The use of causal history explanations increases when the explainer lacks knowledge of the agent's reasons, when the reasons themselves are not the most informative explanation (e.g., when the audience is interested in a "deeper," psychoanalytic or sociological, account of an action), and when the object of explanation is not a single behavioral event but a trend of behaviors (either across time or across agents; see O'Laughlin & Malle, 2002). An explainer might also use a causal history explanation to downplay the agent's subjective and rational decision process (which reasons normally accentuate) and instead point to the "objective" causal determinants of those reasons—a tactic that is often used to defend or excuse undesirable intentional actions (Nelson & Malle, 2002; Wilson, 1997).

The other alternate mode of explanation refers to factors that enabled the action to come about (Malle, 1999). Without such *enabling factors*, there would only be an intention, not a completed action. Thus, enabling factor explanations clarify how it was possible that the agent turned her intention into the intended action (McClure & Hilton, 1997; Turnbull, 1986). For example, "She hit her free-throws because she's practiced them all week." For most social actions, a "How was this possible?" question does not arise (Malle et al., 2000), so enabling factors do not figure prominently in tests of actor–observer asymmetries.

In sum, people use four modes of explaining behavioral events, one for unintentional events and three for intentional events. Actor–observer asymmetries can now be studied both *between* modes and *within* modes. That is, we can ask whether actors and observers differ in the frequency of choosing particular explanation modes and whether, once a given mode is chosen, people's explanations differ in specific features of that mode.

Hypotheses About Actor-Observer Asymmetries

One between-modes hypothesis is straightforward: Because actors explain more unintentional events (and fewer intentional events) than do observers (Malle & Knobe, 1997b), actors will use more cause explanations than will observers. But this asymmetry is plainly due to events explained in the first place, not due to an independent choice of explanation modes.

A more significant between-modes hypothesis involves the choice between reason explanations and causal history of reason (CHR) explanations, which are both applied to intentional events. At least two processes should propel observers to use fewer reasons and more CHR explanations than actors. First, observers have limited access to the actor's subjective reasons, so they must sometimes substitute CHRs for unknown reasons. Second, actors will more often want to highlight the rationality and deliberateness of their actions, which is best achieved by offering reason explanations (Malle et al., 2000). Actors' greater use of reasons constitutes Hypothesis 1 in a series of actor–observer tests we recently conducted (Malle, Knobe, & Nelson, 2001).

The remaining hypotheses all involve within-mode comparisons, beginning with reason explanations. Reasons have the most complex features of all explanation modes, because they are based on the unique folk-conceptual assumptions about how intentional action is generated—by subjective, rational consideration and choice. To adequately describe these features we must distinguish between reasons *as mental states* (beliefs, desires, and valuings) and the *content* of those reasons (Brentano, 1973/1872; Searle, 1983). What the agent rationally considers is not the mental state itself but rather the content of that state (i.e., *what* is believed, *what* is desired). This conceptual distinction between state and content is reflected in people's verbal expression of reason explanations, resulting in three features of reasons on which actors and observer can differ (Malle, 1999). First, any reason appears as one of three types of mental states: a desire ("because she wanted more money"), a belief ("because she thought it would help"), or a valuing ("because she found it interesting"). We call this feature *reason type*. Second, explainers either mark a reason as a subjective mental state by using a mental state verb such as "I wanted," "she thought," "he liked," or else they leave the reason unmarked. This feature captures (the presence or absence of) *mental state markers*. Third, the *reason content* (i.e., *what* is desired, believed, or valued) can be classified, among other ways, as being about the agent or the situation, in line with the classic dichotomy.

Three actor–observer asymmetries can be derived with respect to these features (Malle, 1999). Actors should offer more belief reasons and fewer desire reasons than observers, because belief reasons often capture context-specific facts that are more likely known only to the actor, whereas desires often refer to cultural norms (what people generally want and seek out) that an unknowing observer can more easily infer (Hypothesis 2). Actors should also find it less compelling than observers to highlight the subjectivity of their reasons with mental state markers, because that subjectivity is typically assumed and understood in the context of the explanation (Hypothesis 3).

The next three hypotheses concern the classic person–situation asymmetry in various interpretations. If the classic asymmetry is valid in the context of reasons, observers should cite more person reason content (compared to situation content) than actors (Hypothesis 4). If the asymmetry is valid in the context of mechanical causality (i.e., in cause explanations, CHR explanations, and also the infrequent enabling factor explanations), observers should cite more person causes (compared to situation causes) than actors (Hypothesis 5). A variant of this claim focuses on traits as the critical category in which actors and observers differ: Accordingly, observers should cite more traits (compared to nontraits) among their causal factors than actors do (Hypothesis 6).

Tests and Results

These six hypotheses were tested in four studies (Malle et al., 2001). Study 1 asked participants to recall an instance of having explained one of their own behaviors (actor perspective) and an instance of having explained another person's behavior (observer perspective). Study 2 controlled for the specific behavioral events explained from the two perspectives by presenting participants with three preselected behaviors (two intentional, one unintentional) and asking participants to recall the last time either they themselves (actor condition) or another person (observer condition) performed that behavior and to explain why. Study 3 returned to naturalistic data by extracting spontaneous explanations that occurred in conversation. Study 4 attempted to manipulate the closeness between observers and agents. One group of participants explained behaviors that had occurred in an interpersonal conflict (which they had described earlier on tape). Some of these explanations were from the actor perspective and some from a close observer perspective (i.e., the explaining observer interacted with the agent of that explained behavior and typically knew the agent well). In the second group of participants, each listened to one of the previous conflict descriptions and then explained the very same behaviors that the original participant had explained. These explanations were from a distant observer perspective (i.e., the explainers had not interacted with the agent of the explained behavior and did not know the person).

Table 11.1 summarizes the results of all six hypotheses across the four studies. The first column shows the base rate of each explanation feature in question (i.e., reasons, beliefs, etc.), averaged across all four studies and across both perspectives. The subsequent columns show, separately for each study, the difference in actor percentages and observer percentages for the explanation feature in question. For Hypotheses 1 through 3, differences were predicted to be positive (greater numbers for actors), whereas for Hypotheses 4 through 6, differences were predicted to be negative (i.e., greater numbers for observers).

TABLE 11.1. Six actor–observer differences across four studies

Six Hypotheses:	Base Rates	Actor–Observer Differences				
		Study 1	Study 2	Study 3	Study 4 Distant	Study 4 Close
1 Reasons	71%	**34%**	**16%**	**21%**	**18%**	**16%**
2 Beliefs	47%	**28%**	**14%**	**12%**	**18%**	–8%
3 Unmarked Reasons	46%	**30%**	7%	1%	–2%	4%
Unmarked Beliefs	35%	**37%**	**18%**	**18%**	12%	–1%
4 Person Reason Content	39%	3%	**–17%**	**–11%**	–5%	5%
5 Person Causal Factors	64%	1%	–7%	–9%	4%	2%
6 Traits	14%	–7%	**–10%**	**–19%**	0%	**–14%**

Note: Numbers indicate the difference between actors' percentages and observers' percentages of each explanation feature (predicted to be positive for the first three hypotheses and negative for the next three). Boldface numbers indicate significant differences.

Hypothesis 1 was strongly supported. The rate of reasons was consistently higher among actors (M = 81%) than among observers (M = 61%), even for close observers in Study 4, suggesting that the asymmetry in use of reasons cannot be eliminated by increases in knowledge and intimacy.

Hypothesis 2 was also strongly supported. Actors offered more belief reasons (M = 54%) and fewer desire reasons (M = 36%) than all observer samples (M's = 36% beliefs vs. 52% desires) except for close observers (M's = 57% beliefs vs. 34% desires). This pattern suggests that only close observers, but not distant observers, can have sufficient context-specific and idiosyncratic knowledge about the actor's reasons to formulate a significant number of belief reasons.

Hypothesis 3, examining the use of mental state markers, did not receive consistent support. It is possible that the effect in question is small and subject to substantial variations. More likely, however, the effect does not hold uniformly across all types of reasons. Malle (1999) argued that one function of mental state markers is to highlight the agent's subjectivity and that this highlighting function is more powerful in the case of beliefs than desires (because desires linguistically indicate subjectivity in both the marked and unmarked versions, thus making markers a nondiagnostic feature). We therefore conducted follow-up analyses that tested the mental state marker asymmetry in interaction with reason type (i.e., the three-way interaction between markers, reason type, and perspective). These analyses yielded support for a conditional asymmetry in Studies 1 through 3: Observers used more mental state markers than actors among belief reasons, but not among desire reasons. In Study 4, the means for distant observers pointed in the same direction as in the other studies, but the comparison failed to reach significance. For close observers, no actor–observer difference was found. Apparently, close observers are like actors with respect to both their use of beliefs (see the results for Hypothesis 2) and their use of mental state markers for those beliefs.

Hypothesis 4, testing a person–situation asymmetry in the content of reasons, was generally not supported. Hypothesis 5, testing a person–situation asymmetry for causal factors, was left unsupported in every single study. By contrast, Hypothesis 6, examining the use of traits as causal factors, received noteworthy support. Across all studies, actors mentioned fewer traits (M = 9%) than did observers (M = 18%), but this difference was eliminated in the sample of distant observers (whose trait rate of 6% was as low as that of actors), and it was weaker in Study 1 (where observers often explained actions by agents whom they did not know very well). It appears that for the asymmetry in trait explanations to occur the observer must know the agent well and perhaps have participated in repeated interactions with the agent so that relevant trait knowledge can develop.

To summarize, among the new hypotheses developed within a model of folk explanations, two were strongly supported: Actors use more reasons (and fewer CHR explanations) than observers, and actors use more belief reasons (and fewer desire reasons) than observers. In addition, actors seem to omit mental state markers more often than observers when providing belief reasons (but not when providing desire reasons). Among three variants of the classic person–situation asymmetry, only one was supported: Observers use more trait terms than actors in their cause explanations and CHR explanations, but they all but cease to use traits when they don't know the agent. It is also noteworthy that the overall use of traits in cause and CHR explanations was only 14% (not even counting reason explanations in the denominator), which calls into question the received view that traits are people's "way of packaging the behavior of others" (Hastorf, Schneider, & Polefka, 1970, p. 59) and the "lay view of behavior" (Nisbett, 1980, p. 109). People may well be too quick to infer a trait from a few vivid behaviors, but they do not appear to cite many traits in their explanations of behavior.

To account for the documented actor–observer asymmetries, we may invoke again the epistemic access principle that has served well in accounting for asymmetries at the previous two levels of analysis (i.e., attention to behavioral events and selection of events to explain). Because actors have more access to their own mental states, and especially to their reasons for intentional actions, they readily cite reason explanation, especially the idiosyncratic and context-specific belief reason type. Observers, typically lacking such privileged knowledge, often turn to causal history of reason explanations or, if they do cite reasons, they offer (or perhaps guess) desire reasons, which are more easily derivable from general cultural knowledge (Bruner, 1990). When observers know the agent well, however, they do cite as many belief reasons as do actors themselves.

In addition to this epistemic force, there is also a pragmatic one at play. Actors often design their explanations to serve not only informational but also self-presentational goals. Choosing particular modes and features of explanation thus takes on motivational relevance. Providing reasons, for example, serves to highlight the agent's deliberation and intentional control (Malle, 1999), and belief reasons in particular serve to create an impression of rationality (Malle et al., 2000). So at least the use of belief reasons may be explained both epistemically and motivationally. Only experimental manipulations of explainers' motives and a simultaneous consideration of their knowledge of the agent could disentangle these two forces. But perhaps such disentangling is unrealistic, as the two may not occur independently in natural interactions (e.g., knowing someone well increases the desire to present that person in a positive light).

Finally, we can take up the puzzle that was identified at the end of the last section. There we found that actors in communication seem to explain their own actions (intentional and observable events) to their partner, even though what the partner would need most (and would find most useful) is information about mental states. Now we see that when actors explain their own actions, they do indeed provide a considerable amount of mental state information to their interaction partners: In their action explanations, they cite more than 80% reasons, of which half are the fairly specific and idiosyncratic belief reasons.

CONCLUSIONS

The self is social to the extent that it is represented in an interaction with another person. Social interactions require making sense of both this social self and the other person (Kashima, Kashima, & Clark, this volume), and such sensemaking consists of multiple tasks: allocating attention to different behavioral events in self and other, selecting some of these events for explanation, and constructing for them an actual explanation in private thought or communication. The folk theory of mind and behavior aids in forming integrative representations of self and other when performing these social-cognitive tasks, but two fundamental forces impinge differently on actors and observers: epistemic access and motivational relevance. These forces lead to asymmetries in the kinds of events actors and observers attend to, which events they explain, and how they explain them. The forces themselves have been recognized for a long time in social psychology; but only by considering them in the context of people's own conceptual framework of mind and behavior are we able to track their influence on the cognitive and communicative tools people use in coordinating social interaction.

REFERENCES

Andersen, S. M. (1984). Self-knowledge and social inference: II. The diagnosticity of cognitive/affective and behavioral data. *Journal of Personality and Social Psychology, 46,* 294–307.

Andersen, S. M., Glassman, N. S., & Gold, D. A. (1998). Mental representations of the self, significant others, and nonsignificant others: Structure and processing of private and public aspects. *Journal of Personality and So-*

cial Psychology, 75, 845–861.

Audi, R. (1993). *Action, intention, and reason.* Ithaca, NY: Cornell University Press.

Barr, C. L., & Kleck, R. E. (1995). Self-other perception of the intensity of facial expressions of emotion: Do we know what we show? *Journal of Personality and Social Psychology, 68,* 608–618.

Barresi, J., & Moore, C. (1996). Intentional relations and social understanding. *Behavioral and Brain Sciences, 19,* 107-154.

Brentano, F. C. (1973). *Psychology from an empirical standpoint.* (A. C. Rancurello, D. B. Terrell, & L. L. McAlister, Trans.). New York: Humanities Press. (Original work published 1872)

Bruner, J. (1990). *Acts of meaning.* Cambridge, MA: Harvard University Press.

Bull, P. E. (1987). *Posture and gesture.* (International series in experimental social psychology, Vol. 16). Oxford, UK: Pergamon Press.

Buss, A. R. (1978). Causes and reasons in attribution theory: A conceptual critique. *Journal of Personality and Social Psychology, 36,* 1311–1321.

Davidson, D. (1963). Actions, reasons and causes. *Journal of Philosophy, 60,* 685–700.

DePaulo, B. M. (1992). Nonverbal behavior and self-presentation. *Psychological Bulletin, 111,* 203–243.

Fiske, S. T., & Taylor, S. E. (1991). *Social cognition* (2nd ed.). New York: McGraw-Hill.

Frable, D. E., Blackstone, T., & Scherbaum, C. (1990). Marginal and mindful: Deviants in social interactions. *Journal of Personality and Social Psychology, 59,* 140–149.

Funder, D. C., & Dobroth, K. M. (1987). Differences between traits: Properties associated with interjudge agreement. *Journal of Personality and Social Psychology, 52,* 409–418.

Gilovich, T., Savitsky, K., & Medvec, V. H. (1998). The illusion of transparency: Biased assessments of others' ability to read one's emotional states. *Journal of Personality and Social Psychology, 75,* 332–346.

Goffman, E. (1974). *Frame analysis: An essay on the organization of experience.* Cambridge, MA: Harvard University Press.

Gopnik, A. (1993). How we know our minds: The illusion of first-person knowledge of intentionality. *Behavioral and Brain Sciences, 16,* 1–14.

Gosling, S. D., John, O. P., Craik, K. H., & Robins, R. W. (1998). Do people know how they behave? Self-reported act frequencies compared with on-line codings by observers. *Journal of Personality and Social Psychology, 74,* 1337–1349.

Hastorf, A. H., Schneider, D. J., & Polefka, J. (1970). *Person perception.* Reading, MA: Addison-Wesley.

Heider, F. (1958). *The psychology of interpersonal relations.* New York: Wiley.

Ickes, W. (1993). Empathic accuracy. *Journal of Personality, 61,* 587–610.

Jones, E. E., & Davis, K. E. (1965). From acts to dispositions: The attribution process in person perception. In L. Berkowitz (Ed.), *Advances in experimental social psychology* (Vol. 2, pp. 219–266). New York: Academic Press.

Jones, E. E., & Nisbett, R. E. (1972). The actor and the observer: Divergent perceptions of the causes of behavior. In E. E. Jones, D. Kanouse, H. H. Kelley, R. E. Nisbett, S. Valins, & B. Weiner (Eds.), *Attribution: Perceiving the causes of behavior* (pp. 79–94). Morristown, NJ: General Learning Press.

Jones, E. E., & Thibaut, J. W. (1958). Interaction goals as bases of inference in interpersonal perception. In R. Tagiuri & L. Petrullo (Eds.), *Person perception and interpersonal behavior* (pp. 151–178). Stanford, CA: Stanford University Press.

Locke, D., & Pennington, D. (1982). Reasons and other causes: Their role in attribution processes. *Journal of Personality and Social Psychology, 42,* 212–223.

Malle, B. F. (1999). How people explain behavior: A new theoretical framework. *Personality and Social Psychology Review, 3,* 21–43.

Malle, B. F. (2001). Folk explanations of intentional action. In B. F. Malle, L. J. Moses, & D. A. Baldwin (Eds.), *Intentions and intentionality: Foundations of social cognition* (pp. 265–286). Cambridge, MA: MIT Press.

Malle, B. F. (in press). The relation between language and theory of mind in development and evolution. In T. Givon & B. F. Malle (Eds.), *The evolution of language out of prelanguage.* Amsterdam: John Benjamins.

Malle, B. F., & Knobe, J. (1997a). The folk concept of intentionality. *Journal of Experimental Social Psychology, 33*, 101–121.

Malle, B. F., & Knobe, J. (1997b). Which behaviors do people explain? A basic actor–observer asymmetry. *Journal of Personality and Social Psychology, 72*, 288–304.

Malle, B. F., Knobe, J., Nelson, S. E., & Stevens, S. (2001). *Actor-observer asymmetries in explanations of behavior: New answers to an old question.* Manuscript in preparation, University of Oregon, Eugene.

Malle, B. F., Knobe, J., O'Laughlin, M., Pearce, G. E., & Nelson, S. E. (2000). Conceptual structure and social functions of behavior explanations: Beyond person–situation attributions. *Journal of Personality and Social Psychology, 79*, 309–326.

Malle, B. F., & Pearce, G. E. (2001). Attention to behavioral events during social interaction: Two actor–observer gaps and three attempts to close them. *Journal of Personality and Social Psychology, 81*, 278–294.

McClure, J., & Hilton, D. (1997). For you can't always get what you want: When preconditions are better explanations than goals. *British Journal of Social Psychology, 36*, 223–240.

Mele, A. R. (1992). *Springs of action: Understanding intentional behavior.* New York: Oxford University Press.

Nelson, S. E., & Malle, B. F. (2000, January). *Making excuses: A new look at the self-serving bias in behavior explanations.* Poster presented at the Society for Personality and Social Psychology Annual Conference, Savannah, Georgia.

Nisbett, R. E. (1980). The trait construct in lay and professional psychology. In L. Festinger (Ed.), Retrospections on social psychology (pp. 109–113). New York: Oxford University Press.

Norman, D. A., & Shallice, T. (1986). Attention to action. Willed and automatic control of behavior. In G. E. Schwartz & D. Shapiro (Eds.), *Consciousness and self-regulation* (pp. 1–17). New York: Plenum Press.

O'Laughlin, M., &. Malle, B. F. (in press). How people explain actions performed by groups and individuals. *Journal of Personality and Social Psychology, 82*, 33–48.

Posner, M. I. (1980). Orienting of attention. *Quarterly Journal of Experimental Psychology, 32*, 3–25.

Prentice, D. A. (1990). Familiarity and differences in self- and other-representations. *Journal of Personality and Social Psychology, 59*, 369–383.

Read, S. J. (1987). Constructing causal scenarios: A knowledge structure approach to causal reasoning. *Journal of Personality and Social Psychology, 52*, 288–302.

Rosnow, R. L., & Rosenthal, R. (1989). Definition and interpretation of interaction effects. *Psychological Bulletin, 105*, 143–146.

Searle, J. R. (1983). *Intentionality: An essay in the philosophy of mind.* Cambridge, UK: Cambridge University Press.

Shaver, K. G. (1985). *The attribution of blame: Causality, responsibility, and blameworthiness.* New York: Springer.

Sheldon, K. M., & Johnson, J. T. (1993). Forms of social awareness: Their frequency and correlates. *Personality and Social Psychology Bulletin, 19*, 320–330.

Smart, L., & Wegner, D. M. (1999). Covering up what can't be seen: Concealable stigma and mental control. *Journal of Personality and Social Psychology, 77*, 474–486.

Turnbull, W. (1986). Everyday explanation: The pragmatics of puzzle resolution. *Journal for the Theory of Social Behavior, 16*, 141–160.

Watson, D. (1982). The actor and the observer: How are their perceptions of causality divergent? *Psychological Bulletin, 92*, 682–700.

White, P. A. (1991). Ambiguity in the internal/external distinction in causal attribution. *Journal of Experimental Social Psychology, 27*, 259–270.

Wilson, J. Q. (1997). *Moral judgment: Does the abuse excuse threaten our legal system?* New York: HarperCollins.

Wyer, R. S., Srull, T. K., Gordon, S. E., & Hartwick, J. (1982). Effects of processing objectives on the recall of prose material. *Journal of Personality and Social Psychology, 43*, 674–688.

12

The Social Self in Subjective versus Intersubjective Research Paradigms

WILLIAM ICKES

Introduction
Subjective and Intersubjective Paradigms for the Study
    of Social Cognition
Paradigm-Based Differences in the Social Self
Links to Crossley's (1996) Two Modes of Social Relating
Implications for the Study of Social Psychological Phenomena

INTRODUCTION

*I*n a series of recent articles, my colleagues and I have argued that, historically, there have been two major paradigms for the study of social cognition—a subjective paradigm and an intersubjective paradigm (Ickes & Dugosh, 2000; Ickes & Gonzalez, 1994, 1996). We use the word "paradigms" in the sense intended by Kuhn (1962), that is, to denote broad-scope organizing perspectives for the conduct of research in a given area that are based on fundamentally different assumptions about the nature of the phenomena being studied. In my present remarks, I would like to propose that the differences between the subjective and the intersubjective paradigms have important implications for the *type of social self* and the *mode of social relating* that research participants are likely to experience. In turn, these differences in social self and mode of relating may have important implications for our attempts to study basic social psychological phenomena such as attribution, stereotyping,

Address for correspondence: William Ickes, Department of Psychology, University of Texas at Arlington, Arlington, Texas 76019-0528, USA. E-mail: ickes@uta.edu

prejudice and discrimination (see Smith, this volume, for another example of a metatheoretical position on how the self is conceived).

I will begin by contrasting the two social cognition paradigms in their broadest and most abstract terms. I will then suggest the types of social selves and the modes of social relating that are likely to characterize participants who are tested within each of these paradigms. Finally, I will consider the implications of these social-self and relational-mode differences for the study of certain social psychological phenomena.

SUBJECTIVE AND INTERSUBJECTIVE PARADIGMS FOR THE STUDY OF SOCIAL COGNITION

In our previous articles (Ickes & Dugosh, 2000; Ickes & Gonzalez, 1994, 1996), my colleagues and I have attempted to make explicit a distinction that has seldom been recognized: that, historically, there have been two major paradigms for the study of social cognition. The first is a subjective paradigm that has its origins in mainstream cognitive psychology. This paradigm has been so successful as a model for research that it has dominated and virtually defined the field of social cognition throughout its history. Consistent with its epistemological assumptions, this first paradigm relies on a methodology in which participants are tested individually, in studies designed to ensure the conceptual and statistical independence of each participant's cognitions and behavior from those of the other persons tested. The other contributors to this volume, in fact, generally rely upon this paradigm (see, for example, Smith; Mackie & Smith; this volume).

In contrast, the second paradigm is an intersubjective paradigm that appears to have been invented by interpersonal relations and small groups researchers to enable the study of interaction in dyads and small groups. Compared to the first paradigm, this second paradigm is neither well known nor widely used. In fact, it has imposed so many demands and difficulties on the researcher (i.e., in methodological, practical, statistical, and theoretical terms) that it has won relatively few adherents. Ironically, it is seldom even considered as an alternative paradigm for social cognition research. Consistent with its epistemological assumptions, this second paradigm relies on a methodology in which participants are tested together, in studies designed not only to permit the interdependence of the participants' cognitions and behavior but also to examine these patterns of interdependence as phenomena of fundamental importance to the study of social cognition.

Throughout the rest of this chapter, the term "social" cognition will be used as a convenient shorthand for the subjective social cognition research that is guided by the first paradigm I have described above. The quotation marks are meant to indicate that—because of the subject's independence and separation from others in these single-subject designs—the modifier "social" is of limited or even questionable applicability. In contrast, the term *social* cognition will be used as a convenient shorthand for the intersubjective social cognition research that is guided by the second paradigm I have described above. Here, the italics are meant to indicate that—because of the subject's interdependence and involvement with others in these dyadic or group designs—the modifier *social* is both essential and defining.

In general, then, the term "social" cognition should be taken as equivalent to the seemingly-paradoxical term "subjective social cognition," whereas the term *social* cognition should be taken as equivalent to the seemingly-redundant term "intersubjective social cognition." As we will see, neither the seeming paradox nor the seeming redundancy are accidental.

Essential Differences between the Two Paradigms

The essential differences between the "social" cognition and the *social* cognition paradigms are summarized in Table 12.1. These points of difference, which necessarily overlap each other to some degree, are useful in making explicit the contrasting theoretical, methodological, and statistical assumptions that distinguish the two paradigms.

Contrasting Theoretical Assumptions

As the first two points of comparison in Table 12.1 reveal, implicit in the "social" cognition and *social* cognition paradigms are strikingly different theoretical views about the nature of social cognition. The first paradigm views social cognition as the subjective reactions of a single individual to a pre-programmed, ostensibly "social" stimulus. In contrast, the second paradigm views social cognition as the subjective reactions of at least two individuals to their interaction experience *and* as the shared, intersubjective meaning that these individuals jointly construct through their interaction behavior (Ickes, Tooke, Stinson, Baker, & Bissonnette, 1988; Schutz, 1970; Wegner, Giuliano, & Hertel, 1985).

Consistent with these opposing views, the first paradigm is limited to the study of subjective phenomena occurring at the individual level of analysis, whereas the second paradigm can address both subjective and intersubjective phenomena occurring both at the individual level and at the dyad or group level. As a consequence, researchers who use the first paradigm should find it relatively difficult to produce evidence of emergent, intersubjective phenomena, however intrigued they might be by the possibility that such phenomena exist. In contrast, researchers who use the second paradigm should find it relatively easy to study such intersubjective phenomena, and to begin the long-term task of documenting and analyzing their different forms, origins, dynamics, and consequences.

Table 12.1. Essential Differences between the Two Paradigms

The "Social" Cognition Paradigm	The *Social* Cognition Paradigm
1. Views social cognition as the subjective reactions of a single individual to a pre-programmed "social" stimulus event.	1. Views social cognition as the subjective reactions of at least two individuals to their interaction experience *and* as the shared, intersubjective meaning which they jointly construct through their interaction behavior.
2. Is inherently limited to the study of subjective phenomena, in that phenomena can be observedand assessed only at the individual level.	2. Can be used to study both subjective and intersubjective phenomena, in that phenomena can be observed and assessed both at the individual level and at the dyad or group level.
3. Subjects are tested individually, using single-subject designs and data-analytic models that assume that each subject's cognitive responses are statistically independent from those of other subjects.	3. Subjects are tested together, using dyadic or group designs and data-analytic models that assume that each subject's cognitive responses are statistically interdependent with those of the other dyad or group members.
4. The subject can interact only with people (i.e., experimenters or confederates) whose behavior is constrained by an experimental script and ideally does not vary from one subjectto the next within the same experimental condition. Mutual influence should, ideally, not occur.	4. The subject can interact with one or more other subjects in a relatively naturalistic way that makes it possible for the behavior of each subject to influence the behavior of every other subject within his/her dyad or group. Mutual influence should occur.
5. The statistical interdependence of the subjects' cognitive responses is typically viewed as an undesirable statistical artifact. Such interdependence, if it cannot be avoided by design, is typically regarded as "nuisance variance" that the researcher must attempt to eliminate or control for in the data analyses.	5. The statistical interdependence of the subjects' cognitive responses is typically viewed with great interest, as potential evidence of an intersubjective phenomenon. The variance associated with this interdependence is therefore regarded as "effect variance," not as "error" or "nuisance variance."

Contrasting Methodological Assumptions

As the next two points of comparison in Table 12.1 reveal, the "social" cognition and *social* cognition paradigms also display striking differences in their respective methodologies. In the "social" cognition paradigm, participants are tested individually and can interact only with people (i.e., experimenters or confederates) whose behavior is constrained by an experimental script. In the *social* cognition paradigm, participants are tested together—in dyads or in larger groups—and can interact with each other in a relatively naturalistic way that allows genuine mutual influence to occur. Ideally, at least, mutual influence should not occur in the "social" cognition paradigm; indeed, any evidence that the participant's behavior has altered the behavior of the experimenters, the confederates, or the other participants is typically regarded as a serious methodological problem or design flaw.

Contrasting Statistical Assumptions

As the third and fifth points of comparison in Table 12.1 reveal, the "social" cognition and *social* cognition paradigms reflect different statistical assumptions as well. The "social" cognition paradigm uses data-analytic models which assume that each participant's cognitive responses are statistically independent from those of other participants. If this assumption is violated, the resulting interdependence in the participants' responses is typically viewed as an undesirable statistical artifact (i.e., as "nuisance variance" that the researcher must attempt to eliminate or control for in the data analyses). In contrast, the *social* cognition paradigm uses data-analytic models which assume that each participant's cognitive responses are statistically interdependent with those of the other participants in a dyad or group (e.g., Gonzalez & Griffin, 2000; Kenny, 1988). Indeed, any empirical evidence of such interdependence is typically viewed with great interest, as potential evidence of an intersubjective phenomenon.

The Paradox of Subjective Social Cognition

Given these contrasts between the "social" cognition and *social* cognition paradigms, the seemingly paradoxical nature of subjective social cognition should be evident. Research on subjective social cognition derives from the paradoxical assumption that the best way to study social cognition is to first remove it from the social interaction context in which it naturally occurs. Ironically, however, by attempting to study social cognition outside of its natural context, researchers have severely limited the chances that any genuinely social processes can affect their subjects' cognitive activities (Fiske & Goodwin, 1994; Levine, Resnick, & Higgins, 1993). In addition, they have virtually eliminated the possibility of studying those intersubjective phenomena that various writers (e.g., Asch, 1952; Heider, 1958; Markus & Zajonc, 1985; Mead, 1934) have argued are the ones that make social cognition a unique and distinctive field of research.

Subjective social cognition is the product of remembered or imagined interaction, rather than of real, ongoing interaction (see Table 12.2). It occurs entirely in one person's head, rather than in the intersubjective space that is created when two people jointly construct a shared meaning context through their conversation and nonverbal behavior (Hancock & Ickes, 1996; Schutz, 1970). Metaphorically, it is like the sound of one hand clapping, or like the actor who soliloquizes about relations with characters unseen. On the one hand, it *is*

TABLE 12.2. Subjective versus Intersubjective Social Cognition

Subjective Social Cognition	Intersubjective Social Cognition
1. The product of remembered or imagined, rather than real, ongoing social interaction.	1. The product of real, ongoing social interaction.
2. Occurs in only one person's head and is entirely subjective.	2. Occurs in more than one person's head and is, to some extent, intersubjective as well as subjective.
3. Focuses primarily on either past or potential (future) interaction experiences.	3. Focuses primarily on present interaction experiences.
4. Wide latitude in constructing the other and the other's subjective experience.	4. Narrow latitude in constructing the other and the other's subjective experience.

a genuine aspect of social cognition, reflecting the theoretically important process by which we represent to ourselves the remembered or imagined thoughts, feelings, and behaviors of other people. On the other hand, it is not the only aspect of social cognition, or even the most important one, because it fails to acknowledge—and therefore fails to address—the even more important process by which two or more minds attempt—and often fail—to meet. Paradoxically, however, it is the aspect of social cognition that has dominated researchers' attention for over 50 years.

As Jeremy Dugosh and I have suggested, trying to understand social cognition by studying only its subjective aspects (and simultaneously ignoring its intersubjective aspects) is a bit like practicing swimming on dry land (Ickes & Dugosh, 2000). The swimming, kicking, and breathing motions that one learns to make while practicing swimming on dry land are important—even essential—components of the process of swimming. But, in themselves, they do not confront the would-be swimmer with such crucial aspects of the actual swimming experience as the surface tension of the water, its pressure and drag beneath the surface, and its propensity to flow into any and all bodily orifices within an instant. Analogously, the study of subjective social cognition provides important—even essential—insights about the processes of social cognition as they occur inside one person's head. But, in itself, it does not and cannot inform us about those intersubjective aspects of social cognition that affect the social perceiver just as surely as the surface tension, density, and fluidity of the water affect the swimmer.

The message here should be clear: in its natural form, social cognition occurs in a social environment just as swimming occurs in an aquatic environment. And just as one would never confuse swimming on dry land with the complete, immersive experience of swimming, so one should never confuse the purely subjective aspect of "social" cognition with the complete, immersive experience of social cognition in a genuinely intersubjective context.

PARADIGM-BASED DIFFERENCES IN THE SOCIAL SELF

Given this meta-theoretical background, I would now like to propose that these two contrasting paradigms for the study of social cognition may also differ in the type of social self that is likely to characterize research participants when they are tested within each paradigm. A summary of these hypothesized differences can be found in Table 12.3.

Recall that because the "social" cognition paradigm uses single-subject designs, participants who are tested within this paradigm are not allowed to have spontaneous, naturally-occurring interactions with other people. Instead, the "interactions" they have are subjectively constructed. To the extent that the interactions are imagined rather than real, the participants will experience subjective, rather than intersubjective, social cognition. In most cases, they will be asked to provide self-reports about their anticipated or hypothetical reactions to one or more other participants, while remaining physically separated from those imagined others who presumably bestow upon the situation its nominally "social" character.

As my colleagues and I have recently argued, putting research participants into single-subject studies using the "social" cognition paradigm effectively bestows upon them the social identity of soliloquizing Hamlets who must convey their social experience more through reminiscence or anticipated action than

TABLE 12.3. Hypothetical Paradigm-Based Differences in the Social Self

The "Social" Cognition Paradigm	The *Social* Cognition Paradigm
1. More independent and detached.	1. More interdependent and involved.
2. More egocentric and attuned to one's own subjective reality (solipsism).	2. More altercentric and attuned to the intersubjective reality.
3. Views others in a relatively simplified, stereotypic, and abstract way.	3. Views others in a relatively complex, particularistic, and concrete way.
4. Views others as being compelled by their own "nature" and attributes to think and act the way that they do.	4. Views others as capable of greater self-determination, transcending their own "nature" and attributes to think and act in novel and unexpected ways.
5. More susceptible to fantasy and projective bias.	5. Less susceptible to fantasy and projective bias.
6. Deals with others more as cognitive representations of persons whose own subjectivity can be "constructed" but is not experienced co-actively through the intersubjective exchange.	6. Deals with others more as flesh-and-blood persons whose own subjectivity is experienced co-actively though the intersubjective exchange.

through their actual interactions with others (Ickes & Duck, 2000; Ickes & Dugosh, 2000). Research participants whose social identities are (at least temporarily) cast in this mold are ones who must relate to others as cognitive constructions that exist in their own mind rather than as real, flesh-and-blood persons with whom they are engaged in a dynamic, intersubjective relationship that involves events occurring in the real world and in the other person's mind as well as in their own.

The social self of participants who have been placed in studies using the "social" cognition paradigm is therefore one that is relatively detached, egocentric, and prone to rely on overly simplified, stereotypic constructions of others (see Table 12.3, left column). This social self, because it has been removed from a truly interactive and intersubjective social context, must deal with others primarily as cognitive representations. In most cases, it constructs overly simplified representations of others that tend to confound their objective attributes with the perceiver's own fantasies (constructions, projections, etc.) about how he/she would prefer to see them. Some people are overly idealized; other people are overly demonized; but all people tend to be overly objectified. The general tendency is to perceive others more as stereotyped characters whose attributes compel them to think and act as they do than as self-determining individuals who have a complex subjective life of their own and who are capable of transcending their own "natures" by thinking and acting in novel ways.

In contrast, the social self of people who participate in the spontaneous, naturally occurring interactions of studies using the *social* cognition paradigm tends to be one that is more interdependent and involved (rather than independent and aloof), more altercentric (rather than egocentric), and less likely to rely on overly simplified, stereotypic constructions of others (see Table 12.3, right column). A person experiencing this type of social self tends to perceive the other in a more complex and differentiated way that involves less fantasy and projective bias, and that also gives more credit to the other's own subjectivity as well as to the other's capacity for self-determination and change.

LINKS TO CROSSLEY'S (1996) TWO MODES OF SOCIAL RELATING (INTERSUBJECTIVITY)

Interestingly, some of the key distinctions in Table 12.3 parallel those found in Nick Crossley's (1996) comparison of two modes of intersubjectivity—*egological intersubjectivity* and *radical intersubjectivity*. Drawing his inspiration from similar distinctions made by the philosophers Edmund Husserl and Martin Buber, Crossley has proposed a concept of egological intersubjectivity that appears to have much in common with what I have called subjective social cognition. When participants relate to other people within this mode, they tend to view others as "social objects" that are defined by their objective attributes and their social-category membership. In other words, they relate to the other as a mental representation—as a personality type, a social-category member, or a role-occupant—instead of apprehending the other's subjectivity through their intersubjective exchange. It is perhaps not too much of an oversimplification to say that they relate to their image or mental construction of the other person rather than to the other person directly.

By the same token, Crossley's (1996) concept of radical intersubjectivity appears to have much in common with what I have called intersubjective social cognition. When one person relates to another person within this mode, they tend to transcend the self–other distinction and to experience themselves as constituting *an intersubjective system*. In doing so, they view each other less in terms of their attributes, social categories, and roles, and they more directly "glimpse" or apprehend each other's subjectivity through their intersubjective exchange.

Of these two modes of relating to others, egological intersubjectivity might appear to be the more unnatural—treating other people as mere exemplars of a personality type, a social category, or a social role. However, Crossley (1996) argues that we do this in our everyday life whenever we treat a waiter or a cashier as just a role-occupant—someone whose function is merely to take an order and bring food or to accept our payment and give us a receipt. A more extreme example is the bigot who sees an abstraction—a black or a homosexual whose subjective experience is not seriously considered—rather than seeing a unique human being whose subjective experience must be respected and taken into account. Perhaps the most extreme example is the solipsist—the person who acts as if other people have no subjective experience; they are merely constructions or projections of the solipsist's own mind.

By contrast, radical intersubjectivity doesn't seem so radical at all. Indeed, it seems to be the more natural way to relate to others—accepting that their subjectivity is as real and valid as one's own and cooperating with them to create an "intersubjective system" (Crossley's term) that encompasses and transcends the subjective experience of the individual participants. We should keep in mind, however, that egological intersubjectivity and radical intersubjectivity are theoretical endpoints on what is probably a continuum that includes more mixed and intermediate forms of social relating. These mixed and intermediate forms might be evident, for example, when we at one moment treat the bus driver as a mere role-occupant who takes our change and drives us to our destination, but in the next moment ask about the bus driver's family and express sympathy with his financial problems.

At any rate, there are obvious conceptual parallels between subjective social cognition and egological intersubjectivity on the one hand, and between intersubjective social cognition and radical intersubjectivity on the other hand. These parallels suggest that it might be useful to think about the two modes of relating and their associated forms of social cognition and social self in syndromal terms. From this standpoint, egological intersubjectivity and radical intersubjectivity are different types of psychological syndromes, each associated with a characteristically different type of social self as well as a characteristically different way of thinking about and relating to other people.

Extending this idea, it seems reasonable to suggest that these psychological syndromes can be under either situational or dispositional control. With regard to situational control, when people are physically isolated from others (as in the typical study using the "social" cognition paradigm), their mode of thought becomes one of subjective social cognition, their mode of relating becomes one of egological intersubjectivity, and their social self changes correspondingly. On the other hand, when people are fully immersed in the intersubjective give-and-take of a genuine face-to-face interaction (as in the typical study using the *social* cognition paradigm), their mode of thought becomes one of intersubjective social cognition, their mode of relating becomes one of radical intersubjectivity, and their social self again changes correspondingly.

It is also possible, however, that these same psychological syndromes are associated with the perceivers' own dispositions. For an introverted person who also has a "solipsistic" mindset, the psychological syndrome associated with egological intersubjectivity and subjective social cognition may predominate, whereas for an extraverted person who also seeks interdependence with others, the psychological syndrome associated with radical intersubjectivity and intersubjective social cognition may predominate. These dispositional influences could moderate, or even override, the situational influence of being alone or in face-to-face interaction with others. For example, the person who is both solipsistic and introverted could experience egological intersubjectivity and subjective social cognition even during face-to-face interaction with others, whereas the person who is both interdependence-seeking and extraverted could experience a fantasized version of radical intersubjectivity and intersubjective social cognition even while alone.

IMPLICATIONS FOR THE STUDY OF SOCIAL PSYCHOLOGICAL PHENOMENA

So far, I have proposed that characteristic differences in participants' social selves, mode of social relating, and type of social cognition are linked to the type of research paradigm—subjective or intersubjective—in which they are tested. I would now like to suggest that these characteristic differences might have important implications for our attempts to study basic social psychological phenomena. Some of the more obvious phenomena to consider in this regard include attribution, stereotyping, prejudice, and discrimination.

Attribution

Because participants who are tested within the single-subject designs of studies using the "social" cognition paradigm should experience subjective, rather than intersubjective, social cognition, their attributional behavior should differ in characteristic ways from that of participants who are tested within the dyadic or group designs of studies using the *social* cognition paradigm (see also Malle, this volume). Specifically, as point 4 in Table 12.2 suggests, they should be more susceptible to the actor–observer effect (Jones & Nisbett, 1972) and should therefore make stronger dispositional attributions in interpreting and accounting for other people's behavior. And, as point 5 suggests, their attributions should be also more influenced by their own egocentrism, fantasies, and projective biases. These influences should lead them not only to display a stronger false consensus effect (Marks & Miller, 1987) but also to make egocentric attributions whose content is more obviously colored by their own sources of anxiety and need.

Stereotyping

As point 3 in Table 12.3 suggests, participants who are tested within the single-subject designs of the "social" cognition paradigm should tend to display greater stereotyping than their counterparts who are tested within the dyadic or group designs of the *social* cognition paradigm. Not only should they display a greater tendency to stereotype the imagined interaction partners whom they are asked to rate, but the content of their stereotypes should typically be simpler, less differentiated, and more abstract.

Prejudice and Discrimination

Because they tend to view their imagined interaction partners more stereotypically, individuals who participate in single-subject "social" cognition studies should be more likely to report prejudice and display discrimination toward those whom they stereotype negatively. As the famous study by LaPiere (1934) demonstrated, it is easier to admit prejudice and display discrimination toward negatively stereotyped others when they are merely imagined and subjectively constructed. In contrast, it is more difficult to admit prejudice and display discrimination toward negatively stereotyped others when one is interacting with them face-to-face and therefore must confront—however reluctantly or imperfectly—their own subjective experience during the encounter.

Meta-Theoretical Implications

The LaPiere (1934) study is particularly relevant to the larger theme of this chapter. It was one of the first and most influential studies to alert social scientists to the fact that the research paradigms they adopt can have important implications for the behavior that their research participants will display. From the vantage point of that study, the insight that participants react differently to others in the subjective interactions of the "social" cognition paradigm than in the intersubjective interactions of the *social* cognition paradigm is clearly very old news.

What is new, however, is the attempt to specify more precisely why these different reactions might occur. One answer to this question, suggested in the present chapter, is that different research paradigms can implicate different psychological syndromes, each with its own characteristic mode of social relating, its own characteristic form of social cognition, and its own characteristic type of social self. These latter elements can, in turn, help to account for the different reactions that participants display in "social" cognition versus *social* cognition research.

What is also new is a developing array of methodological paradigms, statistical procedures, and theoretical frameworks that are specifically designed for the study of intersubjective phenomena. For example, a general research paradigm for studying such phenomena has been developed by Ickes and his colleagues, who have extended the unstructured dyadic interaction paradigm (Ickes, 1982, 1983) to assess dyad members' subjective thoughts and feelings, in addition to their overt behavior (Ickes, Robertson, Tooke, & Teng, 1986; Ickes, Stinson, Bissonnette, & Garcia, 1990; Ickes & Tooke, 1988). To date, this paradigm has been used to explore a number of different aspects of intersubjective social cognition. These aspects include empathic accuracy (Ickes, 1993, 1997, 2001), dyadic intersubjectivity (Ickes et al., 1988), and metaperspective taking (Fletcher & Fitness, 1990; Frable, Blackstone, & Scherbaum, 1990; Ickes et al., 1986).

The past 10 to 15 years have also seen the development of powerful new statistical models for investigating intersubjective phenomena such as consensus and meta-accuracy in person perception (Kenny & Albright, 1987; Malloy & Albright, 1990), and "co-orientation" and "shared meaning" effects (Chaplin & Panter, 1993; Kenny & Kashy, 1994). Techniques for studying both within- and between-dyad interdependence (Gonzalez & Griffin, 2000; Kenny, 1988) have also proven useful in identifying *emergent* social phenomena—for example, that mutual gaze is more than the "coincident looking" defined by the joint probability of the participants' individual gazing behavior (Bissonnette, 1992). These methodological and statistical innovations have been further complemented by creative theoretical models such as Wegner, Giuliano, and Hertel's (1985) analysis of transactive memory and other forms of cognitive interdependence in close relationships.

With the advent of these methodological, statistical, and theoretical innovations, it is now easier than it has ever been to study the cognitive and behavioral interdependence that naturally occurs whenever two or more individuals meet and interact together. Researchers who have shied away from studying such phenomena in the past should now feel encouraged to study them. It is my hope that, as they do, the meta-theoretical speculations that have been proposed in the present chapter will eventually be tested through appropriate empirical research. Ideally, the results of this research will enable all of us to make more informed decisions about what kinds of research paradigms are most appropriate for what purposes—decisions that may also implicate different notions of social self (see Otten, this volume). At the least, we should be more cautious about assuming that the findings obtained using one type of paradigm ("social" cognition or *social* cognition) will necessarily generalize to analogue studies conducted within the other type of paradigm.

REFERENCES

Asch, S. E. (1952). *Social psychology.* Englewood Cliffs, NJ: Prentice-Hall.

Bissonnette, V. L. (1992). *Interdependence in dyadic gazing.* Unpublished doctoral dissertation, University of Texas at Arlington.

Buber, M. (1970). *I and thou* (Walter Kaufmann, Trans.). New York: Scribner.

Chaplin, W. F., & Panter, A. T. (1993). Shared meaning and the convergence among observers' personality descriptions. *Journal of Personality, 61,* 553–585.

Crossley, N. (1996). *Intersubjectivity: The fabric of social becoming.* London: Sage.

Fiske, S. T., & Goodwin, S. A. (1994). Social cognition research and small group research, a West Side Story or . . .? *Small Group Research, 25,* 147–171.

Fletcher, G. J. O., & Fitness, J. (1990). Occurrent social cognition in close relationship interaction: The role of proximal and distal variables. *Journal of Personality and Social Psychology, 59,* 464–474.

Frable, D. E. S., Blackstone, T., & Scherbaum, C. (1990). Marginal and mindful: Deviants in social interactions. *Journal of Personality and Social Psychology, 59,* 140–149.

Gonzalez, R., & Griffin, D. (2000). On the statistics of interdependence: Treating dyadic data with respect. In W. Ickes & S. W. Duck (Eds.), *The social psychology of personal relationships* (pp. 181–213). Chichester, UK: Wiley.

Hancock, M., & Ickes, W. (1996). Empathic accuracy: When does the perceiver-target relationship make a difference? *Journal of Social and Personal Relationships, 13,* 179–199.

Heider, F. (1958). *The psychology of interpersonal relations.* New York: Wiley.

Husserl, E. (1960). *Cartesian meditations: An introduction to phenomenology* (Dorion Cairns, Trans.). The Hague, Netherlands: M. Nijhoff.

Ickes, W. (1982). A basic paradigm for the study of personality, roles, and social behavior. In W. Ickes & E. S. Knowles (Eds.), *Personality, roles, and social behavior* (pp. 305–341). New York: Springer-Verlag.

Ickes, W. (1983). A basic paradigm for the study of unstructured dyadic interaction. In H. Reis (Ed.), *New directions for methodology of social and behavioral science* (pp. 5–21). San Francisco: Jossey-Bass.

Ickes, W. (1993). Empathic accuracy. *Journal of Personality, 61,* 587–610.

Ickes, W. (1997). *Empathic accuracy.* New York: Guilford.

Ickes, W. (2001). Measuring empathic accuracy. In J. A. Hall & F. J. Bernieri (Eds.), *Interpersonal sensitivity: Theory and measurement* (pp. 219–241). Mahwah, NJ: Erlbaum.

Ickes, W., Bissonnette, V., Garcia S., & Stinson, L. (1990). Implementing and using the dyadic interaction paradigm. In C. Hendrick & M. Clark (Eds.), *Review of personality and social psychology, Vol. 11: Research methods in personality and social psychology* (pp.

16–44). Newbury Park, CA: Sage.

Ickes, W., & Duck, S. (2000). Personal relationships and social psychology. In W. Ickes & S. W. Duck (Eds.), *The social psychology of personal relationships* (pp. 1–8). Chichester, UK: Wiley.

Ickes, W., & Dugosh, J. (2000). An intersubjective perspective on social cognition and aging. *Basic and Applied Social Psychology, 22,* 157–167.

Ickes, W., & Gonzalez, R. (1994). "Social" cognition and *social* cognition: From the subjective to the intersubjective. *Small Group Research, 25,* 294–315.

Ickes, W., & Gonzalez, R. (1996). "Social" cognition and *social* cognition: From the subjective to the intersubjective. In J. Nye & A. Brower (Eds.), *What's social about social cognition? Research on socially shared cognition in small groups* (pp. 285–309). Newbury Park, CA.: Sage.

Ickes, W., Robertson, E., Tooke, W., & Teng, G. (1986). Naturalistic social cognition: Methodology, assessment, and validation. *Journal of Personality and Social Psychology, 51,* 66–82.

Ickes, W., Stinson, L., Bissonnette, V., & Garcia, S. (1990). Naturalistic social cognition: Empathic accuracy in mixed-sex dyads. *Journal of Personality and Social Psychology, 59,* 730–742.

Ickes, W., & Tooke, W. (1988). The observational method: Studying the interaction of minds and bodies. In S. Duck (Ed.), *The handbook of personal relationships: Theory, research and interventions* (pp. 79–97). Chichester, UK: Wiley.

Ickes, W., Tooke, W., Stinson, L., Baker, V. L., & Bissonnette, V. (1988). Naturalistic social cognition: Intersubjectivity in same-sex dyads. *Journal of Nonverbal Behavior, 12,* 58–84.

Jones, E. E., & Nisbett, R. E. (1972). The actor and the observer: Divergent perceptions of the causes of behavior. In E. E. Jones, D. Kanouse, H. H. Kelley, R. E. Nisbett, S. Valins, & B. Weiner (Eds.), *Attribution: Per-ceiving the causes of behavior* (pp. 79–94). Morristown, NJ: General Learning Press.

Kenny, D. A. (1988). The analysis of data from two-person relationships. In S. Duck, D. F. Hay, S. E. Hobfall, W. Ickes, & B. M. Montgomery (Eds.), *Handbook of personal relationships: Theory, research, and interventions* (pp. 57–77). Chichester, UK: Wiley.

Kenny, D. A., & Albright, L. (1987). Accuracy in interpersonal perception: A social relations analysis. *Psychological Bulletin, 102,* 390–402.

Kenny, D. A., & Kashy, D. A. (1994). Enhanced co-orientation in the perception of friends: A social relations analysis. *Journal of Personality and Social Psychology, 67,* 1024–1033.

Kuhn, T. S. (1962). *The structure of scientific revolutions.* Chicago: University of Chicago Press.

LaPiere, R. T. (1934). Attitudes versus actions. *Social Forces, 13,* 230–237.

Levine, J. M., Resnick, L. B., & Higgins, E. T. (1993). Social foundations of cognition. *Annual Review of Psychology, 44,* 585–612.

Malloy, T. E., & Albright, L. (1990). Interpersonal perceptions in a social context. *Journal of Personality and Social Psychology, 58,* 419–428.

Marks, G., & Miller, N. (1987). Ten years of research on the false consensus effect: An empirical and theoretical review. *Psychological Bulletin, 102,* 72–90.

Markus, H., & Zajonc, R. B. (1985). The cognitive perspective in social psychology. In G. Lindzey & E. Aronson (Eds.), *The handbook of social psychology* (3rd ed., pp. 137–230). New York: Random House.

Mead, G. H. (1934). *Mind, self and society.* Chicago: University of Chicago Press.

Schutz, A. (1970). *On phenomenology and social relations.* Chicago and London: University of Chicago Press.

Wegner, D. M., Giuliano, T., & Hertel, P. T. (1985). Cognitive interdependence in close relationships. In W. Ickes (Ed.), *Compatible and incompatible relationships* (pp. 253–276). New York: Springer-Verlag.

13

Facework and Emotion Work
The Role of Positive Facial Expression in Constituting the Social Self

MARIANNE LaFRANCE

INTRODUCTION

*E*ven though their meaning seems obvious, smiles continue to fascinate both natural and social scientists (Darwin, 1872/1965). At their most straightforward, positive facial displays simply reflect positive affect— people smile because they are happy or amused or pleased (Ekman & Friesen, 1982; Ekman, Davidson, & Friesen, 1990; Ekman, Friesen, & Ancoli, 1980). But, research has also shown that people smile when the expresser feels anything but positive. Results show us, for example, that people smile when they are embarrassed (Edelmann, Asendorpf, Contarello, & Zammuner, 1989), uncomfortable (Ochanomizu, 1991), miserable (Ekman & Friesen, 1982), and apprehensive (Ickes, Patterson, Rajecki, & Tanford, 1982).

In short, smiling may be called into service when a person wants to convey that, even though she feels uncomfortable or miserable, nonetheless she would like others to think that she has her wits about her since she can smile in such a situation. Rather than primarily reflecting underlying positive emotion, smiling

Address for correspondence: Marianne LaFrance, Department of Psychology, Yale University, New Haven, CT 06520, USA. E-mail: marianne.lafrance@yale.edu

is a meta-message, an indicator about how one wants to be taken. Smiling thus falls into the more general domain of strategic self-presentation (Rhodewalt & Tragakis, this volume). In other words, people actively attempt to manipulate social reactions to themselves in order to convey a certain social persona.

In this sense then, smiles are functional. They represent not direct read-outs of underlying emotional feeling but rather indications that the expresser is socially focused. Consider that greetings are associated with smiling (Eibl-Eibesfeldt, 1989), as are persuasion attempts aimed at patients (Burgener, Jirovec, Murrell, & Barton, 1992), students (Zanolli, Saudargas, & Twardosz, 1990), and potential dates (Walsh & Hewitt, 1985). In all these occasions, smiling is used to suggest that one can be trusted.

Thus, smiles present a particular kind of social self rather than being simple reflections of felt positive emotion (Fridlund, 1991). Smiles, more than most other facial displays, are communication acts in which representations are made to other people about how one wants to be taken. Like Kashima and his colleagues (this volume), I hold that smiles are symbols rather than signs. In other words, smiles are representations—they represent how one wishes or needs to be seen rather than signs of what one really is. For example, anthropologists and sociologists have documented numerous instances where people smile because their role or interpersonal situation requires them to do so. Wierzbicka (1994) for one has observed that cheerfulness is mandatory in many cultures.

Within the United States, Hochschild (1983) noted that many workers are required to smile as part of their jobs. For instance, airline flight attendants must smile and smile well. Thus, a flight attendant is trained to "really work on her smiles" and is expected to "manage her heart" in such a way as to create a smile that will seem both "spontaneous and sincere" (Hochschild, 1983, p. 105).

My goal for this chapter is to elaborate on the idea that smiles are often used as a way to get others to see oneself positively. Specifically, I will make the case that people intentionally adopt positive facial displays for rhetorical purposes to further the development of their self-narratives and their social relationships (Sarbin, 1986). By smiling, people communicate that they know the social scripts, and they know that others know the social scripts for conveying agreeableness. In particular, I want to suggest that many social situations impose the obligation to present oneself this way. Moreover, while I see that this obligation is experienced by nearly everybody on some occasions, nonetheless, the obligation to smile is experienced by some people more than others. These people are girls and women.

EXPRESSIVITY DEMAND THEORY

I begin with the assumption that facial displays are typically used to attract and sometimes repel others. As such, facial displays are actively managed by those who display them and are closely monitored by those who see them. Over 30 years ago, Ekman and Friesen (1969) suggested that people do not always show what they feel. What gets expressed facially is guided by display rules that dictate to whom and in what contexts it is appropriate or inappropriate to express various emotion states. For example, upon receiving a disappointing gift, Americans learn that the appropriate response is not a sneer but a smile. I want to stress this social and instrumental nature of smiling. That is, positive facial displays are social conventions aimed at defining a social persona rather than signals about a person's emotional state. In other words, positive facial expressions are often preemptive and ritualized communicative actions aimed at situating the self in a social world.

Three social factors are central in understanding when and why people smile: they are gender norms, situational scripts, and emotional salience. *Gender norms* direct girls and women to be more expressive in general and to smile more in particular. *Situational scripts* indicate whether and how much smiling is to be displayed in particular contexts, roles, or relationships. Third, contexts vary in how much they are marked by *emotional salience*. In contexts where affect is conspicuous, and particularly when tension or sadness is present, smiles are displayed to reduce or redirect the negative feelings. In other words, negative emotion engenders the need for someone to do emotion work. That is, some people (more often women) feel a greater obligation to engage in reassuring behaviors like smiling. Emotion work is designed to reduce tension, restore harmony, and reaffirm social connections.

Gender Expressivity Norms

A key contention of our model is that norms governing facial display in general and smiling in particular are different for females and males. Such gender-based norms for expressivity are both self-imposed (Fiske & Stevens, 1993) and imposed by others (Fischer, 1993). In a recent set of studies, we explored the prescriptive basis of positive facial displays by asking males and females to imagine smiling or not in a number of different contexts. For example, they were instructed to imagine that they smiled or not in response to someone's good news. We predicted that women would anticipate more negative repercussions when they did not smile (LaFrance, 1997).

And that is what we found. Non-smiling females felt significantly less comfortable and less appropriate than non-smiling men. Women also reported that others would regard them as less friendly and genuine and more cold and rude if they did not smile. More to the point, females also believed that the other's impression of them would change more if they did not smile. In contrast, male participants reported that whether they smiled or not was significantly less likely to affect others' impressions of them. In other words, women know well that they should come across as pleasant and that there may be costs if they do not comply. As Biernat and Eidelman (this volume) have shown, stereotypes of one's group play a role in self-evaluation by serving as both interpretative and comparative frames of reference. Other studies also find that women expect fewer rewards and higher costs when their responses to others are insufficiently positive (Stoppard & Gunn-Gruchy, 1993).

And there is evidence that these expectations are based in reality. Deutsch and her colleagues, for instance, found women who do not smile are perceived to be less happy, carefree, and relaxed than non-smiling men (Deutsch, LeBaron, & Fryer, 1987). In fact, Chesler (1972) went so far as to contend that both women and men are "deeply threatened by a female who does not smile often enough" (cited in Henley, 1977, pp. 278–279).

Situational Scripts

Although gender norms for smiling are believed to be fairly ubiquitous, there are some situations that impose the obligation to smile (or to keep smiling in check) on both sexes about equally. These situation-based expectations for positive affect may thus override gender norms and produce comparable positive display in both sexes. Both sexes thus smile a lot or a little or not at all because the situation stipulates appropriate display. Smiling is typically evident at celebratory occasions but attenuated when the context is serious or formal. In other words, women are predicted to smile significantly more than men when the context is *undefined*, in which case gender norms prevail, but they are predicted to smile similarly to men when the situation imposes its own script for whether there should be displays of positive emotion.

Emotion Salience

However, there are situations that are likely to intensify the smiling differences between women and men. Specifically when affect is high, especially negative affect, women will smile more, and the prediction is that women will smile a good deal more than men. As noted earlier, Hochschild (1989) contended that emotion labor is expected more of women than of men, both at home and at work. She wrote, "the world turns to women for mothering, and this fact silently attaches itself to many job requirements" (1989, p. 89). In fact, organizational psychologists report that even within the same occupation, women are expected to perform more emotional labor than men (Adelmann, 1989; James, 1989; Wharton & Erickson, 1993; Wichroski, 1994).

Hochschild (1989) argued that there are two broad ways emotion work is done, namely, *evocation* and *suppression*. In evocation, the individual aims to create an emotion that is not present (e.g., expressing interest or delight in response to others' good news, even when the "news" hold little fascination or delight). Emotion labor can also involve the suppression of negative emotion for others' benefit. For example, several studies find that females subscribe more than males to the need to hide anger with positive affect (Salem, 1998). Smiles are used in the service of both evocation and suppression. And they likely work because seeing a smile on another's face is often enough to engender a brief burst of positive affect in someone else. Especially when someone starts out feeling ill-disposed, a smile from another might engender some positive feeling leading one to feel differently about themselves and others (Forgas, this volume).

In sum, gender norms, situational scripts, and emotion salience combine to explain when women will smile more than men will and when they will not. Gender differences in smiling are predicted to be relatively large where situational scripts are absent or ambiguous because the default option is for women to present themselves as agreeable. Greater smiling by women is expected to be particularly strong in emotionally charged situations because reducing tension or reestablishing harmony is something women are under greater obligation to effect. Only when nonemotionally laden roles or tasks are to be undertaken are men and women expected to show comparable levels of smiling.

META-ANALYIS OF SEX DIFFERENCES IN SMILING

A review of the empirical literature on smiling was conducted to gauge support for these ideas. Specifically, a meta-analysis was undertaken in which all studies that documented an empirical relationship between sex and smiling among adults were retrieved, even if that relationship was not the central one of the investigation. Along with published reports, unpublished materials such as conference papers, theses, and dissertations were also included.

In addition to noting whether women smiled more or less than men, each study was coded for the presence or absence of several moderator variables. Three sets of moderator variables were coded: those reflecting gender norms, those pertaining to situation-based scripts for positive displays, and whether the context was one in which emotion and especially negatively emotion was salient.

Gender-Based Expressivity Moderators

Since no study of sex differences in smiling actually measured the presence of gender norms for positive facial expression, several moderators were coded that served as proxies for these. For example, we measured the degree to which participants were aware of being observed (surveillance moderators) as well as measured the degree to which participants were acquainted with each other (familiarity moderators). Surveillance moderators are based on the premise that greater awareness of being observed should lead to greater adherence to gender-based norms for expressiveness and hence greater smiling differences between women and men. Surveillance moderators included whether subjects knew they were being videotaped, how many others were present, and whether subjects were actively engaged with others. Surveillance moderators draw on the idea that a given social identity (in this case gender identity) will emerge as a dominant self-representation when there are strong contextual cues making that group membership salient (Wright, Aron, & Tropp, this volume). We also measured the level of acquaintanceship subjects had with those who were present. These moderators assume that greater familiarity between participants will lead to lower self-monitoring and reduced need to actualize gender roles.

Situation-Based Expressivity Demands

To assess impact of situational demands, we also used a number of proxy variables. The core idea was to code whether the research context was clearly scripted. For example, a context was scripted if subjects had to complete a particular task (e.g., deceive or teach someone) or perform a particular role (e.g., possessing a higher social power role or being responsible for someone's well-being).

Emotional Salience

Finally, several moderators were coded to assess the degree to which the research context was marked by social tension or negative affect. The prediction was that such emotional contexts would elicit greater smiling by women since it falls more to them to do the emotion work to alleviate negative feelings.

EVIDENCE FOR EXPRESSIVITY DEMAND THEORY

A total of 59,076 participants were included in 143 reports yielding 347 effect sizes. As is typically the case, we used Cohen's d as our measure of effect size. Analysis yielded a mean weighted effect size of $d = .40$. In short, females were found to smile reliably, albeit modestly, more than males. In addition, a homogeneity analysis indicated that the set of effect sizes was heterogeneous—Q_w $(346) = 1391.52, p < .0001$—thus warranting examination of potential moderator variables.

Gender Norms for Smiling

First we looked for evidence bearing on the idea that social prescriptions call for women to show more positive facial displays than men. One way to check on the existence of such expectations was to see whether women smiled more when they knew they were being observed. Specifically, we predicted that sex difference effect size for smiling, favoring greater smiling by women, would be larger when a camera is visible rather than when it is hidden, when participants are with others rather than alone, and when participants are actively engaged with others rather than uninvolved.

There was significant support for all these predictions. Camera visibility produced a significant effect, indicating that as knowledge of being recorded became more apparent, the effect size favoring greater smiling by females became larger. The largest effect size was for the camera-visible situation ($d = .44$) and the smallest when there was no awareness of a camera ($d = .23$).

Presence of others also was a significant moderator. The smallest effect size ($d = .19$) occurred with participants were alone, and the largest occurred when four or more others were present along with the participant ($d = .54$). The prediction was that the difference in smiling would be greater when the participant interacted with others than when the participant was alone, and results show support for that notion.

The effect size for smiling was also greater when participants were more rather than less engaged with others. When participants were unengaged, the effect size was almost zero ($d = .01$). In contrast, when participants are required to interact, the effect sizes differ significantly from zero (co-action, $d = .34$; one-way interaction, $d = .72$; two-way interaction, $d = .39$). When all the interactive situations were compared with the no-engagement condition, the contrast was significant.

Gender norms for expressiveness were also expected to be more salient in interactions with unfamiliar than familiar others. With strangers, there was reason to suspect that participants are more concerned about behaving appropriately and hence that they would be more inclined to adopt gender normative expressive behavior with men smiling less than women. Results bear this out. There was a significant overall between-class effect for acquaintanceship. The largest effect size ($d = .38$) occurred for those with no prior contact and lowest for those who were familiar to each other at the time of the observation ($d = .12$).

In sum, there is clear evidence that women and men display more polarized gender-related behavior, specifically smiling, when they believe they are being evaluated. As Leary (this volume) has argued, people engage in behavior that has the probability of increasing their relational value and social acceptance. A woman who does not smile and a man who does are less likely to elicit social acceptance.

Situational Expressivity Scripts

The second premise has to do with the idea that if males and females are assigned to the same role or required to do the same task, then sex differences in smiling will be considerably smaller than in less scripted contexts where gender norms are expected to reign. Again there is ample support for the prediction that task or role demands substantially reduce the sex difference effect size.

The effect size favoring greater smiling by females was significantly smaller when research participants had the task of deceiving another person than when they were not expressly asked to do this ($d = .19$ and $d = .40$, respectively). Similar results were found when the task was to compete with someone else. During competitive interactions, the effect size assessing sex differences in smiling was significantly smaller than when interactants were not competing. In fact, the effect size was minimal and nonsignificant when the situation involved competition ($d = .06$). The same pattern was observed when the task involved teaching someone. However, one task led to results contrary to prediction. When engaged in persuading another, there was a significantly higher effect size ($d = .54$) than when participants were not focused on being persuasive ($d = .39$).

But two other scripted social roles, namely having social power and providing care-giving, yielded results in line with our thinking about the impact of situational scripts. With respect to interactions where one person has more or less power relative to another person, we predicted that a small sex difference in smiling would exist. When men and women are in high-power roles, they behave "high-power." When they have lower power relative to someone who can control their outcomes, then they behave "low-power." In other words, we predicted that the sex differences in smiling would be much reduced when the sexes had either high or low power relative to one another, because the rules for smiling come from the role rather than from gender scripts. In contrast, we believed that the sex differences would be substantially greater when power was not a relevant issue, that is, when they were on equal footing with one another. In the latter case, women would smile more than men would because there, the default option of gender-appropriate behavior would be in effect.

The results were in accord with such thinking. The largest effect size was observed for equal-power interactants ($d = .41$). In contrast, when participants had higher power than another person, the effect size was predictably smaller ($d = .29$). When they had lower power relative to another, the effect size was somewhat smaller ($d = .38$). The difference between equal power and high power was significant, while the difference between equal power and low power was marginally significant.

For people in caregiving roles such as physicians or therapists or even waiters, results also supported the situational script prediction. In other words, we predicted that when the role calls for nurturing and empathic behavior, smiling is part of the script, and hence the sex differences in such a role would be relatively small since both sexes know the routine. Again, there was solid support for the idea that when men and women are in similar roles, they will smile (or not) because of adherence to the social scripts which override gender prescriptions. We found that the effect size was smaller for caregivers ($d = .22$) than for those not in a caring role ($d = .41$).

Emotion Salience

The final idea involves the impact of emotionally laden situations. We predicted that these situations, however, are likely to accentuate gender differences in smiling. Specifically, when negative affect is high, women will smile more because they feel a stronger obligation to alleviate negative emotion.

Several moderators indicated support for this prediction. First, when situations were coded for presence of social tension, there was a larger effect size (d = .51), showing women smile more men than when the context was one in which the participants were relatively comfortable (d = .41). But there are different kinds of tension. When we coded situations for presence of detectable task tension, such as when there is evaluation apprehension, we saw a different pattern than when the situation was socially tense. Under task tension, there was a smaller effect size than when participants were comfortable with the task. In short, social tension rather than specific task tension is associated with greater differences in positive facial display between women and men, perhaps because in a situation defined as eliciting evaluation apprehension, participants are more concerned with performing the task at hand than with the emotional climate.

Next, we examined the prediction that women smile more when specific negative emotions, such as embarrassment or sadness, have been elicited. In embarrassing situations, we expected that women would smile significantly more than men would. Results bore us out. The size of the gender difference was significantly greater when embarrassment was created (d = .68) than when it was not (d = .39). A similar prediction was made with respect to situations characterized by sadness. Again we found that gender difference in smiling for sad situations (d = .77) is greater than for non-sad situations (d = .40).

Given the logic thus far, it might seem paradoxical for us to now predict a small effect size in smiling in *happy* contexts. We predicted comparable smiling by women and men when a situation is marked by happiness, precisely because smiling is most directly associated with positive affect for both sexes (Ekman et al., 1980). Emotion labor is not required when people are amused or elated. We found no difference in the amount of smiling shown by women and by men in such situations. In fact, when women and men are happy, there are no differences in how much they smile (d = −.04). Similar results were observed when humor was deliberately elicited. Humorous situations were also associated with a significantly lower gender difference (d = .18) in smiling.

There is some evidence, however, that men and women differ in how much they smile when there is *a need to appear to be happy*. Ekman and his colleagues have distinguished between Duchenne and non-Duchenne smiles (Ekman, 1985; Ekman et al., 1990). Duchenne or "felt" smiles reflect genuine pleasure, but non-Duchenne or "false" smiles do not. On the basis of Expressivity Demand Theory, we argued that gender differences would be larger for non-

Duchenne than for Duchenne smiles, since the former are more socially constructed while the latter are more associated with spontaneous happiness. Only two studies could be located with data directly bearing on this question (Hecht & LaFrance, 1998; Levenson, October 13, 1992, personal communication). As predicted, Levenson found no significant gender difference for felt smiles (d = .05) among married couples but a significant gender difference for false or non-Duchenne smiles (d = .24). Hecht and LaFrance (1998) also found no significant gender difference for felt smiles among people with low power or high power (d = 0.00 and d= .07, respectively) but a marginally significant gender difference for false smiles (d = .42).

DISCUSSION

One of the most interesting things about smiling is the range of contexts in which it can be found and the social uses to which it can be put, many of which could not remotely be called happy. Smiling is subject to monitoring, enhancement, and suppression because it is used to represent a social self (Hochschild, 1990). In short, smiling is often an efficient way to represent a positive persona. Sometimes smiles denote happiness; more often, smiling is done to establish social connections or reestablish social harmony.

Do women and men experience comparable obligation to represent a positive social self? Findings from the meta-analysis just described show that women feel a greater obligation to smile than do men. The first premise of Expressivity Demand Theory is that positive displays are expected more often from women than from men. Women are expected more than men to be focused on others, and a smile is an excellent way to communicate that. We predicted and found that the effect size showing more smiling by women was greater when gender norms were implicitly or explicitly highlighted.

The second major tenet of Expressivity Demand Theory speaks to the issue that smiling is also affected by context. Specifically, men and women smile similarly when they are required to engage in the same task, activity, or role. When subjects were given the task of deceiving or competing or teaching, we predicted that the gender difference effect size would be smaller than when no such demand is imposed. Results were supportive, although there was one task that generated results opposite to what we had predicted. When participants' task was to be persuasive, then the effect size for smiling was larger than when participants were not so occupied. One possible explanation for this resides in the fact that persuasion, like leadership, is something that requires women to be more "social" than men, leading to greater smiling (Eagly, Karau, & Makhijani, 1995).

The smiling of women and men was also relatively comparable when they were assigned to the same social role. When men and women had more power or when both had less power than their partner did, there was a smaller effect size than when they were on equal footing with their partner.

The third and final prediction had to do with emotional salience. That smiling is related to emotion, specifically positive emotion, is not in dispute. Instead, the proposal here is that smiling often serves to regulate others' emotions, especially negative ones; however, this particular social function falls to women more than men (Brody & Hall, 1993; Eagly, 1987; Hall, 1984). Several researchers have in fact argued that women will do more emotion management or "tending and befriending" than men both at work and at home (Taylor et al., 2000). The effect size showing women to smile more than men was substantially larger in response to perceptible social tension and when negative emotions were present.

In short, smiles are ways of presenting a self that is attuned to others. They are communicative acts addressed to other people rather than direct reflections of underlying mental states. This is likely true for both women and men even though the evidence shows that women smile more than men do. But of course, this does not mean that women smile more all of the time, nor does it mean that all women smile more than men. But it does mean that smiling for both women and men functions as a way to tie the self to one's social world. As such, smiling can also be work. It is a responsibility; it is something that needs to be done so those social ties can be established and sustained. It especially appears to be women's work.

There is, however, some indication that not all women are happy about the expectation that they be the ones to smile more in general and in particular in response to others' pain and discomfort. Indeed, some have taken issue with what they feel is the pressure to be pleasant. Shulamith Firestone (1970) once called for a "smile boycott," namely the idea that women should only smile when they feel like it.

More work needs to be done with respect to understanding how other expressive displays besides positive ones affect the social self and are affected by it. We also need to understand a good deal more than we do now about why and how positive facial displays are so linked with gender. But whatever the origins, it is clear that a smile boycott by women or men would significantly impact their ability to constitute a viable social self.

REFERENCES

Adelman, P. K. (1989). *Emotional labor and employee well-being*. Unpublished doctoral dissertation, University of Michigan, Ann Arbor.

Brody, L. R., & Hall, J. A. (1993). Gender and emotion. In M. Lewis & J. M. Haviland

(Eds.), *Handbook of emotions* (pp. 447–460). New York: Guilford.

Burgener, S. C., Jirovec, M., Murrell, L., & Barton, D. (1992). Caregiver and environmental variables related to difficult behaviors in institutionalized, demented elderly persons. *Journal of Gerontology, 47,* 242–249.

Darwin, C. (1965). *The expression of the emotions in man and animals.* New York: Appleton. (Original work published 1872)

Deutsch, F. M., LeBaron, D., & Fryer, M. (1987). What is in a smile? *Psychology of Women Quarterly, 11,* 341–352.

Eagly, A. H. (1987). *Sex differences in social behavior: A social role interpretation.* Hillsdale, NJ: Erlbaum.

Eagly, A. H., Karau, S. J., & Makhijani, M. F. (1995). Gender and the effectiveness of leaders: A meta-analysis. *Psychological Bulletin, 117,* 125–145.

Edelmann, R. J., Asendorpf, J., Contarello, A., & Zammuner, V. (1989). Self-reported expression of embarrassment in five European cultures. *Journal of Cross Cultural Psychology, 20,* 357–371.

Eibl-Eibesfeldt, I. (1989). *Human ethology.* New York: Aldine de Gruyter.

Ekman, P. (1985). *Telling lies.* New York: Norton.

Ekman, P., Davidson, R. J., & Friesen, W. (1990). The Duchenne smile: Emotional expression and brain physiology II. *Journal of Personality and Social Psychology, 58,* 342–353.

Ekman, P., & Friesen, W. V. (1969). The repertoire of nonverbal behavior: Categories, origins, usage, and coding. *Semiotica, 1,* 49–98.

Ekman, P., & Friesen, W. V. (1982). Felt, false, and miserable smiles. *Journal of Nonverbal Behavior, 6,* 238–252.

Ekman, P., Friesen, W. V., & Ancoli, S. (1980). Facial signs of emotional experience. *Journal of Personality and Social Psychology, 39,* 1125–1134.

Firestone, S. (1970). *The dialectic of sex.* New York: Bantam.

Fischer, A. H. (1993). Sex differences in emotionality: Fact or stereotype? *Feminism and Psychology, 3,* 303–318.

Fiske, S. T., & Stevens, L. E. (1993). What's so special about sex? Gender stereotyping and discrimination. In S. Oskamp & M. Costanzo (Eds.), *Gender issues in contemporary society* (pp. 173–196). Newbury Park, CA: Sage.

Fridlund, A. J. (1991). Sociality of solitary smiling: Potentiation by an implicit audience. *Journal of Personality and Social Psychology, 60,* 229–240.

Hall, J. A. (1984). *Nonverbal sex differences: Communication accuracy and expressive style.* Baltimore: Johns Hopkins University Press.

Hecht, M. A., & LaFrance, M. (1998). License or obligation to smile: Power, sex and smiling. *Personality and Social Psychology Bulletin, 24,* 1326–1336.

Henley, N. M. (1977). *Body politics: Power, sex, and nonverbal communication.* Englewood Cliffs, NJ: Prentice-Hall.

Hochschild, A. (1983). *The managed heart: Commercialization of human feeling.* Berkeley, CA: University of California Press.

Hochschild, A. (1989). Ideology and emotion management: A perspective and path for future research. In T. Kemper (Ed.), *Research agendas in the sociology of emotions* (pp. 180–203). Albany, NY: State University of New York Press.

Hochschild, A. (1990). Ideology and emotion management: A perspective and path for future research. In T. D. Kemper (Ed.), *Research agendas in the sociology of emotions* (pp. 117–142). Albany, NY: State University of New York Press.

Ickes, W., Patterson, M. L., Rajecki, D. W., & Tanford, S. (1982). Behavioral and cognitive consequences of reciprocal versus compensatory responses to preinteraction expectancies. *Social Cognition, 1,* 160–190.

James, N. (1989). Emotional labour: Skill and work in the social regulation of feelings. *Sociological Review, 37,* 15–42.

LaFrance, M. (1997). Pressure to be pleasant: Effects of sex and power on reactions to not smiling. *Revue Internationale de Psychology Sociale/International Review of Social Psychology, 2,* 95–108.

LaFrance, M., & Hecht, M. A. (1999). Obliged to smile: The effect of power and gender on facial expression. In P. Philippot, R. S. Feldman, & E. J. Coats (Eds.), *The social context of nonverbal behavior* (pp. 45–70). Cambridge, UK: Cambridge University Press.

Ochanomizu, U. (1991). Representation forming in Kusyo behavior. *Japanese Journal of Developmental Psychology, 2,* 25–31.

Salem, J. E. (1998). *Development and validation of a self-report measure of adherence to display rules for the facial expression of emotion*. Unpublished doctoral dissertation, Vanderbilt University, Nashville, TN.

Sarbin, T. (1986). Emotion and act: Roles and rhetoric. In R. Harre (Ed.), *The social construction of the emotions*. London: Blackwell.

Stoppard, J. M., & Gunn-Gruchy, C. D. (1993). Gender, context and expression of positive emotion. *Personality and Social Psychology Bulletin, 19*, 143–150.

Taylor, S., Klein, L. C., Lewis, B. P., Gruenewald, T. L., Gurung, R. A. R., & Updegraff, J. A. (2000). Biobehavioral responses to stress in females: Tend-and-befriend, not fight-or-flight. *Psychological Review, 107*(3), 411–429.

Walsh, D. G., & Hewitt, J. (1985). Giving men the come-on: Effect of eye contact and smiling in a bar environment. *Perceptual and Motor Skills, 61*, 873–874.

Wharton, A. S., & Erickson, R. J. (1993). Managing emotions on the job and in home: Understanding the consequences of multiple emotional roles. *Academy of Management Review, 18*, 457–486.

Wichroski, M. A. (1994). The secretary: Invisible labor in the workworld of women, *Human Organization, 53*, 33–41.

Wierzbicka, A. (1994). Emotion, language and cultural scripts. In S. Kitayama & H. R. Markus (Eds.), *Emotion and culture: Empirical studies of mutual influence* (pp. 133–196). Washington, DC: American Psychological Association.

Zanolli, K., Saudargas, R., & Twardosz, S. (1990). Two-year-olds' responses to affectionate and caregiving teacher behavior. *Child Study Journal, 20*, 35–54.

14

Interpersonal Dynamics of the Self
The Doubly Distributed Approach

YOSHIHISA KASHIMA
EMIKO KASHIMA
ANNA CLARK

INTRODUCTION

S ocial psychology of the self has examined the interplay between social context and self-cognition, primarily focusing on the impact of a variety of interpersonal and intergroup processes on the way in which one regards oneself. This research has put the self squarely within the web of social relationships in which the self is caught by birth or by choice. Yet this conceptual frame of reference misses a significant aspect of the social self as a *human* experience. As George Herbert Mead (1934), the champion of a thoroughly socialized conception of the self, noted, what distinguishes human sociality from that of other social species is symbolic mediation. That is, when we interact with other fellow humans in interpersonal or intergroup context, we act and react to their behavior not as uninterpreted brute force, but as intelligible and meaningful action. As such, the social context in which the self is embedded is saturated with symbolic meaning.

Address for correspondence: Yoshihisa Kashima, Department of Psychology, The University of Melbourne, Victoria 3010, Australia. E-mail: y.kashima@psych.unimelb.edu.au

To use Mead's terminology, human social behavior is a *significant symbol*, which gives rise to the same response not only in the person with whom one interacts but also in one's own self. So, closing and opening the eyelid of one eye quickly while keeping the other open functions as a significant symbol when it elicits the same understanding of "winking" in both the actor and the addressee. If human social behavior on other fellow humans has a psychological influence not by itself *qua* behavior, but as a symbol that stands for something else, it should be understood as a *representation*. Nevertheless, Mead's social behaviorism, as he called his doctrine, declared that it is the socially shared and intersubjective nature of the behavior as representation that made humans' social interaction truly human. For Mead, the kind of social interaction humans have is possible only when the interactants have a mutual understanding of the meaning of each other's action. His point was that the self emerges through meaningful social interaction as an organized whole that reflects the dynamic and yet structured social processes.

Despite this early lead, contemporary social psychology left much of the symbolic aspect of social processes, which may be called cultural processes in one sense of the term (Y. Kashima, 2000), in the background of theoretical and empirical research. Although there have been some encouraging trends (to be reviewed later), this is particularly problematic for research on social self. This is because the human capacity for symbol use may be intimately linked to the human predicament of self-reflexivity, much more so than hitherto acknowledged in social psychology. We argue for the importance of examining the nexus of symbolic mediation and selfhood in this contribution. While critically reviewing existing approaches to the symbolic self, we review our own work on culture and self that involves both empirical and connectionist-inspired simulation research (Kashima & Hardie, 2000; Kashima, Kashima, & Aldridge, 2001; Kashima, Kokubo, et al., 2001; Kashima et al., 1995).

THE SYMBOLIC CONSTRUCTION OF THE SELF

Symbol Use and Self-Cognition

Homo sapiens is one of the very few species known to exhibit the capacity to use symbols. Arguably, we are the only species that does so spontaneously at the level of complexity and flexibility of natural language and cultural symbols (Deacon, 1997). The fundamental competence involved in human symbol use may be a *metarepresentational* capacity, that is, the capacity to represent a representation (e.g., Sperber, 1996; R. A. Wilson, 2000). To illustrate the point, take the example of body piercing in some contemporary industrialized cultures. The fact of piercing one's body at a visible location (e.g., nose, tongue, navel) indicates that one is unique, a nonconformist, and different from "the mass." In other words, it is a representation of one's identity. However, the act of body piercing involves a metarepresentation in that the body piercer knows (or represents the fact) that the body piercing represents his/her identity. In other words, actors must be able to metarepresent in order to make use of cultural symbols as representations.

In fact, prominent discussions about symbols, symbolic communication, and strategic social action revolve around the notion of metarepresentations. To begin, Peirce (1991), a pragmatist philosopher and a contemporary of Mead, defined a symbol as "an object that stands for another to some mind" (p. 141; also see pp. 239–240). In explicating this, he argued that a symbol involves a three-term relationship among a sign, an object, and an interpretant. That is, a sign (e.g., piercing of one's nose) represents an object (e.g., identity of uniqueness and nonconformity), and an interpretant (e.g., a mental representation) represents the sign–object referential relation. For Peirce, symbol use by definition presupposes a metarepresentational capacity.

Symbolic communication often requires a metarepresentational capacity (e.g., Gibbs, 2000; Sperber & Wilson, 1986; D. Wilson, 2000). In interpreting what the speaker meant in his/her utterances, the listener must infer and therefore represent the speaker's intention, which is itself a representation of a sort (especially, see D. Wilson's, 2000, discussion of Grice). Parallel to this, the human capacity to "read" others' minds (i.e., theory of mind; e.g., Leslie, 1987; Perner, 1991; Wellman, 1990; also see Kashima, McIntyre, & Clifford, 1998; Malle & Knobe, 1997) requires a metarepresentational capacity, in which one needs to represent the other people's representations (e.g., beliefs, desires, and intentions). Finally, cultural learning may also require metarepresentational capacity (e.g., Tomasello, Kruger, & Ratner, 1993) because a learner needs to represent a teacher's intention to teach in order to learn from the teacher.

Recent theorizing and empirical evidence in developmental psychology implicates a metarepresentational capacity in the capacity to recognize oneself, which must underlie any self-cognition. Gallup's (1970, 1977) and Lewis and Brooks-Gunn's (1979) early demonstrations suggested that the capacity for self-recognition is rather scarce in nature, exhibited only by chimpanzees, orangutans, and humans older than approximately two years of age (e.g., Gallup & Suarez, 1986, for a review). The mirror self-recognition task is most often used to detect the capacity for self-recognition of human infants and nonhuman primates. An infant (or an animal) is marked on his/her face so that the mark cannot be seen by him/her without a mirror. The infant is then presented with a mirror later on. If the infant can recognize the image in the mirror as oneself, he/she should react to the mark on his/her own face rather than to the image in the mirror. To do this correctly, the infant should be able to realize that the image in the mirror is a representation, or the infant must be able to represent the representation of oneself in the mirror. This implies a metarepresentational capacity (Povinelli, 1995).

To test this, Nielsen, Dissanayake, and Kashima (2000) examined the coemergence of a metarepresentational capacity and the capacity for mirror self-recognition in a longitudinal design in which the development of these abilities within infants was tracked from 15 to 24 months old at the interval of 3 months. To measure metarepresentational capacity, infants' ability to pretend play was examined. In this task, infants were given a toy jug and cup, and asked to give a doll a drink. An infant who successfully displayed a pretend play was deemed to possess a metarepresentational capacity. As Leslie (1987) argued, this type of pretend play requires infants to metarepresent. This is because they must recognize that the toy jug and cup is in fact a representation of a real jug and cup, and that giving the doll a drink is only a representation of really giving someone a drink. Nielsen et al.'s study showed that the developmental trajectories of pretend play and mirror self-recognition closely coincided with each other, and that the age at which pretend play was observed correlated significantly with the age at which mirror self-recognition was displayed. The results imply that the human capacities for self-recognition and metarepresentation are closely linked in child development. If in fact the same metarepresentational capacities underlie both self-recognition and symbol use, it suggests that one cannot have self-cognition without a symbolic capacity.

Gene-Culture Coevolution, and Symbol Use

The close connection between the self and symbol use may be further strengthened by considering the evolutionary basis of symbol use. It is often argued that human social connectedness (Baumeister & Leary, 1995; Caporael, 1997) may have resulted from the human's evolutionary past in which hominids lived in bands of a size of around 30 or macrobands of a size around 300 (Caporael, 1997). As Sedikides and Skowronski (1997) suggested, this social environment may have evolutionarily contributed to the emergence of the symbolic self. Nonetheless, the importance of the *symbolic* environment sustained within bands and macrobands to evolutionary processes is less appreciated in social psychology. It is true that Caporael (1997) pointed to the significance of "shared reality" and "cultural practices" within bands as a factor giving hominids a reproductive advantage. However, she too failed to emphasize the possibility that the shared reality or the symbolic environment per se, once created, could have constituted the environment to which hominids' brains may have had to adapt.

Just such a position, often called gene–culture coevolution, has been outlined by a number of researchers (e.g., Boyd & Richerson, 1985; Durham, 1994). In a nutshell, this position claims that both genetic and symbolic information contributed to the shaping of the contemporary human society. The human genetic makeup not only enables the human sociality but also presupposes it. Without the human sociocultural environment, the human genetic makeup is incomplete. To use the terminology Caporael (1997) urged us, the human genetic makeup and the symbolic environment sustained in the human social organization constitute a *repeated assembly*, a coupling between a genetic possibility and its environment. In particular, it has been argued that the human brain structure and the symbolic environment coevolved. According to this view, the expansion of the brain size, especially that of the frontal cortex, did not so much cause the ability to use symbols, but rather was triggered and facilitated by the human symbolic environment that coevolved with the human social organization.

Deacon (1997) recently made a case for this position using a current knowledge base provided by the development in physical anthropology and evolutionary biology. The hominid social organization was such that relatively exclusive sexual accessibility needed to be maintained between a male and a female for the reproduction and care of their offspring while a band of hominids needed to coordinate their activities to maintain the resource extraction system of hunting and gathering, especially hunting for meat. Deacon argues that something akin to a social contract was necessary to retain the sexual exclusivity while maintaining a cooperative band. This "social contract" is more like a mutually shared representation within a band that this male and this female are bound by a set of obligations (e.g., bringing meat for feeding, sexual exclusivity) and rights (e.g., sexual access, demanding meat for feeding) not only between the mating pair, but also involving the whole of the band. According to Deacon, the learning of this type of representation requires a symbolic capacity. In other words, the evolutionary pressure to balance the trade-off between the sustenance of the cooperative band structure and the assurance of the reproduction of one's own offspring gave rise to the symbolic environment, which in turn gave an additional reproductive advantage for organisms with a brain structure that supports a symbolic capacity.

Symbolic Culture and Self

The symbolic environment with which the human symbolic capacity coevolved is culture in one sense of the term (Kashima, 2000). Culture in this sense provides a symbolic resource with which to construct self-representations (e.g., Bruner, 1990; Smith, 1991). In the current literature of social psychology, however, there have been two clusters of research on the interplay between symbolic culture and self-conception. One cluster adopts a cross-cultural or transhistorical perspective, examining macro-level differences among contemporary cultures and across different historical periods. The other cluster adopts a discursive or social constructionist perspective, detailing micro-level uses of symbolic resources within a particular discursive context. We briefly review them here.

The cross-cultural and transhistorical perspective has been well-represented in recent social psychology around the world (see Y. Kashima, in press; Y. Kashima, Foddy, & Platow, in press, for recent reviews). Following a number of prior theoretical developments (e.g., Hofstede, 1980; Shweder & Bourne, 1982), Triandis (1989) argued that different social conditions (e.g., complexity of social role differentiation, wealth, individualism) tend to make available different types of self-representations, and Markus and Kitayama (1991) theorized that different types of self-representations tend to generate different types of cognitive, affective, and motivational processes. Quite independently, Baumeister (1986) also theorized that different self-conceptions have emerged as culture changed over historical periods (also see Gergen, 1991), especially focusing on the Western European and North American cultural tradition.

Generally, this research tradition emphasized the contrast between a collectivist (interdependent or traditional) and an individualist (independent or modern) self-conception (though there are some important variations among theorists). The collectivist self-conception is said to emphasize the embeddedness of the self in social context, giving a priority to the group goal when it is in conflict with the individual goal. The individualist self-conception, by contrast, stresses the uniqueness and separateness of the self from other individuals, clearly favoring the individual goal pursuit rather than subjecting it to the pursuit of the group goal. Baumeister's point has been that the individualist self-conception emerged out of the breakdown of the traditional or medieval social order in the West through the Enlightenment and Romantic periods. Triandis and Markus and Kitayama suggested that the individualist self-conception predominates in Western Europe and cultures strongly influenced by Western European traditions such as Australia and the United States, whereas the collectivist self-conception is more prevalent in East Asian and Latin American cultures (for reviews, see Y. Kashima, in press; Y. Kashima et al., in press).

In contrast, the discursive and social constructionist perspective on culture and self has been productive especially in European social psychology. Following the lead of Wetherell and Potter (1992) and Edwards and Potter (1992), researchers have examined the way in which social identities and self-categories are used on the fly within particular discursive contexts for various strategic social purposes (e.g., Antaki, Condor, & Levine, 1996; Rapley, 1998; Reicher & Hopkins, 1996a; Reicher & Hopkins, 1996b). This research tradition is similar in spirit to Le Page and Tabouret-Keller's (1985) sociolinguistic project. They characterized "linguistic behaviour as a series of *acts of identity* in which people reveal both their personal identity and their search for social roles" (p. 14). So, language or more generally symbolic culture is seen as providing a variety of symbolic tools with which to project one's personal or social identity on the "stage" of social interaction. A large collection of studies exists in which researchers examined people's uses of linguistic cues (e.g., pronunciation, vocabulary, sentence structure, storytelling) in projecting their personal and social identities such as ethnicity (e.g., Le Page & Tabouret-Keller, 1985; Walters, 1996), gender (e.g., Eckert & McConnell-Ginet, 1999), social role (e.g., Schiffrin, 1996), expertise (e.g., Matoesian, 1999), "nerdiness" (e.g., Bucholtz, 1999), and so on.

Not withstanding their methodological differences, most clearly, these research traditions differ in terms of their preferred units of analysis. The cross-cultural and transhistorical perspective tends to take a culture or historical period as a whole as a unit of analysis, whereas the discursive and social constructionist approach focuses on a particular discourse. As a result, those who take the former approach tend to look for noncontextualized global differences in cultural pattern at the expense of contextual variability within culture; by contrast, the latter approach tends to take pleasure in rich descriptions and interpretations of particularities while abandoning the project of characterizing a general cultural pattern. In this sense, these approaches complement each other.

Nonetheless, there are serious conceptual drawbacks for both approaches. The cross-cultural and transhistorical approach tends to overlook the temporal dynamics as it tends to look for a relatively enduring symbolic system within a society within a historical period. Historical analyses do trace the trajectory of cultural change over a long period of time; however, they usually seek the engine of cultural change outside the symbolic realm such as technological advances, industrialization, and urbanization, for instance. Individuals' concrete social activities in particular contexts are not recognized as a locus of culture change. In contrast, the discursive and social constructionist approach does shed light on the dynamics of culture in its focus on the symbolic construction of the self *in situ*. However, the discursive and social constructionist approach tends to overemphasize the importance of symbolic meaning while leaving behind the embodied nature of the symbolic communication (e.g., Kempen, 1998; Overton, 1997). Although there is a move (e.g., Eckert & McConnell-Ginet, 1999) to ground the discursive approach to a theory of social practice (Lave & Wenger, 1991) that acknowledges the concrete human person's linguistic as well as nonlinguistic activities, this is yet to be realized in research. Our research program has been to develop a theory of the self that can overcome the shortcomings of the current approaches to symbolic culture and self, to which we turn next.

THE DOUBLY DISTRIBUTED APPROACH TO THE MICRO-MACRO PROBLEM IN CULTURE AND SELF

Our major theoretical objective has been to address the sociocultural dynamics involved in the symbolic construction of the self. A central issue in this research program has been a micro–macro problem. Much of the contemporary discussion of culture in psychology has revolved around two conceptions of culture (Y. Kashima, 2000). One conception regards culture as an enduring meaning system (e.g., Triandis, 1994), while the other sees it as the process of meaning-making in particular contexts (e.g., Cole, 1996). The contrast between the cross-cultural/

transhistorical and the discursive/constructionist approaches to culture and self is only a special case of this general split in level of analysis. This micro–macro split is endemic to social science, and to culture theory in particular. Yet, in examining how individuals construct their selves in their ongoing social interaction, it is imperative to address the interface of the macro-level cultural meaning system as symbolic resources and the micro-level meaning-making in symbolically mediated social interaction.

Doubly Distributed Approach

We outline here what we call a doubly distributed approach (Kashima, Kashima, & Aldridge, 2001), which we believe can move us forward in addressing the micro-macro problem in culture and self. According to this view, symbolic meaning is represented in a distributed fashion among individuals and cultural artifacts (distirbuted cognition) as well as within an individual (parallel distributed processing; PDP). A combination of the PDP and distributed cognition approaches helps to address two of the questions in the micro–macro problem: contextualization in cultural learning and representational format of cultural meaning.

The view of culture that emphasizes contextualized meaning-making activities forces us to realize that humans learn culture in specific contexts from other social agents. Once learned, we tend to reproduce learned social activities without perfectly repeating them, that is, with some variation across contexts. Furthermore, we sometimes produce novel social activities, though innovation is unlikely to be completely random (i.e., possibility for "regulated improvisations," Bourdieu, 1977, p. 78). Kashima and Kashima (1999) argued that parallel distributed processing (PDP) mechanisms are suitable for capturing these properties of cultural learning. The PDP approach attempts to model a human cognitive process in terms of a collection of simple information-processing units whose connections are constantly updated as a function of new information (e.g., Rumelhart, McClelland, & the PDP Research Group, 1986). In contrast to localist connectionist networks, which represent a meaningful concept by an individual node, distributed connectionist networks represent a meaningful concept in terms of a pattern of activation over a collection of processing units (e.g., see Read, Vanman, & Miller, 1996; Smith, 1996, for informative reviews).

Yet, the contextualized view of cultural learning poses a problem of how a cultural meaning system may be represented as a macro-level representation. The old-style organic model of culture would not do. Cultural meanings cannot float in the air. A solution offered has been to regard meanings as distributed across individuals and artifacts in a society. This is a claim of the distributed cognition approach (e.g., Hutchins, 1995; see Clark, 1998, for a concise statement; also see Resnick, Levine, & Teasley, 1991). Culturally available knowledge and ideas are not evenly distributed across all members of a society. Clearly, no single person possesses all the knowledge of one culture. Some expertise is acquired by a subset of a society; and presumably a small subset of the entire knowledge available to a society is shared by all. In social psychology, Wegner (1986) called this type of representational format a transactive memory system in which information encoding, storage, and retrieval is distributed across individuals. He argued that people who know each other well can develop a cognitive division of labor so that, for instance, a husband may remember about car-related items (e.g., gasoline price in Orlando) while a wife may remember friends' birthdays (for a recent review on this literature, see Moreland, Argote, & Krishnan, 1996). Furthermore, meaning is represented not only in human minds, but also externally in symbolic forms (e.g., language) and cultural artifacts (e.g., layout of the house). Obviously, these objects cannot be meaningful in the absence of interpreting human minds. Nonetheless, they take on a degree of autonomy. As Durkheim (1882) noted long ago, for those who enter into a society (children, new comers), they do exist as a constraint external to them. Vygotsky (1978) noted that these cultural artifacts provide a tool by which social activities are conducted.

To demonstrate the utility of this way of conceptualizing symbolic culture and its application to the research on culture and self, Kashima, Kashima, and Aldridge (2001) conducted a simple simulation experiment in which a doubly distributed approach was implemented in a connectionist-inspired architecture, which they called the Doubly Distributed Recurrent Network (DDRN; Figure 14.1).

Architecture. In this simulation, a well-known connectionist architecture, a Simple Recurrent Network (SRN; Elman, 1990) was extended so that three SRNs were connected together to form a small "society." SRN is an extension of a standard three-layer feedforward network. It consists of an input layer, a hidden layer, and an output layer, each made up of a set of simple information-processing units. Although the three-layered architecture has not been used in social psychology, it is often used in cognitive science. The hidden layer contains units hidden from the environment with which both input and output layers interface. In a typical three-layer feedforward network, a processing unit receives inputs from connected units, and outputs some activation. The activation spreads forward from the input units through the hidden units to the output units. A unit is activated at a level between 0 and 1 as a non-linear function of the sum of the inputs from all incoming connections. The unit's input to another unit is a function of the product of the activation level and the connection weight. A three-layer feedforward network learns an association between inputs and outputs by adjusting connection weights so that the network can accurately predict on the basis of its inputs the outputs to be learned. The SRN adds context units to a three-layer feedforward network, which also sends acti-

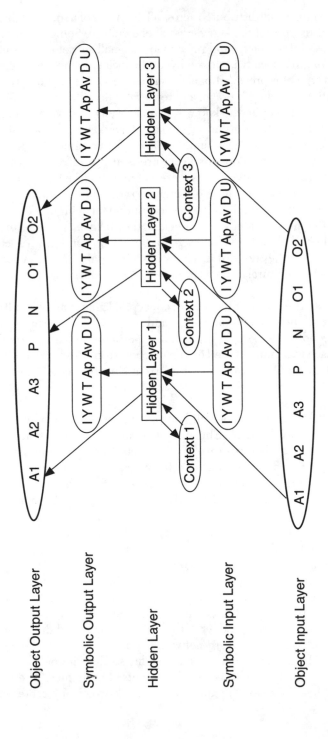

FIGURE 14.1. Schematic picture of doubly distributed recurrent network (DDRN).
Notes. A1 = Actor1, A2 = Actor2, A3 = Actor3, P = Positive Action, N = Negative Action, O1 = Object1, O2 = Object2. I = first-person singular, Y = second-person singular, W = first-person plural, T = third-person plural, T = third-person singular, Ap = approach, Av = avoidance, D = desired object, U = undesired object. This figure was originally published in Kashima, Kashima, and Aldridge (2001).

vation to the hidden units in addition to the input units. This architecture allows the network to learn a sequence of events unfolding over time, for instance, an event 1 leading to event 2, which in turn results in event 3, and so on (see Elman, 1990, 1991, for details).

This architecture not only enables the learning of sequential inputs but also the developing of "internal representations" for the inputs. After the learning is complete, the network propagates activation from the input through hidden to output units when a learned input pattern is presented again. For a given input pattern, then, it produces a corresponding hidden unit activation pattern, which may be interpreted as analogous to an intrapersonal representation of the meaning of the input. In Y. Kashima et al.'s (2001) simulation, SRNs were connected to each other via a simple world made up of objects and a simple symbol system. The object units represent objects in the world with each of the units for a particular object. The object layer in the simulation had seven units, representing seven different objects: Actor1 (A1), Actor2 (A2), Actor3 (A3), positive action (P), negative action (N), Object1 (O1), and Object2 (O2). The symbol layer contained eight symbols: first-person singular (I), second-person singular (You), third-person singular (They—to avoid sexist language), first-person plural (We), approach (Ap), avoidance (Av), desired object (D), and undesired object (U).

Within each SRN, the input units feed into the hidden units, which then feed forward to the output units. In addition, the object units feed into the hidden units of all the nets, which then feed into the output object units. Note that the input units of an individual net do not feed to the hidden units of the other nets, and the hidden units of the given individual net do not feed into the output units of the other nets. This pattern of connections modeled the world in which, though an individual's psychological processes are not directly accessible to other individuals, the objects and symbols are. In the DDRN, then, multiple networks were connected to simulate the learning of social interaction episodes that are constantly encoded and stored not only in each individual's distributed representational system (i.e., each hidden layer), but also in the socially distributed fashion (i.e., across hidden layers).

Inputs. One input to the network is a 31-element vector that reflects one object and its three encodings. The object, Actor1 (A1), may be encoded as *I* (first-person singular) by Actor1, but may be encoded as *You* (second-person singular) by Actor2 and *They* (third person singular) by Actor3. This state of affairs is represented by a vector whose appropriate elements are activated, with all the other elements being zero. One sequence of three inputs constitutes an *action*. The first input represents the actor, the second input represents the behavior, and the third represents the object to which the behavior is directed. Suppose that Actor1 acts positively to Object1, and assume that Object1 is encoded as desired by all the actors. This action is represented by a series of three inputs, assumed to be encoded by Actor1 as "I approach a desired object," but by the other actors as "They (he/she) approach a desired object." Three action types were assumed: individualist action (the actor is a single person whose action is directed to an object), relational action (a single person's action is directed to another person), and collective action (multiple individuals act toward an object, a person, or a group). An episode is a sequence of one or more actions. A one-step episode (i.e., nonresponsive) is a simple action that completes its course by itself. A two-step episode (i.e., responsive) consists of two relational actions that jointly complete one episode. For example, when Actor1 acts negatively to Actor2, and then Actor2 retaliates by acting negatively to Actor1, this sequence constitutes a two-step episode involving two relational actions. The input set consisted of an approximately equal number of actions of the three-action types with each type of action sequences randomly sampled and ordered.

Results. The input sequence was fed to the system six times in the same order, and all possible single- and two-step episodes were fed to the system in a random order without changing the connection weights. The hidden layer activation pattern for each input was then recorded. The pattern was investigated in two ways. First, the collective representations of the DDRN were examined by conducting a multidimensional scaling (MDS) analysis of the activation pattern of all the hidden units together. Second, the individual representations of each SRN embedded in the DDRN were examined by a comparable MDS and a hierarchical cluster analysis. This is the strength of the doubly distributed approach, that is, the possibility of analyzing the collective and individual representations within a single framework.

The MDS solutions of the collective and individual representations are shown in Panels A and B of Figure 14.2. In both collective and individual representations, there are four clear clusters of hidden activation patterns. One cluster represents actions. The other three are one cluster for actors on the right, one cluster for objects on the left, and one cluster for actors as objects (when acts were directed to actors) in between the two. This suggests that (1) the same object in the world can be represented somewhat differently depending on the context (in this case what precedes in the sequence of inputs), and (2) similar types of objects in the world nevertheless can be represented similarly. Collective and individual representations appear to change dynamically as social interactions unfold; however, they are not completely fluid either, as they retain their general configuration. The individual representations in Panel B suggest that there are some individual differences despite the general similarities in the configurations.

The individual representations in each SRN were further investigated by a cluster analysis to look more closely at self-representations developed by each network. The hidden activation patterns for the inputs that represented *I* or *We*

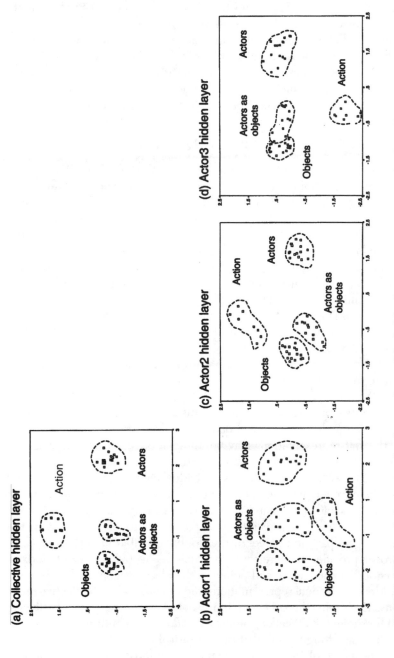

FIGURE 14.2. Multidimensional scaling analyses of the hidden layer activation patterns for the collective and individual representations.

Note: This figure was originally published in Kashima, Kashima, and Aldridge (2001).

for each network showed that for each network three clusters were discernible. First, there was a clear cluster of collective selves. The representations of *We*, where the self was involved in a collective action, clustered separately from the other self-representations. However, there were two additional clusters that may be interpreted as representing individual and relational selves. The relational selves included the representations of *I* where the self was involved in an episode of relational actions, in which relational actions were reciprocated in an interactive fashion. The individual selves included the representations of *I* whose actions were directed to objects or other actors regarded as objects.

Implications of the Doubly Distributed Approach

These results corroborate the tripartite model of the self that is increasingly popular in social psychology. Researchers such as Brewer and Gardner (1986), Kashima et al. (1995), and Triandis (1989) all suggested that there are at least three significant types of self-representations. The one that we prefer (see Kashima, Kashima, & Aldridge, 2001) views the self as a symbolic structure that takes on meaning in relation to other concepts. The individual self represents the self in relation to an objective, as a goal-directed agent; the relational self captures the self in relation to another individual, as a self in interpersonal relationship; and the collective self is the self in relation to a collective, as a member of a social group. The simulation results outlined above show that there exists a physical mechanism that can learn to distinguish these three self-aspects as separable representations.

The current approach makes several important theoretical points. First, these self-representations do not have to be stored in separate locations as contended by Trafimow, Triandis, and Goto (1991), but may be stored in the same processing units in a distributed fashion. This stems from the parallel distributed processing architecture embedded in the doubly distributed approach. Second, the self-representations may be understood as part of the collective social information-processing distributed across individuals. As individual actors engage in their social activities as individuals and as groups, these social behaviors are encoded in terms of meaningful symbols and are represented not only in each of the individual minds, but also across them, an insight that closely parallels that of Mead's. This is the consequence of the distributed cognition perspective again part and parcel of the doubly distributed approach. Third, this approach provides a concrete way in which a collective representation may be understood and analyzed, and points to the close conceptual link between the micro-level individual representations and the macro-level collective representations. Especially, the collective representation may be conceptually akin to what Durkheim (1882) called *conscience collective* a century ago.

Finally, it is fitting to note that our empirical research program based on the tripartite model of the self has been yielding intriguing insights into the mutual constitution of culture and self. To begin, E. Kashima and Hardie (2000) provided a psychometric underpinning to the tripartite model of the self. The measures of individual, relational, and collective selves correlated positively within each category, but not across categories. A multidimensional scaling of a number of scales showed three separate clusters in a two-dimensional space. The first dimension placed the three clusters in the order of individual, relational, and collective. The second dimension distinguished the relational cluster from both collective and individual clusters.

Kashima et al. (1995) administered measures of individual, relational, and collective selves to samples of university students in Australia, the mainland United States, Hawaii, Japan, and Korea. They showed that the measures of the three aspects were only moderately correlated with each other. More important, the measure tapping the significance of the individual self most strongly differentiated Australia and the U.S. samples from the Japanese and Korean samples with the Hawaiian sample in between. Although the relational self was more strongly held by women than men in each of the cultures, this dimension did not distinguish the Western samples from the East Asian samples. It is interesting to note that Kashima and Hardie's data also replicated this finding by showing that females scored higher than males on relational self. Kashima and Hardie found a male tendency to be slightly more collectivist than females when relational tendency was controlled. These results shed light on the recent theoretical development on gender and self that men and women may have different types of social connectedness (Baumeister & Sommer, 1997; Cross & Madson, 1997).

More recently, Kashima, Kokubo, et al. (2001) examined cultural differences between Western and East Asian cultures in individual and collective self. In the current literature, it has often been assumed that Westerners emphasize the individual, agentic self, whereas East Asians regard the collective self as more important. However, in this research, an alternative possibility that urbanism may be responsible for the purported cultural difference is presented. That is, East Asians may have been seen to emphasize their collective selves because their sociocultural enviornment was less urbanized than that of their Western counterparts. To test this, Kashima, Kokuba, et al. took samples from urban areas (Melbourne and Tokyo) and rural areas (Wodonga and Kagoshima) in Australia and Japan. They replicated their previous findings that Australians emphasized individual self more than Japanese whereas there was no urban–rural difference in this regard. They also showed that there was no difference in collective self between the two cultures but that there was a comparable urban–rural difference in both Australia and Japan. In both cultures, a rural sample emphasized collective selves more strongly than an urban sample.

Jointly, the empirical studies provide support for the tripartite division of the self into the individual, relational, and collective aspects. Not only do measures tapping into the separate aspects show relative independence, but they also relate to different sociocultural conditions. To put it simply, the individual self varies as a function of cultural meaning system, between East Asian and Western cultures. The relational self captures gender differences in a systematic fashion at least in the contemporary industrialized cultures. The collective self may change as the social condition becomes more urban. In turn, these results clearly suggest that macro-level sociocultural conditions do influence micro-level self-cognitions.

The doubly distributed approach suggests that people whose behaviors are shaped by the sociocultural conditions (cultural meaning, gender division of labor, and urbanism) may engage in different proportions of individual, relational, and collective social actions. These overt social activities may act as a mediator that links macro-level sociocultural conditions and the emergence of social selves. This hypothesis needs to be empirically investigated. It further implies that these macro-level sociocultural conditions may in turn be maintained by the ongoing social activities—in particular, the relative prominence of individual, relational, and collective social actions—that the actors engage in. The social reality of sociocultural institutions are in fact sustained by the very activities that presuppose the existence of those sociocultural institutions (e.g., Berger & Luckmann, 1967; Giddens, 1979). To the extent that humans tend to reproduce what they have learned in concrete contexts, their behaviors may be self-perpetuating. When these social activities are mutually interlocking and sustaining, the activities may sustain themselves even in the absence of a general intent to sustain them, thus forming self-perpetuating sociocultural processes that link the micro and macro levels of analyses.

REFERENCES

Antaki, C., Condor, S., & Levine, M. (1996). Social identities in talk: Speakers' own orientations. *British Journal of Social Psychology, 35*, 473–492.

Baumeister, R. F. (1986). *Identity: Cultural change and the struggle for self*. New York: Oxford University Press.

Baumeister, R. F., & Leary, M. R. (1995). The need to belong: Desire for interpersonal attachments as a fundamental human motivation. *Psychological Bulletin, 117*, 497–529.

Baumeister, R. F., & Sommer, K. L. (1997). What do men want? Gender differences and two spheres of belongingness: Comment on Cross and Madson (1997). *Psychological Bulletin, 22*, 38–44.

Berger, P., & Luckmann, T. (1967). *The social construction of reality*. London: Penguin Books.

Bourdieu, P. (1977). *Outline of a theory of practice*. (R. Nice, Trans.). Cambridge, UK: Cambridge University Press.

Boyd, R., & Richerson, P. J. (1985). *Culture and the evolutionary process*. Chicago: University of Chicago Press.

Brewer, M. B., & Gardner, W. (1996). Who is this "we"? Levels of collective identity and self representations. *Journal of Personality and Social Psychology, 71*, 83–93.

Bruner, J. (1990). *Acts of meaning*. Cambridge, MA: Harvard University Press.

Bucholtz, M. (1999). "Why be normal?": Language and identity practices in a community of nerd girls. *Language in Society, 28*, 203–223.

Caporael, L. R. (1997). The evolution of truly social cognition: The core configurations model. *Personality and Social Psychology Review, 1,* 276–298.

Clark, A. (1998). Embodied, situated, and distributed cognition. In W. Bechtel & G. Graham (Eds.), *Blackwell companions to philosophy: A companion to cognitive science* (pp. 506–517). Oxford, UK: Basil Blackwell.

Cole, M. (1996). *Cultural psychology.* Cambridge, MA: Belknap Press.

Cross, S. E., & Madison, L. (1997). Models of the self: Self-construals and gender. *Psychological Bulletin, 122,* 5–37.

Deacon, T. W. (1997). *The symbolic species.* New York: Norton.

Durham, W. (1994). *Coevolution.* Stanford, CA: Stanford University Press.

Durkheim, E. (1982). *The rule of sociological method.* London: Macmillan.

Eckert, P., & McConnell-Ginet, S. (1999). New generalizations and explanations in language and gender research. *Language in Society, 28,* 185–201.

Edwards, D., & Potter, J. (1992). *Discursive psychology.* London: Sage.

Elman, J. L. (1990). Finding structure in time. *Cognitive Science, 14,* 179–211.

Elman, J. L. (1991). Distributed representations, simple recurrent networks, and grammatical structure. *Machine Learning, 7,* 195–225.

Gallup, G. G., Jr. (1970). Chimpanzees' self-recognition. *Science, 167,* 86–87.

Gallup, G. G., Jr. (1977). Self-recognition in primates: A comparative approach to the bidirectional properties of consciousness. *American Psychologist, 32,* 329–338.

Gallup, G. G., Jr., & Suarez, S. D. (1986). Self-awareness and the emergence of mind in humans and other primates. In J. Suls & A. G. Greenwald (Eds.), *Psychological perspectives on the self, Vol. 3* (pp. 3–26). Hillsdale, NJ: Erlbaum.

Gergen, K. J. (1991). *The saturated self.* New York: Basic Books.

Gibbs, R. W., Jr. (2000). Metarepresentations in staged communicative acts. In D. Sperber (Ed.), *Metarepresentations* (pp. 389–410). Oxford, UK: Oxford University Press.

Giddens, A. (1979). *Central problems in social theory.* London: Macmillan.

Hofstede, G. (1980). *Culture's consequences.* Beverly Hills, CA: Sage.

Hutchins, E. (1995). *Cognition in the wild.* Cambridge, MA: MIT Press.

Kashima, E. S., & Hardie, E. A. (2000). Development and validation of the relational, individual, and collective self-aspects (RIC) scale. *Asian Journal of Social Psychology, 3,* 19–48.

Kashima, Y. (2000). Conceptions of culture and person for psychology. *Journal of Cross-Cultural Psychology, 31,* 14–32.

Kashima, Y. (in press). Culture and social cognition: Towards a social psychology of cultural dynamics. In D. Matsumoto (Ed.), *Handbook of culture and psychology.* New York: Oxford University Press.

Kashima, Y., Foddy, M., & Platow, M. (in press). *Self and identity: Personal, social, and symbolic.* Mahwah, NJ: Erlbaum.

Kashima, Y., & Kashima, E. S. (1999). Culture, connectionism, and the self. In J. Adamopoulos & Y. Kashima (Eds.), *Social behavior in cultural contexts* (pp. 77–92). London: Sage.

Kashima, Y., Kashima, E., & Aldridge, J. (2001). Towards cultural dynamics of self-conceptions. In C. Sedikides & M. B. Brewer (Eds.), *Individual self, relational self, and collective self: Partners, opponents, or strangers* (pp. 277–298). Philadelphia: Psychology Press.

Kashima, Y., Kokubo, T., Kashima, E., Yamaguchi, S., Boxall, D., & Macrae, K. (2001). *Culture and a tripartite model of self: Are Eastern selves less individualist, more relational, or more collectivist than Western selves?* Manuscript submitted for publication.

Kashima, Y., McIntyre, A., & Clifford, P. (1998). The category of the mind: Folk psychology of belief, desire, and intention. *Asian Journal of Social Psychology, 1,* 289–313.

Kashima, Y., Yamaguchi, S., Kim, U., Choi, S-C., Gelfand, J. M., & Yuki, M. (1995). Culture, gender, and self: A perspective from individualism-collectivism research. *Journal of Personality and Social Psychology, 69,* 925–937.

Kempen, H. J. G. (1998). Mind as body moving in space: Bringing the body back into self-psychology. In H. J. Stam (Ed.), *The body and psychology* (pp. 54–70). London: Sage.

Lave, J., & Wenger, E. (1991). *Situated learning*. Cambridge, UK: Cambridge University Press.

Le Page, R. B., & Tabouret-Keller, A. (1985). *Acts of identity: Creole-based approaches to language and ethnicity*. Cambridge, UK: Cambridge University Press.

Leslie, A. M. (1987). Presense and representation: The origins of "theory of mind." *Psychological Review, 94*, 412–426.

Lewis, M., & Brooks-Gunn, J. (1979). *Social cognition and the acquisition of self*. New York: Plenum Press.

Malle, B. F., & Knobe, J. (1997). The folk concept of intentionality. *Journal of Experimental Social Psychology, 33*, 101–121.

Markus, H., & Kitayama, S. (1991). Culture and the self. *Psychological Review, 98*, 224–253.

Matoesian, G. M. (1999). The grammaticalization of praticipant roles in the constitution of expert identity. *Language in Society, 28*, 491–521.

Mead, G. H. (1934). *Mind, self and society*. Chicago: University of Chicago Press.

Moreland, R. L., Argote, L., & Krishnan, R. (1996). Socially shared cognition at work: Transactive memory and group performance. In J. L. Nye & A. M. Brower (Eds.), *What's social about social cognition?* (pp. 57–84). Thousand Oaks, CA: Sage.

Nielsen, M., Dissanayake, C., & Kashima, Y. (2000). *A longitudinal investigation of the emergence of mirror self-recognition, imitation and pretend play in human infants*. Unpublished manuscript, La Trobe University, Melbourne, Australia.

Overton, W. F. (1997). Beyond dichotomy: An embodied active agent for cultural psychology. *Culture and Psychology, 3*, 315–334.

Peirce, C. A. (1991). *Peirce on signs: Writings on semiotic by Charles Sanders Peirce*. Chapel Hill, NC: The University of North Carolina Press.

Perner, J. (1991). *Understanding the representational mind*. Cambridge, MA: MIT Press.

Povinelli, D. J. (1995). The unduplicated self. In P. Rochat (Ed.), *The self in infancy:*

Theory and research (pp. 161–192). Amsterdam: North-Holland/Elsevier Science .

Rapley, M. (1998). 'Just an ordinary Australian': Self-categorization and the discursive construction of facticity in 'new racist' political rhetoric. *British Journal of Social Psychology, 37*, 325–344.

Read, S. J., Vanman, E. J., & Miller, L. C. (1996). Connectionism, parallel constraint satisfaction processes, and Gestalt principles: (Re)introducing cognitive dynamics to social psychology. *Personality and Social Psychology Review, 1*, 26–53.

Reicher, S., & Hopkins, N. (1996a). Self-category constructions in political rhetoric: An analysis of Tatcher's and Kinnock's speeches concerning the British miners' strike (1984-5). *European Journal of Social Psychology, 26*, 353–371.

Reicher, S., & Hopkins, N. (1996b). Seeking influence through characterizing self-categories: An analysis of anti-abortionist rhetoric. *British Journal of Social Psychology, 35*, 297–311.

Resnick, L. B., Levine, J. M., & Teasley, S. D. (Eds.). (1991). *Perspectives on socially shared cognition*. Washington, DC: American Psychological Association.

Rumelhart, D. E., McClelland, J. L., & the PDP Research Group. (Eds.). (1986). *Parallel distributed processing: Explorations in the microstructure of cognition (Vol. 1)*. Cambridge, MA: MIT Press.

Schiffrin, D. (1996). Narrative as self-portrait: Sociolinguistic constructions of identity. *Language in Society, 25*, 167–203.

Sedikides, C., & Skowronski, J. J. (1997). The symbolic self in evolutionary context. *Personality and Social Psychology Review, 1*, 80–102.

Shweder, R. A., & Bourne, E. J. (1982). Does the concept of person vary cross-culturally? In A. Marsella & G. M. White (Eds.), *Cultural conceptions of mental health and therapy* (pp. 97–137). London: Reidel.

Smith, E. R. (1996). What do connectionism and social psychology offer each other? *Journal of Personality and Social Psychology, 70*, 893–912.

Smith, M. B. (1991). *Values, self and society*. New Brunswick, NJ: Transaction.

Sperber, D. (1996). *Explaining culture*. Oxford,

UK: Blackwell.

Sperber, D., & Wilson, D. (1986). *Relevance*. Oxford, UK: Blackwell.

Tomasello, M., Kruger, A. C., & Ratner, H. H. (1993). Cultural learning. *Brain and Behavioral Sciences, 16*, 495–552.

Trafimow, D., Triandis, H. C., & Goto, G. G. (1991). Some tests of the distinction between the private self and the collective self. *Journal of Personality and Social Psychology, 60*, 649–655.

Triandis, H. C. (1989). The self and social behavior in differing cultural contexts. *Psychological Review, 96*, 506–520.

Triandis, H. C. (1994). *Culture and social behavior*. New York: McGraw-Hill.

Vygotsky, L. S. (1978). *Mind in society*. Cambridge, MA: Harvard University Press.

Walters, K. (1996). Gender, identity, and the political economy of language: Anglophone wives in Tunisia. *Language in Society, 25*, 515–555.

Wegner, D. M. (1986). Transactive memory. In B. Mullen & G. R. Goethals (Eds.), *Theories of group behavior* (pp. 185–205). New York: Springer-Verlag.

Wellman, H. M. (1990). *The child's theory of mind*. Cambridge, MA: MIT Press.

Wetherell, M., & Potter, J. (1992). *Mapping the language of racism: Discourse and the legitimation of exploitation*. London: Harvester Wheatsheaf.

Wilson, D. (2000). Metarepresentation in linguistic communication. In D. Sperber (Ed.), *Metarepresentations* (pp. 411–448). Oxford, UK: Oxford University Press.

Wilson, R. A. (2000). The mind beyond itself. In D. Sperber (Ed.), *Metarepresentations* (pp. 31–52). Oxford, UK: Oxford University Press.

PART III

INTERGROUP, COLLECTIVE, AND CULTURAL ASPECTS OF THE SELF

15

The Social Self and Group Identification
Inclusion and Distinctiveness Motives in Interpersonal and Collective Identities

MARILYNN B. BREWER
CYNTHIA L. PICKETT

INTRODUCTION

The concept of social identity represents an important link between the psychology of the self and the psychology of group behavior and intergroup relations. As originally defined by Tajfel (1981), social identity is " . . . that part of an individual's self-concept which derives from his knowledge of his membership of a social group . . . *together with* the value and emotional significance attached to that membership" (p. 255, emphasis added). This definition implicated cognitive, affective, and motivational processes in the meaning of social identity itself. Nonetheless, further theorizing on the construct (Turner, Hogg, Oakes, Reicher, & Wetherell, 1987) focused almost exclusively on the cognitive bases of social identity, redefining it as a self-representation derived from ingroup–outgroup categorization per se. Taken to its extreme,

Address for correspondence: Dr. Marilynn B. Brewer, Department of Psychology, Ohio State University, 1885 Neil Avenue, Columbus, OH 43210, USA. E-mail: brewer.64@osu.edu

this perspective implies that a salient ingroup–outgroup distinction is both necessary and sufficient to engage self-categorization and associated social identification processes. Indeed, there is evidence that any association between the self and a group label *automatically* activates differential evaluation of the ingroup and outgroup as would be expected if social identity were engaged (e.g., Ashburn-Nardo, Voils, & Monteith, 1999; Otten & Moskowitz, 2000; Otten & Wentura, 1999; see Otten, this volume).

In our view, however, social identification entails more than automatic evaluative biases derived from associations with the self and a positive self-concept. In its more extended meaning, social identity is a transformation of the construal of the self to a level more inclusive than that of the individual self, with a concomitant shift from self-interest to group-interest as the basic motivation for behavior (Brewer, 1991; Kramer & Brewer, 1986; Smith, this volume). Because group identity sometimes entails self-sacrifice in the interests of group welfare and solidarity, understanding why and when individuals are willing to relegate their sense of self to significant group identities requires motivational as well as cognitive analysis. Motivational explanations are needed to account for why ingroup categorization does not always lead to identification and ingroup favoritism and why individuals are more chronically identified with some ingroups rather than others.

MOTIVATIONAL THEORIES OF SOCIAL IDENTIFICATION

The motivational concept most associated with social identity theory is that of self-esteem enhancement. And it is true that initial development of social identity theory (e.g., Tajfel & Turner, 1986; Turner, 1975) implicated self-esteem in postulating a need for "positive distinctiveness" in ingroup–outgroup comparisons. However, it is not clear from these writings whether positive self-esteem was being invoked as a motive for social identity itself or as a motive for ingroup favoritism *given that* social identity had been engaged. Whatever the original intent, subsequent research on the role of self-esteem in ingroup bias has generally supported the idea that enhanced self-esteem may be a *consequence* of achieving a positively distinct social identity, but there is little evidence that the need to increase self-esteem motivates social identification in the first place (Rubin & Hewstone, 1998). To the contrary, there is considerable evidence that individuals often identify strongly with groups that are disadvantaged, stigmatized, or otherwise suffer from negative intergroup comparison (e.g., Crocker, Luhtanen, Blaine, & Broadnax, 1994; Doosje, Ellemers, & Spears, 1995; Turner, Hogg, Turner, & Smith, 1984).

Given the inadequacy of self-esteem as an explanation for why social identity is engaged, other motives have been proposed that do not require positive ingroup status as a basis for attachment to groups and self-definition as a group member. One proposal is that group identity meets fundamental needs for reducing uncertainty and achieving meaning and clarity in social contexts (Hogg & Abrams, 1993; Hogg & Mullin, 1999). In support of this hypothesis, Hogg and his colleagues (Grieve & Hogg, 1999; Mullin & Hogg, 1998) have generated compelling evidence that identification and ingroup bias in the minimal group paradigm are increased under conditions of high cognitive uncertainty, and reduced or eliminated when uncertainty is low. And it is undoubtedly true that one function that group memberships and identities serve for individuals is that of providing self-definition and guidance for behavior in otherwise ambiguous social situations (Deaux, Reid, Mizrahi, & Cotting, 1999; Vignoles, Chryssochoou, & Breakwell, 2000). However, group identity is only one of many possible modes of reducing social uncertainty. Roles, values, laws, and so forth serve a similar function without necessitating social identification processes. Thus, uncertainty reduction alone cannot account for the pervasiveness of group identification as a fundamental aspect of human life.

Uncertainty reduction as a theory of social identity places the explanation for group identification in a system of cognitive motives that includes needs for meaning, certainty, and structure. An alternative perspective is that the motivation for social identification arises from even more fundamental needs for security and safety. Consistent with this idea, Baumeister and Leary (1995) postulated a universal need for *belonging* as an aspect of human nature derived from our vulnerability as lone individuals who require connection with others in order to survive. The connection between the need to belong and basic security motives is supported by results of a study by Cottrell and Leary (2001) who had participants complete an audio version of a measure of the need to be accepted by others in a completely darkened laboratory. Compared to participants who completed the same measure in a lighted room, individuals in the dark room expressed a significantly greater need for social acceptance. Further, as Baumeister, Twenge, and Ciarocco (this volume) have demonstrated, the prospect of social exclusion has fundamental motivational and cognitive consequences.

But belonging alone cannot account for the selectivity of social identification, since any and all group memberships should satisfy the belonging motive. My own theory (Brewer, 1991) postulates that the need for belonging and inclusion is paired with an opposing motive—the need for differentiation—that together regulate the individual's social identity and attachment to social groups.

Optimal Distinctiveness Theory (ODT)

The theory of optimal distinctiveness (Brewer, 1991, 1993; Brewer & Pickett, 1999) is based on the thesis that distinctiveness per se is a factor underlying the selection and strength of social identities, independent of the positive evaluation associated with membership in particular social categories. According to the optimal distinctiveness model, social identities derive "from a fundamental tension between human needs for validation and similarity to others (on the one hand) and a countervailing need for uniqueness and individuation (on the other)" (Brewer, 1991, p. 477). More specifically, it is proposed that social identities are selected and activated to the extent that they help to achieve a balance between needs for inclusion and for differentiation in a given social context.

The basic premise of the optimal distinctiveness model is that the two identity needs (inclusion/assimilation and differentiation/distinctiveness) are independent and work in opposition to motivate group identification. Individuals seek social inclusion in order to alleviate or avoid the isolation or stigmatization that may arise from being highly individuated (Baumeister & Leary, 1995). And researchers studying the effects of tokenism and solo status have generally found that individuals are both uncomfortable and cognitively disadvantaged in situations in which they feel too dissimilar from others. On the other hand, too much similarity or excessive deindividuation provides no basis for comparative appraisal or self-definition, and hence individuals are also uncomfortable in situations in which they lack distinctiveness (Fromkin, 1972; Vignoles et al., 2000). Arousal of either motive will be associated with negative affect and should motivate change in level of social identification.

One dimension along which social identities can vary is the degree of inclusiveness of the social category in which one is classified. Some categorizations refer to broadly inclusive social groupings that include a large number of individuals with only a few characteristics held in common (e.g., gender, racial categories, national groups); other categories are relatively exclusive, based on highly distinctive characteristics or multiple shared features (e.g., deaf persons, Mensa members, Baptist Korean Americans). Within any social context, categories at different levels of inclusiveness can be identified, either hierarchically (e.g., in a gathering of academics, subgroups are differentiated in terms of academic discipline) or orthogonally (e.g., among social psychologists, those who are sailing enthusiasts constitute a cross-cutting category membership). Within a given social context, or frame of reference, an individual can be categorized (by self or others) along a dimension of social distinctiveness–inclusiveness that ranges from uniqueness (i.e., features that distinguish the individual from any other persons in the social context) at one extreme, to total submersion in the social context at the other. Satisfaction of the drive toward social assimilation is directly related to level of inclusiveness, whereas satisfaction of self-differentiation needs is inversely related to level of inclusiveness. The question is, at what level of inclusion are social identities most likely to be established?

According to optimal distinctiveness theory, optimal identities are those that satisfy the need for inclusion within the ingroup and simultaneously serve the need for differentiation through distinctions between the ingroup and outgroups. Individuals will resist being identified with social categorizations that are either too inclusive or too differentiating but will define themselves in terms of social identities that are optimally distinctive. To satisfy the needs simultaneously, individuals will select group identities that are inclusive enough that they have a sense of being part of a larger collective but exclusive enough that they provide some basis for distinctiveness from others.

Testing Motivational Models

One source of evidence for the validity of the optimal distinctiveness model is the pervasive finding in the ingroup bias literature that individuals favor and identify more with relatively small, minority groups compared to large, relatively undistinct majority groups (Bettencourt, Miller, & Hume, 1999; Leonardelli & Brewer, 2001; Mullen, Brown, & Smith, 1992). Furthermore, this preference for minority group identities is stronger when the need for differentiation has been aroused by a recent deindividuation experience (Brewer, Manzi, & Shaw, 1993). However, these studies provide only indirect evidence that needs for inclusion and differentiation are implicated in the selection of distinctive social identities. Membership in small, distinct groups may serve a number of different identity needs, any of which may account for the effect of ingroup size. Thus, more direct tests of the motivational properties of inclusion and differentiation are needed to place ODT on firmer footing as a theory of social identity.

According to Baumeister and Leary (1995) a fundamental human motivation should "elicit goal-oriented behavior designed to satisfy it" (p. 498). Integral to optimal distinctiveness theory (Brewer, 1991) is the idea that the way that humans go about satisfying both their inclusion and differentiation needs is by identifying with social groups that are optimal in being neither too distinct nor too inclusive. Equilibrium is maintained by correcting for deviations from optimality. A situation in which a person is overly individuated will excite the need for assimilation, motivating the person to adopt a more inclusive social identity. Conversely, situations that arouse feelings of deindividuation or overinclusion will activate the need for differentiation, resulting in a search for more exclusive or distinct identities. Thus, the model is testable as a theory of human motivation by demonstrating that deprivation of either the need for inclusion or the need for differentiation results in efforts to achieve or restore optimal social identities.

One method for assessing the motivational properties of inclusion and differentiation is to activate one motive or the other and then test whether individuals shift their social identity preferences in the direction of more or less inclusive groups (depending on which motive has been aroused). Evidence supporting this prediction was obtained in a set of studies by Pickett, Silver, and Brewer (2002). In two studies, activation of the need for inclusion or the need for differentiation was experimentally manipulated by telling participants that their personality type was either very unusual or very common, or by reminding them of past experiences in which they had felt either too different from others or too undifferentiated from others. Following this motive induction, participants rated the importance and level of identification with various social categories to which they belonged, some of which were relatively inclusive (e.g., age cohort, nationality) and some relatively small or exclusive (e.g., honors students, sports club). Consistent with ODT predictions, motive condition and group characteristics interacted to determine importance and identification. In general, participants in the need for differentiation activation conditions increased ratings of their exclusive group memberships and decreased ratings of large, amorphous group memberships in comparison with participants in either the need for inclusion or control (no need arousal) conditions. Participants in the need for inclusion activation conditions, on the other hand, showed greater increases in level of identification with their large social category memberships

A second way in which individuals can respond to arousal of inclusion or differentiation needs is to *redefine* an existing important social identity so that it better satisfies the temporarily activated motive state. One interesting demonstration of this mechanism was obtained in another experiment conducted by Pickett et al. (2002). Following experimental manipulation of need for inclusion or differentiation, participants were asked whether they endorsed policies that would either restrict or enlarge the enrollment in their university, and were also asked to estimate the current size of the university study body. Consistent with ODT, participants in the need for differentiation activation condition endorsed greater restrictiveness of policies compared to those in the need for inclusion or control conditions. Further, participants in the need for assimilation condition perceived the ingroup to be much larger ($M = 44,816$), than did participants in the no need arousal condition ($M = 34,970$), while participants in the need for differentiation condition perceived it to be much smaller ($M = 26,434$). Enrollment records indicate that the actual number of undergraduates at the time the study was conducted was 35,647. Thus, whereas participants in the no need arousal condition were quite accurate in their estimates of ingroup size, participants in the need for assimilation condition tended to greatly *over*estimate ingroup size (by approximately 8,500 students), and need for differentiation participants tended to greatly *under*estimate ingroup size (by approximately 9,500 students). Subjective estimates were apparently influenced by the need to satisfy temporarily activated needs for greater inclusion or greater differentiation.

RESTORING OPTIMAL IDENTITIES: REVIEW OF A RESEARCH PARADIGM

The findings regarding size estimates described above demonstrate how an existing social identity can be modified to meet temporary activation of inclusion or differentiation motives. These results were particularly strong for students who were highly identified with their university to begin with. This effect suggested another research paradigm for assessing the consequences of threatening the optimality of an existing social identity by reducing inclusiveness or distinctiveness of that particular social group. The general logic of this paradigm is represented schematically in Figure 15.1.

The paradigm starts with the assumption that optimal identities are ones that are both sufficiently inclusive and sufficiently differentiated from outgroups to meet both inclusion and differentiation needs. Under these optimal conditions, the opposing motives are balanced, and neither is activated. Hence, salience of an optimally distinctive social identity should be associated with low arousal of identity needs. Given the two criteria for optimality, there are two ways in which the optimality of a given social identity can be threatened or challenged. On the one hand, as represented on the left-hand side of Figure 15.1, the inclusiveness of the individual's group membership can be decreased by assignment to a more distinct (less inclusive) subgroup of the original social category. Such an overly exclusive categorization should arouse the need for inclusion and efforts to restore assimilation to the larger social group. On the other hand, as represented on the right-hand side of Figure 15.1, optimality can be challenged by decreasing the differentiation between the ingroup and a larger more inclusive social category. This should create a state of overinclusiveness and arouse the need for differentiation and similar efforts to restore ingroup distinctiveness.

When an optimal identity is threatened in either case, individuals should show evidence of efforts to subjectively redefine the ingroup in a way that restores both inclusion and differentiation. Interestingly, many of the same mechanisms can serve both purposes. Based on the accentuation principle (Tajfel, 1978), assimilation within categories and contrast between categories are complementary processes. Intragroup assimilation serves to enhance contrast between categories, and intergroup contrast permits assimilation of differences within

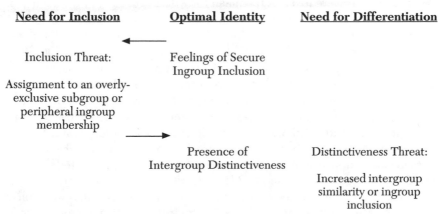

FIGURE 15.1. Motivational model: Basic research paradigm.

category boundaries. As a consequence, either mechanism can enhance ingroup inclusion (assimilation) and intergroup distinctiveness (contrast). Thus, we would predict that threatening optimal identities either by arousing the need for differentiation *or* the need for inclusion should result in efforts to restore the cohesion and solidarity of the ingroup by enhancing ingroup similarity/homogeneity *and* by enhancing ingroup exclusiveness and differentiation from outgroups.

Consequences of Arousing Inclusion and Distinctiveness Motives for Judgments of Group Homogeneity

We designed a study to test the prediction that the desire to achieve greater intragroup assimilation or greater intergroup differentiation would lead to motivated changes in perceptions of group homogeneity (Pickett & Brewer, 2001). Enhancement of both ingroup and outgroup homogeneity increases intergroup contrast, which becomes particularly important when the distinctiveness of a particular social identity is threatened. However, enhancing homogeneity of both ingroup and outgroup also serves the inclusion motive. The perception that "we are all alike" can help to reestablish secure inclusion within the group for an individual whose assimilation motive has been aroused. Further, perceiving the outgroup as homogeneous increases intergroup contrast, which also reinforces intragroup assimilation within the ingroup.

To operationalize the model presented in Figure 15.1, the needs for assimilation and differentiation were manipulated by providing participants with false feedback regarding their score on a previously administered personality test. Participants were also given false feedback regarding the group averages for the ingroup (Arts and Humanities students) on the same test.

Control condition. In the no need arousal (optimal distinctiveness) condition, participants were told that the mean for Arts and Humanities students on the personality test (SAQ) is 62 and that past studies have shown that "one of the areas in which Arts and Humanities students and Natural Sciences students differ is in their scores on the SAQ." The mean for Natural Sciences students was said to be 34. (In this experiment, the relative position of ingroup and outgroup was also varied, but the effects of motive arousal proved to be independent of the implications of relative ingroup–outgroup status.) Below this written information were two curves (containing approximately 20% overlap) that represented the distribution of Arts and Humanities students and Natural Sciences students. Participants' own scores were written in as 61, which placed participants at the mean of the ingroup distribution. It was predicted that participants in this condition would feel fairly satisfied and nonthreatened by this feedback. Their inclusion need would be met by knowing that they are typical of other Arts and Humanities students and their differentiation motive would be met by the clear intergroup distinction between Arts and Humanities students and Natural Sciences students.

Inclusion motive condition. The information given to participants in the inclusion motive condition was identical to the information provided to control participants except that each participant's *own* score on the SAQ was written in as 48. This was designed to make participants feel that they were in the peripheral position within the ingroup, part of a small subgroup at the tail of the ingroup distribution. This feedback was expected to arouse the motive for inclusion and assimilation.

Differentiation motive condition. Similar to the control condition, participants assigned to the differentiation motive condition were told that they scored a 61 on the SAQ. However, in the differentiation motive condition, the distance between Arts and Humanities students and Natural Sciences students on the SAQ was dramatically reduced. The mean for Natural Sciences students was 58, and the curves that represented the distribution of SAQ scores for the two groups overlapped by approximately 80%. Participants were also told that "one of the areas in which Arts and Humanities students and Natural Sciences students do not differ is in their scores on the SAQ." This feedback was intended to threaten ingroup differentiation and was expected to excite participants' need for differentiation.

To test the hypothesis that threats to inclusion or differentiation would motivate increases in perceived ingroup and outgroup homogeneity, two different measures of group homogeneity were included. As an initial measure of perceived ingroup and outgroup homogeneity, we used Park and Judd's (1990) similarity judgment task. In this task, participants were asked to rate (on a 10-point scale) how similar they believed Arts and Humanities students were along four different dimensions—personality, academic ability, social life, and in general. We then repeated the similarity task a second time with Natural Sciences students as the target group. Following the similarity judgments, participants rated the perceived stereotypicality of the ingroup and outgroup, using a version of Park and Judd's (1990) percentage estimates task. In this task, participants received a list of stereotypic traits of Arts and Humanities students followed by a list of stereotypic traits of Natural Sciences students and were asked to estimate the percentage (from 0% to 100%) of students within each of these groups that they believe possess each trait.

Results. Results for both similarity ratings and stereotypicality judgments supported the hypothesis that activation of either inclusion or differentiation motives would increase perceived group homogeneity compared to the control condition. Table 15.1 presents mean similarity ratings for the ingroup on all four dimensions. Ratings of outgroup similarity paralleled the findings for

TABLE 15.1. Perceived Ingroup Homogeneity by Need State
and Similarity Dimension

Need State	Similarity Dimension			
	Personality	Social Life	Academics	In General
Assimilation motive	5.34$_a$	4.33$_{ab}$	5.10$_a$	5.21$_a$
Control	3.92$_b$	4.01$_b$	4.20$_b$	4.21$_b$
Differentiation motive	5.33$_a$	5.04$_a$	5.12$_a$	5.18$_a$

Note. Higher numbers reflect greater perceived ingroup homogeneity. Cell means within the same column that do not share a common subscript differ significantly from each other at the $p < .05$ level. Table reprinted from C. Pickett and M. Brewer "Assimilation and differentiation needs as motivational determinants of perceived in-group and out-group homogeneity" in *Journal of Experimental Social Psychology*, 37, p. 345.

ingroups. Stereotypicality judgments of the ingroup showed the same pattern of effect of need state arousal. Both inclusion motive ($M = 78.38$) and differentiation motive participants ($M = 73.26$) perceived a higher percentage of ingroup members as possessing stereotype-relevant traits than did control participants ($M = 70.41$). (Outgroup judgments did not produce any significant differences as a function of motive activation condition.)

Overall, participants in both the inclusion motive and differentiation motive conditions perceived the ingroup as being more homogeneous than did participants in a control condition in which ingroup salience was equally high but no threats to assimilation or differentiation were present. In addition to enhanced perceptions of ingroup homogeneity, inclusion motive participants in the present study also exhibited heightened perceptions of outgroup similarity. By doing so, participants who found themselves in a distinctive minority within their ingroup were able to distance the outgroup from the ingroup, thus reducing the extent to which their peripheral ingroup position placed them within the region of the outgroup distribution. Differentiation motive participants also exhibited a pattern similar to that of inclusion motive participants in their judgments of ingroup and outgroup homogeneity, supporting our hypothesis that perceiving ingroup and outgroup as high in intragroup similarity serves to restore intergroup differentiation and ingroup distinctiveness.

Effects on Ingroup Exclusion

In the same study described above, we also explored the effects of arousing inclusion and differentiation motives on participants' tendency to protect the boundary between ingroup and outgroup. Again, our prediction was that both forms of identity threat would increase boundary maintenance as a mechanism for enhancing ingroup solidarity and assimilation while increasing intergroup differentiation. To assess restrictiveness, a task originally developed by Yzerbyt and Castano (1998) to examine the ingroup overexclusion effect (Leyens &

Yzerbyt, 1992; Yzerbyt, Leyens, & Bellour, 1995) was used. In this task, participants were presented with a list of 22 stereotypical traits of Arts and Humanities students and were asked to indicate which of the traits they felt were needed in order for someone to be considered an Arts and Humanities student at their university. This task presumes that the more traits a person selects, the more restrictive he/she is being in judging who can be deemed an ingroup member.

Results. As predicted, both assimilation motive participants and differentiation motive participants selected significantly more traits as being necessary for ingroup membership ($M = 5.40$ and $M = 5.01$, respectively) than did control participants ($M = 4.17$). As with the homogeneity judgments, this ingroup exclusion measure demonstrated that participants actively seek to restore ingroup solidarity and distinctiveness when optimal identity is threatened, supporting the motivational model central to optimal distinctiveness theory.

Effects on Self-Stereotyping

Similar arguments can be made for the potential role of self-stereotyping as a mechanism for restoring threatened optimal identities. According to self-categorization theory (Turner et al., 1987), when people adopt a social identity

> there is a perceptual accentuation of intragroup similarities and intergroup differences on relevant correlated dimensions. People stereotype themselves and others in terms of salient social categorizations, and this stereotyping leads to an enhanced perceptual identity between self and ingroup members and an enhanced perceptual contrast between ingroup and outgroup members. (Turner & Onorato, 1999, p. 21)

As one aspect of this self-categorization process, self-stereotyping has the effect of enhancing both intragroup similarity and intergroup differentiation. Thus, we expect that self-stereotyping provides one mechanism through which individuals can maintain or restore an optimal social identity when inclusion or differentiation needs are aroused.

Because of the hypothesized relationship between self-stereotyping and the satisfaction of inclusion and differentiation needs, we predicted that arousal of assimilation and differentiation needs will lead to *increases* in self-stereotyping. The more a person sees group stereotype traits as being descriptive of the self, the more intragroup assimilation this person should be able to achieve. Self-stereotyping enhances the perceptual closeness of the self to the ingroup. Thus, when assimilation needs are heightened, individuals should be motivated to self-stereotype more in relation to that ingroup. By the same logic, arousal of the need for differentiation should have a parallel effect on self-stereotyping. The more that group members perceive themselves (and other group members) in a stereotypical fashion, the more intergroup differentiation they can achieve. To the extent that all group members conform to their respective group stereotypes (see the group stereotype traits as being *self*-descriptive), there should be less overlap between the groups. Thus, in order to satisfy their need for differentiation, individuals should be motivated to self-stereotype in relation to that group in order to achieve greater intergroup differentiation.

Pickett, Bonner, and Coleman (in press) conducted a series of experiments to test this hypothesis. In each study, need activation was experimentally manipulated as in the Pickett and Brewer study described above, although the specific ingroup varied between studies. Self-stereotyping was assessed by asking participants to rate themselves on a long list of personality traits and dispositions that included traits previously identified as stereotypic of the target ingroup and many filler items that were stereotype-irrelevant. The critical measure was the extremity of self-ratings on the stereotypic traits in particular.

For the inclusion need arousal manipulation, the predicted increase in self-stereotyping is particularly counterintuitive. Generally, one would assume that being made aware of one's difference from other group members (as the manipulation in this condition entails) would result in feeling *less* like the prototypical group member and in the belief that the traits typical of the group are less descriptive of oneself. However, because of the relationship proposed by ODT between extreme individuation and the arousal of assimilation needs, we predicted that individuals would react to this feedback by perceiving stereotypical traits of the ingroup as being *more* descriptive of the self.

Consistent with ODT predictions, participants in all three studies (involving three different ingroups and diverse stereotypic traits) exhibited heightened self-stereotyping when either the need for inclusion or the need for differentiation had been activated. (See Table 15.2 for summary of findings.)

Table 15.2. Mean Self-Stereotyping Ratings
(data from Pickett, Bonner, & Coleman, in press)

		Motive Condition		
		Need Inclusion	Control	Need Differentiation
Experiment 1 Ingroup: Honors Students		5.58_a	5.10_b	5.50_a
Experiment 2 Ingroup: University (high identifiers)		5.44_a	4.91_b	5.23_a
Experiment 3 Ingroup: Sorority (high identifiers)	positive	5.61_b	5.07_b	5.71_b
	negative	3.56_{ab}	2.68_b	4.31_a

Note. Higher numbers reflect greater self-stereotyping. Cell means within the same row that do not share a common subscript differ significantly from each other at the $p < .05$ level.

Further, results of Study 3 demonstrated specifically that participants who were high in prior social identification with the target group showed increased self-stereotyping on both positive and negative ingroup traits. The fact that we were able to observe negative self-stereotyping under need arousal conditions testifies to the fundamental nature of inclusion and differentiation needs. Although the desire to view oneself and one's groups positively is quite prevalent (Hogg & Abrams, 1988; Pelham & Swann, 1989), increases in the perceived self-descriptiveness of negative stereotype traits suggests a willingness to forego a certain degree of positive self-regard in the service of other motivations such as assimilation and differentiation which may be more situationally urgent.

EXTENDING OPTIMAL DISTINCTIVENESS THEORY TO THE INTERPERSONAL SELF

As originally conceptualized, the optimal distinctiveness model was intended to be a theory of the motivational underpinnings of the *collective* social self, that is, the self construed as an integral part of a more inclusive social group or social category. More recently, we have considered the possibility that the basic motivational model might be generalized to predict optimal identities at other levels of self-representation as well (Brewer & Gardner, 1996; Brewer & Roccas, 2001). More specifically, we postulate that there are three different self systems—the personal self, the relational self, and the collective self—that serve to regulate individual integrity, maintenance of interpersonal relationships, and maintenance of group memberships respectively. At each level of the self, some tension may exist between assimilating or connecting to others on the one hand, and differentiating or separating the self from others on the other.

According to the original ODT model, optimality at the collective level is regulated by the counterpressures of the need for inclusion (assimilation with others in a larger collective unit) and the need for differentiation (separation from others). Analogous opposing needs for separateness and assimilation may also operate at the levels of individual and relational selves to determine optimal identities at those levels as well.

The postulated opposing motives for each level of self-representation are summarized in Table 15.3. At the collective level, the conflict is between belonging and inclusion on the one hand, and separation and distinctiveness on the other. At the individual level, the needs are expressed in the opposition between the desire for similarity on the one hand and the need for uniqueness on the other (Snyder & Fromkin, 1980). The distinction between inclusion–differentiation and similarity–uniqueness is subtle but important. Similarity refers to the *degree* or extent of overlap between one's own characteristics (attributes, attitudes, etc.) and those of another individual or a group prototype. Inclusion refers to the *number* of others with whom one shares a collective bond (which may be based on a single shared characteristic).

TABLE 15.3. Opposing Drives and Levels of Self-Representation
(from Brewer & Roccas, 2001)

	Motivational Pole	
Level of Self	Separation	Assimilation
Individual	uniqueness	similarity
Relational	autonomy	intimacy/interdependence
Collective	differentiation	inclusion/belonging

At the interpersonal (relational) level, the tension is represented by conflicts between the need for autonomy and the need for interdependence and
intimacy with specific others. At each level, the person must achieve some optimal balance between these conflicting motives for defining self in relation to
others.

Although the three levels of self-representation are hypothesized to be
distinct self-systems, optimality needs play out at each level simultaneously, and
it is reasonable to assume that the way needs for identity and esteem are met at
one level will have some influence on the activation of parallel motives at other
levels. For instance, at the same time that individuals meet needs for inclusion
and differentiation at the collective level by identification with distinctive
ingroups, *within* those groups they will be seeking optimal resolution of their
needs for similarity and uniqueness in comparisons with other individual group
members. When the optimal ingroup is relatively small, distinct, and well-
bounded, the need for intragroup similarity may be more acute than the need
for uniqueness at the individual level. In other words, a high need for distinctiveness at the level of the collective self may be associated with a low need for
uniqueness for the individual self. By contrast, high need for similarity at the
individual level or for autonomy at the relational level may engender high need
for inclusion at the collective level, and a preference for large and relatively
diffuse group identities (Brewer & Roccas, 2001).

Similar parallels between needs underlying interpersonal relationships and
those underlying group identity were drawn by Smith, Murphy, and Coats (1999)
in their work extending attachment theory to the group level. In a program of
three studies, Smith and his colleagues validated a new measure of group attachment, attachment anxiety, and avoidance, modeled after the Romantic Partner Attachment scale (Collins & Read, 1990) developed to assess attachment
styles in close interpersonal relationships. The group attachment scale proved
to have good reliability and predictive and construct validity with respect to
group membership behavior and emotions, and also proved to be distinct from
scores on the relationship attachment measure at the interpersonal level. It
would be of interest in future work to determine whether the different patterns

of attachment at the interpersonal and group levels reflect some kind of complementarity of needs for separation and assimilation at the relational and collective levels of self.

CONCLUSION

In this paper we have highlighted results from a program of research testing the motivational properties of the needs for inclusion and differentiation that underlie the optimal distinctiveness model of social identity and the collective self. The findings across different measures of ingroup identification and solidarity supported our basic assumption that inclusion and differentiation are separable social motives, in that temporary deprivation of either need engages active efforts to satisfy the need and restore equilibrium. Further, although activating inclusion or differentiation involve opposite types of threat to optimal social identity, either one engages similar mechanisms that serve to restore optimal ingroup distinctiveness and inclusiveness. At a more abstract level, these research findings support our general theory that opposing motives underlie a regulatory self-system designed to maintain the individual's connection to social groups that meet basic needs for security and cooperative interdependence with others.

Our future research will be directed toward extending the implications of the optimal distinctiveness model of the social self to other regulatory subsystems of the self, particularly the relational self that regulates interpersonal attachments. Although basic tensions between autonomy and intimacy have long been recognized in the literature on close relationships (e.g., Baxter & Montgomery, 1996), optimal identity models have yet to be tested in this domain.

REFERENCES

Ashburn-Nardo, L., Voils, C., & Monteith, M. J. (1999, May). The role of ingroup favoritism and familiarity in implicit intergroup biases. Paper presented at the meeting of the Midwestern Psychological Association, Chicago, IL.

Baumeister, R. F., & Leary, M. R., (1995). The need to belong: Desire for interpersonal attachments as a fundamental human motivation. *Psychological Bulletin, 117,* 497–529.

Baxter, L. A., & Montgomery, B. M. (1996). *Relating: Dialogues and dialectics.* New York: Guilford.

Bettencourt, B. A., Miller, N., & Hume, D. L. (1999). Effects of numerical representation within cooperative settings: Examining the role of salience in in-group favouritism. *British Journal of Social Psychology, 38,* 265–287.

Brewer, M. B. (1991). The social self: On being the same and different at the same time. *Personality and Social Psychology Bulletin, 17,* 475–482.

Brewer, M. B. (1993). The role of distinctiveness in social identity and group behaviour. In M. Hogg & D. Abrams (Eds.), *Group motivation: Social psychological perspectives* (pp. 1-16). Hemel Hempstead, UK: Harvester Wheatsheaf.

Brewer, M. B., & Gardner, W. (1996). Who is

this "we"? Levels of collective identity and self representation. *Journal of Personality and Social Psychology, 71,* 83–93.

Brewer, M. B., Manzi, J., & Shaw, J. S. (1993). Ingroup identification as a function of depersonalization, distinctiveness, and status. *Psychological Science, 4,* 88–92.

Brewer, M. B., & Pickett, C. L. (1999). Distinctiveness motives as a source of the social self. In T. Tyler, R. Kramer, & O. John (Eds.), *The psychology of the social self* (pp. 71–87). Hillsdale, NJ: Erlbaum.

Brewer, M. B., & Roccas, S. (2001). Individual values, social identity, and optimal distinctiveness. In C. Sedikides & M. Brewer (Eds.), *Individual self, relational self, collective self* (pp. 219–237). Philadelphia: Psychology Press.

Collins, N. L., & Read, S. J. (1990). Adult attachment, working models, and relationship quality in dating couples. *Journal of Personality and Social Psychology, 58,* 644–663.

Cottrell, C. A., & Leary, M. R. (2001, February). Darkness and the need to belong. Paper presented at the annual meeting of the Society of Personality and Social Psychology, San Antonio, TX.

Crocker, J., Luhtanen, R., Blaine, B., & Broadnax, S. (1994). Collective self-esteem and psychological well-being among White, Black, and Asian college students. *Personality and Social Psychology Bulletin, 20,* 503–513.

Deaux, K., Reid, A., Mizrahi, K., & Cotting, D. (1999). Connecting the person to the social: The functions of social identification. In T. Tyler, R. Kramer, & O. John (Eds.), *The psychology of the social self* (pp. 91–113). Mahwah, NJ: Erlbaum.

Doosje, B., Ellemers, N., & Spears, R. (1995). Perceived intragroup variability as a function of group status and identification. *Journal of Experimental and Social Psychology, 31,* 410–436.

Fromkin, H. L. (1972). Feelings of interpersonal undistinctiveness: An unpleasant affective state. *Journal of Experimental Research in Personality, 6,* 178–182.

Grieve, P. G., & Hogg, M. A. (1999). Subjective uncertainty and intergroup discrimination in the minimal group situation. *Personality and Social Psychology Bulletin, 25,* 926–940.

Hogg, M. A., & Abrams, D. (1988). *Social identifications: A social psychology of intergroup relations and group processes.* London: Routledge.

Hogg, M. A., & Abrams, D. (1993). Towards a single-process uncertainty-reduction model of social motivation in groups. In M. Hogg & D. Abrams (Eds.), *Group motivation: Social psychological perspectives* (pp. 173–190). Hemel Hempstead, UK: Harvester Wheatsheaf.

Hogg, M. A., & Mullin, B.-A. (1999). Joining groups to reduce uncertainty: Subjective uncertainty reduction and group identification. In D. Abrams & M. A. Hogg (Eds.), *Social identity and social cognition* (pp. 249-279). Oxford, UK: Blackwell.

Kramer, R. M., & Brewer, M. B. (1986). Social group identity and the emergence of cooperation in resource conservation dilemmas. In H. Wilke, D. Messick, & C. Rutte (Eds.), *Psychology of decisions and conflict. Vol. 3. Experimental social dilemmas* (pp. 205–230). Frankfurt: Verlag Peter Lang.

Leonardelli, G., & Brewer, M. B. (2001). Minority and majority discrimination: When and why. *Journal of Experimental Social Psychology, 37,* 468–485.

Leyens, J.-P., & Yzerbyt, V. (1992). The ingroup overexclusion effect: Impact of valence and confirmation on stereotypical information search. *European Journal of Social Psychology, 22,* 549–569.

Mullen, B., Brown, R., & Smith, C. (1992). Ingroup bias as a function of salience, relevance, and status: An integration. *European Journal of Social Psychology, 22,* 103–122.

Mullin, B-A., & Hogg, M. A. (1998). Dimensions of subjective uncertainty in social identification and minimal intergroup discrimination. *British Journal of Social Psychology, 37,* 345–365.

Otten, S., & Moskowitz, G. B. (2000). Evidence for implicit evaluative in-group bias: Affect-biased spontaneous trait inference in a minimal group paradigm. *Journal of Experimental Social Psychology, 36,* 77–89.

Otten, S., & Wentura, D. (1999). About the impact of automaticity in the minimal group paradigm: Evidence from affective priming tasks. *European Journal of Social Psychology, 29*, 1049–1071.

Park, B., & Judd, C. M. (1990). Measures and models of perceived group variability. *Journal of Personality and Social Psychology, 59*, 173–191.

Pelham, B. W., & Swann, W. B. (1989). From self-conceptions to self-worth: On the sources and structure of global self-esteem. *Journal of Personality and Social Psychology, 68*, 672–680.

Pickett, C. L., Bonner, B. L., & Coleman, J. M. (in press). Motivated self-stereotyping: Heightened assimilation and differentiation needs result in increased levels of positive and negative self-stereotyping. *Journal of Personality and Social Psychology.*

Pickett, C. L., & Brewer, M. B. (2001). Assimilation and differentiation needs as motivational determinants of perceived ingroup and outgroup homogeneity. *Journal of Experimental Social Psychology, 37*, 341–348.

Pickett, C. L., Silver, M. D., & Brewer, M. B. (2002). The impact of assimilation and differentiation needs on levels of group identification and perceptions of ingroup size. *Personality and Social Psychology Bulletin, 28*, 546–558.

Rubin, M., & Hewstone, M. (1998). Social identity theory's self-esteem hypothesis: A review and some suggestions for clarification. *Personality and Social Psychology Review, 2*, 40–62.

Smith, E. R., Murphy, J., & Coats, S. (1999). Attachment to groups: Theory and measurement. *Journal of Personality and Social Psychology, 77*, 94–110.

Snyder, C. R., & Fromkin, H. L. (1980). *Uniqueness: The human pursuit of difference.* New York: Plenum Press.

Tajfel, H. (1978). Social categorization, social identity and social comparison. In H. Tajfel (Ed.), *Differentiation between social groups: Studies in the social psychology of intergroup relations* (pp. 61–76). London: Academic Press.

Tajfel, H. (1981). *Human groups and social categories.* Cambridge, UK: Cambridge University Press.

Tajfel, H., & Turner, J. C. (1986). The social identity theory of intergroup behavior. In S. Worchel & W. G. Austin (Eds.), *Psychology of intergroup relations* (pp. 7–24). Chicago: Nelson-Hall.

Turner, J. C. (1975). Social comparison and social identity: Some prospects for intergroup behaviour. *European Journal of Social Psychology, 5*, 5-34.

Turner, J. C., Hogg, M., Oakes, P., Reicher, S., & Wetherell, M. (1987). *Rediscovering the social group: A self-categorization theory.* Oxford, UK: Blackwell.

Turner, J. C., Hogg, M., Turner, P., & Smith, P. (1984). Failure and defeat as determinants of group cohesiveness. *British Journal of Social Psychology, 23*, 97–111.

Turner, J. C., & Onorato, R. (1999). Social identity, personality and the self-concept: A self-categorization perspective. In T. R. Tyler, R. Kramer, & O. John (Eds.), *The Psychology of the Social Self.* (pp. 11–46). Hillsdale, NJ: Erlbaum.

Vignoles, V. L., Chryssochoou, Z., & Breakwell, G. M. (2000). The distinctiveness principle: Identity, meaning, and the bounds of cultural relativity. *Personality and Social Psychology Review, 4*, 337–354.

Yzerbyt, V. Y., & Castano, E. (1998). *The ingroup overexclusion effect: The role of group identification and group entitativity.* Manuscript submitted for publication.

Yzerbyt, V. Y., Leyens, J.-P., & Bellour, F. (1995). The ingroup overexclusion effect: Identity concerns in decisions about group membership. *European Journal of Social Psychology, 25*, 1–16.

16

I Am Positive and So Are We

The Self as Determinant of Favoritism toward Novel Ingroups

SABINE OTTEN

INTRODUCTION

> *The nature of the self and its relationship to social cognition is the theoretical core of social psychology.*
> —Turner & Oakes, 1997, p. 365

*T*he above statement expresses straightforwardly the relevance of the social self as an issue for social-psychological theorizing and research (for overviews see Baumeister, 1998; Sedikides & Brewer, 2001; Tyler, Kramer, & John, 1999). In this context, the present chapter will investigate how the individual self relates to the collective self, that is, the self as a group member. Moreover, it will be argued that ingroup favoritism can be the result of a close merger between individual and collective self (see also Cooper & Hogg; Mackie & Smith; Smith; Wright, Aron, & Tropp, this volume).

Influential theories on intergroup behavior, especially Social Identity Theory

---

Address for correspondence: Sabine Otten, Department of Psychology, University of Jena, Humboldtstr. 26, 07742 Jena, Germany. E-mail: sabine.otten@uni-jena.de

(SIT; Tajfel & Turner, 1979, 1986) and Self-Categorization Theory (SCT; Turner, Hogg, Oakes, Reicher, & Wetherell, 1987) are essentially theories of the social self. In both theories, the notion of a social identity, defined by group memberships and the evaluations and emotions attached to these membership, is pivotal (Tajfel, 1978; Tajfel & Turner, 1986; Turner, 1999). Whereas SIT is concentrating on the prediction of intergroup relations (see Brown, 2000), SCT's core issue is the more general question of the conditions and the (cognitive) consequences that arise when people categorize themselves as group members with shared characteristics rather than as unique individuals. SCT focuses on social identity as "the cognitive mechanism that makes group behaviour possible" (Turner, 1984, p. 527), while SIT specifically analyzes the motivation to enhance or maintain a positive social identity. Both theories affected the empirical program presented in this chapter; however, due to its emphasis on investigating basic determinants of ingroup favoritism, SIT was most central for deriving the present research questions.

Although much broader in its scope, SIT is closely associated with experiments conducted in the so-called minimal group paradigm (MGP; Tajfel, Billig, Bundy, & Flament, 1971; see also Rabbie & Horwitz, 1969). In this paradigm, participants were anonymously assigned to one of two distinct, novel social categories; there was no intra- or intergroup interaction, no opportunity to directly fulfill self-interests by allocations or evaluations, and no functional relation between the categorization dimension, on the one hand, and the evaluation or allocation dimension on the other hand. Although planned as a baseline to identify subsequently the necessary and sufficient conditions for social discrimination, the minimal group setting did already suffice to elicit ingroup favoritism. Numerous studies have replicated this so-called "mere categorization effect" (see Brewer, 1979; Brewer & Brown, 1998; Brown 2000); however, its interpretation is still controversial.

SIT accounts for this finding by postulating a need for positive social identity (see Brown, 2000; Tajfel & Turner, 1986; Turner, 1999). It is assumed that the self-concept comprises two components—personal and social identity. By treating ingroup members more favorably than outgroup members, social identity can be ensured or enhanced. Thus, establishing positive ingroup distinctiveness serves the general motive of self-enhancement (see Sedikides, 1993; Sedikides & Strube, 1995, 1997). Accordingly, a causal connection between intergroup differentiation and self-esteem is assumed (Brown, 2000, p. 755; see also Abrams & Hogg, 1988; Hogg & Abrams, 1990). As Turner (1999) put it:

> The basic hypothesis, which is at the psychological heart of the theory, is the notion that social comparisons between groups relevant to an evaluation of social identity produce pressures for intergroup differentiation to achieve a positive self evaluation in terms of that identity. (p. 18)

In fact, there is evidence indicating that expressing ingroup bias can enhance self-esteem (Aberson, Healy, & Romero, 2000; Lemyre & Smith, 1985; Oakes & Turner, 1980). However, findings are not unequivocal, especially for the complementary derivation that self-esteem can predict ingroup favoritism (see Crocker & Schwartz, 1985; Crocker, Thompson, McGraw, & Ingerman, 1987; Hogg & Abrams, 1990; Rubin & Hewstone, 1998). Hence, notwithstanding the many successful replications of the "mere categorization effect," its interpretation in terms of a striving for positive social identity is controversial (e.g., Cadinu & Rothbart, 1996; Diehl, 1989; Gaertner & Insko, 2000; Hogg & Abrams, 1990; Messick & Mackie, 1989; Mummendey, 1995). According to Brown (2000), this discussion raises "the possibility of recognising a wider range of cognitive motives associated with social identification than those specified by SIT"(p. 756).

My own research program offers a contribution to such discussion; however, rather than focusing on alternative motivational accounts, it concentrates on basic cognitive processes that might account for ingroup favoritism even in a minimal intergroup situation. Starting from the empirical observation that a favorable attitude toward novel ingroups does not necessitate explicit social comparisons with the outgroup, a model is proposed, in which the self is not seen as immediately motivating or profiting from ingroup favoritism, but rather as a source of information from which the definition of novel own-groups can be derived. More specifically, evidence will be presented with regard to four basic themes:

1. *Positive ingroup default:* Evaluative favoritism toward novel ingroups can emerge immediately after social categorization and without any explicit opportunities to compare with an outgroup.
2. *Implicit associations between ingroup and self:* Response-time evidence implies that there is an overlap between the mental representations of self and ingroup; in case of ambiguous group judgments, ingroup evaluations are facilitated when matching self-ratings (see Smith; Wright et al., this volume).
3. *Self-anchoring:* At least under certain contextual conditions, group members tend to assimilate the ingroup definition to the self-definition in explicit evaluations. Moreover, self–ingroup similarity proved to be an even stronger predictor for ingroup favoritism than the valence of intergroup comparison dimensions.
4. *Self as heuristic:* The process of self-anchoring is affected by the judges' motivation and ability to use heuristics as a means of impression formation on their novel ingroup.

In the following, research findings supporting the above claims will be presented in more detail. Finally, implications for classical theories on intergroup behavior (especially for SIT) and possible directions for future research will be discussed.

POSITIVE INGROUP DEFAULT

According to SIT, social comparison with the outgroup is a most important element in the process by which social categorization can turn into the creation of positive ingroup distinctiveness. Questioning the positive distinctiveness account for ingroup favoritism in the MGP implies doubting the importance of the own group position *in relation to the outgroup*. Thus, the question arises whether individuals who have been assigned to a novel social category will express a biased ingroup evaluation already before having engaged in explicit social comparisons with the outgroup (as typically requested in experiments on intergroup allocations and evaluations). In fact, Maass and Schaller (1991) argued that there is an "initial categorization-based ingroup bias" such that "group members seem to approach their task with the rudimentary hypothesis that their own group is better than the opposing group" (p. 204). Following this logic, favorable ingroup evaluations are the starting point for, rather than the consequence of, comparisons between ingroup and outgroup.

Empirically, these arguments raise the following questions: Can such positive ingroup default be demonstrated even for minimal groups? How can such initial bias be disentangled from bias that is not a starting point but rather a result of a comparison with the corresponding outgroup? Here, paradigms that study judgmental processes on an *implicit level* seemed most appropriate. A pioneering piece of research that provided evidence for the assumed positive ingroup default was conducted by Perdue, Dovidio, Gurtman, and Tyler (1990). These authors demonstrated in learning tasks and lexical decision tasks that (subliminal) global reference to either own-groups ("us") or other-groups ("them") primed positive affect in the former, but rather neutral affect in the latter condition. In sum, their findings imply that words related to ingroups enhance the accessibility of positive trait information.

Perdue and collaborators (1990) did not refer to specific groups in their experiments; instead they used terms like "we" and "us" as ingroup designators and terms like "they" and "them" as outgroup designators. The authors themselves acknowledged that their experiments "do not demonstrate whether it is the in-group and outgroup terms themselves or whether it is the cognitively represented social entities that they signify that are the source of these attitudinal biases" (p. 483). Whereas their findings can be read as evidence for intergroup bias on the implicit level, they do not parallel the minimal group paradigm, where the ingroup–outgroup distinction was conceptually unrelated to existing social schemata. Hence, their data can not demonstrate whether there is such thing as a "positive ingroup default" as the immediate consequence of being categorized as a group member. However, such demonstration was provided in a series of studies by Otten and collaborators (Otten & Moskowitz, 2000; Otten & Wentura, 1999).

Otten and Wentura (1999) conducted two experiments that followed the general logic of the second experiment by Purdue et al. (1990). Instead of using unspecific primes referring to ingroup and outgroup, they subliminally presented the labels of categories, which were introduced in a minimal categorization procedure immediately before the lexical decision task. Again, there was an affective priming effect for ingroup labels such that they facilitated the classification of positive as compared to negative traits, whereas no affective congruency effects emerged for outgroup primes. Moreover, there was a significant correlation between implicit positive ingroup attitudes (as indicated by responses in the lexical decision task) and explicit measures of ingroup preference.

Otten and Moskowitz (2000) provided evidence for an implicit bias toward minimal ingroups in a different paradigm. They combined a minimal categorization procedure with a probe task demonstrating spontaneous trait inferences (STIs; e.g., Uleman, Hon, Roman, & Moskowitz, 1996). The idea was that reference to the minimal ingroup should facilitate spontaneous inferences with regard to positive but not negative traits, whereas valence of traits should not affect STIs about outgroup members. At the beginning of the experiments, participants were individually categorized into a novel social category, allegedly based on their perceptual style when structuring visual information. The second part of the study was introduced as dealing with the structuring of verbal information. The ingroup versus outgroup condition was realized by claiming that the sentences that were presented stemmed from either ingroup or outgroup members who had described activities from their daily life. Following each sentence (which were either trait-implying or not) a target word was presented and participants had to decide quickly whether this word was in the sentence or not. It was hypothesized and found that trait inference would be facilitated (thus interfering with the correct rejection of the word as not in the sentence) by references to the ingroup, but only for traits that were positive and only when presented after trait-implying sentences (for more details, see Otten & Moskowitz, 2000) (see Figure 16.1). The longest response latencies for correctly rejecting trait words were measured when positive traits followed sentences describing ingroup members performing behaviors that implied the respective trait. No effects emerged for sentences describing outgroup members and for non-trait-implying sentences.

Taken together, these experiments provide convincing evidence that there is ingroup favoritism on an implicit level even toward novel laboratory groups. The experiments by Otten and collaborators (Otten & Moskowitz, 2000; Otten & Wentura, 1999) did not involve any explicit social comparison, and they avoided reference to unspecific ingroup and outgroup designators as used by Perdue

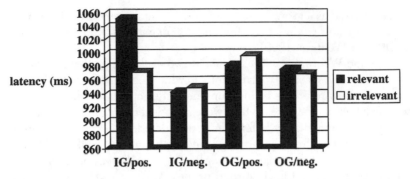

FIGURE 16.1. Mean response latencies as a function of trait relevance, trait valence, and group affiliation (data from Otten & Moskowitz, 2000).

and colleagues (1990); hence, the findings support the assumed positive ingroup default as starting point or baseline rather than result of intergroup evaluations.

However, we are left with the question of which *process* can account for the immediate, automatic emergence of a positive ingroup stereotype. At this point, reference to the self seems plausible and worthwhile. According to Turner and collaborators (e.g. Turner et al., 1987; Turner & Onorato, 1999), when a person identifies with a social group, the perception of self as a person ("me") transforms into the perception of self as a group member ("us"). On the intergroup level of self-categorization, the self is defined by features defining and distinguishing the ingroup as a whole. However, though admittedly a very specific case, in the case of completely novel, minimal groups the reverse path seems to be more plausible: social identity (self as a group member) may form by defining the ingroup in terms of features characterizing the individual self (see Smith, this volume). In fact, Reynolds, Turner, and Haslam (2000) acknowledged this point, stating that in the case of minimal groups the self is the only exemplar available in order to derive the prototype of the novel ingroup. Hence, it will be argued below that the positive value of novel ingroups is based on their association with the typically positively evaluated self (e.g. Baumeister, 1998; Diener & Diener, 1996; Taylor & Brown, 1988).

IMPLICIT ASSOCIATIONS BETWEEN INGROUP AND SELF

Ample evidence for a close link between self-definitions and definitions of own-groups was provided in a series of experiments by Smith and collaborators (Coats, Smith, Claypool, & Banner, 2000; Smith, Coats & Walling, 1999; Smith & Henry, 1996; Smith, this volume). Their research was based upon a paradigm developed by Aron and coworkers in order to demonstrate what they call "self-expansion" in interpersonal relationships (e.g., Aron, Aron, Tudor, & Nelson, 1991;

see also Wright et al., this volume, for an application of this model in the domain of intergroup relations). The cognitive connection between self and ingroup is reflected in response-time evidence: dichotomous judgments of self and ingroup, respectively, were significantly facilitated on those dimensions on which self-definition and ingroup definition (as measured in previously administered questionnaires) matched (see also Smith, this volume). Smith and collaborators (Smith et al., 1999) concluded that self and ingroup are linked in connectionist networks of memory (see Smith, this volume, for a detailed description of the model). When mental representations of self and ingroup overlap, the two stimuli elicit similar patterns of activation. Thereby, activating one concept facilitates congruent responses with regard to the other.

Interestingly, on this implicit level, there is little evidence for systematic links between outgroup and self or outgroup and ingroup. In terms of a need for positive ingroup distinctiveness as assumed by SIT (see above) or the optimal distinctiveness theory by Brewer (1993; see Brewer & Pickett, this volume, for more details), one might have expected a facilitation of responses on trait dimensions characterized by mismatches with the outgroup. However, typically no such evidence was found (Coats et al., 2000; Smith & Henry, 1996; Smith et al., 1999; see Brewer & Pickett, 1999, for one exception).

Although the given evidence on implicit links between self and ingroup is broadly unequivocal, these findings are not yet sufficient to account for ingroup favoritism toward completely novel, arbitrary groups. Smith and collaborators tried to use social categories that were not heavily stereotyped (e.g. students with different majors; members vs. non-members of sororities/fraternities) but not completely novel groups. In fact, the task of evaluating ingroup and outgroup on a large set of trait dimensions can hardly be realized for arbitrary social categories. Therefore, when replicating the study by Smith and collaborators (1999), Epstude and Otten (2000) also refrained from analyzing minimal groups and applied gender as categorization criterion. Instead, as an alternative means to parallel more closely the minimal intergroup setting, we focused on ingroup judgments in a forced-choice response format for those trait dimensions, which, according to previous paper–pencil ratings, were characterized by judgmental *ambiguity*.

Hogg and Mullin (1999; see also Grieve & Hogg, 1999) have demonstrated that uncertainty is an important feature in minimal intergroup settings. Typically, this uncertainty is assumed to stem from the novel, ill-defined social categorization itself (i.e., from novel group members wondering, "Who is this 'we'?") (cf. Brewer & Gardner, 1996, p. 83). However, we argue that uncertainty can also be elicited by focusing on trait dimensions that are not clearly defined for the (realistic) groups in question. Smith and collaborators (e.g. Smith & Henry, 1996; Smith et al., 1999) excluded traits from further analysis that were not clearly judged as applicable or not applicable to the respective targets (answer "4" on the 7-point bipolar scale). However, in our study (Epstude & Otten,

2000) exactly these dimensions were of central interest. Data indicated that judgments about ambiguous traits were facilitated when adapted to self-ratings, thus replicating the pattern of the match–mismatch effect as already obtained for clearly defined traits by Smith and collaborators, 1999. The interaction between type of dichotomous ingroup judgment (response: yes, no) and previous self-rating (trait applies; trait does not apply) was significant for both ambiguous traits and well-defined traits. Again, matches or mismatches with the outgroup evaluation did not affect response latencies. Interestingly, a follow-up study (Otten & Epstude, 2001) revealed that quite similar effects can be found when measuring the response latencies for dichotomous outgroup judgments. Again, matches with the self-evaluation facilitated outgroup judgments for both clearly defined and ambiguous trait dimensions (as defined by the paper–pencil measure). This finding fits arguments by Wright and collaborators (this volume), who suggest that self-expansion does not only apply to ingroups but might also occur for certain outgroups (when there is no intergroup conflict, or even a cooperative intergroup context).

In sum, the findings by Smith and collaborators reveal a firm link between the concepts of self and ingroup (see Smith, this volume). Within the connectionist model, it does not really matter whether the link between the two targets stems from a definition of self in terms of the ingroup (i.e., depersonalization as discussed by SCT; Turner et al., 1987) or whether it stems from a definition of the group in terms of the self, that is, from self-anchoring (see below). In this context, the study by Epstude and Otten (2000) suggests a possibility to disentangle the *direction* of activation patterns that manifest in response latencies.

SELF-ANCHORING IN EXPLICIT MEASURES OF INGROUP FAVORITISM

The findings summarized in the previous section provide convincing evidence for a firm association between self-evaluations on the one hand, and ingroup evaluations on the other hand. Such an implicit link can already account for positive ingroup judgments, as there is much evidence (at least in Western cultures) for the overall tendency to see the self as positive and "above average" (e.g., Alicke, Klotz, Breitenbecher, Yurak, & Vredenburg, 1995; Baumeister, 1998; Matlin & Stang, 1978; Taylor & Brown, 1988; Triandis, 1989). Thus, in the following section more direct tests will be presented, which reveal that assimilating self- and ingroup-definition can account for positive and *positively distinct* ingroup judgments.

"Overall, in-group favoritism in the minimal group paradigm is a well-established phenomenon, but the exact reasons for this favoritism remain unclear" (p. 661). Starting with this critique, Cadinu and Rothbart (1996) suggested an account for favoritism toward minimal ingroups that differs from SIT. In their approach, the process of self-anchoring plays a central role. They argue that in order to give meaning to their novel social category, group members apply a similarity heuristic such that the ingroup is defined as a less extreme (i.e., slightly less positive) copy of the self. In a next step, the outgroup is defined as different from the ingroup: " . . . because self and ingroup are regarded favorably, the outgroup will be regarded, by a principle of differentiation, as less favorable" (Cadinu & Rothbart, 1996, p. 662).

In a series of experiments, Cadinu and Rothbart (1996) collected evidence supporting their model; they categorized participants as members of minimal groups, and measured both self-ratings and ratings about one of the two groups (ingroup or outgroup). Before rating the target group, judges were informed how the respective other group (outgroup or ingroup) had scored on the evaluative dimensions. Accessibility of self-evaluation was varied via the sequence of evaluations (self first, self last). Data indicated that (a) the self-group similarity was much greater for the ingroup than for the outgroup or neutral group; (b) self-anchoring was stronger when self-ratings preceded rather than followed the ingroup ratings, and (c) judgments of the outgroup as well as of neutral groups, but *not* those of the ingroup, followed the differentiation principle.

Notwithstanding the convincing evidence, the paradigm used by Cadinu and Rothbart (1996) might not be optimal to test the assumed processes underlying ingroup favoritism in the minimal group paradigm. Whereas in the original MGP the definition of *both* ingroup and outgroup has to be construed, their self-anchoring studies already provided information about one of the two groups. Besides, self-ratings were obtained *after* social categorization; hence, there is the possibility that self-ratings were already *self-ratings as a group member*; hence, there would be a confound between self-ratings and self–ingroup similarity.

Consequently, Otten (2001) conducted a modified replication of the third study by Cadinu and Rothbart (1996). Participants rated both ingroup and outgroup; therefore, besides the position of the self-rating (before or after the group tasks), the sequence of group ratings (ingroup–outgroup; outgroup–ingroup) was an additional factor. Consistent with Cadinu and Rothbart, findings revealed strong self–ingroup similarity and the most positive ingroup evaluation when the self was rated immediately before the ingroup (see Figure 16.2). Interestingly, data also showed that self-anchoring and intergroup differentiation might be *independent* routes toward positive ingroup distinctiveness: whereas in the self first/ingroup–outgroup condition there was significant ingroup favoritism due to an exceptionally *positive ingroup* rating, in the self last/ outgroup–ingroup condition significant favoritism stemmed from a rather *negative outgroup* judgment.

A different demonstration of the role of self-evaluations for favorable ingroup judgments was provided by Otten and Wentura (2001), who used indi-

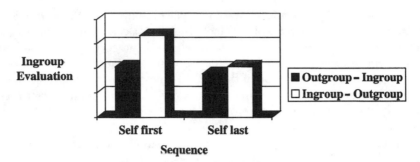

FIGURE 16.2. Ingroup evaluation as a function of evaluative sequence (data from Otten, 2000).

vidual multiple regression analyses in order to demonstrate self-anchoring. In their experiment, participants initially rated themselves on a set of 20 traits (10 positive, 10 negative; embedded in a set of filler items). Then a minimal social categorization was established (allegedly referring to temporal changes in concentration), followed by an "impression formation task" in which the very same traits previously judged for the self were judged whether they applied more to the ingroup or to the outgroup. Thus, similar to intergroup allocation matrices (e.g., Tajfel et al., 1971), ingroup and outgroup were judged simultaneously. Favoritism could be expressed by rating positive traits as more applicable to the ingroup than to the outgroup and negative traits as more applicable to the outgroup than to the ingroup. Hence, valence of traits was expected to predict whether judgments on the intergroup evaluation scales would tend more to the ingroup or more to the outgroup pole.

In individual multiple regression analyses, both self-ratings and valence of traits were tested as predictors of intergroup judgments; both predictors were significant, but self-rating was the more powerful variable. In addition, there was a significant interaction between the two predictors, such that the determination of group ratings by self-ratings was stronger within the domain of positive as compared to negative traits. Nonetheless, self-rating was a significant predictor in both valence conditions. This finding paralleled valence effects as obtained with regard to overall ingroup favoritism. Confirming the typical positive–negative asymmetry in social discrimination (see Mummendey & Otten, 1998; Otten & Mummendey, 2000), favoritism was significantly stronger on positive than on negative trait dimensions. However, in both conditions, the favorable treatment of the ingroup was significant.

The study by Otten and Wentura (2001) indicates that a striving for positive ingroup distinctiveness per se does not suffice to account for ingroup favoritism towards minimal groups. As pointed out elsewhere (e.g., Brown, 2000; Reynolds et al., 2000; Tajfel & Turner, 1986; Turner, 1999), ingroup favoritism is not indiscriminate, but relies on certain conditions. In this context, the present results imply that the (personal) self-image can be an important variable to predict relevant dimensions for ingroup definition and intergroup comparison.

Krueger (1998) subsumed self-anchoring under the more general term of *egocentric social projection*: people tend to project own traits, attitudes, and behavioral intentions onto others (e.g., Clement & Krueger, 2000; Krueger, 1998). The very act of social categorization implies that group members "have reasons to believe that ingroup members share their own response more than outgroup members do" (Krueger, 1998, pp. 221–222). Hence, when comparing ingroup and outgroup judgments, egocentric social projection is *asymmetrical* (Krueger & Clement, 1996; Krueger & Zeiger, 1993; Mullen, Dovidio, Johnson, & Copper, 1992). With minimal groups, this process fosters intergroup differences "where none exist" (Krueger, 1998, p. 228), merely based upon the outgroup's exclusion from the "benefits of projection" (Krueger, 1998, p. 228). Notably, the differences between findings for ingroup and outgroup in nearly all experiments summarized in this chapter (Otten, 2001; Otten & Bar-Tal, 2001; Otten & Moskowitz, 2000; Otten & Wentura, 1999, 2001) is fully consistent with the assumed categorization-based asymmetry in egocentric social projection.

SELF AS HEURISTIC FOR INGROUP EVALUATION

When accounting for ingroup favoritism in the MGP, Cadinu and Rothbart (1996) explicitly referred to heuristic information processing: the ingroup is defined in relation to the self by means of a similarity heuristic (while the outgroup is defined by means of an oppositeness heuristic; see above). Consistently, Krueger (1998) stated that egocentric social projection requires few cognitive resources and is partly based on cognitive simplifications. In conclusion, self-anchoring for ingroup judgments should vary as a function of information-processing effort.

Data in line with this reasoning were provided in a study by Forgas and Fiedler (1996; Experiment 3), who manipulated mood in order to demonstrate that intergroup bias is affected by variations in information processing. There is ample evidence showing that positive mood compared to negative mood decreases processing effort and increases reliance on heuristics (e.g., Clore, Schwarz, & Conway, 1994). Accordingly, Forgas and Fiedler hypothesized that, for minimal groups where the situation does not offer a legitimizing rationale for unequal treatment (Mummendey & Otten, 1998), intergroup bias would be strongest in the positive mood condition. Results confirmed this assumption—under positive mood response, latencies for the evaluation task were shortest and ingroup favoritism was strongest. In addition, and of special importance in the present chapter, increases in favoritism coincided with increases in self-ingroup similarity.

Lay-epistemic motivation is another important variable affecting the probability of heuristic information processing. Moreover, there is evidence that need for cognitive structure (NCS)—that is, the motivation to end up with quick and firm judgments as opposed to judgmental ambiguity (e.g. Kruglanski, 1996)—has an impact on intergroup bias. Shah, Kruglanski, and Thompson (1998) showed that a high need for cognitive structure increased ingroup favoritism, and Otten and collaborators (Otten, Mummendey, & Buhl, 1998) reported decreased ingroup bias when a need to avoid cognitive closure (fear of invalidity) was activated. Research on the effects of an uncertainty reduction motivation on ingroup favoritism in the MGP (Grieve & Hogg, 1999; Hogg & Mullin, 1999) strengthen these findings. Though derived within different theoretical contexts, there is a substantial overlap between the concepts of uncertainty reduction motivation and the need for cognitive closure as determinants of intergroup bias (see Hogg, 2001).

Otten and Bar-Tal (in press) provided a further empirical test of the assumed link between self-anchoring and relative ingroup preference. Recently, Bar-Tal and collaborators demonstrated that cognitive structuring varies not only as a function of NCS but is also affected by the subjectively perceived ability to achieve cognitive structure (AACS; Bar-Tal, 1994; Bar-Tal, Kishon-Rabin, & Tabak, 1997). A series of experiments revealed a significant interaction of NCS and AACS: reliance on heuristics, like schemata or stereotypes, was strongest when both NCS and AACS were high (e.g., Bar-Tal & Guinote, in press; Bar-Tal et al., 1997). Consequently, Otten and Bar-Tal (2001) varied both NCS and AACS in order to test the assumption that the *self* functions *as a heuristic* in minimal ingroup judgments. Self-evaluations were measured before, and ingroup and outgroup ratings right after, the minimal categorization procedure. Consistent with the predictions, regression weights for self-ratings as predictor of ingroup ratings were strongest in the condition with maximum probability of heuristic processing: participants who were under time pressure (high NCS) and who, due to previous experiences in a problem-solving task, were confident about their ability to solve the group-evaluation task (high AACS) were most willing to use the self as anchor for ingroup evaluation. In accordance with most of the studies cited above (e.g., Cadinu & Rothbart, 1996; Otten, 2001; Otten & Moskowitz, 2000; Otten & Wentura, 1999; Perdue et al., 1990; Smith, this volume; Smith & Henry, 1996; Smith et al., 1999), significant effects were found for ingroup ratings but did not apply to outgroup judgments.

SUMMARY AND CONCLUSIONS

The research program summarized above intended to identify factors that provide a convincing account for ingroup favoritism toward minimal groups. Rather than focusing on a motivation for positive social identity and positive ingroup distinctiveness, the main focus was on cognitive factors, namely an automatically generated affective ingroup bias and a generalization from self to novel ingroup. The results can roughly be summarized as follows:

1. There is evidence for a positive ingroup default from two different studies (Otten & Moskowitz, 2000; Otten & Wentura, 1999). Immediately after a minimal categorization procedure, positive ingroup attitudes manifest on implicit measures. Moreover, there is preliminary evidence that this effect corresponds to explicit ingroup preference (Otten & Wentura, 1999).

2. At the same time, there are consistent findings revealing an overlap between the mental representations of self and ingroup (Coats et al., 2000; Smith, this volume; Smith & Henry, 1996; Smith et al., 1999; Wright et al., this volume). Epstude and Otten (2000) extended these results and showed that when there is ambiguity about the ingroup's standing on a certain trait dimension, judgments matching the response to self-ratings are facilitated.

3. Correspondingly, a series of studies on *explicit* evaluations of novel, minimal in- and outgroups indicated a strong relation between self-ratings and ingroup ratings (Cadinu & Rothbart, 1996; Otten, 2001; Otten & Wentura, 2001). The very act of social categorization implies that only ingroup but not outgroup is linked to the self. Hence, only the former but not the latter can profit from a generalization from the typically positive self-image. Both explicit ingroup and outgroup judgments and correlations between self and group evaluations (Otten, 2001) are in accordance with such asymmetrical egocentric projection (Krueger, 1998; Clement & Krueger, 2000).

4. Finally, there is evidence showing that projection from self to minimal ingroup and the resulting positive (and positively distinct) ingroup image are supported by heuristic information processing (Forgas & Fiedler, 1996; Otten & Bar-Tal, 2001). When the probability of heuristic processing was highest, the link between self-ratings and ingroup ratings was closest.

A great merit of the theory of social identity was to direct social psychological researchers' attention to aspects of the *relation* between groups, when discussing intergroup phenomena like social discrimination. Hence, the aspect of social comparison and intergroup differentiation plays a central role in this theory (Tajfel & Turner, 1986; see also Brown, 2000, for a recent summary). The present research program does not intend to question the SIT approach in general. Quite modestly, it started off in order to suggest an alternative explanation for favoritism towards minimal groups. In fact, the findings raise doubts whether social comparison and intergroup differentiation are necessary elements for the emergence of ingroup favoritism in minimal intergroup settings. As Maass and

Schaller (1991) already suggested, favorable ingroup judgments might be the starting point rather than the result of intergroup evaluations.

The minimal group paradigm establishes conditions that are quite unique with regard to the possible interplay between self-definition and (in-)group definition. Typically, it is hard to disentangle whether similarity between self and ingroup arises from group members' defining themselves in terms of their ingroup (self-stereotyping; see Turner et al., 1987) or from defining the ingroup in terms of their personal self (self-anchoring). However, with completely novel, arbitrary ingroups, only self-anchoring but not self-stereotyping is available in order to link self and ingroup, and to give meaning to the new group membership. Hence, reference to personal identity seems necessary in order to establish a novel social identity, and ingroup favoritism might be better understood as intra- (self in relation to other ingroup members) rather than as intergroup process (ingroup in relation to the outgroup). In this vein, the present findings might be read as further support for a primacy of the individual self in social judgment (e.g., Dunning & Hayes, 1996; Gaertner, Sedikides, & Graetz, 1999; Gramzow, Gaertner, & Sedikides, 2001; Sedikides & Gaertner, 2000; Sedikides & Gaertner, 2001; Sedikides & Skowronski, 1993; Simon, 1993; Simon, Pantaleo, & Mummendey, 1995). As Krueger (1998) phrased it: " . . . ingroup favoritism is not only ethnocentric, but also egocentric in nature" (p. 228).

We have demonstrated that varying levels of ingroup favoritism can emerge simply as a function of how close the ingroup judgment is assimilated to the self-judgment, while outgroup judgments and self-ratings need not vary at all (note that in none of the experiments reported above were there any effects of the experimental manipulations on self-ratings). This viewpoint is fully consistent with the finding that variations in ingroup favoritism toward minimal groups stem from variations in ingroup rather than in outgroup treatment (Brewer, 1979). Thus, there can be a positive ingroup without a derogated outgroup; ingroup love must not correlate with outgroup hate (see Allport, 1954; Brewer, 1999). Moreover, as Brewer has shown (see this volume), social identities are affected by two independent motivations: need for inclusion and need for differentiation. Both needs relate positively to ingroup identification and ingroup preference. Need for inclusion is fulfilled by assimilating self and ingroup as suggested by the self-anchoring model. The absence of parallel evidence for attempts to establish intergroup differentiation suggests that the need for inclusion might be more relevant than the differentiation motive during the initial formation of social identity.

Finally, a limitation of the findings summarized in this chapter needs to be stated explicitly. The research program focused on implicit attitudes and on explicit evaluations, but not on intergroup allocations, which is the "classical" dependent variable in experiments on minimal groups. Yamagishi, Jin, and Kiyonari (1999), however, defined only biased intergroup *allocations* as ingroup favoritism, and subsumed biased, nonmaterialistic intergroup *evaluations* under the term "ingroup boasting." Besides, Otten, Mummendey, and Blanz (1995) presented evidence indicating that simple extrapolations from the domain of intergroup allocations to the domain of evaluations (or vice versa) are questionable. However, it seems plausible to argue that the positive ingroup default as demonstrated by Otten and collaborators (Otten & Moskowitz, 2000; Otten & Wentura, 1999) can also affect allocation decisions: positive ingroup treatment would be congruent to the positive affect that is attached to the ingroup. Besides, one might speculate that self-anchoring can affect intergroup allocations by shaping group members' expectations whether their fellow group members will reciprocate ingroup-favoring behavior (see Gaertner & Insko, 2000; Hertel & Kerr, in press). Thus, self-anchoring might mediate between social categorization and allocation bias.

It follows from the above that an important requirement for future research on the relation between personal self, social identity, and ingroup favoritism is a comparison between intergroup allocations and evaluations, and a test of the generalizability of certain effects from minimal groups to naturalistic intergroup settings. While Epstude and Otten (2000) demonstrated self-anchoring in a realistic intergroup context, Forgas and Fiedler (1996) showed that for more realistic groups systematic processing, but for minimal groups heuristic processing, supported ingroup bias and self–ingroup similarity. Moreover, considering Ickes' (this volume) critique about the asocial nature of many studies on the social self, one might wonder whether the self will be considered the prototype of a novel ingroup in situations where other ingroup members are present. Finally, one could ask how the importance of self-anchoring varies during group formation or manifestation of group membership. Clearly, more research is needed to clarify the dynamic and context-specific nature of the links between individual and collective self.

REFERENCES

Aberson, C. L., Healy, M., & Romero, V. (2000). Ingroup bias and self-esteem: A meta-analysis. *Personality and Social Psychology Review, 4*, 157–173.

Abrams, D., & Hogg, M. A. (1988). Comments on the motivational status of self-esteem in social identity and intergroup discrimination. *British Journal of Social Psychology, 18*, 317–334.

Alicke, M. D., Klotz, M. L., Breitenbecher, D. L., Yurak, T. J., & Vredenburg, D. S. (1995). Personal contact, individuation, and the better-than-average effect. *Journal of Personality and Social Psychology, 68*, 804–825.

Allport, G. W. (1954). *The nature of prejudice*. Reading, MA: Addison-Wesley.

Aron, A., Aron, E. N., Tudor, M., & Nelson, G. (1991). Close relationships as including other in the self. *Journal of Personality and Social Psychology, 60*, 241–253.

Bar-Tal, Y. (1994). The effect of need and ability to achieve cognitive structure on mundane decision-making. *European Journal of Personality, 8*, 45–58.

Bar-Tal, Y., & Guinote, A. (in press). Who exhibits more stereotypical thinking? The effect of need and ability to achieve cognitive structure on stereotyping. *European Journal of Personality*.

Bar-Tal, Y., Kishon-Rabin, L., & Tabak, N. (1997). The effect of need and ability to achieve cognitive structuring on cognitive structuring. *Journal of Personality and Social Psychology, 73,* 1158–1176.

Baumeister, R. F. (1998). The self. In D. T. Gilbert, S. T. Fiske, & G. Lindzey (Eds.), *The handbook of social psychology* (Vol. 1, pp. 680–740). New York: McGraw-Hill.

Brewer, M. B. (1979). In-group bias in the minimal intergroup situation: A cognitive-motivational analysis. *Psychological Bulletin, 86,* 307–324.

Brewer, M. B. (1993). The role of distinctiveness in social identity and group behaviour. In M. A. Hogg & D. Abrams (Eds.), *Group motivation: Social psychological perspectives* (pp. 1–16). London: Harvester Wheatsheaf.

Brewer, M. B. (1999). The psychology of prejudice: Ingroup love or outgroup hate? *Journal of Social Issues, 55,* 429–444.

Brewer, M. B., & Brown, R. J. (1998). Intergroup relations. In D. T. Gilbert, S. T. Fiske, & G. Linzdey (Eds.), *The handbook of social psychology* (Vol. 2, pp. 554–594). New York: McGraw-Hill.

Brewer, M., & Gardner, W. (1996). Who is this "We"? Levels of collective identity and self-representation. *Journal of Personality and Social Psychology, 71,* 83–93.

Brewer, M. B., & Pickett, C. L. (1999). Distinctiveness motives as a source of the social self. In T. R. Tyler, R. M. Kramer, & O. P. John (Eds.), *The psychology of the social self* (pp. 71–87). Mahwah, NJ: Erlbaum.

Brown, R. (2000). AGENDA 2000—Social identity theory: Past achievements, current problems and future changes. *European Journal of Social Psychology, 30,* 745–778.

Cadinu, M. R., & Rothbart, M. (1996). Self-anchoring and differentiation processes in the minimal group setting. *Journal of Personality and Social Psychology, 70,* 661–677.

Clement, R. W., & Krueger, J. (2000). The primacy of self-referent information in perceptions of social consensus. *British Journal of Social Psychology, 39,* 279–299.

Clore, G. L., Schwarz, N., & Conway, M. (1994). Affective causes and consequences of social information processing. In R. S. Wyer & T. K. Skrull (Eds.), *Handbook of social cognition* (pp. 323–417). Hillsdale, NJ: Erlbaum.

Coats, S., Smith, E. R., Claypool, H. M., & Banner, M. J. (2000). Overlapping mental representations of self and in-group: Reaction time evidence and its relationship with explicit measures of group identification. *Journal of Experimental Social Psychology, 36,* 304–315.

Crocker, J., & Schwartz, I. (1985). Prejudice and ingroup favoritism in a minimal intergroup situation: Effects of self-esteem. *Personality and Social Psychology Bulletin, 11,* 387–397.

Crocker, J., Thompson, L. L., McGraw, K. M., & Ingerman, C. (1987). Downward comparison, prejudice, and evaluations of others: Effects of self-esteem and threat. *Journal of Personality and Social Psychology, 52,* 907–916.

Diehl, M. (1989). Justice and discrimination between minimal groups: The limits of equity. *British Journal of Social Psychology, 28,* 227–238.

Diener, E., & Diener, C. (1996). Most people are happy. *Psychological Science, 7,* 181–185.

Dunning, D., & Hayes, A. F. (1996). Evidence for egocentric comparison in social judgment. *Journal of Personality and Social Psychology, 71,* 213–229.

Epstude, K., & Otten, S. (2000, June 28–July 1). *The ingroup as part of the self or the self as part of the ingroup? Response time evidence for self-anchoring and self-stereotyping in realistic intergroup contexts.* Paper presented at the 3rd Jena Workshop on Intergroup Processes, Jena, Germany.

Forgas, J. P., & Fiedler, K. (1996). Us and them: Mood effects on intergroup discrimination. *Journal of Personality and Social Psychology, 70,* 28–40.

Gaertner, L., & Insko, C. A. (2000). Intergroup discrimination in the minimal group paradigm: Categorization, reciprocation, or fear? *Journal of Personality and Social Psychology, 79,* 77–94.

Gaertner, L., Sedikides, C., & Graetz, K. (1999). In search of self-definition: Motivational primacy of the individual self, motivational primacy of the collective self, or contextual primacy? *Journal of Personality and Social Psychology, 76,* 5–18.

Gramzow, R. H., Gaertner, L., & Sedikides, C.

(2001). Memory for ingroup and outgroup information in a minimal group context: The self as an informational base. *Journal of Personality and Social Psychology, 80,* 188–205.

Grieve, P. G., & Hogg, M. A. (1999). Subjective uncertainty and intergroup discrimination in the minimal group situation. *Personality and Social Psychology Bulletin, 25,* 926–940.

Hertel, G., & Kerr, N. (in press). On the sufficiency of mere social categorization: In pursuit of the 'elusive' minimal group effect. *Group Dynamics.*

Hogg, M. A. (2001). Subjective uncertainty reduction through self-categorization: A motivational theory of social identity processes. In W. Stroebe & M. Hewstone (Eds.) *European Review of Social Psychology,* (pp. 223–255). Chichester, UK: Wiley.

Hogg, M. A., & Abrams, D. (1990). Social motivation, self-esteem and social identity. In D. Abrams & M. A. Hogg (Eds.), *Social identity theory: Constructive and critical advances* (pp. 28–47). New York: Harvester Wheatsheaf.

Hogg, M. A., & Mullin, B. A. (1999). Joining groups to reduce uncertainty: Subjective uncertainty reduction and group identification. In D. A. Abrams & M. A. Hogg (Eds.), *Social identity and social cognition* (pp. 249–279). Oxford, UK: Blackwell.

Krueger, J. (1998). Enhancement bias in the description of self and others. *Personality and Social Psychology Bulletin, 24,* 505–516.

Krueger, J., & Clement, R. W. (1996). Inferring category characteristics from sample characteristics: Inductive reasoning and social projection. *Journal of Experimental Psychology: General, 128,* 52–68.

Krueger, J., & Zeiger, J. S. (1993). Social categorization and the truly false consensus effect. *Journal of Personality and Social Psychology, 65,* 670–680.

Kruglanski, A. W. (1996). Motivated social cognition: Principles at the interface. In E. Higgings & A. W. Kruglanski (Eds.), *Social Psychology: A Handbook of basic principles* (pp. 493–520). New York: Guilford.

Lemyre, L., & Smith, P. M. (1985). Intergroup discrimination and self-esteem in the minimal group paradigm. *Journal of Personality and Social Psychology, 49,* 660–670.

Maass, A., & Schaller M. (1991). Intergroup biases and the cognitive dynamics of stereotype formation. In W. Stroebe & M. Hewstone (Eds.), *European review of social psychology* (Vol. 2, pp. 189–209). Chichester, UK: Wiley.

Matlin, M. W., & Stang, D. J. (1978). *The Pollyanna principle.* Cambridge, MA: Schenkman.

Messick, D. M., & Mackie, D. M. (1989). Intergroup relations. *Annual Review of Psychology, 40,* 45–81.

Mullen, B., Dovidio, J. F., Johnson, C., & Copper, C. (1992). In-group-out-group differences in social projection. *Journal of Experimental Social Psychology, 28,* 422–440.

Mummendey, A. (1995). Positive distinctiveness and intergroup discrimination: An old couple living in divorce. *European Journal of Social Psychology, 25,* 657–670.

Mummendey, A., & Otten, S. (1998). Positive-negative asymmetry in social discrimination. In W. Stroebe & M. Hewstone (Eds.), *European review of social psychology, Volume 9* (pp. 107–143). New York: Wiley.

Oakes, P. J., & Turner, J. C. (1980). Social categorization and intergroup behaviour: Does minimal intergroup discrimination make social identity more positive. *European Journal of Social Psychology, 10,* 295–301.

Otten, S. (2001). *Why are we so positive? Self-anchoring as a source of favoritism towards novel ingroups.* Unpublished manuscript.

Otten, S., & Bar-Tal, Y. (in press). *Self-anchoring in the minimal group paradigm: The impact of need and ability to achieve cognitive structure.* Unpublished manuscript.

Otten, S., & Epstude, K. (2001). Unpublished data, University of Jena, Germany.

Otten, S., & Moskowitz, G. B. (2000). Evidence for implicit evaluative in-group bias: Affect-biased spontaneous trait inference in a minimal group paradigm. *Journal of Experimental Social Psychology, 36,* 77–89.

Otten, S., & Mummendey, A. (2000). Valence-dependent probability of ingroup-favoritism between minimal groups: An integrative view on the positive-negative asymmetry in social discrimination. In D. Capozza & R. Brown (Eds), *Social identity processes* (pp. 33–48). London: Sage.

Otten, S., Mummendey, A., & Blanz, M.

(1995). Different measures of social discrimination in laboratory settings: Doubts in validity seem advisable. *Revue Internationale de Psychologie Sociale, 2,* 7–21.

Otten, S., Mummendey, A., & Buhl, T. (1998). Accuracy in information processing and the positive-negative asymmetry in social discrimination. *Revue Internationale de Psychologie Sociale, 11,* 69–96.

Otten, S., & Wentura, D. (1999). About the impact of automaticity in the minimal group paradigm: Evidence from affective priming tasks. *European Journal of Social Psychology, 29,* 1049–1071.

Otten, S., & Wentura, D. (2001). Self-anchoring and ingroup favoritism: An individual-profiles analysis. *Journal of Experimental Social Psychology, 32,* 525–532.

Perdue, C. W., Dovidio, J. F., Gurtman M. B., & Tyler, R. B. (1990). Us and them: Social categorization and the process of intergroup bias. *Journal of Personality and Social Psychology, 59,* 475–486.

Rabbie, J. M., & Horwitz, M. (1969). The arousal of ingroup-outgroup bias by a chance win or loss. *Journal of Personality and Social Psychology, 69,* 223–228.

Reynolds, K. J., Turner, J. C., & Haslam, S. A. (2000). When are we better than them and they are worse than us? A closer look at social discrimination in positive and negative domains. *Journal of Personality and Social Psychology, 78,* 64–80.

Rubin, M., & Hewstone, M. (1998). Social identity theory's self-esteem hypothesis: A review and some suggestions for clarification. *Personality and Social Psychology Review, 2,* 40–62.

Sedikides, C. (1993). Assessment, enhancement, and verification determinants of the self-evaluation process. *Journal of Personality and Social Psychology, 65,* 317–338.

Sedikides, C., & Brewer, M. B. (2001). *Individual self, relational self, collective self.* Philadelphia: Psychology Press.

Sedikides, C., & Gaertner, L. (2000). The social self: The quest for identity and the motivational primacy of the individual self. In J. P. Forgas, K. D. Williams, & L. Wheeler (Eds.), *The social mind. Cognitive and motivational aspects of interpersonal behavior*

(pp. 115–138). Cambridge, UK: Cambridge University Press

Sedikides, C., & Gaertner, L. (2001). A homecoming to the individual self: Emotional and motivational primacy. In C. Sedikides & M. F. Brewer (Eds.), *Individual self, relational self, collective self* (pp. 7–23). Philadelphia: Psychology Press.

Sedikides, C., & Skowronski, J. J. (1993). The self in impression formation: Trait centrality and social perception. *Jorunal of Experimental Social Psychology, 29,* 347–357.

Sedikides, C., & Strube, M. J. (1995). The multiply motivated self. *Personality and Social Psychology Bulletin, 21,* 1330–1335.

Sedikides, C., & Strube, M. J. (1997). Self-evaluation: To thine own self be good, to thine own self be sure, to thine own self be true, and to thine own self be better. In M. P. Zanna (Ed.), *Advances in experimental social psychology, 29* (pp. 209–269). New York: Academic Press.

Shah, J., Kruglanski, A. W., & Thompson, E. P. (1998). Membership has its (epistemic) rewards: Need for closure effects on ingroup bias. *Journal of Personality and Social Psychology, 75,* 383–393.

Simon, B. (1993). On the asymmetry in the cognitive construal of ingroup and outgroup: A model of egocentric social categorization. *European Journal of Social Psychology, 23,* 131–147.

Simon, B., Pantaleo, G., & Mummendey, A. (1995). Unique individual or interchangeable group member? The accentuation of intragroup differences versus similarities as an indicator of the individual self versus the collective self. *Journal of Personality and Social Psychology, 69,* 106–119.

Smith, E. R., Coats, S., & Walling, D. (1999). Overlapping mental representaions of self, in-group, and partner: Further response time evidence and a connectionist model. *Personality and Social Psychology Bulletin, 25,* 873–882.

Smith, E. R., & Henry, S. (1996). An in-group becomes part of the self: Response time evidence. *Personality and Social Psychology Bulletin, 20,* 635–642.

Tajfel, H. (Ed.). (1978). *Differentiation between social groups: Studies in the social psychology of intergroup relations*. London: Academic Press.

Tajfel, H., Billig, M. G., Bundy, R. P., & Flament, C. (1971). Social categorization and intergroup behaviour. *European Journal of Social Psychology, 1*, 149–178.

Tajfel, H., & Turner, J. C. (1979). An integrative theory of intergroup conflict. In W. G. Austin & S. Worchel (Eds.), *The social psychology of intergroup relations* (pp. 33–47). Monterey, CA: Brooks/Cole.

Tajfel, H., & Turner, J. C. (1986). The social identity theory of intergroup behavior. In S. Worchel & W. G. Austin (Eds.), *Psychology of intergroup relations* (pp. 7–24). Chicago: Nelson-Hall Publishers.

Taylor, S. E., & Brown, J. D. (1988). Illusion and well-being: A social psychological perspective on mental health. *Psychological Bulletin, 103*, 193–210.

Triandis, H. C. (1989). The self and social behavior in differing cultural contexts. *Psychological Review, 96*, 506–520.

Turner, J. C. (1984). Social identification and psychological group formation. In H. Tajfel (Ed.), *The social dimension: European developments in social psychology* (Vol. 2, pp. 518–538). Cambridge, UK: Cambridge University Press.

Turner J. C. (1999). Some current issues in research on social identity and self-categorization theories. In N. Ellemers, R. Spears. & B. Doosje (Eds.), *Social Identity: Context, commitment, content* (pp. 6–34). Oxford, UK: Blackwell.

Turner, J. C., Hogg, M. A., Oakes, P. J., Reicher, S. D., & Wetherell, M. S. (1987). *Rediscovering the social group. A self-categorization theory*. Oxford, UK: Blackwell.

Turner, J. C., & Oakes, P. J. (1997). The socially structured mind. In C. A. McGarty & S. A. Haslam (Eds.), *The message of social psychology* (pp. 355–373). Oxford, UK: Blackwell.

Turner, J. C., & Onorato, R. S. (1999). Social identity, personality, and the self-concept: A self-categorization perspective. In T. R. Tyler, R. M. Kramer, & O. P. John (Eds.), *The psychology of the social self* (pp. 11–46). Mahwah, NJ: Erlbaum.

Tyler, T. R., Kramer, R. M., & John, O. E. (Eds.). (1999). *The psychology of the social self*. Mahwah, NJ: Erlbaum.

Uleman, J. S., Hon, A., Roman, R. J., & Moskowitz, G. B. (1996). On-line evidence for spontaneous trait inferences at encoding. *Personality and Social Psycholoy Bulletin, 22*, 377–394.

Yamagishi, T., Jin, N. & Kiyonari, T. (1999). Bounded generalized reciprocity: Ingroup boasting and ingroup favoritism. *Advances in Group Processes, 16*, 161–197.

17

Adapting the Self to Local Group Norms
Internalizing the Suppression of Prejudice

CHRISTIAN S. CRANDALL
LAURIE T. O'BRIEN
AMY ESHLEMAN

INTRODUCTION

O ne of the most important questions in psychological theories of the self is "where does the content of the self come from"? Many theories of the self speak to this issue, and they point to a wide variety of sources, but most agree that the content of the self comes from others' vision of us, often referred to as the "looking glass self" (Cooley, 1902; James, 1892; Mead, 1934).

Address for correspondence: Christian S. Crandall, Department of Psychology, University of Kansas, Lawrence, Kansas 66045, USA. E-mail: crandall@lark.cc.ukans.edu

Most of the current research on self is not designed to look at this question, but rather is focused on dynamic processes such as self-protection, self-confirmation, the role of self-esteem, and so on. Theories that guide this research tend to treat the self as preexisting; what is researched is how the self affects other basic processes. Substantially less research has been done on how content of the self gets in there in the first place (but see Cooper & Hogg; Mackie & Smith; Smith; Otten; Wright, Aron, & Tropp; this volume). One good reason for this is that, when we conduct our research, participants tend to bring their selves into the room with them. This makes topics such as self-protection and self-related information processing possible to study, but it interferes with the study of self-creation. In this chapter, we discuss a theory of self that gives one answer to the question of where self-content comes from: the Group Norm Theory of Attitudes (Sherif & Sherif, 1953). The reader may, at this point, wonder why a theory of attitudes might serve as a premise for a self-content theory; it is certainly a good question. We must first convince the reader of the need for the application of attitude theory in the area of the self.

We begin the chapter with a brief overview of the close connectedness between attitudes and the self, based on three things—attitude theories that relate to the self, self-theories that relate to attitudes, and how social influence theories speak to both attitudes and the self. We then describe Sherif and Sherif's (1953) social influenced-based Group Norm Theory of Attitudes and show how it serves as a model for inclusion of content (notably attitudes) into the self. Finally, we report several studies that show how people's attitudes adapt to their group setting and how stages of identification with a group affect people's self-content and self-perceptions.

THEORIES OF ATTITUDES INVOLVE THE SELF

Many attitude theories suggest that attitudes are part of the self, and that to change some central, important attitudes, one might have to change components of the self along with it. Attitudes that relate to the self are sometimes called central attitudes (Judd & Krosnik, 1982); in the early social psychological literature, they were called ego-involving (Sherif & Cantril, 1947). Changing important attitudes involves changing the self; "To unfreeze attitudes that have become central constituents of the self, the sense of identity itself it attacked" (Smith, 1969, p. 94).

The class of *functional theories* of attitudes suggests that attitudes serve several self-relevant purposes. Smith, Bruner, and White (1956) and Katz (1960) suggested that some attitudes serve a social-adjustive function, helping the self fit into a social environment. In Herek's (1986) version of these theories, attitudes that are closely connected to the self are described as having a "symbolic expression function."

Another obvious example is *cognitive dissonance* theory. Implicit in the earliest formulations of dissonance theory is the idea that people change attitudes to protect their internal consistency within the self (see also Cooper & Hogg, this volume). But this is a requirement only to the extent that one values self-consistency. In a later variant of dissonance theory, Aronson (1968) argued that dissonance effects would only occur when the self and its integrity were implicated. When considering two inconsistent cognitions, a third cognition is usually implied, which is that "I am not a fool/hypocrite/liar/loser." If one tolerates one's own self-inconsistency, then dissonance effects do not occur, as Whitman (1855/1982) once observed:

> "Do I contradict myself?
> Very well then, I contradict myself,
>   (I am large, I contain multitudes)."

Several other attitude relevant theories have a large component of "self" to them. *Self-perception theory* (Bem, 1967) revolves around the notion of the self taking action, the self observing action, and then attributing causes to one's own behavior. In self-perception research, the variable that is studied is almost invariably an attitude—the research revolves subtly around the relationship between a person and his/her behavior and how to integrate behavior with the self. *Reactance theory* (Brehm, 1966) suggests that people will actively seek to reestablish a freedom, either in terms of choice or in terms of an important belief, when that threat is to personal, valued, cherished, or self-relevant dimensions (Brehm & Brehm, 1981). Abelson and Prentice (1989) have suggested that attitudes are like personal possession and serve much the same self-definitional function.

THEORIES OF SELF INCLUDE ATTITUDES

There are a number of theories of self-process and structure that include attitudes as an important component. For example, *self-affirmation theory* (Steele, 1988) uses self constructs to explain attitude change, and *symbolic self-completion theory* (Wicklund & Gollwitzer, 1982) treats attitudes as a central part of self-definition (e.g., Schiffmann & Nelkenbrecher, 1994). The large amount of research on self-protective processes (e.g., Crocker & Major, 1989) shows that processes that incorporate, counter, and change information about the self are quite similar in style and substance to research on resistance to persuasion.

The techniques that are used to study self and attitudes overlap, suggesting the phenomena are related in structure and expression. These include priming studies (Milburn, 1987), schema studies (e.g., Markus, 1977), and the measurement and conceptualizations of self-esteem as a self-attitude—treating the self as an object to be evaluated (Rosenberg, 1979). Self theorists in social psychology have often come from the ranks of attitude theory—an incomplete list would include Tony Greenwald, Bill McGuire, Claude Steele, Abe Tesser, Harry Triandis, and Cooper and Hogg within this volume. Finally, if one must resort to the last refuge of self-theorist scoundrels, we might simply wave our hands and claim that attitudes are implicitly contained within the conceptualization of the self developed by William James (1892).

THEORIES OF SOCIAL INFLUENCE SPEAK TO BOTH ATTITUDES AND THE SELF

Theories of social influence are historically hegemonic; that is, they are designed to cover and explain as many psychological phenomena as possible. At this task, they have been remarkably successful, and as we shall argue in this chapter, it is for good reason. Not only are the theories simple and straightforward, but they often accord quite well with the available data.

The Lewin-Festinger Tradition

The Lewin tradition, exemplified by the work of Festinger and his students (e.g., Festinger, Schachter & Back, 1950), showed that rewarding conformity to social norms and punishing deviance—usually by social disapproval or ostracism, and the patterns of communication associated with them—was a powerful explanatory system of social behavior (see also Williams, Wheeler, & Harvey, 2001). This approach led quite quickly to development of a more "self" relevant theory of influence, namely *social comparison theory*. Although often thought of as a self-theory, a careful reading of the original paper and knowing its immediate context (e.g., Festinger, 1950) shows that the theory is more about how people recognize their own deviance, resulting in self-generated conformity. Taken together these two approaches create a theory of influence that accounts for how attitudes are communicated, evaluated, and accepted into the self (or rejected).

Social Identity/Self-Categorization Theory

Social identity theory (SIT; Tajfel & Turner, 1977; Hogg, 2001) and its close cousin, self-categorization theory (SCT; Turner, Hogg, Oakes, Reicher, & Wetherall, 1987), are another example of hegemonic social influence theories (see Turner, 1991) that integrate self, attitudes, and social influence. Both SIT and SCT suggest that, at any given moment, one's self is largely defined by membership in groups, and one's membership in a group involves adhering to the social norms of the group. To the extent that a social group has a norm about a particular attitude (e.g., environmental groups' negative attitudes toward nuclear energy), then identification with that group and its salience within the self will determine how much the individual will also express and internalize that attitude (see Terry & Hogg, 2000, 2001).

CONTENT OF THE SELF

The most important value of social influence models, both in terms of attitudes and in terms of self theory, is that they do what other models of the self do poorly—they account for the *content* of the self. Traditionally, the major theories have given this question short shrift, opting to study process rather than content—it's been a successful strategy. But it has led, to some extent, to pointing to the looking-glass sort of theories (e.g., Cooley & Mead) and a bit of handwaving in that direction.

The class of looking-glass theories has fared poorly in recent years. Research from the social identity tradition (e.g., Simon & Pettigrew, 1990) and research in the social cognition tradition (e.g., Crocker & Major, 1989) suggest that social feedback is often rebuffed rather than incorporated into the self. There is a substantial resistance to negative feedback; Crocker and Major's (1989) review showed that people discount negative feedback, disbelieve it, and devalue its source—this negative feedback often has little or no measurable impact on the self (e.g., Britt & Crandall, 2000; Crandall, Tsang, Harvey, & Britt, 2000). Research in social identity theory suggests that the evaluation one's important groups receives (e.g., race, sexual orientation) is downplayed, and other dimensions that augment self-esteem are enhanced (e.g., Jackson, Sullivan, Harnish, & Hodge, 1996).

Self-discrepant feedback does not typically lower evaluations, but rather leads to attributions for the feedback source (Britt & Crandall, 2000). Under certain circumstances, the response is outright aggression toward someone who expresses a negatively discrepant evaluation (Baumeister, Bushman, & Campbell, 2000; Tice, Twenge, & Schmeichel, this volume). Research in the self-verification tradition (e.g., Swann, 1997) suggests that we often will seek out information or romantic partners who verify our self-views, and we may prefer someone who supports our own negative self-view rather than incorporate a positive message that would require adjustment of our self-image.

GROUP NORM THEORY OF ATTITUDES: HOW (SOME) CONTENT ENTERS THE SELF

We now embark on the discussion of an early social psychological theory that is well-developed and well-supported by the data; it provides an account for the content of the self, and it is almost entirely ignored today—the Group Norm Theory of attitudes (GNT; Sherif, 1948; Sherif & Sherif, 1953). The theory was named by Allport (1954), but we'll introduce the theory in the Sherifs' own words:

> Attitudes toward members of other groups, as well as attitudes toward one's own group, are learned. But attitudes toward members of other groups are not determined so much by experiences while in contact with the group in question as by contact with the attitudes toward these groups prevailing among the older members of the groups in which they develop. (Sherif & Sherif, 1953, pp. 94–95)

The idea is simple—people acquire their attitudes (and beliefs and values and related self-content) by joining groups that have norms that dictate these points of view. Joining a group not only determines who you are, in terms of giving you a label and a feeling of membership, but it also tells you what to think and how to feel. Attitudes such as prejudice come from joining a group and internalizing its attitudes: "The attitude of prejudice is a product of *group membership* . . . the presence or absence of change of attitude and the degree thereof is a function of the degree of assimilation to the atmosphere of the new community" (Sherif, 1948, pp. 66–67). Assimilation to the group entails assimilating its belief, ideals, attitudes, prejudices, and other ways of viewing and valuing the world. This process may be self-conscious at first, but Sherif and Sherif (1953) point out that the process of group influence on the self soon becomes transparent:

> Especially concepts and ideas concerning social relations become, for the individual member, "his own" concepts and ideas. Concerning as they do the characteristics and relations of individuals to other individuals and groups, such concepts, ideas, and approaches to problem situations in every age become part of the individual's personal identity. Once learned—at the time of their development, or later, through books, or from the lips of parents of teachers—they seem as "natural" to the individual as breathing. (pp. 16–17)

Sherif and Sherif (1953) argued that group-based attitudes become so smoothly incorporated that, after a time, the adopted attitude is owned, affirmed, and an unquestioned part of the self.

> In this way, a significant part of the self is formed, from direct adaptation of normatively appropriate beliefs, attitudes, values, and prejudices. In short, attitudes of prejudice, learned chiefly through contact with the norms of social distance prevailing in the group, impressed by the approval of grownups (including parents) for "proper" behavior along with punishment for disapproval for "improper" or "naughty" behavior as well as by sanctions of age-mate groups, come to constitute a part of the individual's very self-identity, of his ego. . . . It is small wonder that they come to be experienced as a "natural" part of oneself—almost as natural as one's name. (Sherif & Sherif, 1953, p. 99)

We restate the theory in the simplest terms. A person enters a group, which has attitude norms. As one comes to identify with this group, one begins to internalize the normatively appropriate attitude. The tension of attitude change may be felt while adopting new attitudes, but once adopted, the social influence source of the attitude is no longer available, and the attitudes appear (and are) genuine, heartfelt—incorporated into the self.

In the remaining body of the chapter, we will review a part of our research program on how people adapt to a group's attitude norms. In particular, we will review research that shows how people adopt norms about prejudice, and the processes they go through internalizing the group's acceptable prejudices and suppressing unacceptable prejudices.

APPLICATIONS OF GROUP NORM THEORY OF ATTITUDES TO INTERNALIZATION OF PREJUDICE

Some obvious hypotheses come out of the GNT. The first one is remarkably simple; the prejudice that people report should map onto the group's social norms for those prejudices. The first study we review compares expression of prejudice to how normatively appropriate it is to have the prejudice.

Expressions of Prejudice and Fit to Norms

To test this, we created a list of 105 different social groups that an undergraduate at the University of Kansas (KU) might feel prejudice toward. These groups ranged from groups toward which negative affect would be quite appropriate (e.g., rapists, child abusers) to groups toward which negative affect is generally inappropriate (e.g., racial groups, the physically handicapped), with many groups in between (e.g., porn stars, politicians, people who smoke, police officers, and people who smell bad).

We measured the normative appropriateness of each prejudice by having a group of over 120 KU undergraduates rate them on a 3-point scale: 2 = "OK to feel negatively toward this group," 1 = "Maybe OK to feel negatively toward this group," and 0 = "Not OK to feel negatively toward this group." We then asked a separate sample of 120-some undergraduates to report, on a feeling thermometer (0–100), how positively they felt toward these same groups (in alphabetical order). Reversing the thermometer scores, high scores now equaling prejudice, we collapsed across subject, and correlated the mean rating of the "norm" score to the mean average prejudice endorsement. We found a correlation of $r = .96$, which is a pretty high rating. In social and personality psychology, we're often quite happy with .30, and with .96, one starts to worry whether or not one has measured the same thing twice. In fact, that's almost exactly the theory—when people report their prejudice-related attitudes, the source of the attitude is not personal experience, it's not rational thought, it's not careful consideration of the merits of a particular group, and it's not a deeply held value system—it's the group norm.

Of course, people's experience of the source of their attitudes may be quite at odds with this account—they might give reasons, rationales, and other delightfully epiphenomenal protocols. But we suggest that people adopt many, if not most of their attitudes from the prevailing group norms; the *very close fit* between what people report, and what people say they should report, is remarkable and leaves little room for idiosyncratic thought, experience, or decision making.

It is not surprising that there is a correlation between norms and attitude expression—it's hard to imagine any theory that would predict otherwise. What is surprising is just how high this correlation is; the sheer size of the correlation supports the GNT. This one study is not an anomaly. For example, in another experiment (Crandall, Eshleman, & O'Brien, in press) the normative appropriateness of prejudice toward a group correlates with how offensive jokes about the group are seen at $r = .82$. Similarly, the normative appropriateness of prejudice correlates with acceptability of discrimination toward groups in housing, dating, and employment at $r = .86$.

Compliance and the Internalization of Social Norms

The social norms that one internalizes vary from group to group, and entrance into a new group involves taking on that group's frame of reference (Cantril, 1941; Sherif & Sherif, 1964). Upon arrival into a new group, there is a transition period during which one learns the group's norms, and should one choose to stay, one begins the process of adaptation and internalization (Kelman, 1961). During this time, the group's norms are salient (Hogg & Abrams, 1988), and people are aware of their deviance—an awareness that contrasts with internalized norms.

When one joins a group, there is a probability that some of the old attitudes will not be welcomed in the new group. As a result, new members are quite likely to suppress their attitudes, or they may directly experience rejection or censure for expression of inappropriate attitudes (Levine & Moreland, 1982). In this early stage, we suggest that outward compliance to new norms will feel, to the suppressor, less like the early process of identification with the group and more like outward pressure to comply with arbitrary norms. As the person begins to identify with the group and take on its norms, compliance turns to identification and internalization—and the sense of external pressure turns to a sense of internal motivation.

This analysis suggests that people will not accurately report on the internal changes that accompany identifying with new groups. When people encounter a new group, especially one that they admire, value, and wish to join, the early desire to fit in (along with the evidence from older group members that they do not share all of the group's attitudes) will feel like an *external* pressure to conform. Later, when the person begins the process of identification with the group, the desire to belong and acquire the new group attitudes will feel like an *internal* motivation to suppress inappropriate attitudes. This analysis suggests a slightly different viewpoint from that taken by the influential analysis of internal and external motivations to suppress inappropriate attitudes of Plant and Devine (1998).

Plant and Devine (1998) developed a scale to differentiate between internal and external motivations to suppress prejudice towards Blacks. The Internal Motivation Scale (IMS) measures the pressure one places on oneself to conform to nonprejudiced standards, and the External Motivation Scale (EMS) measures a sense of pressure to conform to external expectations. We suggest that process of encounter, attraction, and identification with the group "KU students" by new KU undergraduates will determine the reports of internal and external motivation to suppress prejudice.

We tested this idea with about 250 KU undergraduates who filled out the Plant and Devine (1998) scales along with a questionnaire to measure identification with college. We predicted that scores on the Internal Motivation Scale (IMS) would increase as identification with college increased. However, as identification proceeds to the highest level, discrepancies between the group norm and individual attitudes should diminish, and the salience of self-motivated change should shrink. Therefore, at the highest levels of identification, scores on the IMS should begin to decrease.

The perception of external pressure to suppress prejudice against Blacks, without internalization of that attitude, should lead to high scores on the External Motivation Scale (EMS). Because those who do not strongly identify as college students would not be expected to internalize the group's norms, low levels of college identification should be associated with high scores on the EMS.

Because women were more identified with college, and also reported higher levels of suppression, we also analyzed the results separately by sex (the sex difference for IMS was twice the size of the sex difference for EMS). College Identification was correlated with IMS ($r = .25$, and slightly more for males than females).

Because women are more "advanced" in their identification with college, we expected a curvilinear relationship between IMS and College Identification for women: women at the highest levels of identification with college should report lower self-perceived motivation to change their attitudes. When we regressed IMS scores on both a linear and quadratic College Identification term, we found that a linear and a quadratic term were both significant. When identification with the group increased, a sense of internal pressure increased, until very high levels of identification, when reports of internal pressure began to significantly decrease (see Crandall et al., in press, for more details of this analysis).

We admit some surprise, but also excitement that these results conform nicely to our predictions. A similar regression calculated for males showed a linear effect but no quadratic effect, consistent with the interpretation of men's lower College Identification scores indicating substantially less internalization. The pattern for external motivations to suppress was less clear, and differed by gender; as identification increased, external motivation decreased for women but increased for men. These data are consistent with the view that men are in a fairly early stage of adoption of the college's antiprejudice norms, but it's still early to interpret them.

Motives to suppress prejudice reflect the natural history of group identification; external motivation is associated with the early stages of adaptation to a group and precedes internal motivation to conform to group attitudinal norms. Internal motivation to suppress prejudice is associated with a later, self-motivated transformation of attitudes to come in line with group norms. These data do suggest that a process that involves compliance, then identification, and then internalization may take place. It is these three influence processes that serve to make up a substantial amount of self-content.

In the context of this research, we developed our own measure of suppression that focused on internal motivations to suppress prejudice—the Suppression of Prejudice Scale (SPS). It includes items such as "When I meet a person of another race or ethnicity, I try to avoid thinking about their race," "I don't want to appear racist or sexist, even to myself," and "I won't use an ethnic slur, even if it's the word that pops into my head." The SPS was designed to account for a desire to suppress prejudice against many different outgroups.

The 7-item SPS scale correlates with the Modern Racism Scale (MRS) at $r = -.35$, and women reported significantly more suppression than men. Men routinely score higher on the MRS than women (Biernat & Crandall, 1999); in this study the $d = .26$. However, as we have seen, males suppress less than females. To what extent is the difference in racism merely a function of difference in suppression? We removed the variance accounted for by SPS scores and reduced the sex difference to nonsignificance. This suggests that a significant portion of sex differences in racial prejudice may be due to a difference in the amount of suppression of prejudice between the two genders and not due primarily to a difference in the genuine underlying attitudes.

Suppression Scales as Indicators of the Struggle for Internalization

This takes us back to the question of what exactly do suppression scales measure? Certainly people who score high on these measures of suppression report less prejudice toward traditionally studied targets of prejudice. Plant and Devine (1998) and Dunton and Fazio (1997) both found that their suppression scales were negatively correlated with traditional measures of prejudice against Blacks. When we expand our study of prejudice to include the 105 social groups described above, how will measures of the suppression of prejudice behave?

If high suppressors are people who suppress negative thoughts, feelings, and communications toward *all* outgroups, then we would expect suppression scales to be *negatively* correlated with all 105 outgroups. If the internal measures of suppression are indicators of a struggle for the internalization of group norms (as we suggest), then we too predict that high suppressors will report lower levels of normatively inappropriate prejudice (e.g., toward ethnic groups). But, if suppression is a measure of early internalization, high suppressors will report *higher* levels of prejudice toward socially appropriate targets (e.g., criminals social deviants, people whose behavior is politically incorrect). In this case, suppression serves as a marker of the struggle to readjust the self to new group norms and attitudes.

In a study of what suppression scales measure, we used both the SPS and the Dunton and Fazio (1997) Concern scale to measure suppression in about 130 psychology students. Participants also completed a feeling thermometer measure of prejudice toward our 105 target groups (reversed so that high scores equal low evaluations). Because we know from early research what the normatively appropriate level of prejudice expression is for the 105 target groups, we can also compare the fit-to-prejudice norms for high and low suppressors.

If the SPS and the Concern scale simply measure internal drive to suppress prejudice, we should find negative correlations between all 105 targets and the suppression scales. However, if internal suppression scales measure motivation to conform to group prejudice norms, then we should expect a negative correlation between measured suppression and expressions of a prejudice when that prejudice is normatively inappropriate, but a positive correlation between measured suppression and a prejudice when that prejudice is normatively appropriate. The feeling thermometer was reversed so that higher scores represent greater prejudice.

Table 17.1 displays that pattern of correlations. For traditional, normatively inappropriate targets of prejudice (the right-hand of the table), suppression is negatively correlated with expression of prejudice. However, a very different picture emerges from the left-hand half of Table 17.1; when it is normatively appropriate to express a prejudice, we find that high suppressors report *more* prejudice. These data are substantially consistent with the internalization hypothesis; suppressors are acute norm followers. (An overall test of all 105 groups is possible, correlating the normative appropriateness score with that group's correlation between "suppression" and prejudice—this correlation is .69 for SPS and .62 for Concern; see Crandall et al., in press.) These data are quite consistent with the hypothesis that people who report high levels of internal motivation to suppress are people who are very concerned with reporting attitudes that are consistent with, or even extreme versions of, the prevailing group norm.

When only normatively appropriate forms of prejudice are studied, prejudice suppression is virtually indistinguishable from norm following. It is only when appropriate prejudice is included that suppression can be differentiated

TABLE 17.1. Correlations between Internally Motivated
Suppression and Expression of Prejudice among
Normatively Acceptable and Unacceptable Prejudices.

	Acceptable Prejudices		Unacceptable Prejudices
.17	Child abusers	−.29	Fat people
.22	Racists	−.21	Interracial couples
.18	Drunk drivers	−.19	Asian Americans
.17	Kids who steal lunch money	−.22	Hispanics
.24	Men who leave their families	−.25	Black Americans
.15	Liars	−.25	Native Americans
.28	Men who go to prostitutes	−.32	Elderly people
.32	Porn stars	−.27	Mentally retarded people
.24	People who sell marijuana	−.35	Blind people

from norm following. From our research with normatively appropriate targets of prejudice, we know that people who report high levels of prejudice suppression actually report high levels of prejudice. This research suggests that people who report being motivated to suppress their prejudice are people who are motivated to bring their behavior in line with the norms of the group. During this time, the content of self is fluid and marked by some self-doubting. During this time, people are eager to conform to expectations, and adapt themselves to "appropriate" attitudes and behavior.

These data are indirect, though, and we decided to carry out an experiment that more directly tested the notion that people who report high levels of internally motivated prejudice suppression are malleable norm followers.

In many cases, it is difficult for relatively new group members to know which attitudes are normative. Norms can be remarkably malleable, and in certain circumstances the expression of prejudice toward inappropriate targets is tolerated (e.g., in the locker room or at the poker table certain prejudices are tolerated). How will high suppressors act when social norms point to tolerance of vocal racial prejudice? If local social norms are at odds with the overarching societal norms for prejudice, will high suppressors follow the herd?

We selected about 60 students who were either high or low on the SPS. We then presented them with situations that suggested either condemning or condoning racist speech and confidentially recommended responses to racist conduct. If suppression is based on egalitarian convictions, then social influence should play a small role. If suppression is based on a desire to conform to an important reference group, high suppressors will not only condemn racist speech more vigorously, but they will also condone racist speech more tolerantly than low suppressors, depending on the immediate norm of the situation.

Following a technique developed by Blanchard and his colleagues (Blanchard, Crandall, Brigham, & Vaughn, 1994; Blanchard, Lilly, & Vaughn,

1991), we presented participants with a set of attitude "petitions" that asked about the appropriate response to racist conduct. The answers on the petition formed the manipulation; the previous five respondents were either highly condemning of racist speech or highly tolerant of racist speech. A control condition was included where the participant was the "first" to answer the petition.

Blanchard and his colleagues found that a single confederate condemning or condoning racism could dramatically alter tolerance for racist acts. When the confederate condemned racist speech, so too did subjects; when the confederate condoned racist speech, subjects showed great tolerance for it. Using this norm manipulation, we explored whether high suppressors report less overall tolerance of racial prejudice, regardless of the norm of the situation, or whether high suppressors pay more attention to the manipulated social norm and exhibit heightened tolerance of prejudice when the social norm points in that direction.

We replicated the norm manipulation effect produced by Blanchard et al.—participants in the condition where the confederate condemned racism were more condemning of racist conduct, while participants in the condition where the confederate condoned racism were more willing to condone racist conduct, with a control condition falling in the middle.

To test the hypothesis that high suppressors would be more conformist on prejudice-relevant issues, we compared the correlations between suppression and the attitudes toward racist speech. Suppression scores were measured by taking the average of participants' scores on the SPS, Concern scale (Dunton & Fazio, 1997), and the IMS (Plant & Devine, 1998). As one might expect, in the control condition, suppression was negatively correlated with tolerating racist speech. When the previous group members condemned racist speech, suppression was also negatively correlated with tolerating racist speech. The critical test is when the other group members tolerate or *condone* racist speech—what do suppressors do then? We found that suppression was positively correlated with tolerating racist speech, a finding consistent with the notion that suppressors are people highly attuned to the norms of the group. When faced with a normative situation in which their peers clearly established a norm of tolerance for racist speech, the high suppressors are more influenced by the manipulation than the low suppressors, and they express firm opinions of *tolerance* of prejudice. We suggest that high suppressors are more malleable because of the stage of their self-development; they are struggling to bring their selves in line with the group. Evidence of what the group thinks will be substantially more potent to such vulnerable people.

Implications of Research for Attitudes and for the Self

In the struggle to revise the self to meet new demands, a person goes from compliance to identification and internalization, but what the person says about the process may not always quite map on to the psychological process. Compliance may be felt as awkwardness, embarrassment, or feelings of rejection. Identification and internalization may be subjectively experienced as self-motivated change. But when group identification and self-categorization lead to a feeling of attraction to group norms (or to group prototypes; Turner et al., 1987), people will report a willingness and desire to change.

Although the original purpose of this research was to study the influence process on attitudes, it is clear that much can be learned about self-processes by studying attitudes processes. The focus on the self's dynamics has been useful and productive, and there's always room for more of this research. But it is also a good idea to keep one's eyes on the content of the self. How do people come to have their beliefs? How do they come to change their self-images? Which self-images are adapted easily, and which self-images require heavy persuasive pressure? These kinds of questions are useful, although there is much progress to be made yet toward answering them.

The first author's years in graduate school at the University of Michigan were coterminous in social/personality psychology with the upsurge in social cognition and social judgment research (e.g., Nisbett & Ross, 1980), and the depth of despair about self-reported personality measurement and in politics with the revelations of Iran-Contra and arms-for-hostages deals. The common thread among these events was that one simply couldn't trust to be accurate what people said about their plans and motives. Still, one can find meaning in what was said—but it is often not the message's words, but rather in placing the messages in the larger social context, that led to understanding. The same is true with reports of suppression; they are quite meaningful, but they represent a message that in context implies that the suppressor is struggling to acquire a new set of values, beliefs, and attitudes and requires overt suppression of older competing beliefs and attitudes. The changing nature of the self manifests itself in the struggle of internalization.

REFERENCES

Abelson, R. P., & Prentice, D. A. (1989). Beliefs as possessions: A functional perspective. In A. R. Pratkanis & S. J. Breckler (Eds.), *Attitude structure and function. The third Ohio State University volume on attitudes and persuasion* (pp. 361–381). Hillsdale, NJ: Erlbaum.

Allport, G. W. (1954). *The nature of prejudice*. Cambridge, MA: Addison-Wesley.

Aronson, E. (1969). The theory of cognitive dissonance: A current perspective. In L. Berkowitz (Ed.), *Advances in experimental social psychology* (Vol. 4, pp. 1–34). San Diego, CA: Academic Press.

Baumeister, R. F., Bushman, B. J., & Campbell, W. K. (2000). Self-esteem, narcissism, and aggression: Does violence result from low self-esteem or from threatened egotism? *Current Directions in Psychological Science, 9*, 26–29.

Bem, D. (1970). *Beliefs, attitudes, and human affairs*. Belmont, CA: Brooks/Cole.

Bem, D. J. (1967). Self-perception: An alternative interpretation of cognitive dissonance phenomena. *Psychological Review, 74*, 183–200.

Biernat, M., & Crandall, C. S. (1999). Racial attitudes. In J. Robinson, P. Shaver, & L.

Wrightsman, (Eds.) *Measures of political attitudes* (2nd ed., pp. 297–411). New York: Academic Press.

Blanchard, F. A., Lilly, T., & Vaughan, L. A. (1991). Reducing the expression of racial prejudice. *Psychological Science, 2,* 101–105.

Blanchard, F. A., Crandall, C. S., Brigham, J. C., & Vaughn, L. A. (1994). Condemning and condoning racism: A social context approach to interracial settings. *Journal of Applied Psychology, 79,* 993–997.

Brehm, J. W. (1966). *A theory of psychological reactance.* New York: Academic Press.

Brehm, S. S., & Brehm, J. W. (1981). *Psychological reactance: A theory of freedom and control.* New York: Academic Press.

Britt, T. W., & Crandall, C. S. (2000). Acceptance of feedback by the stigmatized and non-stigmatized: The mediating role of the motive of the evaluator. *Group Processes and Intergroup Relations, 3,* 79–96.

Cantril, H. (1941). *The psychology of social movements.* New York: Chapman & Hall.

Cooley, C. H. (1902). *Human nature and the social order.* New York: Scribners.

Crandall, C. S. (2000). Ideology and lay theories of stigma: The justification of stigmatization. In T. Heatherton, J. Hull, R. Kleck, & M. Hebl (Eds.) *The social psychology of stigma* (pp. 126–150). New York: Guilford.

Crandall, C. S., & Eshleman, A. (2000). *The justification-suppression model of prejudice: A general model of the expression and experience of prejudice.* Unpublished manuscript, University of Kansas, Lawrence.

Crandall, C. S., Ehsleman, A., & O'Brien, L. T. (2002). Social norms and the expression and suppression of prejudice: The struggle for internalization. *Journal of Personality and Social Psychology, 82,* 359–378.

Crandall, C. S., Tsang, J., Harvey, R. D., & Britt, T. W. (2000). Group identity-based self-protective strategies: The stigma of race, gender, and garlic. *European Journal of Social Psychology, 30,* 355–381.

Crocker, J., & Major, B. (1989). Social stigma and self-esteem: The self-protective properties of stigma. *Psychological Review, 96,* 608–630.

Dunton, B. C., & Fazio, R. H. (1997). An individual difference measure of motivation to control prejudiced reactions. *Personality and Social Psychology Bulletin, 23,* 316–326.

Festinger, L., Schachter, S., & Back, K. (1950). *Social pressures in informal groups.* New York: Harper & Brothers.

Herek, G. M. (1986). The instrumentality of attitudes: Toward a neofunctional theory. *Journal of Social Issues, 42,* 99–114.

Hogg, M. A. (2001). Self-categorization and subjective uncertainty resolution: Cognitive and motivational facets of social identity and group membership. In J. P. Forgas, K. D. Williams, & L. Wheeler (Eds.), *The social mind: Cognitive and motivational aspects of interpersonal behavior* (pp. 323–349) New York: Cambridge University Press.

Hogg, M. A., & Abrams, D. (1988). *Social identifications.* London: Routledge.

Jackson, L. A., Sullivan, L. A., Harnish, R., & Hodge, C. N. (1996). Achieving positive social identity: Social mobility, social creativity, and permeability of group boundaries. *Journal of Personality and Social Psychology, 70,* 241–254.

James, W. (1892). *Psychology—the briefer course.* New York: Henry Holt.

Judd, C. M., & Krosnick, J. A. (1982). Attitude centrality, organization, and measurement. *Journal of Personality and Social Psychology, 42,* 436–447.

Katz, D. (1960). The functional approach to the study of attitudes. *Public Opinion Quarterly, 24,* 163–204.

Kelman, H. C. (1961). Processes of opinion change. *Public Opinion Quarterly, 25,* 57–78.

Markus, H. (1977). Self-schemata and processing information about the self. *Journal of Personality and Social Psychology, 35,* 63–78.

Mead, G. H. (1934). *Mind, self and society.* Chicago: University of Chicago Press.

Milburn, M. A. (1987). Ideological self-schemata and schematically induced attitude consistency. *Journal of Experimental Social Psychology, 23,* 383–398.

Moreland, R. L., & Levine, J. M. (1982). Socialization in small groups: Temporal changes in individual-group relations. In L. Berkowitz (Ed.), *Advances in experimental social psychology, 15* (pp. 137–192). New York: Academic Press.

Nisbett, R. E., & Ross, L. A. (1980). *Human inference: Strategies and shortcomings of social judgment*. Englewood Cliffs, NJ: Prentice-Hall.

Plant, E. A., & Devine, P. G. (1998). Internal and external motivation to respond without prejudice. *Journal of Personality and Social Psychology, 75*, 811–832.

Rosenberg, M. (1979). *Conceiving the self*. New York: Basic Books.

Schiffmann, R., & Nelkenbrecher, D. (1994). Reactions to self-discrepant feedback: Feminist attitude and symbolic self-completion. *European Journal of Social Psychology, 24*, 317–327.

Sherif, M., & Cantril, H. (1947). *The psychology of ego-involvements; social attitudes & identification*. New York: Wiley.

Sherif, M. (1948). The necessity of considering current issues as part and parcel of persistent major problems: Illustrated by the problem of prejudice. *International Journal of Opinion and Attitude Research, 2*, 63–68.

Sherif, M., & Sherif, C. W. (1953). *Groups in harmony and tension*. New York: Harper.

Sherif, M., & Sherif, C. W. (1964). *Reference groups*. New York: Harper & Row.

Simon, B., & Pettigrew, T. F. (1990). Social identity and perceived group homogeneity: Evidence for the ingroup homogeneity effect. *European Journal of Social Psychology, 20*, 269–286.

Smith, M. B. (1969). *Social psychology and human values*. Chicago: Aldine.

Smith, M. B., Bruner, J. S., & White, R. W. (1956). *Opinions and personality*. New York: Wiley.

Steele, C. M. (1988). The psychology of self-affirmation: Sustaining the integrity of the self. In L. Berkowitz, (Ed.), *Advances in experimental social psychology, Vol. 21* (pp.

261–302). San Diego, CA: Academic Press.

Swann, W. B. (1997). The trouble with change: Self-verification and allegiance to the self. *Psychological Science, 8*, 177–180.

Tajfel, H., & Turner, J. C. (1977). An integrative theory of intergroup conflict. In W. G. Austin & S. Worchel (Eds.), *The social psychology of intergroup relations* (pp. 33–47). Monterey, CA: Brooks/Cole.

Terry, D. J., & Hogg, M. A. (Eds). (2000). *Attitudes, behavior, and social context: The role of norms and group membership*. Mahwah, NJ: Lawrence Erlbaum

Terry, D. J., & Hogg, M. A. (2001). Attitudes, behavior, and social context: The role of norms and group membership in social influence processes. In J. P. Forgas & K. D. Williams (Eds.) *Social influence: Direct and indirect processes* (pp. 253–270) Philadelphia: Psychology Press.

Turner, J. C. (1991). *Social influence*. Pacific Grove, CA: Brooks/Cole.

Turner, J. C., Hogg, M. A., Oakes, P. J., Reicher, S. D., & Wetherell, M. S. (1987). *Rediscovering the social group: A self-categorization theory*. New York: Blackwell.

Whitman, W. (1885/1982). *Complete poetry and collected prose*. New York: Literary Classics/Viking Press.

Wicklund, R. A., & Gollwitzer, P. (1982). *Symbolic self-completion*. Hillsdale, NJ: Erlbaum.

Williams, K. D., Wheeler, L., & Harvey, J. (2001). Inside the social mind of the ostracizer. In J. Forgas, K. Williams, & L. Wheeler (Eds.), *The social mind: Cognitive and motivational aspects of interpersonal behavior* (pp. 294–320). New York: Cambridge University Press.

18

Intergroup Emotions and the Social Self
Prejudice Reconceptualized as Differentiated Reactions to Outgroups

DIANE M. MACKIE
ELIOT R. SMITH

INTRODUCTION

"Well I suppose we would just try to ignore them, like they didn't exist, but if that didn't work we might need to, you know, show them who's boss, and put them in their place a bit, if I was still angry I'd want us to really hurt them, do we have the, you know, upper hand of things, or do they?"
—Student response when asked, "Think about a time when a group to which you don't belong made your group angry —what would your group want to do?"

This research was partially supported by National Science Foundation Grant SBR 9975204 and National Institute of Mental Health grants R01 MH46840 and K02 MH01178. We thank Thierry Devos, Dan Miller, Lisa Silver and Amber Garcia, as well as Heather Claypool, Joe Forgas, and Kip Williams for many valuable and varied contributions to the ideas discussed in this chapter.

Address for correspondence: Diane M. Mackie, Department of Psychology, University of California, Santa Barbara, Santa Barbara, CA 93106-9660, USA. E-mail: mackie@psych.ucsb.edu

*H*ow might social psychologists explain such specific, and conditional, desires to move either away from or against another social group? Most social psychological theories explain discrimination against outgroups as the result of prejudice—a negative evaluation of, dislike for, or antipathy toward a group and its members. Prejudice is seen as a pivotal precursor to discrimination, which can be viewed as evaluation-consistent behavior. This approach has provided many insights. Viewing prejudice in this sense has encouraged the study of a wide range of assumed determinants of prejudice including stereotyping, system justification, and self-esteem needs. It also makes possible the application of sophisticated models of attitude–behavior relations to the issue of whether and when discriminatory behavior will occur (for reviews, see Brewer & Brown, 1998; Dovidio, Brigham, Johnson, & Gaertner, 1996; Fiske, 1998; Glick & Fiske, 1996, 1999; Mackie & Smith, 1998a; Macrae, Stangor, & Hewstone, 1996).

Nevertheless, the adequacy of conceptualizing prejudice as either a positive or negative evaluation, and of viewing discrimination as evaluation-consistent behavior, has been increasingly questioned. One problem with this approach is that it is undifferentiated, in that it provides no theoretical basis for making different predictions about groups who are feared (and thus negatively evaluated) or hated (and thus negatively evaluated). Thus, even more recent extensions of attitude theory that focus on attitudes defined predominantly by affective reactions rather than by cognitions (Dovidio, Esses, Beach, & Gaertner, in press; Esses, Haddock, & Zanna, 1993) do not yet have the theoretical means for differentiating among affective reactions.

A second problem with the approach is that such evaluation is seen as adhering to or being associated with a target category as a whole in an all-or-none manner. Although some more recent approaches to attitude theory make multiple evaluations toward objects possible (Wilson & Hodges, 1992), intergroup theory has tended to rely on more traditional concepts of evaluations as general, enduring, and facilitating response to the category as a whole across time and place (see Smith, 1993, for a broader discussion). Once a negative evaluation becomes associated with the mental representation of a group (and particularly if it becomes automatically activated as part of the mental representation), that group is negatively evaluated, regardless of circumstance. Thus, classic findings that groups are treated differently in different social contexts become difficult to explain (e.g., Minard, 1952).

A third shortcoming is that even when the intensity of such evaluations is taken into account, this approach seems somehow unsuited to account for the virulent nature of some of the acts perpetrated on social groups. Attributing negatively evaluated trait characteristics to groups seems unlikely to be a motivation for those groups to be decimated by "ethnic cleansing" campaigns, or systematically enslaved, tortured, or exterminated (Opotow, 1990a, 1990b; Staub, 1990).

Finally, some commentators have noted that "feelings" of prejudice seem somehow to linger at the affective level, even when cognitions that feed into evaluations are modified (see for example, Dovidio & Gaertner, 1998). Thus, despite their contributions, traditional social psychological approaches to prejudice and discrimination have been of little help in explaining the wide range of ways in which outgroups are devalued, discriminated against, and sometimes decimated, depending on situation, context, and occasion, and sometimes despite considerable change in "rational" bases for thinking about others (Mackie & Smith, 1998a, 1998b; Schneider, 1996; Smith, 1993).

INTERGROUP EMOTIONS THEORY

We have proposed *intergroup emotions theory* (IET; Mackie & Smith, 1998a; Mackie, Devos, & Smith, 2000; Smith, 1993, 1999; Smith & Ho, in press) as an approach with the potential to answer some of these shortcomings. IET proposes that behavioral reactions to social groups are determined by emotional reactions to groups triggered by appraisals of intergroup situations, contexts, and occasions. In that the necessary and sufficient condition for appraising the world in intergroup terms is identification with a social group, IET takes as its foundational assumption that the self is social and that personal and intergroup phenomena are all regulated by mechanisms that are both cognitive and affective and that operate at both individual and group levels (see Smith, this volume). In the rest of this chapter we describe intergroup emotions theory in more detail and then consider results from our current program of research that offer support for many of the theory's key assertions. Finally, we discuss some of the unique aspects of this approach compared to traditional approaches and what other implications might be expected to follow from an intergroup emotions perspective.

According to IET, distinct behavioral reactions to social groups are based on differentiated emotional reactions to those groups. Such emotional reactions come about, in turn, on the basis of appraisals of the consequences of situations and events for the benefit or harm of the groups to which one belongs. In this broad sense, IET is an extension and integration of appraisal theories of emotion to the intergroup relations domain (Mackie & Smith, 1998a; Smith, 1993; see also Dijker, 1987).

Appraisal theories of emotion (Ellsworth & Smith, 1988; Frijda, 1986; Lazarus, 1991; Roseman, 1984; Scherer, 1988; Smith & Ellsworth, 1985) conceptualize personal emotions as complex reactions to specific situations or events that include quite differentiated cognitions, feelings, and action tendencies. Specific emotions experienced by an individual are triggered by appraisals (cognitions or interpretations) of whether an event appears to favor or harm the individual's goals or desires and whether the individual has the resources to cope or not, for example. Other important dimensions of appraisal appear to be the locus of causality of the event or action, as well as the certainty of the outcome. Depending on their particular configuration, cognitive appraisals trigger specific emotional experiences (Ellsworth & Smith, 1988; Roseman, Spindel, & Jose, 1990; Smith & Ellsworth, 1985) and emotion-related behavior tendencies (Frijda, Kuipers, & ter Schure, 1989; Roseman, Wiest, & Swartz, 1994). Anger at another individual, for example, is typically conceptualized as resulting from appraisals that the other has harmed the self and that the self is strong. Such anger in turn leads to tendencies to aggress against that other.

Of course the appraisals that such theories appeal to involve the *individual* self and produce individual emotion. Most appraisal theorists agree in principle that the essence of appraisal involves the question "Does this situation affect me personally?" (Lazarus & Folkman, 1984, p. 31). But as Smith (1993) pointed out, the self implicated in emotion-relevant appraisals need not be only an individual or personal self. Indeed, one of the most powerful transformational notions in contemporary social psychology is the recognition that the self and the social are not in any fundamental way distinct. That is, not only are individuals "in" groups, but groups are "in" individuals.

This recognition is grounded in social identity and self-categorization theories (Tajfel, 1978; Turner, Hogg, Oakes, Reicher, & Wetherell, 1987). According to these theories, the process of social identification leads group members to perceive themselves as interchangeable exemplars of the group rather than as unique individuals. As a result, they highlight the similarities between themselves and other ingroup members (Mackie, 1986; Simon, 1998; Simon, Pantaleo, & Mummendey, 1995). They confuse their own characteristics with those typical of the group (Smith & Henry, 1996). In other words, ingroups and ingroup memberships become part of the self (see also Cooper & Hogg; Otten; Smith; Wright, Aron, & Tropp; this volume). The social extension of the self—the incorporation of an ingroup as part of the self (Smith & Henry, 1996)—provides the means by which an ingroup can acquire affective and emotional significance (Cialdini et al., 1976; Tajfel, 1978).

When groups and group memberships become part of the self in this way, events may be appraised in terms of their implications for such groups. Intergroup appraisals are interpretations of situations or events that bear on group, rather than personal, concerns: such events do not necessarily affect individuals, but may help or hurt their membership groups. There is ample evidence that people can evaluate events as having positive and negative implications for membership groups even when they believe they are personally untouched. For example, people often report that their group is discriminated against, even while feeling that they personally are not (Taylor, 1978). As another example, imagine that you immigrated legally to Australia from New Zealand. A new Australian law is proposed to provide amnesty to all other New Zealanders who are in Australia illegally. Support for such a law, because it is seen as promoting

the ingroup, in all likelihood rests on intergroup appraisals, since
will have no implications for the self personally. Thus the actions of i.
and outgroups may be interpreted in terms of whether they help or har.
ingroup, and whether the ingroup does or does not have the resources to co,
with the action.

Such intergroup appraisals are assumed to trigger group-based, or intergroup, emotions. Following appraisal theories, specific patterns of such appraisals
will trigger specific emotions (Smith, 1993). For example, an action that harms
the ingroup and is perpetrated by a strong outgroup (perhaps suggesting that
the ingroup does not have the resources to cope with the threat) should invoke
fear. On the other hand, when the ingroup is appraised as having the resources
(in terms of numbers, power, or legitimacy) to deal with an outgroup's negative
action, anger is the theoretically more likely emotion to be triggered. Once
again, such emotions may be experienced on behalf of the group, as a function
of group membership, regardless of whether the individual self is implicated or
not. As the home team wins or loses, so too may joy or sadness be experienced,
even by those who never get closer to the action than a television screen (Cialdini
et al., 1987).

Just as individual emotions are self-regulatory, so too do intergroup emotions have a social regulatory function. Extensions of appraisal theories of emotion are particularly useful for the attempt to predict intergroup behavior because they view behavior tendencies as an integral aspect of the emotion. That
is, anger involves the impulse, desire, or tendency to take action against the
source of the anger, just as fear involves the desire to move away from the source
of the fear. Thus intergroup emotions should give rise to specific intergroup
action tendencies, allowing the prediction of which among a range of behavioral options group members are more likely to choose. Importantly, these action tendencies are not just predicted by specific antecedent conditions but are
assumed to be mediated by the experience of a particular emotion. Thus both
prediction of, and intervention in, intergroup action tendencies are possible
from this perspective.

In sum, the experience of intergroup emotion is predicated on social identification. When social identity is salient, intergroup appraisals occur. When
appraisals occur on a group basis, intergroup emotions are experienced: emotions are experienced on behalf of the ingroup, and the ingroup and outgroup
become the targets of emotion. Specific intergroup emotions lead to differentiated intergroup action tendencies and behavior. Such differentiated intergroup
behavior occurs because of and is mediated by specific intergroup emotions
that have been triggered by particular appraisals of situations or events related
to social identity. From the perspective of intergroup emotions then, prejudice
is an emotion experienced with respect to a social identity as an ingroup member, and discrimination is emotion-triggered behavior.

EVIDENCE SUPPORTIVE OF INTERGROUP EMOTIONS THEORY

Several lines of research converge to provide support for the various processes posited by the intergroup emotions approach. In this section we review research from our own laboratories that is consistent with (a) the role of social identification (b) the occurrence of intergroup rather than personal appraisals, (c) the triggering of specific emotional reactions and behavioral tendencies toward groups, and finally (d) the crucial role of intergroup emotions in determining the impact of appraisals on those action tendencies.

The Role of Social Identification

The experience of intergroup emotion is predicated on social identification. It is only when an individual sees himself/herself as an interchangeable member of a group, rather than as an unique individual, that the world can be appraised in terms of group rather than individual outcomes and that emotions can be experienced on behalf of fellow group members, whether or not the individual is directly affected. Cordijn, Wigboldus, Hermsen, and Yzerbyt (1999) provided evidence supportive of this position when they focused participants' attention on either their similarities or on their differences (manipulating social categorization, and at least by intention identity) with people who were harmed by a third party. They found that participants were angrier and less happy when similarities rather than differences with the harmed group were salient. This suggests both that emotions can be experienced on behalf of other group members, and that the emotion experienced will depend on who those others are.

Evidence from our own research program (Silver, Miller, Mackie, & Smith, 2001) is also consistent with the idea that when membership in a group is salient, events that happen to fellow group members, even if not directly to the self, can trigger emotional reactions. In one study, for example, we asked our female participants to imagine that they were walking alone at night down a local street and that they were accosted by another individual who accused them unjustly of breaking his car's side mirror. Given the context—an unsubstantiated accusation made to a lone female on a deserted street at night—our participants imagined that they would feel relatively weak in the situation. Moreover, when asked to report the emotions they thought they would experience in such a situation, participants reported substantial levels of fear and low levels of other negative emotions such as anger, contempt, and sadness. These results thus replicated a decade of research on personal emotion, confirming that appraisals of the potential benefit or threat in a situation, as well as the ability to cope with those potential outcomes, can trigger individual emotions.

Our interest, of course, was whether the same processes occurred when group identifications were salient. In a first set of relevant comparisons we instructed participants to imagine themselves in the same scenario as a single University of California, Santa Barbara (UCSB) student being accosted by a single Santa Barbara Community College (SBCC) student. In a second set of conditions, we asked participants to imagine themselves as one of a group of UCSB students accosted in the same way by a group of SBCC students. We term "mere categorization" conditions the first set of comparisons, in which labeled single members of the groups interact. The conditions involving interactions of multiple group members we refer to as "true intergroup" conditions. As can be seen in Figure 18.1, results in both "group" conditions were very similar to those reported in the individual control condition. Thus, participants imagining themselves as a single group member reported experiencing as much fear as when they imagined themselves as an individual in the situation, whereas those imagining themselves as one of a number group members reported only slightly less fear.

Of course, even in these categorized and intergroup situations, participants were imagining that the events were happening to them personally. In a

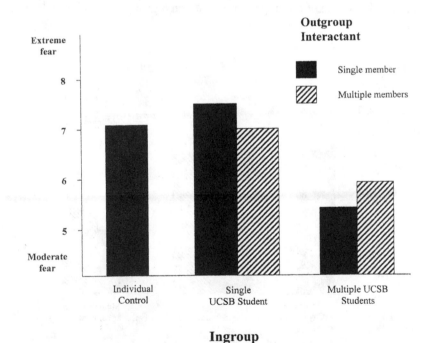

Ingroup

FIGURE 18.1. Reported experience of fear when imagining fear-producing situations involving categorized single and multiple members of the ingroup other than the self in interaction with categorized single and multiple members of the outgroup, compared with interaction between two other individuals (from Silver, Miller, Mackie, & Smith, 2001).

parallel set of relevant conditions, we described exactly the same scenarios—individual, mere categorization, and true intergroup interactions—as if they occurred to other people. In the mere categorization and intergroup conditions, of course, the events impacted other ingroup members but explicitly not the participant herself. Once again we asked participants to report their own emotions (*not* the emotions felt by those involved in the action). Despite finding that less fear overall was reported when the self was not personally involved, the level of fear reported in all comparison conditions was still far above the zero end of the scale, indicating that fear was experienced even when the action did not directly involve the self (the relevant comparisons can be seen in Figure 18.2). Thus, it appears that individual group members do feel emotion on behalf of the ingroup, even when events do not directly impact them. Imagining a single ingroup member other than the self in such a situation resulted in just as much fear being experienced, and even though imagining a group of other ingroup members in the situation evoked significantly less fear, the reported reduction was from near extreme to more moderate fear. The emotions reported in these conditions are thus good evidence for *intergroup* emotion—emotion experienced because of the impact of events on a group to which one belongs (see also Cooper & Hogg, this volume).

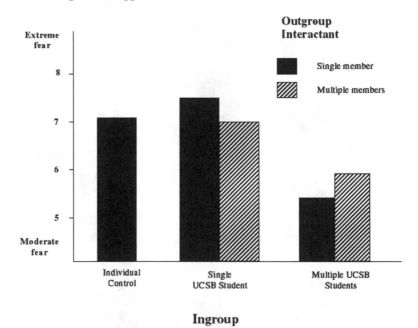

FIGURE 18.2. Reported experience of fear when imagining participation in fear-producing interactions involving categorized single and multiple members of the ingroup and outgroup, compared with interaction between the self and another individual (from Silver, Miller, Mackie, & Smith, 2001).

Two other aspects of these findings are interesting. First, differences in ingroup categorization conditions were much more powerful than differences in outgroup categorization. Such findings resonate with other literature that suggests that the relation between individual and ingroup (rather than the nature of the outgroup) is the driving force in intergroup relations (Allport, 1954: Brewer, 1979; Otten, this volume; Perdue, Dovidio, Gurtman, & Tyler, 1990; Yzerbyt, Castano, Leyens, & Paladino, 2000), but also may require replication in non-scenario paradigms before firmer conclusions can be drawn (see Ickes, this volume). Second, when people are personally involved in intergroup interaction, whether the ingroup context is one of mere categorization or of true intergroup interaction makes only a slight difference. Given this similarity, it appears that the mechanism of activating group membership is enough to invoke the same kinds of processes that might occur in the presence of multiple other-group members. Nevertheless, experienced fear fell significantly—although still being significantly present—when representatives of the ingroup other than the self interacted with the outgroup. Thus it took noninvolvement *and* the presence of multiple ingroup members to reduce experienced fear from very high to only moderately high levels. These differences probably play out particularly in the role of appraisals of the situation, and thus become relevant again in the following section.

Of course the experiments reported here focus on categorization into group membership. As much research suggests (see Hogg & Abrams, 1988, for a review), membership in a group is not the same thing as identification with the group. Different group members may be differentially identified with the group, and IET suggests at least that the more highly identified the member, the more easily intergroup emotions should be experienced (see also Cooper & Hogg, this volume). Although not designed directly to test this idea, results from another series of studies (Mackie et al., 2000) provide some support for the role of identification in producing these effects.

In these studies, participants were asked to identify themselves as members of one or the other of two groups defined by adherence to conflicting values. For example, participants identified themselves as supporting equal rights for homosexuals or opposing such rights. They did this by marking themselves as an X in one of two circles identified by ingroup and outgroup labels. After various manipulations designed to influence appraisals, we measured anger and fear (in Studies 1 and 2) and anger and contempt (in Study 3) toward the outgroup. The relevant finding for our purposes here was that the relationship between appraisals and emotions was significantly, although not completely, mediated by identification.

Evidence for Intergroup Appraisals

According to IET, group membership turns appraisal into an intergroup activity. Events are now assessed as either helping or hurting the ingroup, as being caused by the ingroup or outgroup, or as suggesting ingroup or outgroup strength, for example. We have studied intergroup appraisals in two different ways.

First, we asked participants to recall, and then describe, situations in which they experienced, for example, anger, disgust, fear, happiness, or pride, either as an individual or as a member of a group (Silver et al., 2001). Participants then made several ratings of their descriptions, including questions about relevant dimensions of appraisal. Analyses of these ratings show appraisals predictable from interpersonal appraisal theory. That is, events that lead to anger appear to involve threat, assumed intention, and a sense of strength (i.e., that there are resources to cope with the threat). Events eliciting fear, on the other hand, involve threat, uncertainty, and a pervasive feeling of weakness. The findings were consistent and compelling: ratings of appraisal dimensions differed significantly between the different emotions, but produced very few interactions with whether participants described individual or intergroup situations. Thus, as we had predicted, intergroup situations, at least those involving emotion, appear to be appraised in ways similar to interpersonal situations and along dimensions previously identified as important in interpersonal emotion contexts.

There was one consistent area in which appraisals differed between individual and group contexts, however. When we asked about situations that triggered anger or disgust at the self or ingroup, ratings of self-blame and self-responsibility were reliably higher in the individual than in the group situation. This makes sense because situations involving the ingroup allow for diffusion of responsibility. One can feel that one's group has done something wrong but distance oneself from personal responsibility at least to an extent, but such distancing is much less possible when one has personally committed a negative act. Nevertheless, this one systematic difference merely highlighted the uniformity of the other results: virtually no reliable differences in appraisals of individual versus intergroup situations.

We have also studied intergroup appraisals by describing intergroup situations that feature different dimensions of appraisal and assessing whether they evoke different emotions. Mackie et al. (2000), for example, manipulated the perception of ingroup or outgroup strength in a situation of intergroup threat. Once participants had identified themselves as members of one of two opposing groups, we manipulated the collective support apparently enjoyed by the ingroup. We did so by exposing participants to a series of alleged newspaper headlines, which appeared to reflect popular and political support either for their own group or for the outgroup. In one case, for example, participants read 16 headlines such as "Assembly Passes Gay Equal Rights Bill" or "Gay Activists Given Hearing by Governor" or "Polls Show Majority Support Equal Rights for Gay Couples." These were intermingled with only 3 headlines proclaiming sentiments like "Court Turns Back Gay Rights Appeal." In the other condition, the ratio of supportive to nonsupportive headlines was reversed. This technique reliably induced appropriate perceptions that the ingroup or outgroup was in a position of relative strength. We then assessed emotions felt toward the outgroup. With all else held constant, the manipulation of perceived ingroup versus outgroup strength had profound effects on experienced emotions. Those perceiving the ingroup to be strong reported considerable anger at the other group, whereas those in the weak condition reported none. Thus, how intergroup situations are appraised on critical dimensions can trigger quite different intergroup emotions, consistent with a key tenet of IET.

The Occurrence of Intergroup Emotion and Associated Intergroup Action Tendencies

The argument that different appraisals of intergroup situations produce differentiated intergroup emotions is also a critical assertion of the IET approach. The argument is not just that different appraisals produce different emotions, but that they produce quite distinct negative emotions, rather than a generalized negative reaction. The best evidence for this assertion comes from Mackie et al. (2000). In all three studies, participants were asked to describe their emotions on a number of Likert scales. Analyses of responses to these questions revealed clearly differentiated negative emotions. For example, principal components factor analyses revealed that responses to items related to fear (fearful, anxious, worried, frightened) were closely related to one another but quite different from the closely related responses to items tapping anger (annoyed, irritated, angry, mad) or contempt (disgusted, contemptuous, repulsed). In addition, confirmatory factor analyses showed that a two-factor model in which the factors were correlated provided a much better fit to the data (across several experiments) than a one-factor model. Thus, although there is clearly some overlap between at least these two negative intergroup emotions, anger and fear are clearly differentiated. Moreover, specific manipulations of intergroup appraisals increased reported experience of fear while decreasing anger, and vice versa. Far from producing generalized negative affect, our manipulations indicated that quite different, quite separate, and quite specific negative emotions could be generated. These results were confirmed in Silver et al. (2001). Factor analyses once again indicated that intergroup anger and fear were quite separate and that particular appraisal dimensions affected one without affecting the other.

A different kind of evidence for the occurrence of intergroup emotions comes from the recall paradigm studies already described (Silver et al., 2001). When participants described situations in which they had experienced an emotion either as an individual or as a group member, and then rated the intensity of that emotion, only a single significant difference between the individual and group conditions was found. Consistent with the appraisal differences noted earlier, participants rated themselves as experiencing less guilt in situations where they experienced guilt as a group member rather than as an individual. For all other emotions assessed, however, there were no significant differences in the intensity of feelings experienced in personal and intergroup situations.

The overall picture from analyses of intergroup emotions is clear. Different intergroup situations can trigger separate, different, and distinct emotions directed toward the outgroup and ingroup. With the exception of guilt, these emotions don't differ in intensity from the same emotions experienced in individual situations. Moreover, these emotions do not seem to be a by-product of generalized negative evaluation: different negative emotions increase or decrease depending on the situation quite independently of one another.

Our interest in intergroup emotions was of course prompted by emotions' association at the interpersonal level with action tendencies—the desire, urge, or intention to take a particular form of action. The data from studies completed so far provide consistent evidence that different intergroup emotions are associated with quite distinct action tendencies. In Mackie et al. (2000), for example, we asked participants to indicate desires to take a number of different kinds of actions, ranging from leaving the outgroup alone (items like "I want to avoid/have nothing to do with/keep at a distance from/get away from them.") to trying to hurt them (items such as "I want to confront/oppose/argue with/attack them."). Factor analysis indicated that the items representing moving away from the other group were closely associated and quite distinct from the multiple closely associated items that reflected movement against the other group. Moreover, manipulations of appraisals that made the ingroup appear strong and that produced anger increased the desire to take action against the outgroup, while having no impact on behavioral tendencies to avoid the outgroup.

Similar results came from the study in which conditions designed to suggest ingroup weakness produced fear. In these conditions, participants indicated wanting to move away from the outgroup and certainly showed no desire to confront it. Thus both sets of studies indicated that manipulation of intergroup appraisals and emotions could be used to predict quite specific patterns of intergroup behavior, at least in terms of action tendencies. And once again, additional cross-methodological convergent evidence was provided by our recall studies (Silver et al., 2001). When participants rated how likely they would be to perform a series of either approach or avoidance kinds of behaviors in situations prompting a wide range of emotions, there were once again few differences between individual and intergroup conditions. When it came to arguing with, confronting, and attacking, for example, people reported as much willingness to do so in the intergroup as interpersonal condition.

Of course, action tendencies do not always translate into actual behavior. However, even prediction of the desire or intention to take certain kinds of action is a significant advance in the intergroup sphere. The assumed (and demonstrated) association between emotions and specific action tendencies also allows the theoretical weight of other approaches, such as the extensive literature on the consistency between intentions and behavior, to be brought to bear in the intergroup domain.

The Crucial Function of Intergroup Emotion

The defining feature of IET is the argument that the impact of intergroup appraisals on intergroup behavior is mediated by intergroup emotions. Evidence for this relationship is provided by performing path analytic assessments of the extent to which the impact of intergroup appraisals on intergroup action tendencies is mediated by the experience of the appropriate emotion. Strong evidence that emotions significantly mediated this relationship came from our study of intergroup fear in mere categorization and true intergroup contexts. As noted above, participants reported appraisals of weakness, experienced emotions and desired action tendencies in these various conditions. As can be seen in Figure 18.3, the impact of appraisals of ingroup weakness on action tendencies was significantly mediated by the emotion of fear, both in conditions involving the self (upper panel) and, although more weakly, in conditions in which the self was not involved (lower panel).

Similar evidence came from our manipulations of whether the ingroup was in a relatively strong versus weak position vis-à-vis the outgroup as a result of social support (Mackie et al., 2000). In this case, the mediational analyses indicated that the effects of perceived ingroup strength on offensive action tendencies were substantially mediated by anger. Importantly, other analyses indicated that even though the emotions of anger and contempt had not been distinguishable in these studies, the desire to move away from the group, and only this action tendency, was mediated by contempt for the outgroup. These results confirm the hypothesis that the impact of intergroup appraisals on intergroup action tendencies is caused by the experience of a distinct intergroup emotion.

Such findings demonstrate that intergroup emotions mediate peoples' desires, impulses, or tendencies to act toward outgroups in particular ways. But perhaps the most compelling evidence of the crucial mediational role played by intergroup emotions comes from a recent study on the impact of actual intergroup contact. Recent research indicates that intergroup friendships are particularly effective in reducing prejudice (Pettigrew, 1997; Wright, Aron, McLaughlin-Volpe, & Ropp, 1997). We wondered what role intergroup emotions might play in this apparently successful means of moving beyond prejudice. Smith, Miller, and Mackie (2001) asked college students how frequently they experienced specific positive and negative emotions in past encounters with African Americans and when thinking about African Americans as a group. We also measured students' acquaintances and close personal friendships with that group and general liking for the group. Regression analyses confirmed earlier research in indicating that the closeness of a personal friendship was the only measure that successfully predicted generally positive or negative liking

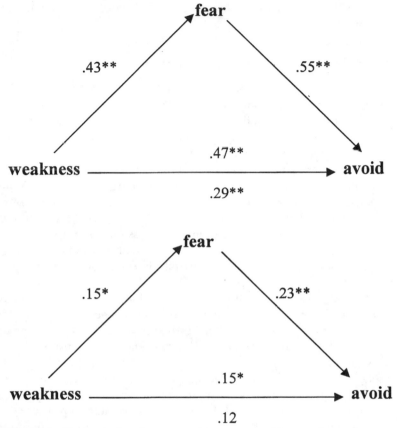

FIGURE 18.3. Evidence that the reported experience of fear mediates the impact of appraisals of weakness on the desire to avoid the outgroup for situations in which the self is (upper panel) and is not (lower panel) involved (from Silver, Miller, Mackie, & Smith, 2001). Coefficients are significant at $p < .001$ (°°) or $p < .05$ (°). Z-tests significant at $p < .001$ and $p < .12$ for the self-involved and non-self-involved conditions respectively indicate a significant drop in the relationship between *weakness* and the tendency to *avoid* when the mediational path through *fear* is included.

for the outgroup. Most importantly for IET, the impact of such closeness on attitudes toward African Americans was significantly mediated by the participants' emotional reactions in intergroup interactions: a decrease in negative intergroup emotions experienced in intergroup interactions mediated the effect of closeness on the traditional measure of prejudice.

In sum, these studies demonstrate the validity and usefulness of intergroup emotions theory as regards the ability to predict specific intergroup action tendencies (specifically, the desires to move against or away from the outgroup) from intergroup emotions (such as anger and fear) and to trigger those intergroup emotions via intergroup appraisals (relative strength or weakness, perceptions of fairness and uncertainty, etc.). In particular, the results provide evidence for the key assertion of the theory: it is the experience of the intergroup emotion that determines how intergroup appraisals will be translated into action tendencies toward the outgroup.

UNIQUE CONTRIBUTIONS OF INTERGROUP EMOTIONS THEORY

IET is distinct from previous approaches to understanding prejudice in several ways, and thus can also generate as-yet-unexplored research hypotheses. First, responses to different outgroups under different circumstances can be differentiated. Rather than prejudice being merely "negative," specific patterns reflecting different emotions such as anger, fear, or disgust, and associated action tendencies, should be identifiable. As exemplified by the respondent whose quote opened this chapter, feelings about a group, and the action that one might want to take toward them, differs by time and circumstance.

Second, with intergroup appraisals dictating emotions and action tendencies, stereotypes can be usefully seen also as end-products, rather than only as precursors of prejudice. That is, groups may be seen as weak because we feel angry toward them, as having frightening characteristics because they frighten us, and so forth.

Third, group members may experience the range of distinct emotions about the ingroup as well as the outgroup (e.g., ingroup pride, ingroup guilt). Focus on the ingroup provides a new model for viewing the emotional (rather than simply evaluative) component of group membership. Focus on the outgroup provides new theories of prejudice and discrimination.

Fourth, this new model allows for the possibility that an outgroup may be stereotyped in positive ways yet still generate negative emotions (as strong, but therefore frightening, for example). As Smith (1993) pointed out, this helps explain the puzzle of ambivalent intergroup relations such as those experienced by "model" minorities.

Fifth, this approach suggests an integration of the emotion-coping literature into intergroup relations, suggesting a range of ways (emotion-based or problem-based) in which people can negotiate the emotional consequences of intergroup relations. Integration of this literature alone, for example, might generate unique interventions to improve intergroup relations.

Finally, this approach puts emphasis on the social regulatory function of social emotions. That is, just as emotion is seen as regulating personal behavior and interpersonal interaction, so too can intergroup emotion be seen as regulating group behavior and intergroup interactions. We have, of course, focused on the latter, tracing the role of appraisals of what events mean for the ingroup on the production of emotions toward the outgroup that then can guide interaction with them. However, IET also presupposes a similar range of and role for emotions within the ingroup. Feelings of "identification" with various ingroups and a deeper understanding of the *social self* might be better understood in terms of the emotions generated about that group—ingroups about which we feel pride, joy, gratitude, or shame may all have different effects on our group-mediated behavior. Thus IET is also a profoundly functional theory, in that cognitive, affective, individual, and intergroup processes are seen as integrated for the purposes of regulation. At the intergroup level, as at the individual level, "feeling is for doing," just as thinking is.

REFERENCES

Allport, G. W. (1954). *The nature of prejudice*. New York: Addison-Wesley.

Brewer, M. B. (1979). Ingroup bias and the minimal intergroup situation: A cognitive motivational analysis. *Psychological Bulletin, 86*, 307–324.

Brewer, M. B., & Brown, R. J. (1998). Intergroup relations. In D. T. Gilbert & S. T Fiske (Eds.), *The handbook of social psychology* (Vol. 2, 4th ed., pp. 554–594). Boston: McGraw-Hill.

Cialdini, R. B., Borden, R. J., Thorne, A., Walker, M. R., Freeman, S., & Sloan, L. R. (1976). Basking in reflected glory: Three (football) field studies. *Journal of Personality and Social Psychology, 34*, 366–375.

Cialdini, R. B., Schaller, M., Houlihan, D., Arps, K., Fultz, J., & Beaman, A. L. (1987). Empathy-based helping: Is it selflessly or selfishly motivated? *Journal of Personality & Social Psychology, 52*, 749–758.

Dijker, A. J. (1987). Emotional reactions to ethnic minorities. *European Journal of Social Psychology, 17*, 305–325.

Dovidio, J. F., Brigham, J. C., Johnson, B. T., & Gaertner, S. L. (1996). Stereotyping, prejudice, and discrimination: Another look. In C. N. Macrae, C. Stangor, & M. Hewstone (Eds.), *Stereotypes and stereotyping* (pp. 276–322). New York: Guilford.

Dovidio, J. F., Esses, V. M., Beach, K. R., & Gaertner, S. L. (in press). The role of affect in determining intergroup behavior: The case of willingness to engage in intergroup contact. In D. M. Mackie & E. R. Smith (Eds.), *Beyond prejudice: Differentiated reactions to social groups*. Philadelphia: Psychology Press.

Dovidio, J. F., & Gaertner, S. L. (1998). On the nature of contemporary prejudice: The causes, consequences, and challenges of aversive racism. In J. L. Eberhardt & S. T. Fiske (Eds.), *Confronting racism: The problem and the response* (pp. 3–32). Thousand Oaks, CA: Sage.

Ellsworth, P. C., & Smith, C. A. (1988). From appraisal to emotion: Differences among unpleasant feelings. *Motivation & Emotion, 12*, 271–302.

Esses, V. M., Haddock, G., & Zanna, M. P. (1993). Values, stereotypes, and emotions as determinants of intergroup attitudes. In D. M. Mackie & D. L. Hamilton (Eds.), *Affect, cognition, and stereotyping: Interactive processes in group perception* (pp. 137–166). New York: Academic Press.

Fiske, S. T. (1998). Stereotyping, prejudice, and discrimination. In D. T. Gilbert & S. T. Fiske (Eds.), *The handbook of social psychology* (Vol. 2, 4th ed., pp. 357–411). Boston, MA: McGraw-Hill.

Frijda, N. H. (1986). *The emotions*. Cambridge, UK: Cambridge University Press.

Frijda, N. H., Kuipers, P., & ter Schure, E. (1989). Relations among emotion, appraisal, and emotional action readiness. *Journal of Personality & Social Psychology, 57*, 212–228.

Glick, P., & Fiske, S. T. (1996). The ambivalent sexism inventory: Differentiating hostile and benevolent sexism. *Journal of Personality & Social Psychology, 70*, 491–512.

Glick, P., & Fiske, S. T. (1999). Sexism and other "isms": Interdependence, status, and the ambivalent content of stereotypes. In W. B. Swann, Jr., L. A. Gilbert, & J. Langlois (Eds.), *Sexism and stereotypes in modern society: The gender science of Janet Taylor Spence* (pp. 193–221). Washington, DC: American Psychological Association.

Gordijn, E. H., Wigboldus, D., Hermsen, S., & Yzerbyt, V. (1999). Categorization and anger: The influence of negative intergroup behavior. In D. Van Knippenberg, C. K. W. De Dreu, C. Martin, & C. Rutte (Eds.), *Fundamental social psychology* (pp. 13–23). Tilburg, Netherlands: Tilburg University Press.

Hogg, M. A., & Abrams, D. (1988). *Social identifications*. London: Routledge.

Lazarus, R. S. (1991). Cognition and motivation in emotion. *American Psychologist, 46,* 352–367.

Lazarus, R. S., & Folkman, S. (1984). Coping and adaptation. In W. G. Gentry (Ed.), *The handbook of behavioral medicine* (pp. 282–325). New York: Guilford.

Mackie, D. M. (1986). Social identification effects in group polarization. *Journal of Personality and Social Psychology, 50,* 720–728.

Mackie, D. M., Devos, T., & Smith, E. R. (2000). Intergroup emotions: Explaining offensive action tendencies in an intergroup context. *Journal of Personality and Social Psychology, 79,* 602–616.

Mackie, D. M., & Smith, E. R. (1998a). Intergroup cognitions and intergroup behavior: Crossing the boundaries. In C. Sedikides, J. Schopler, & C. A. Insko (Eds.), *Intergroup cognition and intergroup behavior* (pp. 423–450). Hillsdale, NJ: Erlbaum.

Mackie, D. M., & Smith, E. R. (1998b). Intergroup relations: Insights from a theoretically integrative approach. *Psychological Review, 105,* 499–529.

Macrae, C. N., Stangor, C., & Hewstone, M. (Eds.). (1996). *Stereotypes and stereotyping.* New York: Guilford.

Minard, R. D. (1952). Race relationships in the Pocahontas coal field. *Journal of Social Issues, 8,* 29–44.

Opotow, S. (1990a). Moral exclusion and injustice: An introduction. *Journal of Social Issues, 46,* 1–20.

Opotow, S. (1990b). Deterring moral exclusion. *Journal of Social Issues, 46,* 173–182.

Pettigrew, T. F. (1997). Generalized intergroup contact effects on prejudice. *Personality and Social Psychology Bulletin, 23,* 173–185.

Perdue, C. W., Dovidio, J. F., Gurtman, M. B., & Tyler, R. B. (1990). Us and them: Social categorization and the process of intergroup bias. *Journal of Personality and Social Psychology, 59,* 475–486.

Roseman, I. J. (1984). Cognitive determinants of emotion: A structural theory. *Review of Personality & Social Psychology, 5,* 11–36.

Roseman, I. J., Spindel, M. S., & Jose, P. E. (1990). Appraisals of emotion-eliciting events: Testing a theory of discrete emotions. *Journal of Personality & Social Psychology, 59,* 899–915.

Roseman, I. J., Wiest, C., & Swartz, T. S. (1994). Phenomenology, behaviors, and goals differentiate discrete emotions. *Journal of Personality & Social Psychology, 67,* 206–221.

Scherer, K. R. (1988). Criteria for emotion-antecedent appraisal: A review. In V. Hamilton & G. H. Bower (Eds.), *Cognitive perspectives on emotion and motivation* (pp. 89–126). Dordrecht, Netherlands: Kluwer Academic Publishers.

Schneider, D. J. (1996). Modern stereotype research: Unfinished business. In C. N. Macrae, C. Stangor, & M. Hewstone (Eds.), *Stereotypes and stereotyping* (pp. 419–454). New York: Guilford.

Silver, L. A., Miller, D. A., Mackie, D. M., & Smith, E. R. (2001). The nature of intergroup emotions. Unpublished manuscript, University of California, Santa Barbara.

Simon, B. (1998). Individuals, groups, and social change: On the relationship between individual and collective self-interpretations and collective action. In C. Sedikides & J. Schopler (Eds.), *Intergroup cognition and intergroup behavior* (pp. 257–282). Mahwah, NJ: Erlbaum.

Simon, B., Pantaleo, G., & Mummendey, A. (1995). Unique individual or interchangeable group member? The accentuation of intragroup differences versus similarities as an indicator of the individual self versus the collective self. *Journal of Personality & Social Psychology, 69,* 106–119.

Smith, C. A., & Ellsworth, P. C. (1985). Patterns of cognitive appraisal in emotion. *Journal of Personality & Social Psychology, 48,* 813–838.

Smith, E. R. (1993). Social identity and social emotions: Toward new conceptualizations of prejudice. In D. M. Mackie & D. L. Hamilton (Eds.), *Affect, cognition, and stereotyping: Interactive processes in group perception* (pp. 297–315). San Diego, CA: Academic Press.

Smith, E. R. (1999). Affective and cognitive implications of a group becoming a part of the self: New models of prejudice and of the self-concept. In D. Abrams & M. A. Hogg (Eds.), *Social identity and social cognition* (pp. 183–196). Malden, MA: Blackwell.

Smith, E. R. (2001, May). *Overlapping mental representations of the self and group: Evidence and implications.* Paper presented at Sydney Symposium on Psychology, Sydney, Australia.

Smith, E. R., & Henry, S. (1996). An ingroup becomes part of the self: Response time evidence. *Personality & Social Psychology Bulletin, 22,* 635–642.

Smith, E. R., & Ho, C. (in press). Prejudice as intergroup emotion: Integrating relative deprivation and social comparison explanations of prejudice. In I. Walker & H. Smith (Eds.), *Relative deprivation: Specification, development, and integration.* Boulder, CO: Westview Press.

Smith, E. R., Miller, D. A., & Mackie, D. M. (2001). *Intergroup contact, friendship, and prejudice: Role of intergroup emotions.* Unpublished manuscript, Purdue University, West Lafayette, IN.

Staub, E. (1990). Moral exclusion, personal goal theory, and extreme destructiveness. *Journal of Social Issues, 46,* 47–64.

Tajfel, H. (1978). *Differentiation between social groups: Studies in the social psychology of intergroup relations.* New York: Academic Press.

Taylor, J. A. (1978). The relationship between the contact variable and racial stereotyping in school-aged children. (Doctoral dissertation, University of South Carolina, 1978). *Dissertation Abstracts International, 39,* 1550.

Turner, J. C., Hogg, M. A., Oakes, P. J., Reicher, S. D., & Wetherell, M. S. (1987). *Rediscovering the social group: A self-categorization theory.* New York: Blackwell.

Wilson, T. D., & Hodges, S. D. (1992). Attitudes as temporary constructions. In L. L. Martin & A. Tesser (Eds.), *The construction of social judgments* (pp. 37–65). Hillsdale, NJ: Erlbaum.

Wright, S. C., Aron, A., McLaughlin-Volpe, T., & Ropp, S. A. (1997). The extended contact effect: Knowledge of cross-group friendships and prejudice. *Journal of Personality and Social Psychology, 73,* 73–90.

Yzerbyt, V. Y., Castano, E., Leyens, J.-Ph., & Paladino, P. (2000). The primacy of the ingroup: The interplay of entitativity and identification. *European Review of Social Psychology, 11,* 257–295.

19

Dissonance Arousal and the Collective Self
Vicarious Experience of Dissonance Based on Shared Group Membership

JOEL COOPER
MICHAEL HOGG

INTRODUCTION

The candidate for political office prepares to climb to the podium. You and he have been longstanding members of the same trade union. You, he, and the union have traditionally opposed free trade zones. But today he has been invited to address the Chamber of Commerce to express his views. He begins to speak, and you realize that he is extolling the virtues of lowered tariffs and reduced trade restrictions. He is speaking contrary to the position you know he holds privately.

The authors wish to thank Michael Norton and Benoit Monin whose ideas and experimental work were fundamental to this chapter.

Address for correspondence: Department of Psychology, Princeton University, Green Hall, Princeton, NJ 08544-1010, USA. E-mail: jcoops@princeton.edu

*T*he scenario described above can lead easily to a prediction based on the social psychological principle of cognitive dissonance (Festinger, 1957). Because of his counterattitudinal advocacy, the candidate should experience dissonance and change his attitude to become privately more in favor of free trade alliances. A second question is more intriguing, yet less obvious. Will you, by dint of observing your fellow union member make a dissonance-arousing speech, also experience dissonance? We believe that the answer is yes. In this chapter, we develop support for the proposition that the fusing of the individual self with one's social group causes an individual to experience what other members of the group are experiencing (see also Otten; Smith; Wright, Aron, & Tropp; this volume). Membership in a common group establishes the psychological conditions that permit attitude-discrepant behavior by one member of a group to be experienced vicariously as dissonance by other members of the group: in the example above, the witness to his fellow partisan's dissonant behavior will experience dissonance vicariously and consequently will be motivated to change his own attitude toward free trade.

DISSONANCE THEORY EVOLVES: FROM INSIDE THE HEAD TO THE SOCIAL SELF

Cognitive dissonance theory has had a long and productive history. As all students of social psychology know, Festinger (1957) conceived of dissonance as a state of arousal that occurs when cognitive elements are inconsistent with each other. Proposing that the arousal was aversive, Festinger reasoned that dissonance leads to a motivation to reduce that arousal, whether by cognitive change, by adding new cognitive elements, or by altering the importance of the cognitive elements. With numerous twists and turns, this formulation has served as a guidepost for understanding dissonance reduction processes. One of the brilliant features of Festinger's theory was to represent a social situation in the cognitive field of an individual actor. The relationship among behavioral acts, emotions, and attitudes could be studied because they were all representations that existed inside the head: so too were people, events, and other aspects of the social environment. The relationship between perceived events and a person's attitudes or feelings could be studied in a rough mathematical formula because all elements existed in the same representational dimension. Thus, for Festinger, dissonance was merely a matter of considering pairs of elements in the representational field, determining their consistency or inconsistency, and thus arriving at a prediction of the magnitude of the dissonance.

But dissonance has evolved in its long history from a theory solely about cognitions in the head to a theory that is inextricably connected to the concept of the self. Elliot Aronson (1968) was perhaps the first to point out that not all cognitions are created equal in their impact on dissonance arousal, and suggested that cognitions about the self must be part of the equation if dissonance is to be aroused. Similarly, Steele's (1988) theory of self-affirmation placed dissonance reduction strictly in the service of protecting and enhancing the self. Cooper and Fazio (1984) conceived of dissonance as emanating from the recognition of being responsible for bringing about an unwanted or aversive event. Cooper and Fazio's notion that dissonance is dependent on the personal responsibility of the actor also fashions dissonance as a process intimately intertwined with the concept of self. Finally, Stone and Cooper's (2001) recent self-standards approach to dissonance strengthens the theoretical bond between dissonance and self by specifying the aspects of self that must become cognitively accessible for particular behaviors to lead to dissonance.

We propose an expansion of dissonance theory based on recent conceptions of the self as a dynamic social entity (Abrams & Hogg, 2001). In particular, we build on the recognition that people have different conceptions of self that derive from specific aspects of the social context, and that self-conception can be based on commonalities among people who belong to the same social or cultural groups (see Brewer & Pickett; Smith; and Wright et al.; this volume). By expanding dissonance theory to include collectively shared conceptions of self, we predict that dissonance can be experienced on behalf of other people—that is, it can be experienced vicariously.

Dissonance by Conjoint Responsibility

The dissonance process in the context of group membership has not received much empirical attention. Ironically, one of the earliest studies supporting Festinger's theory of cognitive dissonance was conducted in an in vivo social group. In the mid-1950s, Ms. Marion Keech's "Seekers" prophesied a cataclysm that would terminate life on Earth. Festinger, Riecken, and Schachter (1956) reported that the members of the Seekers sought social support as a way of reducing dissonance, once their central belief was shown to be false. However, the focus of dissonance research soon shifted to the study of the individual and, with few exceptions, little further attention was paid to the in vivo social group (see Cooper & Stone, 2000, for a review).

In the few instances in which group membership was studied as a factor in dissonance, individuals were typically made conjointly responsible for the aversive outcome of the dissonant behavior. For example, Zanna and Sande (1987), varied whether participants were acting on their own or in groups while engaging in inconsistent behavior. Their results showed that dissonance was experienced by people in groups, although some individuals diffused responsibility in group settings and did not experience dissonance. Sakai (1999) asked participants to accompany a confederate who was deceiving someone into believing that a boring experimental task was interesting. Sakai found that bonding into two-person units caused the participant to experience dissonance, even though it was always the confederate who made the attitude-discrepant statement. The work of Festinger et al. (1956), Sakai (1999), and Zanna and Sande (1987) all show that dissonance can be experienced in group settings. These studies all share the common feature that individuals were jointly responsible for the dissonance-producing acts. Our current theoretical notion expands dissonance beyond instances of conjoint responsibility among members of a group. We take the position that the processes of social categorization and social identity make joint membership in a common group sufficient to motivate one person in a social group to experience dissonance vicariously—merely because they share a group-based bond with an actor who is engaged in dissonant behavior.

Dissonance by Social Identification

The ability to experience the thoughts and feelings of another person, to take them on as one's own, forms the crux of vicarious dissonance. To an impressive extent, empathic bonds occur in a variety of situations. Aron, Aron, and their colleagues (e.g., Aron, Aron, Tudor, & Nelson, 1991; Wright et al., this volume) have shown that empathic bonds arise between people in close personal relationships. Cialdini and his colleagues (e.g, Cialdini, Brown, Lewis, Luce, & Neuberg, 1997) have shown that empathic bonds influence people's altruistic decisions to help other people. We believe that the empathic bonds that develop among members of a social group lead people to share the experiences of their fellow group members, including the aversive motivational experience of cognitive dissonance.

In groups, social identity and social categorization processes assimilate the individual's perception of his/her own self and the perception of fellow group members to the prototype of the group (Hogg, 2001c, in press; Hogg & Abrams, 1988; Tajfel & Turner, 1979; Turner, Hogg, Oakes, Reicher, & Wetherell, 1987). The "you and I" that characterize the individual's self-conceptions become transformed into the "we" of the collective self (Hogg, 2001c). The self-concept, in other words, is extended to incorporate the other (Cadinu & Rothbart, 1996; Simon, 1997; Simon & Hastedt, 1999; Smith & Henry, 1996; Wright, et al., this volume). As Mackie and Smith (this volume) put it, not only are individuals "in" groups, but groups are "in" individuals. Unique individuals, then, can become psychologically joined as representatives of the same group, paving the way for vicarious experience.

Groups have their greatest impact on group members who are highly identified with their group (Hogg & Hardie, 1991): Mere membership in a group may establish the necessary condition for empathic bonds to occur, but the degree of empathy will be determined by the degree of psychological identification people feel for their group. Research has shown that high identifiers are more influenced by group norms and standards (Terry & Hogg, 1996, 2001). It is they who are more likely to experience the "oneness" or empathic bond with the prototypical group member. We expect that vicarious dissonance will occur most strongly for people who strongly identify with their group.

Recent theorizing about attitudes in the field of social identity (see Hogg, 2001a; Terry & Hogg, 2001; Terry, Hogg, & White, 2000) provides a further motivation for group members to be motivated by vicarious dissonance. Group identifications serve an important adaptive function by allowing us to assess the accuracy and validity of our attitudes and behaviors: indeed, our need to reduce conceptual uncertainty about the self is a primary purpose of identification (Hogg, 2000, 2001a). Observing group members with whom one identifies behaving in ways that fail to reflect their true attitudes undermines this central function of group identification and may increase subjective uncertainty. Arousal caused by uncertainty about the outcomes of one's own behavior is aversive (Sorrentino, Short, & Raynor, 1984). The highly-identifying witness to a group member's dissonant actions, then, is subject not just to aversive dissonance arousal, but also to aversive uncertainty arousal, making the need for arousal reduction even more pressing.

In summary, when people identify with a social group, processes unfold that make it likely they will experience what other prototypical group members experience. Because of people's tendency to engage in social categorization and to fuse their individual selves to the group prototype, we suggest that people who witness a fellow group member engaging in dissonance-producing behaviors will experience dissonance vicariously. And the greater the level of identification an individual has with a group, the greater the level of vicarious dissonance.

VICARIOUS DISSONANCE: EMPIRICAL TESTS

We conducted four studies (reported below) that explored the vicarious dissonance concept (Norton, Monin, Cooper, & Hogg, 2001): our goal was to establish the conditions that simulate the scenario described in the opening of this chapter. In our initial investigation, we set out to have a research participant observe a member of his/her group making a statement on a meaningful issue that the participant knew was counterattitudinal. To accomplish this, we enlisted volunteer participants at Princeton University to participate in an experiment testing the existence of "linguistic subcultures." At Princeton, incoming students are randomly placed in residential colleges that then form the basis of social life for the freshmen who live, eat, and socialize there. We told participants that we were studying how linguistic differences develop between social groups and that we were particularly interested in assessing different linguistic patterns that might develop among different residential colleges. This provided a way for us to highlight the important social groups to which our student-participants belonged. Our purported hypothesis also allowed us to justify why we needed students to listen to and rate audio tapes made by other students.

Participants were run in dyads and were always told that the other participant has been randomly assigned to record a speech, while they would be doing the rating, and were further told that they would not have to make a speech themselves. They were told that speakers knew that other students were rating their tapes, and were then informed that their speaker was either from their ingroup (same residential college) or outgroup (different residential college). We assessed our participants' level of identification with their college (Hogg, Cooper-Shaw, & Holzworth, 1993) and expected high identifiers who heard an ingroup member to be most susceptible to vicarious dissonance.

Participants heard another student give a counterattitudinal speech (a speech in favor of a tuition increase). Some students knew that the speaker was a member of his/her own residential college or was a member of a different college. In addition, we manipulated the decision freedom that the speaker had to make the speech. Half of the participants heard the speakers choose to make the speech, while the other half heard the speaker simply accede to the experimenter's instructions. In all conditions, the taped interaction made it clear that the speaker disagreed with the position taken in the speech.

If vicarious dissonance exists, then it should be experienced by students who heard their ingroup member deliver a counterattitudinal speech. These students should change their attitudes in the direction of the speech, especially if they felt strongly attracted to their group. And, as depicted in Figure 19.1, that is precisely what happened. Students who were affiliated with their residential college (high identifiers) and who heard a fellow college member behave in a way that was attitude-discrepant changed their own attitude in the

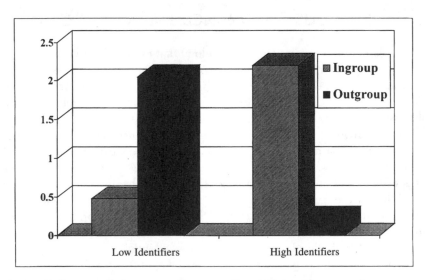

FIGURE 19.1. Attitude change as a function of level of identification and group membership of speaker.

direction of the speech. They became more favorable to the position that tuition should be increased. No such change occurred for the high identifying students who heard exactly the same speech given by a member of a different residential college. These results suggest an answer to the question raised in the opening scenario of this chapter. It seems that the union member indeed would have been motivated to change his attitudes on the free trade issue.

Our results also show an unpredicted reversal for low identifying students. They experienced more change from observing outgroup members. As we confirmed with additional survey data, most low identifiers were those who actually wished they were in a different residential college. They did not like the group to which they had been randomly assigned and, instead, identified with other residential colleges. For low identifiers, the technical ingroup was the psychological outgroup; the technical outgroup was their psychological ingroup, accounting for the interaction shown in Figure 19.1. Overall, the predictions of the vicarious dissonance analysis were supported by the attitude change results.

Was it Really Dissonance?

The finding that attitude change occurred for people who heard members of a group with which they identified give a counterattitudinal speech is consistent with our notion of vicarious dissonance. But not quite. Half of our participants heard the speechmaker being given a choice about whether to make the pro-tuition speech, and the other half heard the experimenter merely tell the speaker to make the speech. There are myriad dissonance experiments that show that the personal experience of dissonance depends upon the perception of choice (e.g, Linder, Cooper, & Jones, 1967). Yet, choice did not have that effect on the observation of counterattitudinal behavior. Without differences between choice and no-choice conditions, the possibility exists that participants were merely persuaded more by the words of a speech that were given by ingroup members rather than outgroup members. It is possible that people's biases to perceive arguments presented by ingroup members as superior (e.g., Wilder, 1990) may have led to greater attitude change.

There are additional factors that may have contributed to greater attitude change for high identifiers who heard speeches from ingroup members. For example, messages from ingroup members are often more deeply processed (Mackie & Smith, this volume; Mackie, Worth, & Asuncion, 1990) than similar messages from outgroup members. So, too, are unexpected or unanticipated messages (e.g., Eagly, Wood, & Chaiken, 1978; Smith & Petty, 1996) processed more deeply. Perhaps hearing a speech by an ingroup member favoring a tuition increase was so unexpected that it caused greater attention to, and deeper processing of, the pro-tuition arguments. It became apparent that, in order to rule out interpretations based on differential persuasion, we needed to remove the actual speech from our procedure, and play only the taped interaction between the student and the experimenter during which the student agreed to make the speech. As we view it, attitude change that stems from vicarious dissonance is independent of processing effects. It occurs when we witness someone with whom we identify engaging in dissonant behavior. Just as the aversiveness of agreeing to perform counterattitudinal behavior, and not the performance itself, induces dissonance on an individual level (Linder, Cooper, & Wicklund, 1968), so too should witnessing agreement induce vicarious dissonance in an observer. Although analyses of speech ratings in our experiment did not reveal any differences for perceived speech quality as a function of its being delivered by an ingroup member rather than an outgroup member, only eliminating the speech—and thus the information contained within that speech—can allow us to rule out this interpretation.

IN PURSUIT OF VICARIOUS DISSONANCE: FURTHER STUDIES

We conducted a second experiment (Norton et al., 2001) with two goals in mind. The first was to eliminate the speech from the procedure so the participant only processed the cognition that the speaker had *agreed* to make a counterattitudinal speech. The second was to make certain that the speaker was in the throes of cognitive dissonance by clearly manipulating whether the speaker agreed or disagreed with the position of the speech. Although a speech may be counterattitudinal for the majority of a group, it is not necessarily counterattitudinal for every member. We systematically varied whether the topic of the speech was counterattitudinal or proattitudinal for the group member whom the participant observed.

The results of this second study provide strong support for the centrality of dissonance processes to the attitude change we observed in Study 1. As shown in Figure 19.2, participants who heard an ingroup member agree to make a counterattitudinal speech changed their own attitudes to become more consistent with the position that the group member was to advocate. The actual words of the speech were not important, as attested to by the fact that participants did not hear the actual speeches. And, as in the first experiment, only people who were highly attracted to their group showed the vicarious dissonance effect. What is particularly interesting about these data is that participants only experienced vicarious dissonance if the speech was dissonant for the speaker. If the speaker personally believed in the argument he/she agreed to make, then it caused little attitude change in the observer, even though the speech was contrary to the participant's attitude. Only if the speaker was behaving in a way that was likely to cause dissonance for himself/herself did the observer feel the motivation to change his/her attitude.

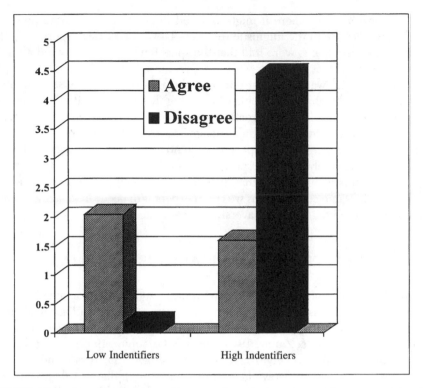

FIGURE 19.2. Attitude change as a function of speaker's opinion and participant's level of indentification.

Vicarious Dissonance and Aversive Consequences

A great deal of research has demonstrated that behavior that produces an aversive consequence leads to dissonance and subsequent efforts to reduce that dissonance (see Cooper & Fazio, 1984). Cooper and Worchel (1970) showed that aversive consequences are necessary to produce dissonance, and Scher and Cooper (1989) showed that producing an unwanted event is both necessary and sufficient to produce dissonance over and above cognitive inconsistency. The question is, does vicarious dissonance function in the same way?

In a third experiment (Norton et al., 2001), we manipulated whether the speaker's counterattitudinal behavior was likely to lead to an unwanted consequence. Participants were again told that they would be listening to speeches made by other students as part of an investigation of linguistic subcultures. Each participant heard an ingroup member make a speech contrary to his/her attitudes on a campus issue. As in the first two studies, half of the participants heard the experimenter tell the ingroup member that the speech would be sent to the Dean's office where it might be used to create an unwanted policy in addition to its use in the linguistic research. However, in this experiment, the remaining participants were told that the speech would be destroyed after its use in the linguistics study.

Once again, we found that our procedure successfully aroused cognitive dissonance in the observer. People who felt highly identified with their ingroup changed their attitude in the direction of the forthcoming speech by the ingroup member. As predicted, the attitude change occurred when the speaker was told that the Dean would read his speech, while no attitude change occurred when the speech was solely for the purpose of the linguistic research. The importance of these results is the finding that dissonance occurred in the observer under precisely the same conditions as we could expect it to occur in an actor—when the behavior led to unwanted, aversive consequences.

THE EXPERIENCE OF VICARIOUS DISSONANCE

How does dissonance feel? Festinger hypothesized that dissonance is an unpleasant state of tension, and several studies, using both physiological and self-report measures, have corroborated his speculation (Elliot & Devine, 1994; Higgins, Rhodewalt, & Zanna, 1979; Losch & Cacioppo, 1990). Using that description, a number of investigations have shown that dissonance can be misattributed to a wide array of environmental stimuli that are alleged to produce the same feeling. For example, Fazio, Zanna, and Cooper (1977) told writers of attitude-discrepant essays that the heat in the room in which they were writing might produce unpleasant arousal. That information was sufficient to permit participants to misattribute their arousal to the hot room rather than their dissonant act.

Is vicarious dissonance experienced in the same way? In the second study that we described in this chapter, we ran an additional set of conditions. We gave half of the participants a standard misattribution stimulus (e.g., Fazio et al., 1977). We told them that the conditions in the room often make people feel tense and uncomfortable. This information, which typically eliminates personal dissonance, had no impact on vicarious dissonance. Participants continued to show attitude change despite the presence of an external stimulus that could account for their unpleasant feelings. The persistence of vicarious dissonance, despite the availability of a misattributional stimulus, suggests that vicarious dissonance may be experienced differently from personal dissonance. We suggest that the experience of vicarious dissonance is based not only on the direct experience of unpleasant arousal but also on an empathic understanding of the actor's dilemma. Rather than making the observer feel precisely the way the actor feels, vicarious dissonance is based in part on a mental representation of the actor's experience.

In a final study, we found evidence for the notion that vicarious dissonance is related to empathic reactions (Norton et al., 2001). We again created the conditions for vicarious dissonance by using the linguistic subcultures paradigm. This time, we created new measures designed to assess the participants' own positive and negative affect, the participants' attributions of the affect that the actor was experiencing, and the *vicarious* affect that they believed they would feel if they were doing what the actor was asked to do. We found that attitude change in the vicarious dissonance paradigm was related to the experience that participants believed they would feel if they were in the actor's place. Participants who were highly attracted to their group and who observed an ingroup member behaving counterattitudinally felt that they would feel considerable negative emotion if they were in their group member's shoes. Most importantly, the degree of this negative affect was significantly related to the magnitude of attitude change.

Vicarious negative affect (or the negative affect participants reported they would feel if in the actors' shoes) was also related to individual differences in empathy as measured by Davis's Interpersonal Reactivity Index (Davis, 1983, 1994). In particular, our measure of vicarious affect was related to the Empathic Concern scale of the IRI that assesses the tendency "to experience feelings of sympathy and compassion for unfortunate others." Thus, individuals who were predisposed to connect empathically with others in distress reported higher levels of negative vicarious affect, and this vicarious negative affect was then related to attitude change.

VICARIOUS DISSONANCE: INTERGROUP OR INTERPERSONAL?

We have taken the position that group identification expands the social self and that the occurrence of vicarious dissonance depends on this expanded sense of self. The work of Wright et al. (this volume) and Mackie and Smith (this volume) have made similar proposals in their analyses of emotions and prejudice. But an intriguing question remains: Does the expanded sense of self produce vicarious dissonance as a function of *intergroup* identification, or will any *interpersonal* attraction accomplish the same goal? Ultimately, this is an empirical question that can be answered by additional research. However, we have reason to speculate that group identification is not just a sufficient condition but a necessary one for the existence of vicarious dissonance. In the research described in this chapter, attitude change by vicarious dissonance was not related either to attitude similarity nor to liking for the speaker, two common markers of interpersonal closeness. In the unfolding of social identity processes, other people impact our attitudes (Deaux, 1993) and reduce our attitudinal uncertainty (Hogg, 2000) only when they are part of our self-defined social identity.

Although liking, familiarity, and even nominal group membership are often seen as adequate markers of social identity, it is only when people identify strongly with their group that the fusion of self and other that typifies social identity occurs. The results of our studies are consistent with the notion of group-based social identification in that vicarious dissonance occurred only when people observed the counterattitudinal behavior of a speaker who was part of their own, self-defined, and important social group.

CULTURE AND THE TWO DISSONANCES

Recent interest in the cultural generality of social psychological phenomena is particularly apt when applied to cognitive dissonance. Due to the differing construals of the self that predominate in different cultures, processes that rely on self-conceptions may well vary. Markus and Kitayama (1991) have argued that, in western cultures such as Europe and North America, the self is conceived as independent. People typically assess the meaning of their attitudes, behaviors, and emotions by engaging in personal referencing rather than referencing their social context of social groups. By contrast, people in Eastern cultures, typified by the countries of eastern Asia, have more interdependent selves, relying on social referencing to assess meaning in their social world.

Although there have been some studies that found evidence for the occurrence of personal dissonance in Asian cultures (e.g., Sakai, 1999), the findings have not been consistent. Heine and Lehman (1997) looked for evidence of cognitive dissonance in a group of Japanese students. They found that a dissonance-producing choice that created attitude change among European-Canadian students did not lead to attitude change among the Japanese. Kitayama, Suzuki, Conner, and Markus (2001) found that Japanese students showed attitude change after a dissonance-producing choice, but only if those instructions specifically primed social relationships.

We suggest that vicarious dissonance may be more prevalent in eastern cultures than western cultures. Interdependent selves may be more likely to empathize with fellow group members. Precisely because people in interdependent cultures are more likely to engage in social referencing, they may be more likely to experience what their fellow ingroup members experience and consequently be more susceptible to vicarious dissonance. The findings we have presented in this chapter show that people in western cultures do experience vicarious dissonance. However, the more interdependent nature of the social self in eastern cultures may amplify and expand the prevalence of vicarious dissonance in those cultures. Our understanding of cognitive dissonance processes and their relationship to the social self would benefit from further research on cross-cultural differences in vicarious dissonance.

REFERENCES

Abrams, D., & Hogg, M. A. (2001). Collective identity: Group membership and self-conception. In M. A. Hogg & R. S. Tindale (Eds.), *Blackwell handbook of social psychology: Group processes* (pp. 425–460). Oxford, UK: Blackwell.

Aron, A., Aron, E. N., Tudor, M., & Nelson, G. (1991). Close relationships as including other in the self. *Journal of Personality and Social Psychology, 60,* 241–253.

Aronson, E. (1968). Dissonance theory: Progress and problems. In R. Abelson, E. Aronson, W. McGuire, T. Newcomb, M. Rosenberg, & P. Tannenbaum (Eds.), *Theories of cognitive consistency: A sourcebook* (pp. 5–27). Chicago: Rand McNally.

Cadinu, M. R., & Rothbart, M. (1996). Self-anchoring and differentiation processes in the minimal group setting. *Journal of Personality and Social Psychology, 70,* 661–677.

Cialdini, R. B., Brown, S. L., Lewis, B. P., Luce, C., & Neuberg, S. L. (1997). Reinterpreting the empathy-altruism relationship: When one into one equals oneness. *Journal of Personality and Social Psychology, 73,* 481–494.

Cooper, J., & Fazio, R. H. (1984). A new look at dissonance. In L. Berkowitz (Ed.), *Advances in experimental social psychology* (Vol. 17, pp. 229–268). San Diego, CA: Academic Press.

Cooper, J., & Stone, J. (2000). Cognitive dissonance and the social group. In D. J. Terry & M. A. Hogg (Eds.), *Attitudes, behavior, and social context: The role of norms and group membership* (pp. 227–244). Mahwah, NJ: Erlbaum.

Cooper, J., & Worchel, S. (1970). The role of undesired consequences in the arousal of cognitive dissonance. *Journal of Personality and Social Psychology, 16,* 312–320.

Davis, M. H. (1983). Measuring individual differences in empathy: Evidence for a multidimensional approach. *Journal of Personality and Social Psychology, 44,* 113–126.

Davis, M. H. (1994). *Empathy: A social psychological approach.* Boulder, CO: Westview.

Deaux, K. (1993). Reconstructing social identity. *Personality and Social Psychology Bulletin, 19,* 4–12.

Eagly, A. H., Wood, W., & Chaiken, S. (1978). Causal inferences about communicators and their effect on opinion change. *Journal of Personality and Social Psychology, 36,* 424–435.

Elliot, A. J., & Devine, P. G. (1994). On the motivational nature of cognitive dissonance: Dissonance as psychological discomfort. *Journal of Personality and Social Psychology, 67,* 382–394.

Fazio, R. H., Zanna, M. P., & Cooper, J. (1977). Dissonance and self-perception: An integrative view of each theory's proper domain of application. *Journal of Experimental Social Psychology, 13,* 464–479.

Festinger, L. (1957). *A theory of cognitive dissonance.* Evanston, IL: Row, Peterson.

Festinger, L., Riecken, H. W., & Schachter, S. (1956). *When prophecy fails.* Minneapolis, MN: University of Minnesota Press.

Heine, S. J., & Lehman, D. R. (1997). Culture, dissonance, and self affirmation. *Personality and Social Psychology Bulletin, 23,* 389–400.

Higgins, E. T., Rhodewalt, F., & Zanna, M. P. (1979). Dissonance motivation: Its nature, persistence and reinstatement. *Journal of Experimental Social Psychology, 15,* 16–34.

Hogg, M. A. (2000). Subjective uncertainty reduction through self-categorization: A motivational theory of social identity processes. *European Review of Social Psychology, 11,* 223–255.

Hogg, M. A. (2001a). Self-categorization and subjective uncertainty resolution: Cognitive and motivational facets of social identity and group membership. In J. P. Forgas, K. D. Williams, & L. Wheeler (Eds.), *The social mind: Cognitive and motivational aspects of interpersonal behavior* (pp. 323–349). London: Cambridge University Press.

Hogg, M. A. (2001b). Social categorization, depersonalization, and group behavior. In M. A. Hogg & R. S. Tindale (Eds.), *Blackwell handbook of social psychology: Group processes* (pp. 56–85). Oxford, UK: Blackwell.

Hogg, M. A. (2001c). Social identity and the

sovereignty of the group: A psychology of belonging. In C. Sedikides & M. B. Brewer (Eds.), *Individual self, relational self, collective self* (pp. 123–143). Philadelphia: Psychology Press.

Hogg, M. A. (in press). Social identity. In M. Leary & J. Tangney (Eds.), *Handbook of self and identity.* New York: Guilford.

Hogg, M. A., & Abrams, D. (1988). *Social identifications: A social psychology of intergroup relations and group processes.* London: Routledge.

Hogg, M. A., Cooper-Shaw, L., & Holzworth, D. W. (1993). Group prototypicality and depersonalized attraction in small interactive groups. *Personality and Social Psychology Bulletin, 19,* 452–465.

Hogg, M. A., & Hardie, E. A. (1991). Social attraction, personal attraction, and self-categorization: A field study. *Personality and Social Psychology Bulletin, 17,* 175–180.

Kitayama, S., Suzuki, T., Conner, A., & Markus, H. R. (2001). *Culture, self and dissonance: Post-decisional attitude change in Japan and the Untied States.* Unpublished manuscript, Kyoto University, Japan.

Linder, D. E., Cooper, J., & Jones, E. E. (1967). Decision freedom as a determinant of the role of incentive magnitude in attitude change. *Journal of Personality and Social Psychology, 6,* 245–254.

Linder, D. E., Cooper, J., & Wicklund, R. A. (1968). Pre-exposure persuasion as a result of commitment to pre-exposure effort. *Journal of Experimental Social Psychology, 4,* 470–482.

Losch, M. E., & Cacioppo, J. T. (1990). Cognitive dissonance may enhance sympathetic tonus, but attitudes are changed to reduce negative affect rather than arousal. *Journal of Experimental Social Psychology, 26,* 289–304.

Mackie, D. M., Worth, L. T., & Asuncion, A. G. (1990). Processing of persuasive in-group messages. *Journal of Personality and Social Psychology, 58,* 812–822.

Markus, H. R., & Kitayama, S. (1991). Culture and the self: Implications for cognition, emotion and motivation. *Psychological Review, 98,* 224–253.

Norton, M. I., Monin, B., Cooper, J., & Hogg, M. A. (2001). *Vicarious dissonance: Attitude change from the inconsistency of others.* Unpublished manuscript.

Sakai, H. (1999). A multiplicative power-function model of cognitive dissonance: Toward an integrated theory of cognition, emotion, and behavior after Leon Festinger. In E. Harmon-Jones & J. Mills (Eds.), *Cognitive dissonance theory: Progress on a pivotal theory in social psychology* (pp. 267–294). Washington DC: American Psychological Association.

Scher, S. J., & Cooper, J. (1989). The motivational basis of dissonance: The singular role of behavioral consequences. *Journal of Personality and Social Psychology, 56,* 899–906.

Simon, B. (1997). Self and group in modern society: Ten theses on the individual self and the collective self. In R. Spears, P. J. Oakes, N. Ellemers, & S. A. Haslam (Eds.), *The social psychology of stereotyping and group life* (pp. 318–335). Oxford, UK: Blackwell.

Simon, B., & Hastedt, C. (1999). Self-aspects as social categories: The role of personal importance and valence. *European Journal of Social Psychology, 29,* 479–487.

Smith, E. R., & Henry, S. (1996). An in-group becomes part of the self: Response time evidence. *Personality and Social Psychology Bulletin, 22,* 635–642.

Smith, S. M., & Petty, R. E. (1996). Message framing and persuasion: A message processing analysis. *Personality and Social Psychology Bulletin, 22,* 257–268.

Sorrentino, R. M., Short, J. C., & Raynor, J. O. (1984). Uncertainty orientation: Implications for affective and cognitive views of achievement behavior. *Journal of Personality and Social Psychology, 46,* 189–206.

Steele, C. (1988). The psychology of self-affirmation: Sustaining the integrity of the self. In L. Berkowitz (Ed.), *Advances in experimental social psychology, Vol. 21* (pp. 261–302). Hillsdale, NJ: Erlbaum.

Stone, J., & Cooper, J. (2001). The self-standards model of cognitive dissonance. *Journal of Experimental Social Psychology, 37,* 228–243.

Tajfel, H., & Turner, J. C. (1979). An integrative theory of intergroup conflict. In W. G. Austin & S. Worchel (Eds.), *The social psychology of intergroup relations* (pp. 33–47). Monterey, CA: Brooks/Cole.

Terry, D. J., & Hogg, M. A. (1996). Group norms and the attitude–behavior relationship: A role for group identification. *Personality and Social Psychology Bulletin, 22,* 776–793.

Terry, D. J., & Hogg, M. A. (2001). Attitudes, behavior, and social context: The role of norms and group membership in social influence processes. In J. P. Forgas & K. D. Williams (Eds.), *Social influence: Direct and indirect processes* (pp. 253–270). Philadelphia: Psychology Press.

Terry, D. J., Hogg, M. A., & White, K. M. (2000). Attitude-behavior relations: Social identity and group membership. In D. J. Terry & Hogg, M. A. (Eds.), *Attitudes, behavior, and social context: The role of norms and group membership* (pp. 67–93). Mahwah, NJ: Erlbaum.

Turner, J. C., Hogg, M. A., Oakes, P. J., Reicher, S. D., & Wetherell, M. S. (1987). *Rediscovering the social group: A self-categorization theory.* New York: Blackwell.

van Knippenberg, D., & Wilke, H. (1992). Prototypicality of arguments and conformity to in-group norms. *European Journal of Social Psychology, 22,* 141–155.

Wilder, D. A. (1990). Some determinants of the persuasive power of in-groups and out-groups: Organization of information and attribution of independence. *Journal of Personality and Social Psychology, 59,* 1202–1213.

Zanna, M. P., & Cooper, J. (1974). Dissonance and the pill: An attribution approach to studying the arousal properties of dissonance. *Journal of Personality and Social Psychology, 29,* 703–709.

Zanna, M. P., & Sande, G. N. (1987). The effects of collective actions on the attitudes of individual group members: A dissonance analysis. In M. P. Zanna, J. M. Olson, & C. P. Herman (Eds.), *Social influence: The Ontario symposium, Vol. 5. Ontario symposium on personality and social psychology* (pp. 151–163). Hillsdale, NJ: Erlbaum.

20

Including Others (and Groups) in the Self

Self-Expansion and Intergroup Relations

STEPHEN C. WRIGHT
ART ARON
LINDA R. TROPP

INTRODUCTION

*T*he idea that the self extends beyond the confines of the individual person, to include more than personal characteristics and attributes, is now a common theme in many social psychological analyses of the self (e.g., Abrams & Hogg, 2001; Brewer & Gardner, 1996; Deaux, 1996; Taylor & Dubé, 1986; Turner, Oakes, Haslam, & McGarty, 1994). Cross-cultural analyses (e.g., Markus & Kitayama, 1991; Triandis, 1989) and especially the social identity (Tajfel & Turner, 1979) and self-categorization (Turner, Hogg, Oakes, Reicher, & Wetherell, 1987) perspectives have been especially influential in focusing attention on the socially extended nature of the self. The initial formulation of

Address for correspondence: Stephen Wright, Psychology Department, Social Science
II, University of California, Santa Cruz, CA 95064, USA. E-mail: swright@cats.ucsc.edu

social identity theory was not intended as a general theory of the self. However, one of its cornerstone idea—that group memberships are meaningful and valued aspects of the self—has sparked considerable theorizing and rethinking about the nature of the self (e.g., Brewer, 1991; Oakes, Haslam & Turner, 1994; Simon, 1999).

At the same time, the idea that the self extends beyond the individual person is an essential assumption of another line of research and theory, one rooted in the study of interpersonal relations. Aron and Aron (1986, 1996) proposed a model of interpersonal relationships that holds that when two individuals become close, the other is "included" in the self. Although the language is somewhat different, the two perspectives share the conception of a self that contains aspects of other social entities—the ingroup in the case of social identity theory and the close other in the case of the Aron and Aron model. However, an important difference is found in the motives that the two perspectives see as driving the inclusion of other entities in the self. While a number of other motives have been proposed (we will consider some these in more detail later), the social identity perspective has been dominated by the self-esteem or self-enhancement hypothesis that holds that we have a basic need for positive self-esteem, and that joining and identifying with groups is one way to meet this need (see Rubin & Hewstone, 1998). Aron and Aron (1986, 1996), on the other hand, theorize that the inclusion of others in the self is motivated by a need for self-expansion. The basic premise of the *self-expansion model* is that people seek to enhance their potential efficacy by expanding the self to include material and social resources, perspectives, and identities that will facilitate achievement of goals (for a recent elaboration of the motivational aspect of the model, see Aron, Norman, & Aron, 1998). Thus, self-expansion in pursuit of greater general self-efficacy is a central human motivation, and one way to achieve expansion is through the development of close relationships in which the other is included in the self. However, extending this perspective to the domain of group processes and intergroup relations makes apparent the possibility that another means of self-expansion is to include relevant *groups* in the self.

In this chapter, we briefly consider a number of ways that the self-expansion model might be adapted and integrated with the study of group processes and intergroup relations. First, we consider the utility of conceptualizing ingroup identification as the inclusion of ingroup in the self, and we discuss how the self-expansion motive might influence self-categorization and ingroup identification. Second, we describe possible applications of the inclusion of other in the self and self-expansion motives to the improvement of intergroup relations. Specifically, we examine how the inclusion of other in the self might be associated with positive intergroup contact effects, and we propose an extension of the self-expansion model to explain why, under certain circumstances, we might have a strong positive interest in, and even liking for, outgroups.

INGROUP IDENTIFICATION:
INCLUDING THE INGROUP IN THE SELF

One of social identity theory's key contentions is that the self includes not only a set of unique individual characteristics (i.e., personal identities), but also includes aspects that connect the individual to others through shared group memberships (i.e., social identities). Which of these many self-aspects will become the dominant self-representation in a given circumstance is determined by both the situational/contextual cues that focus attention on that self-aspect and the accessibility of that self-aspect for the particular individual (see Abrams & Hogg, 2001; Simon & Kampmeier, 2001; Turner, et al., 1987). Thus, a given social identity will emerge as a dominant self-representation when there are strong contextual cues making that group membership salient and when that group has particular psychological significance for the individual. The bulk of the research in the social identity tradition has focused on the contextual factors that make a given ingroup more salient and meaningful (see Hogg, 2000; Oakes, 2001). However, several researchers have considered the role of *ingroup identification*—the individual's chronic psychological connection with a specific ingroup (e.g., Branscombe & Ellemers, 1998; Deaux, 2000; Ellemers, Spears, & Doosje, 1997; Tropp & Wright, 1999).

Despite increased attention to ingroup identification, the meaning and parameters of the concept remain somewhat obscure (Ellemers, Kortekaas, & Ouwerkerk, 1999; Jackson & Smith, 1999). We believe this confusion stems in part from two ambiguities in the definition and use of the term. First, some authors use ingroup identification in a very general sense to refer to the present strength of a social identity, that is, the degree to which a category membership serves as immediate dominant self-representation (e.g., Hogg, 2001; Ellemers, Spears, & Doosje, 1999). In this use, identification is the combined influence of contextual and individual characteristics. Certainly, we recognize that the present importance of a social identity is to a great extent determined by the immediate social context. However, we also see benefits to distinguishing between the influences of immediate context and an individual's chronic psychological attachment to the group. Thus, we limit our use of the term "ingroup identification" to refer to that part of the strength of a social identity that arises from the individual's chronic ongoing connection to the specific ingroup (e.g., Deaux, 2000).

In addition, it is productive to distinguish between *self-categorization*, *collective self-esteem* (e.g., Luhtanen & Crocker, 1992), and *ingroup identification*; where self-categorization represents the simple recognition or awareness that one is a member of the group, collective self-esteem represents how positively or negatively one evaluates that group membership, and ingroup identification involves the degree to which the person feels an enduring sense of interconnectedness between himself/herself and the group. Thus, while necessary, self-categorization is not sufficient for ingroup identification. Nor is a positive evaluation of the ingroup sufficient to produce ingroup identification. In fact, a positive evaluation may not be necessary for ingroup identification. Thus, we believe that at its most basic level, ingroup identification represents the *degree to which the ingroup is included in the self.*

This definition of ingroup identification is consistent with, although more specific than, Tajfel's (1981) initial formulation of the concept of social identity. However, this definition derived more directly from Aron and Aron's (1986, 1996) conception of including other in the self. Aron and Aron use the term "inclusion of *other* in the self" to refer to the interconnectedness of self and other in close relationships. When people become close, rather than being perceived as separate beings, self and other are regarded as "overlapping selves," where aspects of the close other are considered part of the self. In fact, interpersonal closeness is defined by the degree of other–self overlap.

In a variety of studies, Aron, Aron, Tudor, and Nelson (1991) have demonstrated that close others function cognitively like self, while nonclose others do not. For example, Aron et al. (1991, Experiment 3) proposed that if close others are included in the self, individuals should respond more slowly, when rating the self, to characteristics that produce an *inconsistency* between oneself and the close other, since this inconsistency would interfere with cognitive processing. Conversely, individuals should respond more quickly to characteristics that produce *consistency* between oneself and the close other, as no such interference would take place. Participants rated the extent to which a series of characteristics were descriptive of themselves and of their spouse. Then, a reaction-time procedure was used to measure the speed of participants' "me/not me" judgments for these characteristics. Indeed, participants were slower in responding to characteristics that produced an inconsistency between self and spouse compared to characteristics for which perceptions of self and spouse were consistent. Smith and Henry (1996; see also Otten, this volume; Smith, this volume; Smith, Coats, & Walling, 1999) adopted this paradigm to study relationships between representations of the self and the ingroup. Consistent with the inclusion-of-ingroup-in-the-self hypothesis, they found that responses were slower for traits that produced an inconsistency between ratings of self and ingroup than for traits that were consistent for self and ingroup. Match or mismatch between self and an outgroup had no such effects.

Recently, Tropp and Wright (2001) have extended this approach to consider more directly the role of ingroup identification. Just as research has demonstrated that the degree of interpersonal closeness moderates the self–other overlap effects (Aron & Fraley, 1999; Smith et al., 1999; Smith, this volume), Tropp and Wright (2001) predicted that ingroup identification, defined as the degree to which the ingroup is included in the self, should moderate the effect found by Smith and his colleagues (see Smith, this volume) and by Otten and her colleagues (see Otten, this volume). In order to operationalize the conception of ingroup identification as the inclusion of the ingroup in the self, Tropp and Wright adapted Aron, Aron, and Smollan's (1992) Inclusion of Other in the Self Scale (IOS Scale). The IOS Scale is a one-item scale on which participants describe the closeness of their relationship by selecting from seven pairs of circles representing various degrees of overlap between self and other. After demonstrating that this scale performs as well or better than other measures of closeness, Aron et al. (1992) concluded that its effectiveness suggests that this metaphor of overlapped selves may actually reflect how relationships are cognitively represented. In Tropp and Wright's (2001) adaptation, referred to as the Inclusion of the Ingroup in the Self Scale (IIS), the pairs of circles represent varying degrees of overlap between the self and a specified ingroup (see Figure 20.1). A series of studies using responses from samples of women and ethnic minority groups establish the construct validity, the concurrent and discriminant validity, and the test-retest reliability of the IIS. Most importantly, though, the results suggest that the IIS may capture the essence of interconnectedness between self and ingroup underlying the construct of ingroup identification (see Tropp & Wright, 2001, for an extended discussion).

Using the IIS as a pretest and the reaction-time procedure used by Smith and Henry (1996), Tropp and Wright (2001, Study 1) tested the hypothesis that cognitive representations of the self and ingroup would be less strongly connected among those low in ingroup identification compared to those who were more strongly identified with the ingroup. Thus, inconsistencies in ratings of a trait for self and ingroup should have little influence on reactions times for "me/not me" judgments of these traits among low identifiers. However, inconsistencies between self and ingroup ratings should impede reaction times among high identifiers. The results supported this prediction. As shown in Figure 20.2, participants with high IIS scores responded significantly slower to self-descriptive characteristics that were not descriptive of the ingroup (i.e., where ratings of the self and ingroup were inconsistent) than to characteristics that were both self-descriptive and ingroup-descriptive (i.e., where ratings of the self and

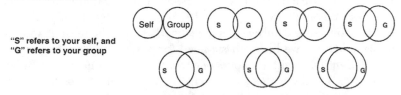

FIGURE 20.1. The Inclusion of the Ingroup in the Self (IIS) Scale. (The label of "group" can be replaced with a specific ingroup [i.e., ethnic label, gender, student affiliation, etc.].)

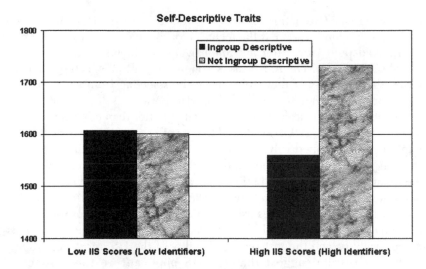

FIGURE 20.2. Mean reaction time by high and low identifiers for self-descriptive traits that were either descriptive or nondescriptive of the ingroup.

ingroup were consistent). In contrast, participants with low IIS scores showed virtually no difference in reaction times for self-descriptive characteristics that were or were not descriptive of the ingroup (i.e., where ratings of the self and ingroup were either consistent or inconsistent). This suggests that for people low in ingroup identification (as measured by the IIS), the ingroup is not adequately included in the self-concept to produce the self/ingroup confusion found among those high in ingroup identification. These findings illustrate the importance of studying cognitive representations not only in terms of group membership but also in terms of the degree to which individuals include that group as part of their self-concepts.

Motivation for Ingroup Identification

A model of ingroup identification must consider not only the impact of ingroup identification, but also motivation. Why do people join and identify with groups? Social identity theory (Tajfel & Turner, 1979) proposes two basic motivations for identification: *self-enhancement* and *distinctiveness*. The self-enhancement hypothesis holds that we have a basic need for positive self-esteem, and that joining and identifying with groups is one way to meet this need (see Rubin & Hewstone, 1998). Thus, we seek to belong to groups that are positively valued compared to relevant outgroups because these memberships provide us with a positive social identity. The second motive, distinctiveness, contends that we seek groups that provide adequate contrast with comparison outgroups. Thus, groups that are clearly distinguishable from relevant outgroups are preferred. Both these motives are thought to influence not only joining and identification with groups, but also the individual's understandings of the intergroup relations and intergroup behavior, producing ingroup bias and actions that increase intergroup contrasts.

The self-enhancement motive has received considerable attention, but reviews of the research have revealed inconsistencies. It appears that when intergroup comparisons result in the perception that the ingroup holds higher status than a comparison outgroup, self-esteem is enhanced (e.g., Lemyre & Smith, 1985). However, there appears to be little consistent evidence that self-enhancement is the only or even the primary motivation for identification with a group. Numerous authors have pointed out that people often show strong identification with groups that are recognized to hold low status positions (e.g., Mlicki & Ellemers, 1996; Rubin & Hewstone, 1998).

The distinctiveness motive has been considered in a number of ways. First, there is some evidence that an outgroup that is seen to be "too similar" to the ingroup can raise identity threats and efforts to increase the distinctive character of the ingroup (Jetten, Spears & Manstead, 1997; Spears, Doosje, & Ellemers, 1997). Self-categorization theory focuses on the role of group distinctiveness in meeting the need for self-explanation and self-evaluation. Self-categorization provides meaningful information about the social world and about our place in it. Ingroups that are well differentiated from other groups can provide explicit and unambiguous information about who belongs, and perhaps more importantly, whether we belong. Thus, if identification is motivated by a need for meaning, groups that are well differentiated from other groups are more likely to attract our identification.

Hogg and his colleagues (see Hogg, 2000, 2001; Hogg & Abrams, 1993) have extended the self-categorization idea that self-categorization and ingroup identification serve an explanatory function. Rather than distinctiveness, self-esteem, or simple explanation, Hogg and his colleagues focus on ways that categorization (and especially self-categorization) serves to reduce subjective uncertainty. From this perspective, we engage in social categorization primarily to simplify the complexities of the social world. Similarly, identification with the ingroup is motivated by the need to clarify important concerns about the state of that world. Supporting this view, Grieve and Hogg (1999) and Mullin and Hogg (1999) have demonstrated in a number of studies that self-categorization occurs and ingroup identification increases when uncertainty is high and decreases when uncertainty is low.

Brewer and her colleagues (e.g., Brewer, 1991; Brewer & Pickett, 1999, this volume) have also extended social identity theory's focus on distinctiveness in the theory of optimal distinctiveness. Here, distinctiveness is seen as one need that stands in constant opposition to a need for inclusion or belonging (see also Leary, this volume). Thus, identification is motivated both by a need for differentiation from other social entities and by a need to be part of a larger social entity. Findings that smaller minority groups tend to attract stronger identification than larger majority groups is seen as evidence for the optimal distinctiveness model. There is also evidence that priming inclusion needs can heighten identification with larger more inclusive groups, while priming distinctiveness needs can heighten identification with relatively smaller more exclusive groups (see Brewer & Pickett, this volume, for a review).

Thus, the self-enhancement and group distinctiveness motives originally proposed by social identity theory have been supplemented and challenged by other perspectives regarding the motivation for ingroup identification. In the next section, we propose an additional motive, self-expansion, and consider briefly how the self-expansion model compares with some of these other perspectives.

Self-Expansion as a Motivation for Ingroup Identification

The self-expansion model proposes that we have a strong motive to expand the self and that one way to achieve this is to include others in the self. In doing so, we take on the resources, perspectives, and identities and of the other, thus making them part of who we are. The motive that underlies the desire for self-expansion is an increase in one's sense of general self-efficacy. Extending the self-expansion perspective from the domain of interpersonal relationships to group processes, we propose that ingroup identification (including the ingroup in the self) is, at least in part, the result of self-expansion motives. That is, we seek to include groups in the self because doing so increases our confidence that we can meet the demands of our world and achieve goals. Several interesting connections can be drawn between self-expansion motives and the other major perspectives on motivation for ingroup identification.

Self-Expansion, Uncertainty Reduction, and Ingroup Identification

Interestingly, the self-expansion and uncertainty reduction models share some basic tenets. First and foremost, both postulate something like a need for control as the basic underlying motivate. Hogg (2001) wrote that "uncertainty about one's attitudes, beliefs, feelings and perceptions, as well as about oneself and other people, is aversive . . . because it is ultimately associated with reduced control over one's life" (p. 478). Similarly, Aron, Aron, and Norman (2001) wrote that "people seek to expand the self in the sense that they seek to enhance their potential efficacy by increasing the physical and social resources, perspectives, and identities that facilitate achievement of any goal that might arise" (p. 227).

There is a long and extensive literature on the importance of perceived control (see Skinner, 1992). Feelings of uncontrollability have numerous negative consequences (e.g., Abramson, Seligman, & Teasdale, 1978; Deci & Ryan, 1991; Dweck & Leggett, 1988; Seligman, 1975), and the desire for control can be a powerful motivator (Stevens & Fiske, 1995). In some cases, control motives can lead one to seek knowledge that will explain the present distribution of outcomes, or even better, allow one to predict subsequent outcomes (Fiske & Depret, 1996). Thus, need for control is associated with information seeking in an effort to explain and predict events.

Hogg's (2001) subjective uncertainty reduction model is clearly consistent with this desire for control. Knowing what the relevant group boundaries are and to which group one belongs allows one to explain important aspects of the social world and even to predict subsequent events. In addition, self-categorization evokes group norms that prescribe specific responses to events and, thus, increase our sense of control over future outcomes. We might conclude that it is the feelings of uncontrollability that result from subjective uncertainty that provide the primary motivation for ingroup identification; that is, the subjective uncertainty reduction motive may essentially represent an attempt to increase one's sense of control.

Self-expansion is also directly linked to control motives. In addition to acquiring knowledge that will provide explanation and prediction, control motives also inspire efforts to acquire the resources and status that allow one to directly influence the environment to ensure that it provides the desired outcomes. Expanding one's resources by including the group in the self, increases the likelihood that one will be able to exert direct control over self-relevant events. Thus, it appears that both uncertainty reduction and self-expansion perspectives share the view that identification arises in part from a desire to increase one's sense of control.

The two perspectives also describe a similar relationship between their respective motives and self-enhancement. Hogg (2001) proposed that uncertainty reduction may underlie the self-enhancement associated with identification because high self-esteem is contingent upon self-certainty. Thus, increases in self-esteem associated with ingroup identification may not result directly from that group membership, but rather as the indirect result of the greater self-clarity and self-certainty that membership provides. Similarly, self-expansion sees self-enhancement as a by-product of self-expansion. Aron, Paris, and Aron (1995) found that after falling in love (and thus presumably including another in the self) there was an increase in perceived self-efficacy and an associated increase in self-esteem. They concluded that this occurs because people feel good about themselves to the extent that they possess the resources needed to accomplish their goals. Similarly, identification with a group (including the group in the self) should enhance self-esteem because the newly acquired resources increase self-efficacy. Thus, both models see the self-enhancement that can result from ingroup identification as a by-product of satisfying a more basic motive (uncertainty reduction or self-expansion).

However, the two perspectives have a somewhat different general focus. Uncertainty reduction paints a picture of the person locked in a constant battle against an insecure and anxiety-provoking world—as facing a ceaseless tide of uncertainty, confusion, and angst. Although Hogg (2001) recognized that we may at times experience a background of relative certainty, the focus is clearly on our quest to solve existing problems with uncertainty and insecurity. The self-expansion model, on the other hand, portrays the individual as much more secure and represents our interactions with the world as much more appetitive. Ordinarily, the individual seeks novelty and opportunity. The difference between these perspectives is not inconsistent with the distinction made by Higgins (1998) between promotional and preventative regulatory systems (see also Smith, this volume). Like the preventative system, uncertainty reduction focuses on avoiding negative outcomes and ensuring security. By contrast, like the promotional system, self-expansion focuses on continual growth.

Perhaps because of these different foci, the two perspectives produce some divergent predictions. Because uncertainty reduction focuses on the need for understanding and clarity, it predicts that we will tend to identify with groups that are *consistent* with our existing self-perceptions, as these groups validate and clarify our self-knowledge and, thus, create the greatest certainty. Thus, similar and familiar groups will be preferred. In the case of the self-expansion model, the motivation is to expand the self. Thus, groups that are to some degree *divergent* from the present self may be more attractive. That is, rather than preferring groups that easily validate our present self-conceptions, we may seek group memberships that add new self-aspects, perhaps even challenging the present self-concept.

However, this divergence in perspective is not as extreme as it initially appears. Although we have focused on the appetitive aspects of the self-expansion model, the theory also proposes the opponent process of self-integration. Self-expansion must be followed by periods of integration where newly acquired self-aspects are integrated into existing self-schema. Self-expansion that is too rapid or extensive to allow adequate integration is distressing, even aversive. Similarly, the uncertainty reduction approach could be extended to consider situations where the individual experiences relative certainty and security, and then seeks a broader array of self-categorizations to shield against future challenges and uncertainties. This idea is consistent with Linville's (1985) notion that having a diverse self (one with more identities) can be adaptive, as other aspects of the self can buffer threats to a particular self-aspect.

In sum, the self-expansion and uncertainty reduction models, despite their entirely different pedigrees (intergroup relations and social identity for uncertainty reduction, and interpersonal relations and intimacy for self-expansion), share a number of very similar notions on the nature of the self and the motivations associated with self processes.

Self-Expansion, Optimal Distinctiveness, and Ingroup Identification

The basic prediction of optimal distinctiveness theory appears to be that groups that most consistently balance inclusiveness and distinctiveness needs should attract the greatest identification. The central idea of a push and pull of opposing motives found at the heart of optimal distinctiveness is also central to the self-expansion model. Restraining the desire for self-expansion is the need to integrate newly acquired self-aspects. Like the opposition of inclusiveness and differentiation, the opposition of expansion and integration determines the type of, the number of, and the pace at which groups can be included in the self. For example, highly inclusive groups and/or groups with prototypes that differ greatly from the present self-schema would be difficult to integrate and thus may not be readily or deeply included in the self.

In addition, Brewer and Pickett (this volume) argue that the need for inclusiveness results from "an even more fundamental need for security and safety" and explicitly connect this to the idea that belongingness needs arise from the vulnerability of lone individuals (Baumeister & Leary, 1995; see also Williams, Wheeler, & Harvey, 2001). This language is not inconsistent with self-expansion's central motive of enhancing one's general efficacy. In addition, Brewer's suggestion that large highly inclusive groups are best able to meet belongingness needs is consistent with the view that in general larger more inclusive groups would provide the greatest opportunity for self-expansion. Thus, the two perspectives provide very similar explanations for why we seek membership in larger inclusive groups.

However, self-expansion motives seem inconsistent with the optimal distinctiveness model's need for personal uniqueness. The active pursuit of the perspectives and identities of others (and groups) proposed by self-expansion implies that we are quite willing to sacrifice independence and uniqueness in favor of a larger more diverse self. The self-expansion model's explanation for attraction to smaller more exclusive groups would be similar to that proposed by Hogg's subjective uncertainty reduction model. Smaller more exclusive groups are likely to have clearer, better articulated prototypes than larger more inclusive groups. Thus, these smaller groups will make easily apparent the resources, perspectives, and identities that would be gained through group membership.

In short, optimal distinctiveness and self-expansion share some similarities in their structure and propose similar explanations for the appeal of larger more inclusive groups. However, the uniqueness motive central to optimal distinctiveness theory has no analogous process in the self-expansion model.

Summary

The idea of including other in the self fits nicely into social psychology's general understanding of ingroup identification, and the self-expansion model provides novel and potentially useful explanations for ingroup identification processes. Although consistent with some aspects of other motivational models of ingroup identification, the self-expansion perspective yields a number of divergent hypotheses. Our general view is that self-expansion complements these other models by providing an alternative explanation for why people join groups and why some group memberships have such a significant influence on thoughts, attitudes, and actions.

SELF-EXPANSION, INCLUDING OTHERS IN THE SELF, AND IMPROVING INTERGROUP RELATIONS

Intergroup Contact and Including Others in the Self

Recently, we have investigated the utility of the self-expansion model in explaining the dynamics associated with intergroup contact. The intergroup contact hypothesis has been among the most enduring theoretical perspectives in the study of intergroup relations (Allport, 1954; Amir, 1976; Hewstone & Brown, 1986; Miller & Brewer, 1984; Pettigrew, 1986, 1998; Stephan, 1987). Essentially, it proposes that, under specific circumstances, contact between members of different groups reduces negative intergroup attitudes. Recently, the contact hypothesis has experienced something of a renaissance fueled by a number of interesting new lines of research (e.g., Brown, Vivian, & Hewstone, 1999; Gaertner & Dovidio, 2000; Pettigrew & Tropp, 2000).

We have been particularly interested is recent work by Pettigrew (1997, 1998; see also Herek & Capitanio, 1996) suggesting that interpersonal friendship may be the particular form of contact most likely to produce a generalized reduction in prejudice (that is, reductions in prejudice toward the outgroup as a whole). Using data from a large international European sample, Pettigrew (1997) demonstrated that having an outgroup friendship predicted lower levels of subtle and blatant prejudice, greater support for pro-outgroup policies, and even generalized positive attitudes toward outgroups not involved in the contact. Having a cross-group coworker or neighbor produced much smaller effects than cross-group friendships (see Hamberger & Hewstone, 1997, for a complementary analysis of this data).

Pettigrew (1997) focused on the importance of positive affect associated with interpersonal friendship, and proposed that this affect leads to generalized empathy and identification with the outgroup. However, no clear mechanism is provided to describe how this generalization occurs. Why should positive affect toward an individual produce empathy or identification with the outgroup as a whole? We propose that the notion of including the other in the self provides a basis for such a mechanism. The logic is this: when one becomes close to a member of an outgroup, aspects of the outgroup member are included in the self. When that individual's social identity (his/her group membership) is made salient, that social identity may also be included in the self. Thus, through the close friend, the outgroup is included in the self and is then accorded some of the benefits usually accorded to the self (i.e., positive biases in attribution and resource allocation, feelings of empathy with their troubles, taking pride in their successes, generously sharing resources, etc.).

It is important to explicate what we mean by "including the outgroup in the self." Sometimes, this can mean actually acquiring membership in that group. For example, forming a close relationship with someone may give us real entrée into some of that person's groups (e.g., friendship groups, clubs, even his/her family should we marry). In other cases, actual membership in the outgroup is unlikely (e.g., ethnic, national, or occupational groups). Here, the connection involves psychological identification with the outgroup, such that events that effect the group now have personal meaning. In this case, the group is included in the self even though the person may be keenly aware that he/she is not actually included in the group.

Thus, "inclusion of other in the self" provides a mechanism to explain how friendship with a single outgroup member can lead to improved attitudes and actions toward the outgroup as a whole. Notice, this mechanism focuses on the importance of *interpersonal closeness* in the cross-group relationship. Including the other in the self is reserved for those with whom we share a *close* relationship. Thus, superficial or nonfriendly cross-group interactions should not serve to produce the necessary link between self and the other's group.

With inclusion of other in the self as the theoretical basis, we have carried out a number of studies that have attempted to clarify the role of cross-group friendship—and more specifically interpersonal closeness—in cross-group contact effects. Since our basic prediction is that it is the sense of intimacy and resulting inclusion of the other in the self that is responsible for the more positive intergroup attitudes, it was first necessary to demonstrate the direct role of intimacy per se in intergroup contact effects. The correlation between friendship and positive intergroup attitude found in the existing research literature can not explicitly rule out the possibility that intimacy and positive intergroup attitudes both result from greater quantity of contact or greater number of outgroup contacts (e.g., the development of a social network in the outgroup). McLaughlin-Volpe, Aron, Wright, and Reis (2000) have completed two questionnaire studies (one involving interethnic attitudes and another using attitudes toward rival universities), and a third study using a diary procedure (a version of the Rochester Interaction Record method, Reis & Wheeler, 1991; see also Williams et al., 2001). In all three studies, having outgroup friends was associated with less prejudice. More importantly, the amount of outgroup contact and the number of outgroup friends had little influence on prejudice. Rather, it was the extent to which one included a particular member of the outgroup in the self that predicted differences in prejudice toward that specific outgroup, such that the more inclusion of other in the self, the less prejudice. Also, in the diary study, structural equation modeling analyses suggested unique causal paths in both directions—including others in the self led to reduced prejudice, and reduced prejudice led to including others in the self. However, the path from inclusion to reduced prejudice was stronger and more consistent. Finally, in each study there was a significant interaction in predicting prejudice between number of interactions and inclusion of other in the self. When inclusion of other in the self was high, the more interactions, the less prejudice. However, when inclusion of other in the self was low, more interactions had either no impact on prejudice or actually lead to *greater* prejudice. In sum, the findings from all three studies are consistent with the inclusion of other in the self perspective and provide evidence of the importance of interpersonal closeness in intergroup contact effects.

While these findings are very encouraging, they all involve cross-sectional data and, like earlier survey data (Pettigrew, 1997), cannot unambiguously answer the question of causal direction. The alternative causal hypothesis, that those low in prejudice seek outgroup friends while those high in prejudice avoid outgroup members, is also very reasonable. To address this issue, Wright and Van der Zande (1999) used a laboratory procedure to demonstrate experimentally the causal direction from friendship to more positive intergroup attitudes. European American (White) women were randomly paired with either a cross-group (Asian-American or Latina) or a same-group (White) partner. Over an 8-week period, the partners met 4 times to engage in a series of friendship-building activities. Feelings of closeness were measured following each of the four activities. After the final meeting, under the guise of an unrelated second study, participants completed several measures of intergroup attitudes.

The data from the White participants showed that women in both same-group (White/White) partnerships and cross-group (White/Latina, White/Asian) partnerships developed strong feelings of closeness with their partners (i.e., we were able to produce relatively strong feelings of interpersonal closeness between same-group and cross-group randomly assigned pairs in the laboratory). More importantly, a number of measures showed that White women who became close with a Latina or Asian-American woman held significantly more positive intergroup attitudes than did White women who made friends with another White women. For example, those who had made outgroup friends indicated lower endorsement of several "anti-minority" policies—policies that had been the subject of recent highly publicized electoral propositions in California (where this study was conducted). Also, compared to those making an ingroup friend, those who made an outgroup friend reported lower feelings of anxiety at the prospect of cross-ethnic interactions. The least obvious, and perhaps most behavioral, measure was Haddock, Zanna, and Esses's (1993) "budget-cutting task." Participants were asked to assist the university in deciding how to distribute anticipated budget cuts to 15 student organizations. The task asked participants to redistribute resources among the organizations such that they cut a total of $5,000 from the total budget. The list of organizations included the "Latino/Chicano Student Association" and the "Asian & Pacific Islander Student Alliance." Figure 20.3 shows that participants who had made an Asian-American or Latina friend cut significantly less money from the organization representing that friend's ethnic group. Thus, the results clearly support the claim that making an outgroup friend leads to improvements in White participants' attitudes toward the outgroup as a whole.

Finally, feelings of closeness to the cross-group partner appear to be directly involved in the improvement in intergroup attitudes. For participants in the cross-group condition, there was a significant positive correlation between reported closeness to partner and intergroup attitudes. This is consistent with the claim that interpersonal closeness mediates the effect of the friendship-making manipulation on generalized intergroup attitudes.

Self-Expansion and Outgroup Orientation

The social psychology literature is replete with explanations for outgroup intolerance and even hatred. Mechanisms range from evolutionary predisposition, to personality characteristics, to basic cognitive and motivational processes, to abstract principles and political orientations. Compared to this multilevel conglomeration of reasons to avoid and even persecute outgroups, we find almost no explanations for why people might tolerate, let alone seek out, positive interactions with outgroups. It seems that abstract, even esoteric beliefs about justice and equality are the meager sandbags standing against a torrent of more

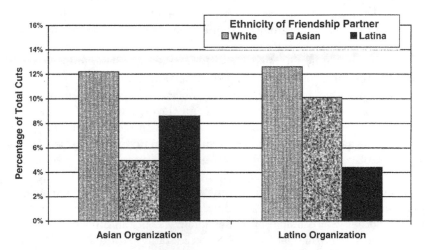

FIGURE 20.3. White participants' percentage budget cut to each of the Asian and Latino student organizations.

basic processes that lead inevitably toward negative intergroup relations. However, as Pettigrew (1997) asked "beyond media headlines of intergroup turmoil, most groups throughout the world achieve some degree of stability and mutual acceptance in their interactions. Why?" (p. 182). One explanation for our apparent inability to answer Pettigrew's query might be that in our efforts to explain the most problematic aspects of intergroup relations (prejudice and hatred), we have failed to as deeply consider the more mundane (tolerance and stability).

We propose that self-expansion may provide one example of a basic human motivational process that would predict an appetitive interest in outgroups and, thus, stands as an opponent to the many motivations to avoid and persecute outgroups. The logic follows directly from the basic premise of the self-expansion model—that people seek to expand the self and thus seek relationships with others that increase their constellation of resources, perspectives, and identities. Others who share most of our present perspectives and identities provide only limited potential for self-expansion, while those with divergent perspectives and identities provide the greatest opportunity for self-expansion. Thus, at least initially, we should be drawn to others who are highly divergent from ourselves. Groups whose identities, perspectives, and resources are detached from one's own should be particularly appealing. This perspective provides a potential explanation for the billions of dollars spent annually by people travelling to "exotic" places. Admittedly, many tourists prefer to simply observe from the comfort of a bus or a hotel that mirror their own culture. However, many seek to immerse themselves to some degree in the host culture and to "get to know" the local residents. This inclination toward those who are different is consistent with self-expansion motives.

This basic assumption provides the foundation for a variety of more complex hypotheses. Space considerations preclude a full analysis of all the implications of this model for intergroup relations. Nonetheless, we will briefly review a few examples. First, the self-expansion model recognizes that self-expansion needs are restrained by the need for self-integration, making unbridled self-expansion stressful. Thus, we would predict that outgroups will be most appealing when we have not just experienced significant self-expansion in other domains. For example, someone who has recently taken a new job, fallen in love, or moved to a new city might seek interactions with ingroup members with whom forming a relationship would demand only limited additional self-expansion. On the other hand, individuals who are securely entrenched in their present social world might be drawn to outgroup members. Thus, interest in outgroups may be moderated by recent and ongoing self-expansion in other domains.

Secondly, self-expansion in one domain may result in the loss of self-aspects in another. For example, if an academic accepts an offer from another university, he/she has an opportunity for considerable self-expansion. The new group offers a variety of resources, perspectives, and identities not presently available. However, there is also considerable potential for reduction in the self.

She/he must sacrifice the identities and resources provided by the present institution, by the present friendship groups, and so forth. Thus, we would predict a kind of cost–benefit analysis whereby the potential for self-expansion offered by including a new group in the self is weighed against the potential for self-loss. Similarly, forging a connection with an outgroup may be unappealing if the relationship between that group and my present ingroup is extremely negative. Including such an outgroup in the self risks rejection by my present ingroup and the loss of that self-aspect. Thus, the degree to which including the outgroup in the self will result in a net expansion of the self is in part determined by the state of relations between that outgroup and present ingroups.

There are numerous other potential applications of this perspective. However, even from these few examples it is clear that self-expansion paints the outgroup in a very different light than most other models of intergroup relations. Certainly, the appeal of the outgroup is restricted by other considerations, such as the need for self-integration and the possible loss of other important self-aspects. Nonetheless, the self-expansion model represents contact with outgroups as an attractive social experience. Outgroups, *because of their divergence from the present self*, provide an interesting and appealing opportunity for self-expansion.

SUMMARY AND CONCLUSIONS

In this chapter, we have briefly considered a number of ways that the self-expansion model might be adapted and integrated with ideas from the study of group processes and intergroup relations. We propose that the concept of including others in the self can be extended to provide a useful model of how ingroups become part of the self-concept. In addition, self-expansion motives provide a novel motivational account of ingroup identification, one that may prove a valuable complement to other existing perspectives. We have also considered how self-expansion and including other in the self provide potential mechanisms to explain how generalized positive intergroup attitudes can result from interpersonal cross-group contact. Finally, with its focus on the appeal of entities that have the potential to expand the self, self-expansion provides a refreshing contrast to most discussions of motivation in intergroup relations. The self-expansion model portrays outgroups as possible targets of interest rather than targets of indifference and intolerance.

We share the enthusiasm of others in this collection (Brewer & Pickett; Mackie & Smith; Smith; all this volume) for the possibility of illuminating similarities and consistencies in the processes that guide interpersonal and intergroup phenomena. However, we have also attempted to represent the unique ways in which group memberships and intergroup relations influence the specifics of how these common underlying processes manifest themselves.

REFERENCES

Abrams, D., & Hogg, M. A. (2001). Collective identity: Group membership and self-concept. In M. A. Hogg & S. Tindale (Eds.), *Blackwell handbook of social psychology Vol. 2: Group processes* (pp. 425–460). Oxford, UK: Blackwell.

Abramson, L., Seligman, M., & Teasdale, J. (1978). Learned helplessness in humans: Critique and reformulation. *Journal of Abnormal Psychology, 87,* 49–74.

Allport, G. (1954). *The nature of prejudice.* Reading, MA: Addison-Wesley.

Amir, Y. (1976). The role of intergroup contact in change or prejudice and ethnic relations. In P. A. Katz (Ed.), *Towards the elimination of racism* (pp. 245–308). Elmsford, NY: Pergamon.

Aron, A., & Aron, E. N. (1986). *Love as the expansion of self: Understanding attraction and satisfaction.* New York: Hemisphere.

Aron, A., & Aron, E. N. (1996). Self and self-expansion in relationships. In G. J. O. Fletcher & J. Fitness (Eds.), *Knowledge structures in close relationships: A social psychological approach* (pp. 325–344). Mahwah, NJ: Erlbaum.

Aron, A., Aron, E. N. & Norman, C. (2001). Self-expansion model of motivation and cognition in close relationships and beyond. In M. S. Clark & G. J. O. Fletcher (Eds.), *Blackwell handbook of social psychology Vol. 2: Interpersonal processes.* Oxford, UK: Blackwell.

Aron, A., Aron, E. N., & Smollan, D. (1992). Inclusion of Other in the Self Scale and the structure of interpersonal closeness. *Journal of Personality and Social Psychology, 63,* 596–612.

Aron, A., Aron, E. N., Tudor, M., & Nelson, G. (1991). Close relationships as including other in the self. *Journal of Personality and Social Psychology, 60,* 241–253.

Aron, A., & Fraley, B. (1999). Relationship closeness as including other in the self: Cognitive underpinnings and measures. *Social Cognition, 17,* 140–160.

Aron, A., Melinat, E., Aron, E. N., Vallone, R., & Bator, R. (1997).The experimental generation of interpersonal closeness: A procedure and some preliminary findings. *Person-*

ality and Social Psychology Bulletin, 23, 363–377.

Aron, A., Norman, C. C., & Aron, E. N. (1998). The self-expansion model and motivation. *Representative Research in Social Psychology, 22,* 1–13.

Aron, A., Paris, M., & Aron, E. N. (1995). Falling in Love: Prospective studies of self-concept change. *Journal of Personality and Social Psychology, 69,* 1102–1112.

Baumeister, R. F. (1998). The self. In D. T. Gilbert, S. T. Fiske, & G. Lindzey (Eds.), *The handbook of social psychology Vol. 1* (4th ed., pp. 680–740). Boston: McGraw-Hill.

Baumeister, R. F., & Leary, M. R. (1995). The need to belong: Desire for interpersonal attachments as a fundamental human motivation. *Psychological Bulletin, 117,* 497–529.

Blake, R. R., Shepard, H. A., & Mouton, J. S. (1964). *Managing intergroup conflicts in industry.* Houston, TX: Gulf.

Branscombe, N. R., & Ellemers, N. (1998). Coping with group-based discrimination: Individualistic versus group-level strategies. In J. K. Swim & C. Stangor (Eds.), *Prejudice: The target's perspective* (pp. 243–266). San Diego, CA: Academic Press.

Brewer, M. B. (1991). The social self: On being the same and different at the same time. *Personality and Social Psychology Bulletin, 17,* 475–482.

Brewer, M. B. (1979). In-group bias in the minimal intergroup situation: A cognitive-motivational analysis. *Psychological Bulletin, 86,* 307–324.

Brewer, M. B., & Gardner, W. (1996). Who is this "we"? Levels of collective identity and self-representations. *Journal of Personality and Social Psychology, 71,* 83–93.

Brewer, M. B., & Pickett, C. L. (1999). Distinctiveness motives as a source of the social self. In T. R. Tyler, R. M. Kramer, & O. P. John (Eds.), *The psychology of the social self* (pp. 47–69). Mahwah, NJ: Erlbaum.

Brown, R., Vivian, J., & Hewstone, M. (1999). Changing attitudes through intergroup contact: The effects of group membership salience. *European Journal of Social Psychology, 29* 741–764

Deaux, K. (1996). Social identification. In E.

T. Higgins & A. W. Kruglanski (Eds.)m *Social psychology: Handbook of basic principles* (pp. 777–798). New York: Guilford.

Deaux, K. (2000). Models, meanings and motivations. In D. Capozza & R. Brown (Eds.), *Social identity processes: Trends in theory and research* (pp. 1–14). Thousand Oaks, CA: Sage.

Deci, E. L., & Ryan, R. M. (1991). A motivational approach to self: Integration in personality. In R. Dienstbier (Ed.), *Nebraska Symposium on motivation: Volume 38. Perspectives on motivation* (pp. 237–288). Lincoln, NE: University of Nebraska Press.

Dweck, C. S., & Leggett, E. L. (1988). A social-cognitive approach to motivation and personality. *Psychological Review, 95,* 256–273.

Ellemers, N., Kortekaas, P., & Ouwerkerk, J. W. (1999). Self-categorization, commitment to the group and group self-esteem as related but distinct aspects of social identity. *European Journal of Social Psychology, 29,* 371–389.

Ellemers, N., Spears, R., & Doosje, B. (1997). Sticking together or falling apart: In-group identification as psychological determinant of group commitment versus individual mobility. *Journal of Personality and Social Psychology, 72,* 617–626

Ellemers, N., Spears, R., & Doosje, B. (1999). Introduction. In N. Ellemers, R. Spears, & B. Doosje (Eds.), *Social identity: Context, commitment, content* (pp. 1–5). Oxford, UK: Blackwell.

Fiske, S. T., & Depret, E. (1996). Control, interdependence and power: Understanding social cognition and its social context. In W. Stroebe & M. Hewstone (Eds.), *European Review of Social Psychology* (Vol. 7, pp. 31–61). Chichester, UK: Wiley.

Gaertner S. L., & Dovidio, J. F. (2000). *Reducing intergroup bias: The common ingroup identity model.* Philadelphia: Psychology Press.

Grieve, P., & Hogg, M. A. (1999). Subjective uncertainty and intergroup discrimination in the minimal group situation. *Personality and Social Psychology Bulletin, 25,* 926–940.

Haddock, G., Zanna, M. P., & Esses, V. M. (1993). Assessing the structure of prejudicial attitudes: The case of attitudes towards homosexuals. *Journal of Personality and Social Psychology, 65,* 1105–1118.

Hamberger, J., & Hewstone, M. (1997). Interethnic contact as a predictor of blatant and subtle prejudice: Tests of a model in four West European nations. *British Journal of Social Psychology, 36,* 173–190.

Heider, F. (1958). *The psychology of interpersonal relations.* New York: Wiley.

Herek, G. M., & Capitanio, J. P. (1996). "Some of my best friends": Intergroup contact, concealable stigma, and heterosexuals' attitudes towards gay men and lesbians. *Personality and Social Psychology Bulletin, 22,* 412–424.

Hewstone, M., & Brown, R. (1986). *Contact and conflict in intergroup encounters.* Oxford, UK: Blackwell.

Higgins, E. T. (1998). Promotion and prevention: Regulatory focus as a motivational principle. In M. P. Zanna (Ed.), *Advances in experimental social psychology* (Vol. 30, pp. 1–46). New York: Academic Press.

Hogg, M. A. (2000). Self-categorization and subjective uncertainty resolution: Cognitive and motivational facets of social identity and group membership. In J. P. Forgas, K. D. Williams, & L. Wheeler (Eds.), *The social mind: Cognitive and motivational aspects of interpersonal behavior* (pp. 323–349). New York: Cambridge University Press.

Hogg, M. A. (2001). Subjective uncertainty reduction through self-categorization: A motivational theory of social identity processes. In W. Stroebe & M. Hewstone (Eds.), *European Review of Social Psychology, 11* (pp. 223–255). Chichester, UK: Wiley.

Hogg, M. A., & Abrams, D. (1993). Towards a single-process uncertainty-reduction model of social motivation in groups. In M. A. Hogg & D. Abrams (Eds.), *Group motivation: Social psychological perspectives* (pp. 173–190). London: Harvester Wheatsheaf.

Jackson, J. W., & Smith, E. R. (1999). Conceptualizing social identity: A new framework and evidence for the impact of different dimensions. *Personality and Social Psychology Bulletin, 25,* 120–135.

Jetton, Y., Spears, R., & Manstead, A. S. R. (1997). Distinctiveness threat and prototypicality: Combined effects on intergroup discrimination and collective self-esteem. *European Journal of Social Psychology, 27,* 635–657.

Lemyre, L., & Smith, P. M. (1985). Intergroup discrimination and self-esteem in the minimal group paradigm. *Journal of Personality and Social Psychology, 49,* 660–670.

Linville, P. W. (1985). Self-complexity and affective extremity: Don't put all of your eggs in one cognitive basket. *Social Cognition, 3,* 94–120.

Luhtanen, R, & Crocker, J. (1992). A collective self-esteem scale: Self-evaluation of one's social identity. *Personality and Social Psychology Bulletin, 18,* 302–318.

Markus, H. R., & Kitayama, S. (1991). Culture and the self: Implications for cognition, emotion, and motivation. *Psychological Review, 98,* 224–253.

McLaughlin-Volpe, T., Aron, A., Wright, S. C., & Reis, H. T. (2000). *Intergroup social interactions and intergroup prejudice: Quantity versus quality.* Manuscript under review.

Miller N., & Brewer, M. B. (1984). *Groups in contact: The psychology of desegregation* New York: Academic Press.

Mlicki, P. P., & Ellemers, N. (1996). Being different or being better? National stereotypes and identifications of Polish and Dutch students. *European Journal of Social Psychology, 26,* 97–114.

Mullen, B., Brown, R., & Smith, C. (1992). Ingroup bias as a function of salience, relevance, and status: An integration. *European Journal of Social Psychology, 22,* 103–122.

Mullin, B.-A., & Hogg, M. A. (1999). Motivations for group membership: The role of subjective importance and uncertainty reduction. *Basic and Applied Social Psychology, 21,* 91–102.

Oakes, P. (2001). The root of all evil in intergroup relations? Unearthing the categorization process. In R. Brown & S. Gaertner (Eds.) *Blackwell handbook of social psychology (Vol. 4): Intergroup processes* (pp. 3–21). Oxford, UK: Blackwell.

Oakes, P. J., Haslam, S. A., & Turner, J. C. (1994). *Stereotyping and social reality.* Oxford, UK: Blackwell.

Pettigrew, T. F. (1986). The contact hypothesis revisited. In M. Hewstone & R. Brown (Eds.), *Contact and conflict in intergroup encounters* (pp. 169–195). Oxford, UK: Blackwell.

Pettigrew, T. F. (1997). Generalized intergroup effects on prejudice. *Personality and Social Psychology Bulletin, 23,* 173—185.

Pettigrew, T. F. (1998). Intergroup contact theory. *Annual Review of Psychology, 49,* 65–85.

Pettigrew, T. F., & Tropp, L. (2000). Does intergroup contact reduce prejudice? Recent meta-analytic findings. In S. Oskamp (Ed.), *Reducing prejudice and discrimination: Social psychological perspectives* (pp. 93–114). Mahwah, NJ: Erlbaum.

Reis, H. T., & Wheeler, L. (1991). Studying social interaction with the Rochester Interaction Record. In M. P. Zanna (Ed.), *Advances in experimental social psychology* (Vol. 24, pp. 269–318). San Diego, CA: Academic Press.

Rubin, M., & Hewstone, M. (1998). Social identity theory's self-esteem hypothesis: A review and some suggestions for clarification. *Personality and Social Psychology Review, 2,* 40–62.

Seligman, M. E. P. (1975). *Helplessness: On depression, development and death.* San Francisco: Freeman.

Simon, B. (1999). A place in the world: Self and social categorization. In T. R. Tyler, R. M. Kramer, & O. P. John (Eds.), *The psychology of the social self* (pp. 47–69). Mahwah, NJ: Erlbaum.

Simon, B., & Kampmeier, C. (2001). Revisiting the individual self: Towards a social psychological theory of the individual self and the collective self. In C. Sedikides & M. B. Brewer (Eds.), *Individual self, relational self, collective self* (pp. 199–218). Philadelphia: Psychology Press.

Skinner, E. A. (1992). Perceived control: Motivation, coping, and development. In R. Schwarzer (Ed.), *Self-efficacy: Thought control of action* (pp. 91–106). Washington, DC: Hemisphere.

Smith, E., Coats, S., & Walling, D. (1999). Overlapping mental representations of self, in-group, and partner: Further response time evidence and a connectionist model. *Personality and Social Psychology Bulletin, 25,* 873–882.

Smith, E., & Henry, S. (1996). An in-group becomes part of the self: Response time evaluation. *Personality and Social Psychology Bulletin, 22,* 635–642.

Spears, R., Doosje, B., & Ellemers, N. (1997). Self-stereotyping in the face of threats to group status and distinctiveness: The role of group identification. *Personality and Social Psychology Bulletin, 23*, 538–553.

Steele, J. L. (1999). *Cognitive mechanisms of attitude change in close relationships*. Unpublished doctoral dissertation, State University of New York at Stony Brook.

Stephan, W. G. (1987). The contact hypothesis in intergroup relations. In C. Hendrick (Ed.), *Group processes and intergroup relations. Review of personality and social psychology, Vol. 9* (pp. 13–40). Beverly Hills, CA: Sage Publications.

Stevens, L. E., & Fiske, S. T. (1995). Motivation and cognition in social life: A social survival perspective. *Social Cognition, 13*, 189–214.

Tajfel, H. (1981). *Human groups and social categories*. Cambridge, UK: Cambridge University Press.

Tajfel, H., & Turner, J. C. (1979). An integrative theory of intergroup conflict. In W. G. Austin & S. Worchel (Eds.), *The social psychology of intergroup relations* (pp. 33–47). Monterey, CA: Brooks/Cole.

Taylor, D. M., & Dubé, L. (1986). Two faces of identity: The "I" and the "We". *Journal of Social Issues, 42*, 81–98.

Triandis, H. C. (1989). The self and social behavior in differing cultural contexts. *Psychological Review, 96*, 506–520.

Tropp, L. & Wright, S. C. (1995, July). *Inclusion of ingroup in the self: Adapting Aron & Aron's IOS Scale*. Paper presented at the meeting of the American Psychological Society, New York, NY.

Tropp, L. R., & Wright, S. C. (1999). Ingroup identification and relative deprivation: An examination across multiple groups social comparisons. *European Journal of Social Psychology, 29*, 707–724.

Tropp, L. R., & Wright, S. C. (2001). Ingroup identification as inclusion of ingroup in the self. *Personality and Social Psychology Bulletin, 27*, 585–600.

Turner, J. C., Hogg, M. A., Oakes, P. J., Reicher, S. D., & Wetherell, M. S. (1987). *Rediscovering the social group: A self-categorization theory*. New York: Blackwell.

Turner, J. C., Oakes, P. J., Haslam, S. A., & McGarty, C. (1994). Self and collective: Cognition and social context. *Personality and Social Psychology Bulletin, 20*, 454–463.

Williams, K. D., Wheeler, L., & Harvey, J. (2001). Inside the social mind of the ostracizer. In J. Forgas, K. Williams, & L. Wheeler (Eds.), *The social mind: Cognitive and motivational aspects of interpersonal behavior* (pp. 294–320). New York: Cambridge University Press.

Wright, S. C., & Van der Zande, C. C. (1999, October). *Bicultural friends: When cross-group friendships cause improved intergroup attitudes*. Paper presented at the meeting of the Society for Experimental Social Psychology, St. Louis, MO.

21

Putting Our Selves Together
Integrative Themes and Lingering Questions

CONSTANTINE SEDIKIDES

Introduction
The Tripartite Self
Self and Motivation
Self and Affect
Epilogue
Final Observation

INTRODUCTION

*I*n a recent article, Abraham Tesser (2000) pointed out that the empirical output on the self has increased threefold in the last three decades, far exceeding the growth rate of empirical publications in psychology as a whole. He also remarked that one out of seven recent publications in psychological journals examined aspects of the self. The splendid collection of 21 chapters in this volume pays tribute to the polymorphous diversity of research on the self.

Despite their conceptual and empirical diversity, the chapters appear to have overlapping elements. My task in this chapter is to highlight the emerging integrative themes, offer commentary, dwell on enduring questions, and point to future research directions. It is a task undertaken with pleasure and anticipation.

Address for correspondence: Constantine Sedikides, Department of Psychology, Southampton University, Highfield Campus, Southampton, UK. E-mail: cs2@soton.ac.uk

THE TRIPARTITE SELF

In a recent edited volume, Marilynn Brewer and I (Sedikides & Brewer, 2001) adopted a tripartite definition of the self in terms of its individual, relational, and collective representational aspects (Brewer & Gardner, 1996; Kashima & Hardie, 2000). The individual self refers to one's unique set of attributes, which are derived from interpersonal comparison and differentiation processes. The relational self refers to a set of attributes that are shared with significant others; this type of self is achieved through assimilation processes and the formation of attachment bonds. Finally, the collective self refers to a constellation of attributes that are shared with an ingroup but are distinctly different from those of antagonistic outgroups; this type of self is attained via intergroup comparison processes.

Certainly, this is not the first time that the self has been conceptualized as a trichotomy. For example, similar classifications include the material, social, and spiritual self (James, 1890/1983); the id, ego, and superego (Freud, 1901/1965); the actual, ideal, and ought self (Higgins, 1987); and the reflexive consciousness, interpersonal roles, and executive function (Baumeister, 1998). However, we (Sedikides & Brewer, 2001) reasoned that our endorsed notion of the self-system as consisting of the three semi-autonomous but highly interactive aspects mentioned above (i.e., individual, relational, and collective) was timely, generative, and sufficiently broad to encompass much of the relevant empirical literature and thus bring about a measure of theoretical coherence.

The chapters in the present volume seem to fit nicely into the Sedikides and Brewer (2001) trichotomy, a perceived fit that will comprise the running theme of my commentary. This fit is illustrated compellingly by Y. Kashima, E. Kashima, and Clark (this volume). They embrace a distributed cognition approach to explore the three types of self. According to their doubly distributed model, meaning (a term reflecting subjective experience) is constructed both intra-individually (parallel distributed processing) and on the basis of the interplay between the individual and his/her culture (distributed cognition). Y. Kashima et al. report strong support for the tripartite classification of the self. The individual self varies substantially as a function of culture (e.g., East vs. West), the relational self varies along the lines of gender division of labor, whereas the collective self varies according to group size and population trends (e.g., rural vs. urban environment).

Individual versus Collective Self

The current volume, however, not only confirms the tripartite classification, but it also enriches it and challenges it. To begin with, Ickes (this volume) argues that a researcher can study the self in terms of two broad and mutually exclusive research paradigms, the subjective and intersubjective. The former focuses on the independent person as the unit of analysis, on subjective experience, and on how the person perceives others, interprets their behavior, remembers their actions, responds to them, and attempts to influence them. This paradigm is driven by the assumption that the individual self has predictive utility with regard to human functioning. The latter paradigm focuses on the dyad as the unit of analysis, on intersubjective experience, and on mutual and interdependent perceptions, construals, responses, and influences. This paradigm is based on the assumption that the relational self is a potent predictor of human functioning.

Ickes (this volume) seems to polarize the issue in order to illustrate effectively the pros and cons of the subjective and intersubjective paradigms. This polarization is useful but does not reflect the reality of the intellectual landscape. Indeed, there are few if any researchers who conceive of the individual self as totally independent, uninfluenced by social interactions, and in a static association with the relational or collective self. Nor are there any relationships researchers who deny categorically the relevance of subjective experience. In his provocative thesis, however, Ickes goes beyond useful conceptual polarization. He endorses unequivocally the intersubjective paradigm while castigating the subjective paradigm.

As a commentator, I can comfortably afford to be magnanimous about this issue. I think that both research paradigms have contributed valuable insights into the nature of the self and that both are dearly needed. Granted, the importance of social interactions cannot be underestimated. For example, Malle (this volume) has highlighted the flexibility and influencability of the self (be it individual, relational, or collective) in the context of social interactions where both actors and observers strive to explain each other's intentions and overt behaviors by deploying a powerful inferential tool—what Malle termed the *folk theory of mind and behavior*. Nevertheless, I believe that social interactions would be uninterpretable, thoroughly confusing, and nonconsequential if they occurred in the absence of subjective experience (Bless & Forgas, 2000; Y. Kashima et al., this volume). It is subjective experience that provides the fodder for social interactions to shape the self. Subjective experience intervenes between social stimuli and social behavior, and it causes behavior. In summary, subjective experience is the necessary medium through which social interactions sculpt the self. Incidentally, I should clarify that I am echoing my (and my collaborators') theoretical bias, which lies somewhere in the middle of the subjective and intersubjective research paradigms, with an emphasis on one's phenomenological experience and self-regulatory system as the basis for self-definition (Gaertner, Sedikides, & Graetz, 1999; Sedikides & Gaertner, 2000, 2001).

Indeed, people seem to have great difficulty escaping their own phenomenology. Gilovich (this volume) describes a program of research on the spotlight effect that documents the consistency and persistence with which people use the individual self (and their phenomenological experience) in understanding social reality. According to the spotlight effect, people overestimate the degree to which others attend to, evaluate, and remember their physical appearance and overt behavior. For example, participants overestimate (a) the extent to which others remember them wearing a specific T-shirt (picturing either a popular or a controversial celebrity), (b) the salience of their own input to a group discussion, (c) the salience of their physical absence in a group, and (d) the severity of others' evaluation of their absence. In fact, people are so wrapped up into their own perspective that they typically fail to adjust sufficiently from their own phenomenology toward approximating others' perceptions of themselves. People do not have an accurate view of how they are seen by others (Kenny & DePaulo, 1993).

Otten's chapter (this volume) is another example of the pervasiveness and inescapability of human egocentricity. The thrust of her argument is that people project the individual self into the collective self. (For similar arguments, see Gramzow, Gaertner, & Sedikides, 2001; Krueger, 1998.) When the collective self is ambiguous, as in the case of novel ingroups, people use the individual self as a source of definition for the collective self. The cognitive representation of the individual self forms the basis for the cognitive representation of the collective self. Self-liking is spontaneously translated into ingroup liking, a phenomenon that explains the presence of ingroup favoritism in the absence of intergroup comparison (e.g., Brewer, 1979).

That the two types of self share attributes and characteristics and that the collective self acquires psychological relevance when it is incorporated into the individual self are some of the main foci of the chapter by Wright, Aron, and Tropp. Smith (this volume) is concerned with the same issues, while emphasizing a dynamic and flexible interplay between the individual and collective self. Smith adopts a distributed connectionism approach. Distributed connectionist models reject the traditional concept of symbolic representational structure (i.e., information-bearing nodes bound together via linkages) and endorse the notion that representations are patterns of activation (changeable from moment to moment) among nodes that have no fixed meaning. These units are linked through weighted and unidirectional connections. Each unit sends output and receives input. Activation patterns change rapidly, but the connection weights (the carriers of long-term knowledge) are more permanent. Smith's conceptualization can account for the individual self's sensitivity to social contextual configurations, such as a salient outgroup or group identification (Wright et al., this volume). According to this view, the individual and collective self rely on the same underlying pool of attributes, and one or the other (i.e., units) are activated depending on contextual features (which reflect connection weights). In all, Smith stresses the continuity between the individual and collective self.

Continuity, however, oftentimes travels a bumpy road. Crandall, O'Brien, and Eshleman (this volume) provide a useful analysis of this process. They discuss the psychological mechanisms of compliance, identification, and internalization. When a highly valued collective self is incorporated hastily into the self-system (e.g., the nouveau riche bigot relocating into an egalitarian neighborhood), compliance processes are activated: the person succumbs to external pressures to go along with the group norms even if this means suppressing inappropriate attitudes (e.g., prejudice). The process of identification follows, during which the person is internally (rather than externally) motivated to conform to group norms and suppress inappropriate attitudes. Only at an advanced internalization stage will the person restore the balance between internal and external motivation for having or expressing socially appropriate attitudes. From the perspective of the current discussion, the internalization stage reflects the fusion of the collective and individual self (Wright et al., this volume).

Biernat and Eidelman (this volume) are concerned with the conditions under which fusion (i.e., assimilation) versus contrast occurs in reference to the individual and collective selves. They emphasize the role of context in self-definition. Biernat and Eidelman demonstrate that whether the individual self will be assimilated with or contrasted from the collective self depends on contextual features, such as objective versus subjective response scales and solo versus non-solo group status. Let us consider the example of a gender-mixed group. Whether women will rate themselves as inferior leaders (with "leader" being a male stereotypic attribute) depends on whether women use an objective scale (i.e., rankings) versus a subjective scale (i.e., ratings) and on whether they have a solo status or not. When using an objective scale, women self-stereotype; that is, they endorse an undesirable collective self (i.e., poor leader) as part of the individual self because they compare with men. Additionally, self-stereotyping is more pronounced when women occupy a solo status. When using a subjective scale, however, women do not self-stereotype. This is because they compare with other women.

Relational Self

So far, I have discussed mostly the interplay between the individual and collective self. However, several chapters also point to the psychological importance of the relational self (e.g., Y. Kashima et al., this volume). Indeed, when participants are negated of their desired relational self (i.e., when they are socially excluded), they respond in an extraordinary manner: they display an impaired sense of time (i.e., they report that time passes slowly), show a lack of orientation toward the future, manifest deteriorated self-regulatory skills (i.e., proneness to quitting as task difficulty increases), experience a drop in self-esteem, and behave in a less prosocial and more antisocial manner (Baumeister, Twenge,

& Ciarocco, this volume; Leary, this volume; Tice, Twenge, & Schmeichel, this volume; for a general and systematic investigation, see Williams, 2002).

Additional Issues

The research presented in this volume advances substantially our understanding of the individual, relational, and collective self. More importantly, the research raises several interesting issues. One issue concerns the definition of the relational self. In some cases, this type of self is defined in terms of specific dyadic bonds of attachment (e.g., Y. Kashima et al.; Leary; Smith; Wright et al.), whereas in other cases it is defined in terms of a general connectedness with others (e.g., Baumeister et al.; Malle; Tice et al.; see also LaFrance; all this volume)—a definition not markedly different from that of public individual self (e.g., Gilovich). Perhaps the relational self should be reconceptualized as a two-component construct, with one component referring to specific dyadic relationships and the other component referring to generalized relational affiliations. If so, it would be worth clarifying the antecedents and consequences of these two possible relational selves, as well as the various ways in which they interplay with the individual and collective self.

Another important issue that the research presented in this volume raises is that of interrelatedness among the individual, relational, and collective selves. In some chapters, this interrelatedness is depicted as cooperative (Otten; Smith; Wright et al.; see also Cooper & Hogg and Mackie & Smith), in others as antagonistic (Crandall et al.; Ickes; see also Brewer & Pickett), and still in others as symbiotic (Gilovich; Kashima et al.; see also Forgas, and LaFrance). One resolution of this debate would be to propose that typically this interrelatedness is symbiotic, with context (e.g., Biernat & Edelman) determining the transformation of the relation into a cooperative or an antagonistic one. For example, when responding to objective scales, a participant's positive individual self ("leader") conflicts with a negative collective self ("poor leader"). However, when responding to subjective scales, the participant's individual and collective selves are in total harmony, as they are both positive ("leader"). Nevertheless, this issue invites clarification of the nature of context per se, a topic to which I will return in the *Epilogue*.

SELF AND MOTIVATION

Although at several historical junctions in social and personality psychology the assertion that the self is woven into the motivational system would constitute heresy, such a statement is now considered rather trite. A sizable portion of the literature in the last 15 years has addressed the link between motivation and the self, and chapters in this volume honor this tradition. I will discuss this link around two themes: avoidance and approach motivation.

Avoidance Motivation

Relevant chapters discuss avoidance motivation under the rubric of self-protection and differentiation motives. Indeed, the spotlight effect (Gilovich, this volume) can be partly conceptualized as self-protective thinking and behaving. An exaggerated sense of the degree to which others notice and remember a person's appearance and behavior may derive, in part, from the person's implicit desire to avoid negative consequences such as derogation, confrontation, and social exclusion. Arguably, then, the spotlight effect is an implicit and pre-emptive deference gesture to an audience, with deference being a prima facie self-protective act.

A fascinating behavioral strategy in the service of self-protection is self-handicapping, the strategy of setting up obstacles to one's performance as a fallback excuse in the case of failure. Hirt and McCrea (this volume) address the question of exactly which aspect of the self does a self-handicapping behavior protect. They conclude that self-handicapping protects one's perception of the self as competent in an important performance domain. Rhodewalt and Tragakis (this volume) wonder about the circumstances under which self-handicapping is most likely to occur. They show that self-handicapping is exacerbated when a person regards competence as a fixed and unmodifiable attribute, while simultaneously endorsing performance goals as opposed to mastery goals. Interestingly, self-handicapping is a strategy that can protect not only the individual, but also the relational self: self-handicapping behavior intensifies when one's reputation in the relevant performance domain is at stake.

Differentiation is another example of avoidance motivation. This construct is elaborated upon in Brewer and Pickett's (this volume) treatment of optimal distinctiveness theory. These researchers maintain that, when temporarily deprived, the social motive of differentiation or distinctiveness (i.e., considering the self as unique, separate, and different from others) propels self-definition away from the collective self and toward the individual self.

Approach Motivation

The discussion of the link between approach motivation and the self is centered around the motives of self-expansion, self-enhancement, and self-inclusion. Wright et al. (this volume; see also chapters by Cooper & Hogg, Smith, and Mackie & Smith) embrace a theoretical framework according to which self-expansion motivation is the engine that powers (a) affiliation with the ingroup, (b) affiliation with a specific member of the outgroup, and (c) affiliation with that outgroup. In fact, Wright at el. demonstrate that interpersonal closeness with an outgroup member increases behavioral contact with that outgroup. Their research is a clear depiction of the three types of self—individual, relational, and collective—in a mutually beneficial alliance.

The work of Otten (this volume), Smith (this volume), Biernat and Eidelman (this volume), and LaFrance (this volume) is relevant to the self-enhancement motive. Otten argues that the motive of enhancement of the individual self is transformed into the motive of enhancing the collective self when persons join novel ingroups (even in the absence of outgroups). In a similar vein, Smith discusses how the motive of expansion of the individual self has implications for the motive of enhancement of the collective self. For example, expanding the individual self to incorporate an ingroup can lead to behaviors that benefit the ingroup, such as favoritism and altruism. Biernat and Eidelman's work raises an interesting implication: people will self-enhance when the context allows it. People have more room to self-enhance when rating themselves on subjective scales, and they do so (i.e., they do not self-stereotype). LaFrance considers the role of smiling in enhancing the relational self. Her argument is that the act of smiling projects a positive persona upon others, presents a self that is attuned to others, and thus functions to affirm relational ties and establish relational harmony. More specifically, LaFrance focuses on gender differences in smiling. In a discussion reminiscent of Biernat and Eidelman's (this volume) shifting standards model, LaFrance documents that women are expected and feel obligated to smile more often than men: Non-smiling women and over-smiling men are less likely to elicit social acceptance and inclusion compared to over-smiling women and non-smiling men, respectively.

Brewer and Pickett (this volume) are concerned with the self-inclusion motive. In reference to optimal distinctiveness theory, they propose that self-inclusion (i.e., considering the self as similar to others and seeking validation from others) is a need that is independent of and in opposition with the need for differentiation. The tension between these two needs is manifested in experiments (detailed by Brewer & Pickett) that demonstrate that temporary suppression of the need for inclusion pushes self-definition away from the individual and toward the collective self, thus establishing psychological equilibrium.

Additional Issues

Research on the motive of self-protection is garnering renewed interest (Baumeister, Smart, & Boden, 1996; Pyszczynski, Greenberg, & Solomon, 1997; Sedikides & Green, 2000). It is now well-established that people use a variety of clever tactics to protect the self, of which the spotlight effect and self-handicapping are two. An additional tactic worth exploring is people's deft utilization of the social context. For example, taking off from Biernat and Eidelman's chapter, will women (or men, for that matter) express a tactical (i.e., self-protective) preference for subjective over objective response scales, when threatened?

Of course, even the most canny self-protective move will occasionally fail. What are the consequences of such a breakdown in self-protection? The research of Baumeister et al. (this volume) and Tice et al. (this volume) provides an answer. When no clear self-protective mechanism is viable any longer—as depicted by the phenomenon of social exclusion—people will resort to antisocial behavior (e.g., cheating on a test) or, even worse, to aggressive behavior (e.g., criticizing, antagonizing, and harming others). From this standpoint, antisocial or aggressive behavior is seen as a socially clumsy attempt to reaffirm the autonomy, positivity, and agency of the self. Despite its clumsiness, however, this behavior can be effective in achieving one's immediate goals (Jones & Pittman, 1982), although to the frequent detriment of broader or long-term objectives.

It is worth noting that, besides self-protection and self-differentiation, an additional avoidance motive has received extensive research attention. This is the motive of uncertainty reduction. Self-definition can shift from the individual to the collective self when uncertainty is high compared to low (Hogg, 2001a). Joining a group can contribute a degree of clarity to one's understanding of the social environment.

Research on the self-enhancement motive has also flourished in the last decade. People are remarkably shrewd tacticians when it comes to elevating the positivity of the self, be it individual (Sedikides, 1993), relational (Rusbult, Van Lange, Wildschut, Yovetich, & Verette, 2000), or collective (Hogg, 2001b). However, besides self-enhancement (and self-expansion as well as self-inclusion), another approach motive deserving of empirical attention is self-improvement (Sedikides, 1999; Sedikides & Strube, 1997). The motive to improve and experience a sense of progress may underlie not only individual behavior (e.g., pursuing a college degree), but also relational behavior (e.g., dating a prospective partner that is similar to one's ideal self) and collective behavior (e.g., joining a group that offers the promise of challenging team activities).

SELF AND AFFECT

The link between the self and the affective system is another focus of this volume. This is a timely issue in social and personality psychology, as indicated by the markedly increased empirical attention that the topic of affect has recently received (e.g., Forgas, 2000, 2001). I will structure my discussion of the link between affect and the self around two themes: First, is affect regarded as an independent or a dependent variable? Second, to which type of self does affect refer?

Forgas (this volume) conceptualizes and operationalizes affect as an independent variable. Forgas reports empirical evidence for the pervasive and congruent (i.e., similarly valenced) influence of affect on the self, including self-referent judgments, attributions about one's behavior, interpretations of own behaviors, decisions affecting the self, and communication of self-relevant information (e.g., self-disclosure). However, affective influences on the self are not uniformly congruent. In support of his affect infusion model, Forgas reports that sad or happy moods will impact on the self in a congruent way under two circumstances: (a) when a substantial degree of self-construction is required (i.e., when people are relatively uncertain as to whether they possess a given attribute and are motivated to find out), and (b) when there are no overriding motivational forces at work.

In research in which affect is conceptualized as a dependent variable, the self typically assumes the status of an intervening variable (e.g., Rusting, 2001). Negative affectivity—associated with (a) the spotlight effect, such as anxiety and worry (Gilovich, this volume); (b) the failure of self-handicapping, such as low self-esteem (Hirt & McCrea, this volume; Rhodewalt & Tragakis, this volume); and (c) social exclusion, such as emotional numbness/passivity (Baumeister et al., this volume) and low self-esteem (Leary, this volume)—is due to the mediating influence of the self. The chapter by Cooper and Hogg (this volume) is another case in point. In their prototypical experiment, participants who strongly identify with their ingroup and observe an ingroup member expressing counterattitudinal views report that they would experience negative emotions themselves if they were in the position of that ingroup member. More importantly, the more negative the emotions that participants report that they would experience, the more counterattitudinal their own views become. The role of the self as an intervening construct in this research is highlighted by the fact that participants experience cognitive dissonance vicariously on behalf of a member of a *valued* ingroup, that is, a group that they have incorporated into their self-system.

Mackie and Smith (this volume) push this argument further by demonstrating that people can experience affect on behalf of a valued ingroup even when the affect-eliciting event is irrelevant to them personally. Guided by their intergroup emotions theory, Mackie and Smith demonstrate that (a) emotions can underlie favoritism toward the ingroup and discrimination toward the outgroup, (b) different emotions (e.g., fear, anger, disgust) are associated with different behavioral responses to the outgroup, and (c) stereotypes can be conceptualized not only as a precursor but also as a result of discrimination.

To which type of self does affect refer? The chapters illustrate the links between affect and all three types of self. Specifically, affect is linked to the individual self (Forgas; Gilovich; Hirt & McCrea; Rhodewalt & Tragakis), relational self (Baumeister et al.; Forgas; Leary), and collective self (Cooper & Hogg; Forgas; Mackie & Smith). Moreover, researchers emphasize that affect can spill over from one type of self to another (e.g., from the individual to the relational self; Gilovich; Leary), and from the individual to the collective self (Cooper &

Hogg; Mackie & Smith). These turns and twists clearly demonstrate the relevance of affect for the self-system, and vice versa.

EPILOGUE

The present volume has initiated an active, timely, and multi-voiced dialogue on the nature of the self, its link with motivation, and its link with affect. The volume sharpens the ongoing debate surrounding enduring problems in the field and promises to inform the agenda for the next wave of research on the self. Four issues, in particular, deserve careful empirical scrutiny.

Interplay between Relational and Collective Self

The first issue involves the interplay between the relational and the collective self. Several chapters address this interplay (Wright et al., Mackie & Smith; Smith) and offer the useful insight that psychological closeness to a member of the outgroup increases liking for that outgroup. Stated otherwise, a relational self fosters the development of a collective self.

Given the ebb and flow of interpersonal relationships, however, it is likely that the dyadic bond with the outgroup member will not last forever. What will happen when this bond is severed? Will liking for the outgroup be reduced, be replaced by indifference, or give way to resentment? Also, consider the case in which a person is affiliated with two members of the outgroup, and one affiliation is positive whereas the other is negative. How will these mixed-valence relationships influence perceptions of and behavior toward the outgroup? Will negative exemplars be given disproportionate weight when forming an impression of the group? Will this depend on the level of abstractness or concreteness of group representation? Finally, can sentiment for the outgroup as a whole be positive despite the presence of antagonistic dyadic relationships with one or more specific members of that group? Empirical attention to these issues promises to clarify further the interplay between the relational and collective self.

Motive Conflict

Another set of questions pertains to conflict among self-motives. Both avoidance (self-protection, self-differentiation) and approach (self-expansion, self-enhancement, self-inclusion) motives fuel the individual, relational, and collective self. These motives, however, often conflict. The conflict can be a function of self type and motive type. Furthermore, the conflict can be either within-self or between-self.

Within-self conflict refers to motive antagonism within a single self type. This kind of conflict is further subdivided into within-motive and between-motive

Table 21.1. Illustration of Self x Motive Conflict

| | | Self Type | | |
		Individual	Relational	Collective
Motive Type	Avoidance	1	2	3
	Approach	4	5	6

conflict. *Within-motive conflict* refers to the opposition of one avoidance motive with another (or of one approach motive with another) in reference to a single type of self (i.e., conflict that is restricted to a single cell of Table 21.1). For example, self-protection may be in opposition to self-differentiation: a person may desire to protect the individual self from others, an act that can be incompatible with differentiating the individual self from others; likewise, a person may desire to expand but also enhance the individual self—two action tendencies that are often incompatible. *Between-motive conflict* refers to the opposition between an avoidance motive (e.g., self-protection) and an approach motive (e.g., self-expansion) in reference to a single type of self. For example, a person may be motivated both to protect the individual self from potentially harmful dyadic relationships but also to expand the individual self through association with a physically attractive other (Sedikides & Green, 2000).

Between-self conflict refers to motive antagonism involving more than one self type. This kind of conflict is also subdivided into within-motive and between-motive conflict. *Within-motive conflict* refers to opposition among avoidance motives (or among approach motives) in regard to more than one self type. For example, a person may desire to protect simultaneously the individual, relational, and collective self (Sedikides, Campbell, Reeder, & Elliot, 1998) or enhance simultaneously the three selves (Pemberton & Sedikides, 2001), an act that is often incompatible and requires delicate balancing. This type of conflict is represented in terms of single rows in Table 21.1 (i.e., cells 1–3, or cells 4–6). *Between-motive conflict*, on the other hand, refers to opposition between one (or more) approach and one (or more) avoidance motives in reference to multiple types of self. Such a pattern of conflict can be complex. An example involves activation of the self-protection motive for the individual self, the self-enhancement motive for the relational self, and the self-inclusion motive for the collective self (i.e., cells 1–5–6). That is, a participant may simultaneously desire to protect the self from possible failure at a difficult test through self-handicapping behavior, present the self favorably (i.e., as an intelligent person) to a senior student, and realize that performance on the test and the impression that the senior student forms of him will likely determine inclusion in a highly desirable group (e.g., a high-status fraternity).

Obviously, motive conflict can assume various shapes and forms. An ambitious undertaking would be the development of a topography of conflictual patterns of interrelatedness among self-motives. Such an approach, albeit cumbersome, has the potential to lead to a systematic investigation of motive interplay and to yield new insights in our understanding of the motivational and self systems. At the very least, such an approach will help enrich the research agendas on this issue.

Interplay between Motivation and Affect

For historical, conceptual, and measurement reasons, the motivational and affective systems have each been granted a distinct psychological status in social and personality psychology. The traditional practice of treating motivation and affect as independent is reflected in textbooks, monographs, scholarly meetings of professional associations, and several programs of research. This approach certainly has been prolific. More recently, however, researchers have been moving beyond this artificial dichotomy and toward posing questions relevant to the interplay between the two systems (e.g., Higgins, 1987; Higgins & May, 2001; Williams, 2002). This tendency is reflected in the present volume (e.g., Baumeister et al.; Cooper & Hogg; Forgas; Hirt & McCrea). A common thread in this tendency is the recognition that the construct of self can bring together these separate research traditions.

Self-motives do have affective consequences: avoidance or approach motivation per se can reduce negative feelings or increase positive feelings, respectively. To make matters more complicated, the motivational and affective systems appear to have an interactive influence on the three types of self. To illustrate, let me revert to the motive type x self type classification depicted in Table 21.1. What sort of feelings can within-self (either within-motive or between-motive) conflict induce? Also, what kind of feelings can between-self (either within-motive or between-motive) conflict induce?

Arguably, such patterns of motive antagonism can evoke the entire gamut of emotions, including blended emotions. Take the case of between-self and between-motive conflict outlined in the prior section labeled *Motive Conflict*. A participant was motivated to protect the self from performance failure, impress a high-status other, and join a desirable group. The self-protection motive for the individual self, the self-enhancement motive for the relational self, and the self-inclusion motive for the collective self were in stark opposition. Protection of the self from failure (e.g., self-handicapping) would increase self-esteem and possibly elevate mood, failure to impress the important other would likely lead to shame and self-loathing, whereas exclusion from an appealing group would lead to emotional numbness and passivity. Furthermore, these feelings would be experienced simultaneously. This is clearly an intricate and textured emotional quilt, one that is not easily classifiable under existing conceptual affective categories (i.e., single emotions, such as fear, happiness, or anger).

In summary, the self has the potential to serve as the construct that will unify, or at least bridge the gap, between motivation and emotion. An explicit recognition of this potential can lead to challenging empirical pursuits, thus pushing the boundaries of knowledge on motivation, emotion, and also the self.

Clarifying the Nature of Context

When referring to the interrelatedness among the individual, relational, and collective self, I proposed that this interrelatedness generally be regarded as symbiotic, with context effecting its transformation into cooperative or antagonistic. However, what is the nature of context per se? More importantly, what is context for? In the spirit of this volume, the answer is that context is for self-construction. Humans have a vested interest in (especially positive) self-construction, and this intrinsically motivated activity takes place and is subject to both internal and external forces.

An example of internal context is affect (Forgas, this volume; Mackie & Smith, this volume). Affective context can influence the kind of self that is constructed. For instance, under the influence of sad mood, one will rate the self as complaining, whereas under the influence of positive mood the self will be judged as uncomplaining (Sedikides & Green, 2001). Motivation can also be construed as internal context. The end-product of the self-construction process (e.g., is the self thrifty or generous?) often hinges on the type of motive (e.g., protection vs. expansion) that is momentarily activated.

External context can be generally classified as non-social or social. An example of non-social context is the type of response scales employed (Biernat & Eidelman, this volume). Another example is the neatness and orderliness of one's physical surroundings. Social context refers the presence of others. Examples include such variables as type of group status (solo vs. non-solo; Biernat & Eidelman, this volume), type of living environment (urban vs. rural; Y. Kashima et al., this volume), group structure (inclusive vs. non-inclusive; Brewer & Pickett, this volume), and task type. The last variable is discussed by LaFrance (this volume). She reports that, when the task structure is rigid (e.g., to teach, to deceive), no reliable gender differences in smiling are obtained; however, when the task structure pertains to mending relationships and managing emotions, women smile more often than men.

FINAL OBSERVATION

The authors of the 21 chapters in the volume converge in successfully elucidating the antecedents, correlates, and consequences of the social self. The authors engage in bold theorizing, report compelling empirical findings, and draw far-reaching conclusions. The outcome is an involving scholarly exchange that will, no doubt, stir up controversy and serve as a benchmark for future research. Judging from this volume, the topic of the self has an exciting present and a promising future.

REFERENCES

Baumeister, R. F. (1998). The self. In D. T. Gilbert, S. T. Fiske, & G. Lindzey (Eds.), *The handbook of social psychology* (pp. 680–740). New York: Oxford University Press.

Baumeister, R. F., Smart, L., & Boden, J. M. (1996). Relation of threatened egotism to violence and aggression: The dark side of self-esteem. *Psychological Review, 103*, 5–33.

Bless, H., & Forgas, J. P. (Eds.). (2000). *The message within: The role of subjective experience in social cognition and behavior.* Philadelphia: Psychology Press.

Brewer, M. B. (1979). In-group bias and the minimal intergroup situation: A cognitive motivational analysis. *Psychological Bulletin, 86*, 307–324.

Brewer, M. B., & Gardner, W. (1996). Who is this "we"?: Levels of collective identity and self-representation. *Journal of Personality and Social Psychology, 71*, 83–93.

Forgas, J. P. (2000). *Feeling and thinking: The role of affect in social cognition.* New York: Cambridge University Press.

Forgas, J. P. (Ed.). (2001). *The handbook of affect and social cognition.* Mahwah, NJ: Erlbaum.

Freud, S. (1901/1965). *The psychopathology of everyday life.* New York: Norton.

Gaertner, L., Sedikides, C., & Graetz, K. (1999). In search of self-definition: Motivational primacy of the individual self, motivational primacy of the collective self, or contextual primacy? *Journal of Personality and Social Psychology, 76*, 5–18.

Gramzow, R. H., Gaertner, L., & Sedikides, C. (2001). Memory for ingroup and outgroup information in a minimal group context: The self as an informational base. *Journal of Personality and Social Psychology, 80*, 188-205.

Higgins, E. T. (1987). Self-discrepancy: A theory relating self and affect. *Psychological Review, 94*, 319–340.

Higgins, E. T., & May, D. (2001). Individual self-regulatory function: It's not "we" regu-

lation, but it's still social. In C. Sedikides & M. F. Brewer (Eds.), *Individual self, relational self, collective self* (pp. 47–67). Philadelphia: Psychology Press.

Hogg, M. A. (2001a). Subjective uncertainty reduction through self-categorization: A motivational theory of social identity processes. *European Review of Social Psychology, 11*, 223–255.

Hogg, M. A. (2001b). Social identity and the sovereignty of the group. In C. Sedikides & M. F. Brewer (Eds.), *Individual self, relational self, collective self* (pp. 123–143). Philadelphia: Psychology Press.

James, W. (1890/1983). *The principles of psychology.* Cambridge, MA: Harvard University Press.

Jones, E. E., & Pittman, T. S. (1982). Toward a general theory of strategic self-presentation. In J. Suls (Ed.), *Psychological perspectives on the self* (Vol. 1, pp. 231–262). Hillsdale, NJ: Erlbaum.

Kashima, E. S., & Hardie, E. A. (2000). Development and validation of the relational, individual, and collective self-aspects (RIC) scale. *Asian Journal of Social Psychology, 3*, 19–48.

Kenny, D. A., & DePaulo, B. M. (1993). Do people know how others view them? An empirical and theoretical account. *Psychological Bulletin, 114*, 145–161.

Krueger, J. (1998). Enhancement bias in the description of self and others. *Personality and Social Psychology Bulletin, 24*, 505–516.

Pemberton, M., & Sedikides, C. (2001). When do individuals help close others improve?: Extending the self-evaluation maintenance model to future comparisons. *Journal of Personality and Social Psychology, 81*, 234–246.

Pyszczynski, T., Greenberg, J., & Solomon, S. (1997). Why do we need what we need? A terror management perspective on the role of human social motivation. *Psychological Inquiry, 8*, 1–20.

Rusbult, C. E., Van Lange, P. A. M., Wildschut, T., Yovetich, N. A., & Verette, J. (2000). Perceived superiority in close relationships: Why it exists and persists. *Journal of Personality and Social Psychology, 79,* 521–545.

Rusting, C. (2001). Personality as a mediator of affective influences on social cognition. In J. P. Forgas (Ed.), *The handbook of affect and social cognition* (pp. 371–391). Mahwah, NJ: Erlbaum.

Sedikides, C. (1993). Assessment, enhancement, and verification determinants of the self-evaluation process. *Journal of Personality and Social Psychology, 65,* 317–338.

Sedikides, C. (1999). A multiplicity of motives: The case of self-improvement. *Psychological Inquiry, 9,* 64–65.

Sedikides, C., & Brewer, M. B. (Eds.). (2001). *Individual self, relational self, collective self.* Philadelphia: Psychology Press.

Sedikides, C., Campbell, W. K., Reeder, G., & Elliot, A. J. (1998). The self-serving bias in relational context. *Journal of Personality and Social Psychology, 74,* 378–386.

Sedikides, C., & Gaertner, L. (2000). The social self: The quest for identity and the motivational primacy of the individual self. In J. P. Forgas, K. D. Williams, & L. Wheeler (Eds.), *The social mind: Cognitive and motivational aspects of interpersonal behavior* (pp. 115–138). Cambridge, UK: Cambridge University Press.

Sedikides, C., & Gaertner, L. (2001). A homecoming to the individual self: Emotional and motivational primacy. In C. Sedikides & M. F. Brewer (Eds.), *Individual self, relational self, collective self* (pp. 7–23). Philadelphia: Psychology Press.

Sedikides, C., & Green, J. D. (2000). On the self-protective nature of inconsistency/negativity management: Using the person memory paradigm to examine self-referent memory. *Journal of Personality and Social Psychology, 79,* 906–922.

Sedikides, C., & Green, J. D. (2001). Affective influences on the self-concept: Qualifying the mood congruency principle. In J. P. Forgas (Ed.), *The handbook of affect and social cognition* (pp. 145–160). Mahwah, NJ: Erlbaum.

Sedikides, C., & Strube, M. J. (1997). Self-evaluation: To thine own self be good, to thine own self be sure, to thine own self be true, and to thine own self be better. In M. P. Zanna (Ed.), *Advances in experimental social psychology, 29* (pp. 209–269). New York: Academic Press.

Smith, E. R., & Henry, S. (1996). An in-group becomes part of the self: Response time evidence. *Personality and Social Psychology Bulletin, 22,* 635–642.

Tesser, A. (2000). On the confluence of self-esteem maintenance mechanisms. *Personality and Social Psychology Review, 4,* 290–299.

Williams, K. D. (2002). *Ostracism: The power of silence.* New York–: Guilford Publications.

Author Index

Subject Index